BUTLER'S
LIVES OF THE SAINTS

NEW

FULL EDITION

JUNE

BUTLER'S
LIVES OF THE SAINTS

NEW FULL EDITION

Patron
H. E. CARDINAL BASIL HUME, O.S.B.
Archbishop of Westminster

BUTLER'S
LIVES OF THE
SAINTS

NEW
FULL EDITION

JUNE

Revised by
KATHLEEN JONES

BURNS & OATES

THE LITURGICAL PRESS
Collegeville, Minnesota

First published 1997 in Great Britain by
BURNS & OATES
Wellwood, North Farm Road,
Tunbridge Wells, Kent TN2 3DR

First published 1997 in North America by
THE LITURGICAL PRESS
St John's Abbey, Collegeville,
Minnesota 56321

Butler's *Lives of the Fathers, Martyrs and other principal Saints* ... first published
1756-9. First revised edition, *Butler's Lives of the Saints*, ed. Herbert Thurston,
S.J., 1926-38, copyright © Burns, Oates & Washbourne Limited. Second revised
edition, ed. Herbert Thurston, S.J., and Donald Attwater, 1954-8, copyright ©
Burns & Oates Limited.

ISBN 0 86012 255 7   Burns & Oates
ISBN 0-8146-2382-4   The Liturgical Press

The emblems appearing at the foot of some pages are taken from W. Ellwood Post,
Saints, Signs and Symbols: A Concise Dictionary. © Copyright 1962, 1974 by
Morehouse Publishing, with the permission of the publishers. Sources of other
illustrations are credited on their respective pages.

Library of Congress Catalog Card Number: 95-81671

Typeset by Search Press Limited
Printed in the United States of America

CONTENTS

(Entries in capital letters indicate that the saint or feast is commemorated throughout the Roman Catholic Church with the rank of Solemnity, Feast, Memorial or Optional Memorial, according to the 1969 revised Calendar of the Latin [Roman] Rite of the Catholic Church, published in the Roman Missal of 1970, or that the saint is of particular importance for the English-speaking world. These entries are placed first on their dates. All others are in chronological order, by date of death.)

Contents

Contents

PREFACE

The celebration of saints' days in June includes the great feast of SS Peter and Paul, on the 29th. Among other well-known saints in the month are John the Baptist; Barnabas; Boniface, the Apostle of Germany; Columba, "the glory of the Celtic Church"; and the silver-tongued and much-loved Antony of Padua. The earliest martyrs are the Martyrs under Nero, among whom Peter and Paul were numbered. Others who died for their faith include St Alban, proto-martyr of Britain; SS John Fisher and Thomas More; four nuns of Arras executed in the final throes of the French Revolution; and the Martyrs of Uganda, St Charles Lwanga and companions, killed on the orders of King Mwanga in 1886 and commemorated in the Universal Calendar on 3 June.

To do any sort of justice to these and many other remarkable characters in a single volume is a challenge. They are not standardized figures in plaster or stained glass. They are fully human, with personalities so strong that some of them seem to leap off the page and claim one's attention. All of them are dedicated to something greater than their own comfort and satisfaction. Many have a remarkable degree of courage. They teach, they preach, they heal the sick, they protect the vulnerable and help the needy. They often seem to have a special relationship with the natural world—with birds and animals, with mountains and deserts and forests; but their most outstanding common characteristic is their vitality. There is something truly creative in the way they live and face up to the basic problems of living and dying.

In earlier centuries accounts of the lives of the saints made theology real and accessible to a largely unlettered public. Travellers went on pilgrimages to shrines in distant places and brought back new treasures and new stories of martyrdom and reputed miracles. Relics were eagerly sought after to give a focus for devotion in a new church or cathedral. At a popular level stories of saints from their homeland were recounted round the campfire by soldiers on campaigns; on the roads by merchants, pilgrims, and travellers; and on deck at night by seafarers slowly making their way round the Mediterranean. Oral tradition has played a considerable part in preserving and spreading knowledge of those whom the Church has come to honour.

Preface

The development of mass literacy has not made the lives of the saints less valuable. Any journalist or television presenter knows that abstract issues have to be personalized if they are to be understood. We still learn best through the example of others. Through these lives we can draw on a vast treasury of Christian experience in many generations and many societies over nearly two thousand years of human history. The saints bring theology to the human level, to the concrete and actual problems of living the Christian life. New theological work in the analysis of religious experience and in the nature of spirituality now draws increasingly on biographical accounts of the saints for evidence.

For the saints whose feasts occur in June, as for others, that evidence is often less complete than we should like, and there is still more to be discovered. Though there is a vast literature on the life of St Peter, there are still unanswered questions. How strong is the evidence that he was with the Church in Rome? How certain can we be, after all the excavations and the scientific tests, that the relics enshrined in the great Roman basilica that bears his name are really his? There are eighty-six known early manuscripts on the life of St Alban, but who exactly was he; and was Amphibalus a person or, as one writer has suggested, an emperor's greatcoat?

For some of the less well-known saints we are often dependent on oral tradition, and this has its own limitations: was St Moluag known as "the son of Lismore" or "the sun of Lismore"? Did St Antonina come from the island of Cea in the Aegean, from Nicaea, or from Ceja in Spain? Perhaps we shall never be quite certain. Some lives were recorded only after centuries of recounting by word of mouth had obscured or elaborated the original story.

Even when the Lives were finally set down in records, there were opportunities for misunderstanding. Manuscripts were passed from monastery to monastery and painfully copied by hand. The ability to transcribe accurately was highly valued, but standards of learning varied. Mistakes crept in, and sometimes dubious additions were made. Monk-chroniclers were often much more interested in producing an account that would be edifying to the faithful than in keeping strictly to the facts. Folklore easily became interwoven with history. Modern historiographers have to know their chroniclers: they have had to learn whom to trust and whom to doubt.

The quest for historical accuracy is a comparatively modern development—though not as recent as is sometimes assumed. The editors of the June volumes of the *Acta Sanctorum* published in the 1660s were already trying to distinguish between a *vita fide*, which could be relied upon, a *vita suspecta*, which could not, and a *vita multa fabulosa*, which took off into the realms of fantasy and legend. An exacting standard for modern scholars was set by Fr Hippolyte Delehaye of the Society of Bollandists (1859-1941). As his collaborator and biographer Fr Peeters writes, Delehaye "felt the ugliness of an error or a defect to the very fibres of his being." Yet this precise and rigorous Jesuit scholar was neither an iconoclast nor a cynic. He understood the value of legends in describing how the saints had been understood and venerated through the centuries; and he knew the importance of detective work, sifting through the evidence to find the real person behind the stories.

Scholars will continue to look for new interpretations, new evidence, new insights. Sometimes we see in a glass darkly—or, as the *New Jerusalem Bible* has it, "We see a dim reflection in a mirror." Sometimes we can brush away centuries of cobwebs, correct misapprehensions, find a new approach to an old subject. The study of the saints provides a unique focus for meditation and devotion and a basis for future research.

This volume on the June saints owes much to the help and advice of friends and colleagues. Special thanks are due to Edward and Anne Clay of Kampala, who made a journey to Namugongo to verify information on the Martyrs of Uganda; to Pirrko Carpenter of the Chydenius Institute, Kokkola, Finland, for assistance with St Sergius and St Germanus of Valaam; to the duke of Argyll and Alastair Livingstone, baron of Bachuil, for the story of St Moluag's crozier; to Jane Kelsall, art historian of Saint Albans, who cleared up a number of obscurities in the accounts of St Alban; to Dom Henry Wansbrough, O.S.B., for learned comments on the biblical entries; to Dr Lucy Cohen of The Catholic University of America (Washington, D.C.) for her interest and for reading and commenting on drafts; and to Paul Burns, general editor of this series, for his unfailing support and for drawing my attention to some very interesting saints whom I might otherwise have missed.

---

10 February 1997, Feast of St Scholastica

Kathleen Jones

Abbreviations and Short Forms

A.A.S.	*Acta Apostolicae Sedis, Commentarium officiale.* Rome, 1908-.
AA.SS.	*Acta Sanctorum*, 64 vols. Antwerp, also Rome and Paris, 1643-. June volumes published 1867. Page and volume numbers may vary in different editions.
AA.SS.OSB.	L. d' Achéry and J. Mabillon (eds.), *Acta Sanctorum Ordinis Sancti Benedicti*, 9 vols. Paris, 1668-1701.
Anal.Boll.	*Analecta Bollandiana* (1882-).
Anstruther	G. Anstruther, O. P., *The Seminary Priests*, 4 vols. Ware, Ushaw and Great Wakering, 1968-77.
A.S.C.	G. N. Garmonsway (trans. and ed.), *The Anglo-Saxon Chronicle.* London, 1972.
Auréole Séraphique	Léon de Clary, O.F.M., *Auréole Séraphique*, Eng. trans., *Lives of the Saints and Blessed of the Orders of St Francis*, 4 vols. Taunton, 1887.
Bardenhewer	O. Bardenhewer, *Geschichte der altkirchlichen Literatur.* Freiburg, 1913-32.
B.D.E.C.	J. Gillow (ed.), *Biographical Dictionary of English Catholics*, 5 vols. London and New York, 1887-93.
Bede, *H.E.*	The Venerable Bede, *Historia Ecclesiastica.* Various editions.
B.G.	S. Baring Gould, *Lives of the Saints*, 12 vols. London, 1872-9, rp. 1907.
B.G.F.	S. Baring Gould and J. Fisher, *Lives of the British Saints*, 14 vols. 1907-13.
B.H.G.	Society of Bollandists, *Bibliotheca Hagiographica Graeca.* 3d ed., Brussels, 1957.
B.H.L.	Society of Bollandists, *Bibliotheca Hagiographica Latina*, 2 vols. Brussels, 1898-1901.
B.H.O.	Society of Bollandists, *Bibliotheca Hagiographica Orientalis.* Brussels, 1910, rp. 1970.
Bibl.SS.	*Bibliotheca Sanctorum*, 12 vols. Rome, 1960- 70; Suppl. 1, Rome, 1987.
Capgrave	John Capgrave, *Chronicle of England*, ed. F. C. Hingeston. London, 1858. See also *N.L.A.*
Christian Worship	L. Duchesne, *Christian Worship and its Evolution*, trans. M. L. McClure, 5th ed. London, 1919.
C.M.H.	*Commentarius Perpetuus in Martyrologium Hieronymianum*, ed. H. Delehaye, P. Peeters et al.: in *AA.SS.*, vol. 64. 1940.

C.T.S.	Catholic Truth Society.
D.A.C.L.	F. Cabrol and H. Leclercq (eds.), *Dictionnaire d'archéologie chrétienne et de liturgie.* Paris, 1907-36.
D.C.B.	W. Smith and H. Wace (eds.), *Dictionary of Christian Biography,* 4 vols. London, 1877-87.
D.Cath.Biog.	J. J. Delaney and J. E. Tobin (eds.), *Dictionary of Catholic Biography.* London, 1961.
D.E.C.H.	S. L. Ollard and G. Crosse (eds.), *Dictionary of English Church History.* London and Oxford, 1912; 3d ed. 1971.
de Villegas	Alonso de Villegas Selvado, *Flos Sanctorum* (1623). Eng. trans., *The Lives of the Saints, E.R.L.* 356, 1977.
D.H.G.E.	A. Baudrillart et al. (eds.), *Dictionnaire d'histoire et de géographie ecclésiastique,* Paris, 1912-.
D.H.E.E.	Q. A. Vasquez, T. H. Martínez, *Diccionario de Historia Eclesiastica de España,* 4 vols. Madrid, 1972.
Dict.Hag.	Dom Baudot, O.S.B. (ed.), *Dictionnaire hagiographique.* Paris, 1925.
Dict.Sp.	M. Viller *et al., Dictionnaire de spiritualité.* Paris, 1937.
D.N.B.	Leslie Stephen *et al.* (eds.), *Dictionary of National Biography.* London, 1885-.
D.N.H.	F. Holböck (ed.), *Die neuen Heiligen der katholischen Kirche.* Stein am Rhein, 1994.
D.T.C.	A. Vacant, A. Mangenot, and E. Amann (eds.), *Dictionnaire de théologie catholique,* 15 vols. Paris, 1903-50.
Duchesne, *Fastes*	L. Duchesne, *Fastes épiscopaux de l'ancienne Gaule,* 3 vols. 4th ed., Paris, 1908.
Dufourcq	A. Dufourcq, *Etude sur les Gesta Martyrum Romains,* 4 vols. Paris, 1900-10.
E.H.R.	*English Historical Review,* 1886-.
E.R.L.	D. M. Rodgers (ed.), *English Recusant Literature, 1558-1640.* Ilkley and London, 1970-.
España Sagrada	Enrique Florez, *España Sagrada: Indice.* Madrid, 1877, 2d. ed. 1946.
Eusebius, *H.E.*	Eusebius of Caesarea, *Historia Ecclesiastica.* Various editions: see N.P.N.F. 1.
F.B.S.	Marion A. Habig, *The Franciscan Book of Saints.* Revised ed., Chicago, 1979.
Florence of Worcester, *Chronicon.*	Various editions.

Golden Legend	Jacob de Voragine, *The Golden Legend*, trans. W. G. Ryan. Princeton ed., 2 vols., 1993.
Haddan and Stubbs	A. W. Haddan and W. Stubbs, *Councils and Ecclesiastical Documents*, 3 vols. Oxford, 1869-78.
Hefele-Leclercq	C. J. Hefele, *Histoire des Conciles d'après les documents originaux*, ed. H. Leclercq *et al.* Paris, 1907-.
Heist, V.S.H.	W. W. Heist, *Vita Sanctorum Hiberniae*, 2 vols. Brussels, 1965.
Hieronymianum	see *C.M.H.*
Histoire littéraire	Benedictines of Saint Maur, *Histoire littéraire de la France*. Paris, 1865-1945.
H.S.S.C.	F. Chiovaro *et al.* (eds.), *Histoire des saints et de la sainteté chrétienne*. Paris, 12 vols., 1972-88.
Irish Saints	D. Pochin Mould, *The Irish Saints*. Dublin and London, 1964.
Jaffé	P. Jaffé, *Regesta Pontificum Romanorum*. 1885, 2 vols., rp. Graz, 1956.
Jerome	*Viri illustri, The Lives of Illustrious Men*: see N.P.N.F. 3. Other works, N.P.N.F. 6.
K.S.S.	A. P. Forbes (ed.) *Kalendars of Scottish Saints*. Edinburgh, 1872.
L.E.M. 1	Bede Camm (ed.), *Lives of the English Martyrs*, first series, 2 vols. London, 1904-5.
L.E.M. 2	E. H. Burton and J. H. Pollen, *Lives of the English Martyrs*, second series, on the martyrs declared Venerable 1583-8. London, 1915.
L. D. H.	J. Torsky (ed.), *Lexicon der deutschen Heiligen*. Cologne, 1959.
Lib. Pont.	L. Duchesne (ed.), *Liber Pontificalis*. Paris, 1886.
Liber Pontif.	Raymond Davis (ed.*)*, *The Book of Pontiffs: Liber Pontificalis*. Liverpool, 1989.
Mann	H. K. Mann, *The Lives of the Popes in the Middle Ages*, 16 vols. London, 1922-.
M.G.H.	G. Pertz et al. (eds.), *Monumenta Germaniae Historiae, Scriptores*, 64 vols. Hanover, 1839-1921. Sub-series include *Auctores Antiquissimi, Epistolae Selectae*, and *Scriptores Rerum Merovingicarum*.
M.M.P.	R. Challoner, *Memoirs of Missionary Priests*, new ed. by J. H. Pollen. London, 1924.
Mortier	D. A. Mortier, *Histoire des maîtres généraux O.P.*, 4 vols. Paris, 1923.

N.C.E.	*New Catholic Encyclopedia*, 14 vols. New York, 1967.
N.D.B.	*Neue deutsche Biografie*. Berlin, 1952-.
N.D.S.	D. Attwater, *A New Dictionary of Saints*, ed. J. Cumming, Tunbridge Wells and Collegeville, Minn., 1993.
N.L.A.	C. Horstmann (ed.), *Nova Legendae Angliae*, 2 vols. Oxford, 1901.
N.P.N.F.	P. Schaff and H. Wace (eds.), The Nicene and Post-Nicene Christian Fathers, 1887-1900: 2d series rp., Grand Rapids, Michigan, 1979. vol. 1, Eusebius of Caesarea, *Historia Ecclesiastica*; vol. 2, Socrates, *Historia Ecclesiastica*; Sozomen; *Historia Ecclesiastica*; vol. 3, Jerome, *Viri illustri*, Rufinus, *Historia Ecclesiastica*; vol. 4, Theodoret; *Historia Ecclesiastica*; vol. 10, Ambrose, *Principal Works and Letters*.
N.S.B. 1	Thierry Lelièvre, *100 nouveaux saints et bienheureux de 1963 à 1984*. Paris, 1983.
N.S.B. 2	Thierry Lelièvre, *Nouveaux saints et bienheureux de 1984 à 1988*, Paris, 1989.
O.D.C.C.	F. L. Cross and E. A. Livingstone (eds.), *The Oxford Dictionary of the Christian Church*. Oxford and New York, 1957; 2d ed., 1974; 3d ed., 1997.
O.D.P.	J. W. Kelly (ed.), *The Oxford Dictionary of Popes*. Oxford, 1986.
O.D.S	D. H. Farmer (ed.), *The Oxford Dictionary of Saints*. Oxford and New York, 3d ed., 1992.
Origines du culte	H. Delehaye, *Les origines du culte des martyrs*. Brussels, 1911.
Pastor	L. Pastor, *History of the Popes from the Close of the Middle Ages*, 40 vols., various eds. and trans. 6th ed., London, 1938.
P.B.	F. Guérin (ed.), *Vie des Saints des Petits Bollandistes*, 17 vols. Paris, 1880.
P.G.	J. P. Migne (ed.), *Patrologia Graeca*, 112 vols. Paris, 1857-66.
P.L.	J. P. Migne (ed.), *Patrologia Latina*, 221 vols. Paris, 1844-64.
Plummer, *V. S. H.*	C. Plummer, *Vitae Sanctorum Hiberniae*, 2 vols. Oxford 1910, 2d ed., 1968.
Procter	J. Procter (ed.), *Short Lives of the Dominican Saints*. London, 1900.

Propylaeum	H. Delehaye (ed.), *Propylaeum ad Acta Sanctorum Decembris*: *AA.SS.*, 65. Brussels, 1940.
Quentin	H. Quentin, *Les martyrologes historiques du Moyen Age*. Paris, 1908.
Rev.Bén.	*Revue Bénédictine*, 1885-.
R.H.E.	*Revue d'histoire ecclésiastique*, 1900-.
Roscarrock	Nicholas Roscarrock, *Lives of the Saints: Cornwall and Devon*, Devon and Cornwall Record Society, new series 35, ed. Nicholas Orme. Exeter, 1992.
R.P.S.J.	H. Foley (ed.), *Records of the English Province of the Society of Jesus*, 8 vols. Roehampton, 1879.
R.S.	Rolls Series: *Rerum Britannicum Medii Aevi Scriptores*, H. M. Stationery Office. London, 1858-.
Rufinus, *H.E.*	See N.P.N.F. 3.
Ruinart	T. Ruinart, *Acta Martyrum Sincera*. Paris, 1859.
Saints in Italy	Lucy Menzies, *The Saints in Italy*. London, 1924.
S.B.I.	A. Bond and N. Mabin, *Saints of the British Isles*. Bognor Regis, 1980.
Socrates, *H.E.*	See N.P.N.F. 2.
Sozomen, *H.E.*	See N.P.N.F. 2.
Stanton	R. Stanton, *A Menology of England and Wales*. London, 1892.
Synax.Const.	*The Synaxary of Constantinople*, in H. Delehaye (ed.), *Propylaeum ad Acta Sanctorum Novembris*, *AA.SS.*, 64. Brussels, 1902.
Wadding	L. Wadding, *Annales seu Trium Ordinum a S. Francisco Institutorum*, 25 vols. Rome, 1931-47.
William Worcestre	*Itineraries*, ed. J. H. Harvey. Oxford, 1969.

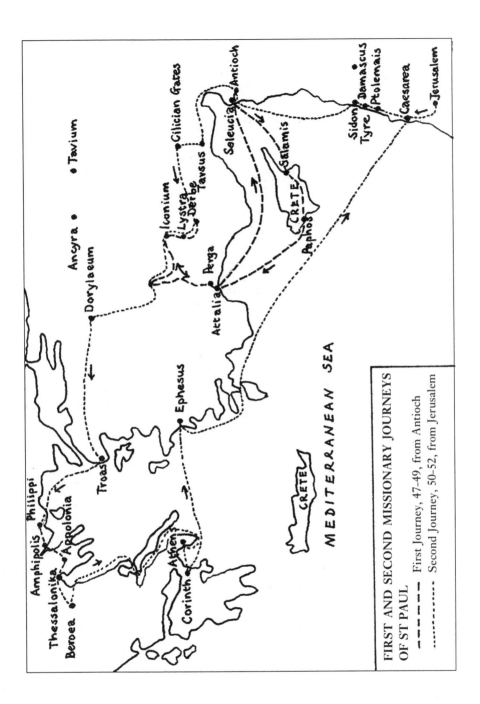

FIRST AND SECOND MISSIONARY JOURNEYS
OF ST PAUL

- - - - First Journey, 47-49, from Antioch

·········· Second Journey, 50-52, from Jerusalem

MEDITERRANEAN SEA

Thessalonika
Amphipolis
Philippi
Apollonia
Beroea
Athens
Corinth
Troas
Ephesus
Dorylaeum
Ancyra
Tavium
Iconium
Lystra
Derbe
Tarsus
Cilician Gates
Attalia
Perga
Seleucia
Antioch
Salamis
CRETE
Paphos
Sidon
Damascus
Tyre
Ptolemais
Caesarea
Jerusalem
CRETE

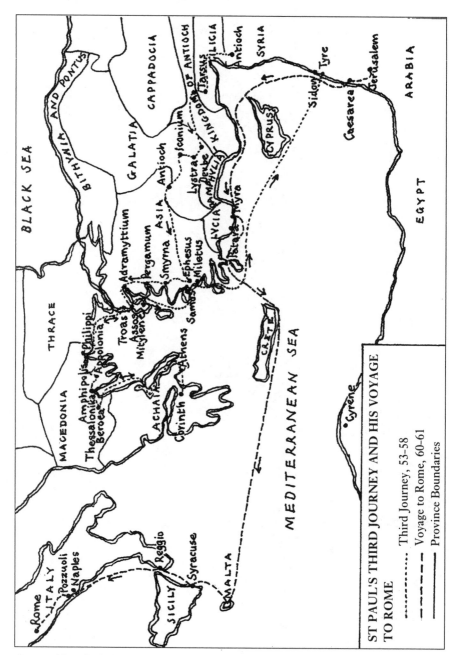

ST PAUL'S THIRD JOURNEY AND HIS VOYAGE
TO ROME

.... Third Journey, 53–58

– – – – Voyage to Rome, 60–61

———— Province Boundaries

Source: New Catholic Encyclopedia

1

ST JUSTIN MARTYR (*c*.100-65)

Justin was a Greek from Samaria who became a Christian about the year 135. He is the first notable Christian philosopher. His extensive writings, undertaken at a time when the early Church faced many pressures, show a fearless and unprejudiced search for truth and an attempt to reconcile the new Christian truths with traditional Hellenistic metaphysics.

He was born at Nablus (Shechem, or Flavia Neapolis) in Samaria. He was not a Jew, either by birth or by religion. He was a Greek, and he was given a classical Greek education. He studied rhetoric, poetry, and history and then turned to philosophy, searching, as he says himself, for "the vision of God." He travelled widely, joining philosophy schools in Ephesus and Alexandria, and he was attracted in turn to the schools of the Stoics, the Peripatetics, and the Pythagoreans. He found the Stoic philosophy too arid, the Peripatetic teacher too keen on material rewards, the Pythagorean too broad in his approach, for he demanded a knowledge of geometry, music, and astronomy as a prerequisite to philosophical study. In Platonism, Justin found some of the answers to the questions he was asking, and he was trained in dialectic. In the *Dialogue with Trypho*, he says: "The perception of incorporeal things quite overwhelmed me, and the Platonic theory of ideas added wings to my mind, so that in a short time, I imagined myself a wise man. So great was my folly that I fully expected immediately to gaze upon God."

One day while walking by the seashore, probably at Ephesus, he met a "respectable old man of meek and venerable mien" who told him about the Hebrew prophets and Christianity. Justin writes, "My spirit was immediately set on fire, and an affection for the Prophets and for those who are friends of Christ took hold of me; while pondering on his words, I discovered that his was the only sure and useful philosophy."

In Christianity he found the answer to his search. He taught at Ephesus. Jerome (30 Sept.), writing about him some two centuries later, says that he practised "as a philosopher, and wearing the garb of a philosopher," the traditional and distinctive philosopher's cloak. He debated publicly with the Jews, with the Gnostics, and with those who worshipped the Roman gods. In about the year 150 he went to Rome, where he taught Christian apologetics, founded a school of philosophy, and wrote his major works.

While the Apostolic Fathers, such as Pope St Clement of Rome (23 Nov.), St Ignatius of Antioch (13 Oct.), and St Polycarp (23 Feb.), wrote theology for the early Christian communities, Justin wrote an intellectual defence of Christian beliefs against outside attack.

He is said to have lived a very ascetic and austere life. His pleasure was in the cut and thrust of intellectual exchange, and he was constantly involved in controversy and public debate. He opposed the teaching of Crescens the Cynic, whom he described as "the lover not of wisdom but of false opinions," and he stated "I expect to be the victim of a plot and to be affixed to the stake . . . perhaps even by Crescens, that lover of fanfare and ostentation." Jerome says that Crescens was involved in Justin's arrest. Justin's fearless defence of Christianity and his thorough demolition of his opponents must have made him many enemies. His martyrdom took place in the reign of Marcus Aurelius, and an authentic record of the proceedings survives. He stated his beliefs, refused to sacrifice to the Roman gods, and accepted suffering and death as the means to salvation. He was beheaded with six other Christians about the year 165.

Justin wrote many works, of which only his two *Apologies* and the *Dialogue with Trypho* survive, together with some works of more doubtful attribution: the *Exhortation to the Greeks*; the *Discourse to the Greeks*; and *The Monarchy*, subtitled *The Rule of God*. Justin's literary work is of particular importance for three reasons: first, he gives us a vivid picture of the early Church under pressure from its opponents; second, he provides some insights into its worship; third, he sees Platonic thought and Christian revelation as two streams of knowledge sent by God, mutually reinforcing. Some later commentators have suggested that he ignores fundamental differences between the two, but his integrative vision was to have a profound effect on later writers such as Augustine of Hippo (28 Aug.) and Thomas Aquinas (28 Jan.).

Christianity was only one of the many religious systems that competed in the eastern part of the Roman Empire in his day, and it was neither respectable nor acceptable to Roman society. Rumours circulated that Christians practised incest and cannibalism, and their secret meetings were held to be subversive. The rites of Baptism and the Eucharist were thought to be black magic. Respectable citizens may not have taken the Roman gods very seriously, but they took the view that the ceremonial buttressed the existing order and held the empire together. Christians were often called "atheists" because they refused to subscribe to public worship. Justin brushes these slanders aside, commenting that they may be true of some of the Gnostic sects but that Christians worship only the supreme God and his revelation to mankind in Christ. He insists that Christians pay their taxes, are honest in trade, and live peaceably with their fellows.

He has little to say about miracles, which, in the context of his time, might have been regarded as magic. Instead he describes the whole tradition of the Jewish prophets and their fulfilment in the earthly life of Christ. He refers to the cave where Jesus was born and the place of his execution—both already holy places for Christians. The emperor Hadrian had erected a temple to

2

Adonis on the site of the Nativity and a statue of Jupiter and a temple to Venus on the site of Calvary to discourage veneration; but as Jerome was to comment later, this merely marked the sites out for worshippers and for future generations.

Justin taught from a living tradition, for the evidence of the evangelists had not yet taken the form of the New Testament as we know it, and he may not even have seen the Gospels in written form. He taught that God sent his prophets to predict the coming of Christ to the Jews and the Greek philosophers, such as Socrates and Plato, to prepare the minds of the Graeco-Roman world for his message; and when the time was fulfilled the *Logos* came into the world—Light of Light, like the flame kindled from one torch by another. Christ is the new Adam, and his mother Mary the new Eve. The Incarnation is not a break in history but the fulfilment of history. By the mystery of Christ crucified, God has broken the power of sin and evil and offers redemption to the whole human race. The resurrected Christ will come to judge the living and the dead. The rites of Baptism and the Eucharist are carefully described to distinguish them from other rituals of the time, such as those of the Mithraists: Baptism is a new birth, and the Eucharist is participation in the life of Christ himself.

Because of his devotion to truth, Justin is an excellent and reliable witness. He gives us an insight into the life and doctrines of the Church only a century after the crucifixion and sets out a theology of history that was to be elaborated by later Christian writers but not superseded.

Eusebius, *H.E.*, 4, 8 and 16–18; Jerome, ch. 23; *AA.SS.*, Apr., 2, pp. 105-30, and June, 1, pp. 16–32. Modern Lives by M. J. Lagrange (1914); C. C. Martindale (1923); E. Goodenough (1930); L. W. Barnard (1967). See also Bardenhewer, 1, pp. 190–241; A. L. Williams, *Justin Martyr: The Dialogue with Trypho* (New York, 1930); T. B. Falls, *The Writing of Saint Justin Martyr* (New York, 1948); H. Chadwick, "Justin Martyr's Defence of Christians," *Bulletin of the John Ryland's Library* 47 (1965), pp. 275-97.

St Pamphilus and Companions, *Martyrs* (309)

The historian Eusebius of Caesarea was a pupil, a friend, and perhaps a kinsman of Pamphilus. He admired his teacher greatly and wrote his life in three volumes; St Jerome knew this work, but it has since disappeared. When Pamphilus died Eusebius styled himself Eusebius Pamphili in his honour.

Pamphilus came of a rich and well-regarded Phoenician family in Berytus (Beirut). He studied in his native city and then went to continue his studies in the great catechetical school at Alexandria. He moved to Caesarea, where he was ordained priest, and spent the rest of his life there. He was known as the greatest biblical scholar of his age, and his work in examining and correcting manuscripts led to the collation of the best texts of the Bible then known. This provided a foundation for the work which Jerome (30 Sept.) was to carry out later in the fourth century. Pamphilus founded a school of sacred literature and built up a library which survived until the seventh century, when it was destroyed by the Arabs.

Pamphilus was known as a very hard worker, transcribing many documents with his own hand and having copies made in his school for dissemination elsewhere. He seems to have been the most generous of men, using his wealth for the benefit of others. He often gave copies of manuscripts away without payment in order to encourage biblical study. He treated his slaves as members of his family and gave money freely to his relatives, his friends, and the poor.

In 307 or 308 Urbanus, the governor of Palestine, had him arrested for refusing to sacrifice to the Roman gods. He was tortured and imprisoned but refused to give way. During his imprisonment, which lasted nearly two years, he collaborated with Eusebius, who may also have been a prisoner, in writing the *Apology for Origen*. Pamphilus had come under the influence of Origen's pupil Pierius during his time at Alexandria. He greatly admired Origen's works, many of which he had caused to be transcribed.

Toward the end of 309 Urban's successor as governor had him brought to trial with two other Christians, Valens and Paul of Jamnia. Valens was an elderly deacon who was said to have committed the whole of the Bible to heart, and Paul preached with great fervour. All three were condemned to death. Their behaviour at the trial was so inspiring that other Christians supported them, and they were also condemned. Porphyrius, a gifted young scholar who was one of Pamphilus' pupils, asked, when his teacher was sentenced, for permission to bury his body. He also was arrested and cruelly tortured to death. Seleucus, who saw Porphyrius die and brought news of his witness to the other Christians, was arrested. The governor, furious to find that even his own favourite servant, an old man named Theodulus, was a Christian and had embraced one of the martyrs, had Theodulus crucified. Pamphilus, Valens, Paul, and Seleucus were all beheaded, with some others whose names have not survived. There are thought to have been eleven martyrs in all. Their bodies were thrown out for the wild beasts to devour, but were rescued and given decent burial by the Christian community, at great risk.

Eusebius describes Pamphilus as "the glory of the Caesarean church, illustrious for every virtue, especially for absolute unworldliness, philosophic conduct, and self-discipline, thorough devotedness to the study of the scriptures, untiring energy in all that he undertook, generosity to the poor, and ready kindness to all who came near him."

Eusebius, *De Martyribus Palestinae*, chs. 7-9. The Latin text is in *AA.SS.*, June, 1, pp. 60-9. The Greek text is in *Anal.Boll.* 16 (1897), pp. 113-39. See also *C.M.H.*, p. 218; Ruinart, pp. 363, 366-7; Bardenhewer, 2, pp. 242-7; *B.G.*, June, pp. 2-3; *D.C.B.*, 4, pp. 178-9. Pamphilus is commemorated in the early *Syriac Breviarum* and in the *Hieronymianum*, pp. 100-1. The latter includes Delehaye's commentary.

St Wite (date unknown)

Very little is known about this saint, but her cult is of great antiquity. The village of Whitchurch Canonicorum in Dorset is thought to take its name from her. It is mentioned as Hwitan Cyrcian in the will of King Alfred, so the name was well known in the ninth century. The church is dedicated to St Wite (the Latin form of her name, Candida, is not known until the sixteenth century), and her shrine is in the north transept. This consists of a fourteenth-century coffin covered by a marble slab, on a thirteenth-century base. There is no inscription, but it has long been known locally as the saint's shrine.

When repairs were being carried out in the north transept in 1900, the coffin was opened at one end. Inside were pieces of bone, teeth, wood, and lead (presumably all that remained of an earlier coffin), and a leaden casket with the inscription *Hic Reqesct Reliqe Sce Wite*, containing more bones. The inscription is in twelfth- or thirteenth-century raised lettering. These bones were not disturbed, and the coffin was replaced after cleaning. Apart from the tomb of St Edward the Confessor (13 Oct.), this is the only shrine known to survive intact from the Anglo-Saxon period.

In the twelfth century Sir Robert de Mandevil bequeathed an estate to "St Wita or the church at Whitchurch." Robert Pyke, who died in 1531, asked that his body be buried in the chancel of "Saincte White of Whitechurch."

Several theories have been put forward about Wite's identity: that she was a West Saxon woman of whom no other record is known; that she was a Welsh or Breton saint whose relics were given by King Athelstan to the church which his grandfather Alfred had founded; that she was the much-married St Gwen Teirbron of Cornwall and Brittany (Gwen means "white," and this saint is called Candida or Blanche in Brittany); that she was in fact a man, to be identified with St Witta or Albinus, an Anglo-Saxon monk who became bishop of Bursburg in Hesse about 760; or that Wite simply means "white" and is not the name of a man or a woman. The word is such a common one that many explanations are possible, and there are, as the previous editors of this work concluded, "no solid grounds for speculation" about any of them. However, St Wite's relics are mentioned by both William Worcestre and John Gerard, who calls her St Vita. Gerard says: "The virgin Vita was the daughter of a west of England king, and many churches were dedicated to her under the name of Witchurch."

St Thomas More (22 June) mentions a sixteenth-century local custom of offering the saint cakes and ale on her feast-day.

William Worcestre, pp. 73 and n., 123 and n.; John Gerard, *Autobiography* (1950 ed.), p. 50; B.G.F., 8, pp. 68-9; O.D.S., p. 492.

SS Proculus the Soldier, *Martyr* (*c.* 304), **and Proculus of Bologna,** *Bishop and Martyr* (*c.* 542)

Proculus "the Soldier" was at one time the principal patron of Bologna, and his story has been confused with that of a bishop of the same name who lived some two and a half centuries later. The military Proculus is thought to have been an officer in Diocletian's army and to have been martyred about the year 304. Tradition is that he was beheaded, but St Paulinus of Nola (22 June), writing in the late fourth or early fifth century, says in a poem that he was crucified. The clerical Proculus was born in Bologna and became bishop in 540. He was martyred by the Goths some two years later.

At the end of the fourteenth century the Benedictines built a church in Bologna, to which the relics of the two saints were taken. They were placed in the same tomb. The church received the title of St Proculus or San Proclo, commemorating both. In Italy they are known as "San Proclo Soldato" and "San Proclo Vescovo" to distinguish them, and their cult spread to other cities. Fr Delehaye takes the view that St Proculus of Pozzuoli and St Proculus of Ravenna may be identified with the soldier, and St Proculus of Terni with the bishop. They are sometimes found together in paintings of the Bolognese school.

C.M.H., p. 219; *B.H.L.*, 2, pp. 1012-3; *AA.SS.*, June, 1, pp. 48-50 (Proculus the Soldier), and pp. 77-80 (Proculus, bishop of Reggio). The latter entry deals with the cult and the confusion between the two. *Origines du culte*, pp. 300-1, 316, 328; *Saints in Italy*, pp. 369-70.

St Caprasius of Lérins, *Abbot* (430)

Caprasius was the spiritual director and teacher of St Honoratus of Arles (16 Jan.). He gave up great worldly prospects to live as a hermit on the Iles de Lérins, off the Mediterranean coast of Gaul. There he was visited by Honoratus and his brother Venantius, two young men who sought to learn from him. When the brothers felt that they were called to go to the East, Caprasius accompanied them. They endured considerable hardships and privations; their health suffered, and when they were in Greece, Venantius died. Caprasius and Honoratus returned to Gaul and lived for some time in the hills above Fréjus before deciding to return to Lérins in order to live a very austere life according to the example of the Desert Fathers. Others joined them, and inspired by the Rule of St Pachomius (9 May), they decided to form a community like the monastery of Tabbenisi in Egypt, where a number of small religious houses were organized under a common Rule and a single superior.

It seems that Caprasius never actually acted as superior of what was to become a famous monastic institution. Perhaps he was too old, or perhaps it was Honoratus who had the necessary gifts of administration; but Caprasius is reckoned as the founder and first abbot of Lérins, presumably because he continued to be Honoratus' director and so indirectly that of the whole community.

The *laudatio* delivered by St Hilary of Arles (5 May) after his death praised

Caprasius for his great sanctity. This is our chief source of information about him. Hilary was a former monk of Lérins, related to Honoratus, and he succeeded him as bishop of Arles. The influence of Lérins, which was to spread through Gaul and the Celtic Church in Ireland and Britain, owed much to the example of Caprasius as its first spiritual guide.

B.H.L., 1, pp. 234-5; *AA.SS.*, June, 1, pp. 75-7, is based on an ancient manuscript from the abbey of Lérins; *C.M.H.*, pp. 218-9; Duchesne, *Fastes*, 2, pp. 144-7; H. Moris, *L'abbaye de Lérins* (1909); A. C. Cooper-Marsdin, *History of the Islands of the Lérins* (1913); J-J. Antier, *Lérins, l'île sainte de la Côte d'Azur* (1988).

St Wistan (850)

Wistan (Wystan, Winston) was a prince of the royal family of Mercia. His father, Wigmund, died in 839, and Wistan succeeded his grandfather, Wiglaf, as king of Mercia in 840. He was still young, and his mother, Elfleda, ruled as regent for a time.

Berhtic (Brifardus), another member of the royal family, wanted to marry Elfleda. Wistan forbade the marriage, ostensibly on the grounds of consanguinity: Berhtic was a kinsman, and his godfather. He may have distrusted Berhtic, who was ambitious and wanted to seize power. If so, he had good reason: in 850, Berhtic ferociously murdered Wistan and three of his knights at Wistanstow—probably Wistow in Leicestershire. Wistan is said to have been scalped. His body was buried in the royal monastery at Repton with those of his father and grandfather.

The abbots of Evesham supported Canute and later the Norman kings. Royal favour made it possible for them to acquire the relics of Anglo-Saxon saints. In 1019 Abbot Aelfweard, who subsequently became bishop of London, asked King Canute for Wistan's relics, and Canute agreed to their transfer from Repton. In 1075 another abbot, Ethelwig, collaborated with the Norman barons in suppressing the Revolt of the Three Earls, and four years later he became royal justiciar for Shropshire, Herefordshire, Worcestershire, Staffordshire, Warwickshire, Oxfordshire, and Gloucestershire. When Archbishop Lanfranc's commission investigated the cults of Anglo-Saxon saints and abolished many, the monks of Evesham were allowed to keep most or all of their relics. Those of St Egwin of Worcester (30 Dec.) were taken on tour to provide money for a new abbey church.

A curious legend from Wistow is that on the anniversary of Wistan's death a light hovered over the spot where he was killed and a crop of human hair grew from the ground. In fact, several kinds of fungus have a hairlike appearance, dark or blond, so there may be a natural explanation for the latter phenomenon. It was said to have been verified by a commission sent to Wistow by Baldwin, archbishop of Canterbury; but verification would have been difficult, since the "hair" was visible for only one hour in the year and then disappeared again.

There are three ancient dedications to Wistan—Wistow and Wigstow in Leicestershire and Wistanstow in Shropshire.

Evesham Chronicle (R.S. 35), ed. W. D. Macray, pp. 325-7; *N.L.A.*, 2, pp. 522-30; *AA.SS.*, June, 1, pp. 83-4. In his preface to the Rolls Series edition of the *Evesham Chronicle* (p. xxxix), Macray notes that the story of the hair, which appears in the *Chronicle*, is omitted from *N.L.A.* and *AA.SS.* Florence of Worcester, *Chronicon, an.* 850; William Worcestre, p. 165; *B.H.L.*, 2, p. 1295; *Anal.Boll.* 58 (1940), pp. 90-103; D. Rollason, *The Search for St Wystan* (1981). For fungi, see Roger Phillips, *Mushrooms and Other Fungi of Great Britain and Europe* (1981), pp. 67, 75, and 117. For Ethelwig, see F. M. Stenton, *Anglo-Saxon England*, Oxford History of England (1947), pp. 612, 623.

St Simeon of Syracuse (1035)

A Life, still extant, was written soon after Simeon's death by his friend Eberwin, abbot of Tholey and St Martin's at Trier, at the request of Archbishop Poppo of Trier. The curious and adventurous circumstances of Simeon's career are thus very well attested.

Simeon was born in Syracuse in Sicily. His father was Greek, and at the age of seven he was taken to Constantinople to be educated. When he was old enough he decided that he had a vocation to the solitary life, so he went on a pilgrimage to the Holy Land and planned to settle there. He lived with a hermit by the river Jordan and later entered a monastery near Mount Sinai. With the abbot's permission, he spent two years as a solitary in a cave by the Red Sea and then some time in a hermitage near the top of Mount Sinai, but when he returned to the monastery he was given a commission which led him into a different sort of life. He and another monk were charged to go to Normandy to collect tribute from Duke Richard II. The money was urgently needed for the support of the community.

The two monks set out, but their ship was captured by pirates, who murdered the passengers as well as the crew. Simeon escaped by jumping overboard and swimming ashore. He made his way on foot to Antioch, where he met Richard, abbot of Verdun, and Eberwin, abbot of St Martin's, on their way home to France from Palestine. The three men became friends and agreed to travel together, but at Belgrade they were separated. The French pilgrims were allowed to proceed, but Simeon and a monk named Cosmas, who had joined the party, were arrested. When they were finally freed, they made a long and painful journey through the mountainous terrain of what is now Bosnia to the coast, encountering robbers and much hardship before they were able to take a ship for Italy. Eventually they reached Rome and pressed on to the south of France, where Cosmas died. Simeon traversed France and at last reached Normandy, only to discover in Rouen that Duke Richard was dead and that his successor, either Richard III (1026-7) or his brother Robert I (1027-35), father of William the Conqueror, refused to pay the tribute.

Simeon had travelled some four thousand miles to carry out his commission, and years must have elapsed since the time he left Mount Sinai. He went to consult his friends Abbot Richard of Verdun and Abbot Eberwin of Trier. At Trier he was introduced to Archbishop Poppo, who was about to undertake a pilgrimage to Palestine. The archbishop asked Simeon to accompany him as a guide, and—this time in company and well protected—he made the journey back to the Holy Land. We do not know whether he returned to his former monastery in Sinai, but when the archbishop made his way back to Trier, Simeon went with him.

There he at last found the solitude he desired after his years of travel. He was allowed to live as a hermit in a tower near the city's Porta Nigra, and the archbishop himself carried out the enclosure. He spent the rest of his life in penance, prayer, and contemplation. His life was not without its trials: he endured many temptations and sometimes assaults from the local populace. On one occasion, a rumour that he was practising black magic led to an attack in which he was assaulted with stones and missiles, but in time he was recognized as a holy man. When he died, Abbot Eberwin closed his eyes, and his funeral was attended by the entire population. The Porta Nigra became known as St Simeon's Gate. Archbishop Poppo wrote his biography and promoted his cause at Rome. He was canonized in 1042, only seven years after his death. The first recorded solemn canonization, by Pope John XV, was that of St Ulric, bishop of Augsburg (4 July), and Simeon's canonization by Pope Benedict IX is generally regarded as the second.

The Latin biography written by Abbot Eberwin is given in *AA.SS.*, June, 1, pp. 86-100. See also E. W. Kemp, *Canonisation and Authority* (1948), pp. 60-1; *Anal.Boll.* 68 (1950), pp. 181-96; *N.D.S.*, p. 290.

St Eneco of Oña, *Abbot* (1057)

Eneco (Iñigo, Ignatius) was a monk of the abbey of San Juan de la Peña in Aragon and the baptismal patron of St Ignatius of Loyola (31 July). According to one account he had been prior for some time when he felt the call to the solitary life he had practised before entering the monastery. He was allowed to live as a hermit in the mountains of Aragon, and he developed a great reputation for sanctity and austerity. King Sancho of Castile, who supported the Cluniac Rule and introduced it into his dominions, determined that Eneco should go to take charge of a monastery at Oña, which was to be brought into conformity to the Rule. The monastery, founded by the king's father-in-law, Count Sancho of Castile, about the year 1010, was said to have become lax in its observances. King Sancho had sent monks from San Juan de la Peña to replace the nuns and appointed a new abbot, García, a disciple of St Odilo of Cluny (1 Jan.); but García died before his work was completed, and so the king sent envoys to Eneco asking him to take his place.

Eneco, clinging to his life of solitude, refused; and he changed his mind only after King Sancho personally made the journey to his remote hermitage to

9

persuade him. Once committed, he made an excellent abbot. The Rule was restored, the numbers of monks increased, controversies were settled, and Eneco acquired a statesmanlike reputation for reconciling bitter divisions between groups and individuals far beyond the walls of the monastery. He seems to have been a man of great tolerance and gentleness of character: it is said that when he died even Jews and Moors lamented his death. Many local legends grew up around him.

Eneco is mentioned in the calendar of Oña, a twelfth-century Franco-Hispanic calendar, and there is evidence of his cult. He is thought to have been canonized by Pope Alexander III (1159-81), but there is some obscurity about the date. It is known that in 1259 Pope Alexander IV granted an indulgence to pilgrims who visited the church at Oña "on the feast of Blessed Eneco, confessor, former abbot of the said monastery."

AA.SS., June, 1, pp. 104-23; Fidel Fita, *Boletín de la real Academia de la Historia* 27 (1895), pp. 76-136, and 38 (1901), pp. 206-13; *C.M.H.*, p. 219; *D.H.G.E.*, 15, 458; *D.H.E.E.*, 2, p. 109; *P.B.*, 6, pp. 17-18; *España Sagrada*, 27, pp. 142-75; E. W. Kemp, "Pope Alexander III and the Canonisation of Saints," *Transactions of the Royal Historical Society*, 4th series, 27 (1945), pp. 13-28. For the connection with St Ignatius Loyola, see *Anal.Boll.* 52 (1934), p. 448, and 69 (1951), pp. 295-301.

St Theobald of Alba (1150)

Devotion to Theobald Roggieri centres on Vico, near Mondovi, where he was born, and Alba, where he spent most of his life. He is honoured throughout Piedmont as the patron of cobblers and porters. The only known account of his life, published in 1626 by D. Passoni, is claimed to be based on authentic documents, but these were not located at the time of publication and have not subsequently come to light. According to Passoni's account Theobald came of a relatively wealthy family and received a good education, but he felt that a Christian should live simply and humbly. He went to Alba and was apprenticed to a shoemaker. He was so successful at this trade that when his master was dying, the old man asked him to marry his daughter and take over the business. Theobald, who had taken a vow of celibacy, did not want to distress his master, so he temporized until after the funeral. Then he handed over all his earnings to the widow, asking her to distribute them among the poor, and left Alba, penniless, to make a pilgrimage to Compostela.

He had no ambition to be a worldly success, even as a shoemaker. When he returned, he abandoned his trade and hired himself out as a porter, carrying sacks of corn and other goods. He gave two-thirds of his earnings away, slept on the ground, and practised other austerities. His way of life brought him into contact with many sick and poor people, whom he cared for. Once in his life he uttered a curse—we do not know whom he cursed, or why, but in expiation he undertook to sweep out the cathedral church of San Lorenzo and to tend its lamps for the rest of his life.

Commentators have tended to be suspicious of this narrative because of the alleged disappearance of Passoni's documentary sources; but the story is so modest, so specific, and so lacking in the extravagant legends that often become attached to the lives of medieval saints that this may not be a reason for disbelieving it. Theobald's relics were said to have been discovered in Alba in 1429.

For Passoni's Life, see *AA.SS.*, June, 1, pp. 132-44, which gives a Latin translation of the original Italian. There are a number of small devotional booklets, some of comparatively recent dates, but these all rely on Passoni as the only available source. *Saints in Italy*, p. 427; *N.D.S.*, p. 300.

Bd John Storey, *Martyr* (1571)

Born about 1504 and educated in law at Oxford, John Storey proceeded to a lectureship in law after graduation. He was known as "the most noted civilian and canonist of his time." He became Oxford's first Regius Professor of Civil Law, and for two years he was principal of Broadgates Hall, now Pembroke College. He took Henry VIII's Oath of Supremacy (perhaps, like many other clerics and academics, hoping that the king's quarrel with the pope would pass), but he was very uneasy about the king's claims and the breach with the papacy.

In 1537 he resigned his academic appointments, which placed him in a prominent and vulnerable position if he should be regarded as a dissident. He married, was admitted to Doctors' Commons, and began to practise as an advocate. He entered Parliament as the member for Hindon in Wiltshire, and in the first Parliament of Edward VI he strongly opposed the Act of Uniformity of 1549 and the new *Book of Common Prayer*, both of an extreme Protestant nature. The House of Commons was incensed at his speeches, and he was committed to the Tower of London for three months. When he was released he went to Louvain, where many opponents of the new régime were based.

Queen Mary's accession in 1553 marked a rise in his fortunes. He returned to England and was appointed chancellor of the dioceses of Oxford and London and dean of the Arches. These were the major legal posts within the church structure. At first the return to Catholicism proceeded peacefully; but when Mary married Philip of Spain in 1554, the previous violence against Catholics was replaced by an equal violence against Protestants. Latimer, bishop of Worcester, and Ridley, bishop of London, were convicted of heresy and went to the stake in 1555, and Thomas Cranmer, archbishop of Canterbury, followed in 1558. Edmund Bonner, the restored bishop of London, had himself been incarcerated in the Marshalsea Prison in Edward VI's time, and he had no mercy on those who had persecuted him. In his capacity as chief legal officer, Storey took a major part in prosecuting those who refused to abandon their Protestant beliefs. He acted as Queen's Proctor at Cranmer's trial. In all, some three or four hundred people are thought to have been burned at the stake.

Storey lived on into the reign of Elizabeth I and remained in England after her accession, when many Catholics fled to the Continent. He was still a member of Parliament, and he opposed the new Act of Supremacy in the House of Commons. He was imprisoned, first in the Fleet and then in the Marshalsea, but managed to escape and found his way back to Louvain. There he and his family were wretchedly impoverished. He was reduced to becoming a pensioner of the king of Spain and took a post which involved searching English ships in Antwerp harbour for contraband and heretical books. This proved his undoing. While he was searching the hold of an English ship, the hatches were closed, and the ship sailed for England.

At Yarmouth he was arrested and charged with treason. One of the people who attended his trial in Westminster Hall (in disguise, because he too was a suspected person) was Edmund Campion (1 Dec.). Storey refused to plead at his trial, saying that he was no longer an English citizen but a subject of the king of Spain. He also claimed that he had been responsible for saving the lives of many Protestants: for example, when twenty-eight people were condemned to be burned, he and the abbot of Westminster had made representations to the papal legate, Cardinal Pole, on the grounds that the accused did not know what they were doing. They had gone together to the queen, who pardoned them all save one, "an old woman that dwelt about Paul's Churchyard; she would not convert, and therefore was burned."

Storey continued: "Yea, it was my procurement that there should be no more burnt in London; for I saw well that it would not prevail, and therefore we sent them into odd corners, into the country." There is no reason to doubt this: the violence and barbarity on both sides in this conflict were such as to appall even those whose positions forced them to take part; John Storey had held a position of such prominence in Queen Mary's reign that his plea had no effect. He was condemned to death, and he died at Tyburn.

The account in *L.E.M*, 2, pp. 14-110, is based on contemporary records. See also for general background J. H. Pollen, *The English Catholics in the Reign of Elizabeth* (1920); J. Bossy, *The English Catholic Community 1570-1850* (1975).

Bd Hannibal di Francia, *Founder* (1851-1927)

Annibale Maria di Francia was born in Messina, and he was only nine years old when Garibaldi's troops swept through Sicily on their way to unify Italy. In this troubled and impoverished port he grew up as a free-thinker without religious affiliation, satisfying his instincts for ritual through Freemasonry. The call to a religious vocation was, as he noted later, "unexpected"; but when it came it was "most sure," and it changed his whole life.

He was ordained in 1878 and sent to one of the poorest quarters of the area, where he worked among the peasantry and had a particular care for orphaned children. As Pope John Paul II said at his beatification, he had grown up with the knowledge that the harvest was rich, but the labourers were few (Matt. 9:37-8).

In a life of unremitting labour for his people he met and worked with Melanie Calvat, the mystic of La Salette. She helped to inspire him to found an Order for women, the Daughters of the Holy Zeal, and then only two months later, the Rogationist Fathers. The two Congregations now have a total of approximately one thousand members in many countries, including Italy, Spain, Brazil, the United States, Australia, Argentina, the Philippines, and Ruanda.

Fr di Francia died on 1 June 1927 at the age of seventy-six, a year after establishing the world's first shrine dedicated to prayer for vocations.

A.A.S. 84, (1992), pp. 109-11; *D.N.H.*, 3, pp. 226-30; *Osservatore Romano*, 1 Oct. 1990.

ST JUSTIN MARTYR (pp. 1-3)
Gold pen, sword with gold hilt and silver blade,
on red field.

13

2

SS MARCELLINUS AND PETER, *Martyrs* (304)

Marcellinus and Peter are among the saints commemorated daily in the Roman Canon of the Mass. Marcellinus was a prominent priest in the city of Rome, and Peter is said to have been an exorcist. He is sometimes known as Petrus Exorcista. They are said to have been arrested and put in prison during the persecutions of Diocletian, where they bore witness to the Faith and made many converts, including the jailer Arthemius and his wife and daughters. They were condemned to death by a magistrate named Severus or Serenus, taken secretly to a wood called the Silva Nigra, and there beheaded. The intention was that their place of execution should not be known, but the executioner, who subsequently became a Christian, revealed it. Two devout women, Lucilla and Firmina, rescued their bodies and gave them a decent burial in the catacomb of St Tiburtius on the via Laviana. It was thought at one time that forty-four other martyrs died with Marcellinus and Peter, but this is due to a misreading of the *Hieronymianum*.

Their memory was venerated by the Christian community in Rome. Constantine built a church over their tomb, and his mother, St Helena (18 Aug.), was buried there about the year 330. Pope Damasus (11 Dec.), who was born about the time of the martyrs' death, said that he had heard the details of the execution from the executioner himself. During his pontificate (366-84) Damasus opened the catacombs and composed epitaphs for many martyrs. Inscriptions such as *Sancte Petr(e) Marcelline, suscipite vestrum alumnum* are still in existence, and a catacomb near the tomb of the empress Helena, about two miles from the Porta Maggiore, bears their names. Part of the tomb forms a church named for SS Peter and Marcellinus.

In 827 Pope Gregory IV sent some of the saints' relics to Charlemagne's court to provide a focus for devotion in one of the many monasteries he had built or restored. They were eventually enshrined at Seligenstadt, near Frankfurt-am-Main, with great ceremony, and contemporary accounts have been preserved; but a sarcophagus also said to contain relics lies in a transept of the cathedral at Cremona. In art the two are represented together, robed as priests and carrying the palms of martyrdom.

M.G.H., Scriptores, 15, pt. 1, pp. 238-64; *AA.SS.*, June, 1, pp. 166-204; *C.M.H.*, p. 220; *B.H.L.*, 2 pp. 776-7; *Anal.Boll.* 26 (1907), pp. 478-81; *B.G.*, June, p. 19; *Saints in Italy*, pp. 353-4; *O.D.S.*, p. 317; *Bibl.SS.*, 8, 657.

The Martyrs of Lyons and Vienne (177)

The letter which describes the persecution, trial, and execution of Bishop Pothinus and the martyrs of Lyons and Vienne during the reign of Marcus Aurelius was addressed by the survivors to the churches of Asia and Phrygia. It has been preserved in the *Ecclesiastical History* of Eusebius of Caesarea and is of unquestionable authenticity. It gives the earliest evidence of an organized Church community in Gaul. Pothinus was probably the elder of whom his successor, St Irenaeus, said that he had "listened to those who had seen the Apostles."

Lyons, on the right bank of the Rhône, and Vienne, on the left bank, formed the terminus of the trade route to the East. Among their populations would have been many Greek and Levantine Christians. The letter gives a vivid account of the persecution. It started with social ostracism: Christians were "excluded from the houses, the baths, and the market." Then there were insults, then Christians were stoned and their houses plundered. Rumours as to what Christians believed and what they did must have been circulating around the two towns, gaining in extravagant detail as they went. All that anyone actually knew was that Christians formed a society within a society, that they were in one another's confidence, and that they carried out some sort of ritual in private. It was said that they had committed treason against the emperor because they refused to worship the Roman gods. Later they were accused, according to the writers of the letter, of "feeding on human flesh like Thyestes and committing incest like Oedipus, as well as other abominations which it is unlawful even for us to think of, and which we can scarcely believe ever to have been perpetrated by men." No charge was too fantastic to be levelled against them.

The allegations were taken up officially. Representative Christians were taken to the forum and publicly questioned while surrounded by an infuriated mob. A young Christian in the crowd, Vettius Epagathus, was so appalled at the unfairness of the questioning that he begged to be allowed to defend the accused, and when that was denied he took his place with them. They were all consigned to prison, and ten of them abjured. "Then were we all greatly distraught," says the letter, "not from fear of the torments which were to come upon us, but from looking to the end and dreading lest others should fall away. However, day by day there were taken up those who were worthy to fill up their number, until there had been gathered from the two churches all their most earnest and active members."

To prevent the prisoners from escaping, their servants were also arrested. Many of the servants were not Christians, and in fear that they might be implicated some were prepared to swear that the Christians had practised all sorts of abominations. The prisoners were tortured. Bishop Pothinus, who was ninety years old, was dragged before the governor in front of a howling mob. When asked, "Who is the God of the Christians?" he replied, "If you are

worthy, you shall know." He was kicked and beaten until he was nearly unconscious, and two days later he died from his injuries. A deacon named Sanctus,
who was burned with hot irons, could only repeat, "I am a Christian." A frail
slave girl named Blandina repeated over and over, "I am a Christian, and
nothing vile is done among us."

Sanctus, Blandina, Maturus (who was newly baptized), and Attalus of
Pergamos were all exposed to the beasts in the amphitheatre. They endured a
whole day of mauling, to the entertainment of the mob, before they were
finally brought forward for execution; but Attalus, who was a Roman citizen,
was removed and sent back to prison to await the emperor's command, and the
beasts refused to touch Blandina. The dreadful litany of violence went on, and
both were eventually killed in the amphitheatre with many others.

Throughout, the martyrs showed a remarkable charity to their persecutors
and to those who lapsed from their faith under pressure. They prayed for both,
showed no superiority, and went humbly and firmly to their deaths. The letter
continues: "They asked for life, and God gave it to them: they shared it with
their neighbours, and departed to God in every way victorious. Having always
loved peace and having ever commended peace to us, they went in peace to
God."

The Romans did all they could to suppress any commemoration of the acts
of the martyrs. The letter ends by describing how their bodies were "burned
and reduced to ashes, and swept into the Rhône . . . so that no trace of them
might appear on earth." Eusebius of Caesarea says that the Christians of Lyons
and Vienne sent this record of their martyrs' sufferings to the churches in Asia
and Phrygia, recording the events in great detail, because they were determined that the record should survive—as it did, in his own *History.*

The dungeons in which the martyrs were imprisoned lie beneath the church
of the abbey of Ainay at Lyons. They adjoin a crypt which was used as a chapel
until the French Revolution. At that time the chapel was desecrated, but it has
now been restored. The amphitheatre where the martyrs suffered survives as a
substantial ruin.

The letter to the Eastern churches is in Eusebius, *H.E.*, 5, 1, in N.P.N.F.; B.G., June, pp.
7-17, has a translation. See also Ruinart, pp. 109-17; H. Quentin in *Anal.Boll.* 39 (1921),
pp. 113-8, and cf. *C.M.H.*, p. 220; Bardenhewer, 2, pp. 609-20; A. Chagny, *Les martyrs de
Lyon* (1936). There has been some controversy over the date of the martyrdoms: see H. I.
Marrou in *Anal.Boll.* 71 (1953), pp. 5-20.

St Erasmus, *Bishop and Martyr* (? 303)

Little is known of the life of St Erasmus. He is said to have been bishop of
Formiae in the Campagna and to have been martyred. His name occurs in the
martyrology of Jerome and in the Old English martyrology of the ninth century. Pope Gregory the Great (3 Sept.) referred to his relics being venerated at
Formiae, but when the Saracens sacked the town in 842 his relics were trans-

lated by the Gauls to Gaeta, where he became the patron saint.

If facts are few, legends have proliferated. Erasmus has been confused with a Syrian bishop of the same name who fled during the persecutions of Diocletian to become a hermit on Mount Lebanon and was martyred there. As St Elmo, Erasmus became the patron saint of sailors. In the mixing of languages in the ports and on board ships with multinational crews, Erasmus became Eramus, Ermus, Ermo, and finally Elmo or Telmo. One legend describes him as preaching from the masthead of a ship during a thunderstorm. The blue electrical discharges that are sometimes seen on the masts or rigging of a ship after a storm were called "St Elmo's fire" and thought to be a sign of his protection.

There was further confusion during the period of Portuguese naval supremacy, when Portuguese sailors adopted St Peter Gonzalez (14 April) as their patron, and the two saints were often thought to be the same.

Representations in art frequently show the original St Erasmus, as the patron saint of sailors, with a windlass bearing a coiled rope as his emblem.

C.M.H., pp. 219-20; *AA.SS.*, June, 1, pp. 206-14; *B.H.G.*, 1, pp. 182-3; R. Flahault, *S. Erasme*(1895); *Bibl.SS.*, 4, 1288-93; *Origines du culte*, pp. 302, 307-8; Quentin, pp. 334, 429, 515; B.G., June, pp. 20-1; *Saints in Italy*, pp. 153-4; *D.H.G.E.*, 15, 666-7; *O.D.S.*, pp. 159-60.

The legend is commemorated in Rome by a mosaic above an altar in St Peter's and a painting in the Vatican by Nicholas Poussin. There is a sculpture in the chapel of Henry VII in WestminsterAbbey, and paintings by Cranach, Grünewald, and Dirk Bouts also survive.

St Eugenius I, *Pope* (657)

In the year 654 Pope St Martin I (13 Apr.) was removed from office by the exarch of Ravenna, the Eastern emperor's representative in Italy. The emperor, Constans II, was a supporter of the Monothelite heresy, the proposition that though Christ had two natures, human and divine, he had only one will, the divine will. Constans was probably more concerned with ecclesiastical politics than with theological dogma: he wanted an amenable pope in Rome. Pope Martin was not prepared to support him, and Eugenius, an elderly Roman presbyter, was expected to be a mild and saintly man who would do as he was told.

There has been some debate over whether Eugenius was a pope properly elected by the clergy and people to prevent the appointment of a Monothelite candidate or whether he was an antipope foisted on the Church by the emperor. The determining factor seems to be that Pope Martin, who had been banished, apparently agreed to abdicate, for it is recorded that he prayed "for the one who is now ruling the Church." However, he was known to be subjected to intense pressure: he died of ill treatment and starvation in 656, and, technically, Eugenius did not become pope until his death.

Once in office, Eugenius proved unexpectedly resolute and resisted the emperor's demands. When Eugenius sent legates to Constantinople they were sent back with instructions from the emperor that the new pope should declare himself in communion with the Byzantine patriarch, Peter, who was pursuing a policy of deliberate ambiguity about the Monothelite formulation. A letter from the patriarch was publicly discussed in the church of St Mary Major, and the clergy and laity who attended were so angered by its contents that they refused to allow Eugenius to say Mass until he had promised to reject the proposal.

Defying the emperor was extremely dangerous, but fortunately the emperor's attention was elsewhere. He was engaged in a campaign against the Arabs, and Pope Eugenius survived until his own death three years later. He is thought to have been the pope who received St Wilfrid (12 Oct.) on his first visit to Rome as a young man. The monk Eddi, who wrote Wilfrid's Life, mentions the visit but not the name of the pope—perhaps because of the uncertain status of Eugenius at the time.

AA.SS., June, 1, pp. 214-6; *Lib.Pont.*, 1, p. 341-2; Jaffé, 1, p. 234; Mann, 1, pt. 1, pp. 406-12; *C.M.H.*, p. 220; Eddi, *Life of Wilfrid*, ed. B. M. Colgrave (1927, rp. 1985), p. 13; *Anal.Boll.* 65 (1947), p. 320; *O.D.P.*, p. 75.

St Stephen of Sweden, *Bishop and Martyr* (? 1075)

Little information has survived about this Stephen, who was known as the apostle of the Helsings. He was a monk at the Saxon monastery of Corbey and was sent as a missionary bishop to Sweden, probably by the bishop of Bremen. He is said to have been the first to take Christianity to Helsingland and to have been very successful for a time in suppressing the worship of the Norse gods. He was martyred by the Norsemen either at Uppsala or at Noroda in Helsingland.

It is possible that his story has been confused with that of another Bishop Stephen, who lived earlier. The tomb of one or other St Stephen was venerated at Norrala until the Reformation, but it has now disappeared.

AA.SS., June, 1, pp. 226-9, has an account by the chronicler Adam of Bremen. There are brief mentions in *M.G.H., Scriptores*, 7, pp. 366 and 378; *C.M.H.*, p. 221; *N.D.S.*, p. 295.

St Nicholas the Pilgrim (1094)

Nicholas Peregrinus was a devout and simple-minded young Greek. His parents despaired of teaching him anything and set him to mind the sheep at the age of six. Perhaps he was aware of his own limitations, for he constantly cried *Kyrie eleison*. His mother thought he was mad and threw him out at the age of twelve. Then, repenting of her action, she induced the monks of Sterion to take him in and care for him; but the monks also became impatient with him and his continual cries of *Kyrie eleison*, and they let him wander away. He lived in a cave with his brother George, uttering his strange cries and making crude wooden crosses. The local priests denied him the Sacrament, thinking that he was devil-possessed, and he determined to go to Italy.

He was treated very badly on the ship during the voyage, but eventually he landed in southern Italy, where he had no friends or relations. He lived at Otranto for a time and then wandered about Apulia, living on alms. He wore a single garment which reached only to his knees, carried a cross in his right hand, and cried *Kyrie eleison* as he went along. He carried apples and other things to please the children who flocked around him in the streets echoing his chant. Some people were kind to him. Others thought he was a tramp or a lunatic and handled him roughly.

Nicholas was so puzzling to a society that knew nothing about arrested mental development that eventually the archbishop of Trani asked to see him. He arrived, still crying *Kyrie eleison*. The archbishop questioned him and thought that he was devout; but Nicholas' attention wandered while he was still being interviewed, and he went skipping off with the children, forgetting the archbishop. Apparently he was happy for three days, but on the fourth he fell ill, and he died at Trani.

After his death many legends circulated about him, and he came to be venerated because of the miracles attributed to his intercession. He was canonized by Pope Urban II in 1098. His emblem is a Greek cross, and he is depicted in art surrounded by a crowd of children. The considerable space devoted to him in the *Acta Sanctorum* reflects the perplexity of the chroniclers.

AA.SS., June, 1, pp. 229-54; A. di Jorio, *Della Vita di S. Nicolao Pellegrino* (1879); B.G., June, pp. 394-5; *N.D.S.*, p. 235. See also E. W. Kemp, *Canonisation and Authority* (1948), pp. 67-8 and 163-5.

Bd Sadoc and Companions, *Martyrs* (1260)

In the year 1221 at the second general chapter of his Order, which was held in Bologna, St Dominic (8 Aug.) charged his friars to go out into the world to preach the gospel. One band of missionaries was sent to Hungary and the land of the Tartars—a region where St Dominic had greatly wished to go himself. They were under the leadership of a Hungarian friar named Paul, who was to found the first Dominican province in his own country. Among the most successful of the missionaries was a young man named Sadoc, who was probably also a Hungarian. After he had preached in Hungary he moved on to Sandomir in Poland, where he founded a Dominican priory, of which he became the superior. In 1260 the Tartars besieged and captured Sandomir. It is said that on the day before their martyrdom a novice went to the middle of the choir to sing the names of the martyrs to be commemorated by the Order, and he added, "At Sandomir, the passion of forty-nine martyrs." There were forty-nine friars present. The prior told them all to prepare for death. They spent the night in prayer, and on the following day they were all cut down at Compline while singing the *Salve Regina*. Only one friar, who hid in the belfry, escaped to tell the tale.

A decree of indulgence conceded by Pope Boniface I in 1295 speaks only of a massacre in Sandomir, without particular reference to the Dominicans. However, the cult of Bd Sadoc and his companions was confirmed by Pope Pius VII (1800-23), and we can assume that the evidence presented then was sufficient to support at least the outlines of the story.

AA.SS., June, 1, pp. 258-60; Mortier, 1, pt. 1, pp. 152, 529, and 3, 29; Procter, pp. 163-5; I. Taurisano, *Catalogus Hagiographicus O. P.* (1918), p. 16, gives the names of the martyrs; B.G., June, p. 21.

Bd John Pelingotto (1304)

John Pelingotto was the son of a prosperous merchant of Urbino, but from his early years he cared nothing for worldly success and making money. He would have lived as a hermit had his parents not determinedly opposed this. He stayed at home but shut himself up to live a life of prayer and austerity. Then he felt a call to go out into the world and serve poor and sick people. To the mortification of his parents, he gave them much of his own food and the clothes off his back, going hungry and wearing old pieces of sacking himself.

His parents were anxious about the extremes to which John's sense of unworthiness took him. Once on Passion Sunday he went to the cathedral with a rope tied around his neck to indicate that he was the worst of criminals. While in the cathedral he went into an ecstasy (or fell into a catatonic state), which lasted for hours and from which he was roused with difficulty. On another occasion, in bitterly cold weather, he went into the marketplace and spent the day with a crowd of beggars and petty thieves. He was finally rescued by his parents in a very debilitated condition.

A solution to his problems came when he became a Franciscan tertiary. With the spiritual support of the Franciscan Rule he was able to live a Christian life helping those poorer than himself. He came to be venerated in Urbino as a holy man and a prophet. His cult is long-standing and was approved in 1918.

AA.SS., June, 1, pp. 144-51, has a Life by a contemporary. See also Wadding, 6, pp. 38-42; *A.A.S.* 10 (1918), pp. 513-6; *Dict.Hag.*, p. 366; *F.B.S.*, pp. 410-11.

Bd Herculanus of Piegaro (1451)

Herculanus, born at Piegaro on the borders of Umbria and Tuscany, entered the Franciscan Convent of the Observance in Sarteano, where he became a disciple of Bd Albert of Sarteano. He accompanied Albert to the East to take possession of the Holy Places when the Franciscans were granted their custody, and he also went with him to Egypt. For a time after his return to Tuscany he lived a life of retirement and prayer; but when he was sent out to preach, he became one of the foremost preachers of the fifteenth century, speaking eloquently of the suffering of Christ and the people's need for salvation. His sermons and addresses were so powerful that his listeners were frequently reduced to tears and inspired by his example to reform their lives. He lived a life of great austerity, eating only a little bread and some vegetables, and sometimes going without food for days at a time.

On one occasion he was preaching at Lucca during Lent when the Florentines besieged the city. The people were running out of provisions and on the point of surrender when he promised them that if they did penance until Easter, the city would be saved. This attracted a great following, and his prophecy was fulfilled: the Florentines raised the siege.

In Lucca he begged from door to door for the poor of the city. The people of Lucca were so impressed with his ministry that they raised money for new Franciscan convents. Herculanus was appointed commissary, and for some four years he governed three communities he had founded in Tuscany. He spent his last years in the convent he had founded in Castelnuovo. His beatification by Pope Pius IX took place in 1860.

Mariano of Florence in *AA.SS.*, May, 6, pp. 849-51; Wadding, 12, pp. 122-3; *Auréole Séraphique*, 2, pp. 297-300; *F.B.S.*, pp. 400-2.

Martyr's palms and crown,
for THE MARTYRS OF UGANDA (over page).
Wood engraving by Frank Martin.

3

SS CHARLES LWANGA AND COMPANIONS,

The Martyrs of Uganda (1886)

These saints, of whom Joseph Mkasa and Charles Lwanga are the best known, are venerated as the proto-martyrs of Black Africa. After the publicity attending Stanley's discovery of the Scottish missionary David Livingstone at Ujiji in 1871, missions were sent out from Europe in response to the needs of the "dark continent." The first Catholic missions among the Baganda, the people of southern Uganda, were established by Cardinal Lavigerie's White Fathers in 1879. The *kabaka*, or king of the Baganda, Mtesa, was not unfriendly, and for a time the missions flourished; but when he died in October 1884, he was succeeded by his eighteen-year-old son, Mwanga. The boy had attended mission classes but was said to be "wayward and flighty" and unable to concentrate.

Mwanga was subject to many pressures, not least from those counsellors who feared that the foreigners would "eat the country" and take it over for themselves. In the "scramble for Africa" both the British and the Germans were making inroads into the territory, while Emin Pasha was known to be making his way southward up the Nile from Egypt. The power and status of witch doctors and fetishists were threatened, and Mwanga was easily persuaded that the ancestors were angry at the desertion of the old ways.

In 1885 the newly-appointed Anglican bishop, James Hannington, decided to make his way to Buganda through the land of the Masai tribesmen, which had so far been free from European intervention. News of this approach immediately aroused apprehension among Mwanga's advisers: other missionaries had come from the south, around the edges of Lake Victoria, and the Masai territory was Buganda's "locked back door," closed to foreigners. A letter warning Hannington not to take this route apparently never arrived, and he and his party were seized and murdered on Mwanga's orders. Fr Lourdel of the White Fathers noted in his diary: "Hannington murdered . . . Beginning of Mwanga's cruelties. Alas, it will not be the last."

The *kabaka*'s personality began to deteriorate. He smoked hemp, he drank alcohol in quantity, and his behaviour became irrational and arbitrary. His own failure to learn to read and write increased his anger against the missionaries as he saw them teaching the young men of his court. His fury was roused when he demanded sexual favours from the young pages at his court and was refused. He is said to have learned these practices from traders from the north, since they were not common among his own people. Christian boys, on the instruction of the missionaries, would not give way to his demands, and this led to murderous outbursts of rage in which he would seize a boy and ask, "Do you read?" meaning, "Are you a Christian?"

The master of the pages, Joseph Mkasa, was himself a Catholic and a catechist. He taught the younger pages, protected them against the *kabaka*, and openly reproached the *kabaka* for his debauchery and his complicity in the murder of Bishop Hannington. He was seized on a pretext and beheaded on 15 November 1885. In the following May, the *kabaka* sent for a young page named Mwafu and was told that he had been receiving instruction from another, Denis Sebuggwawo. Denis was sent for, and the *kabaka* thrust a spear through his throat. That night guards were posted round the palace to prevent anyone escaping, witch doctors were sent for, and the drums beat to summon the executioners.

Charles Lwanga had succeeded Joseph Mkasa as master of the pages; he too was a Catholic. By night he secretly baptized four young catechumens including Kizito, who was only thirteen and whom he had repeatedly saved from the *kabaka*'s attacks. In the morning all the pages were commanded to appear before the *kabaka*, and the Christians were ordered to separate themselves from the rest. The oldest was Charles Lwanga and the youngest Kizito. Mwanga asked them if they intended to remain Christians. They answered that they did, and Mwanga's reply was, "Then put them to death!"

The appointed place of execution, Namugongo, was more than sixteen miles from Munyonyo, on Lake Victoria, where the arrests took place. It was a *matámbiro*, or place of ritual sacrifice. Three youths were killed on the road. The rest were cruelly imprisoned for seven days and made to help construct a huge pyre. On Ascension Day, 3 June 1886, Charles Lwanga was brought out first, and died by slow fire. His last words were *Katonda wange*, "My God." Then the rest were brought out, stripped of their clothes, bound, and each wrapped in a mat of reeds. They were stacked on the pyre, and it was set alight. One boy, Mgaba, was first killed by a blow on the neck by order of his father, who was the chief executioner. The rest were burned alive, to the sound of the ritual chants of the executioners.

One executioner is reported to have said later: "We have killed many people, but never such as these. On other occasions, the victims did nothing but moan and weep. . . . There was not a sigh, not even an angry word. All we heard was a soft murmur on their lips. They prayed until they died."

Other Christians were also put to death. A leader among the Catholics was Matthias Murumba, an assistant judge, who was executed with great cruelty. Another older victim was Andrew Kagwa, chief of the Kigowa, who had gathered a large group of catechumens around him. Many others had to go into hiding, and the lives of the missionaries and their converts were endangered over several years. In 1888 Mwanga conceived a plan for taking all the religious leaders, Christian and Muslim, and throwing them to the crocodiles, but his rule ended before he could put this into effect. There was a rebellion, a period of Muslim rule, and a war, following which British suzerainty was accepted in 1890.

There has been much discussion about the denominational composition of the group executed at Namugongo. Fr J. P. Thoonen of the Mill Hill Fathers, after reading missionary diaries and the records of the Apostolic Process of 1913-14, comes to the conclusion that there were twelve Catholics in addition to Charles Lwanga, ten or eleven other Christians, and seven or eight who were accused of having Christian sympathies but were unbaptized. The full lists of martyrs kept at Namugongo include some other Christians who were killed around the same time: twenty-two Catholics and twenty-four Protestants in all. Records show that there was not another mass execution after that of 3 June 1886.

"A well which has many sources never runs dry. When we are gone, others will come after us." These were the words of one of the martyrs, Bruno Serúnkuma, to his brother Bosa. In January 1890 there were estimated to be ten thousand Christians in Buganda. Mwanga's outburst of savagery and the witness of the martyrs led to a great increase in Christian believers. There are both Catholic and Protestant shrines at Namugongo, and both have become centres of devotion—many thousands of Christians make pilgrimages to them on the martyrs' feast-day. The magnificent Catholic shrine, in the shape of a pyre, has the story of the martyrdoms carved on the great doors. The Catholic martyrs were solemnly beatified by Pope Benedict XV on 6 June 1920 and canonized on 8 October 1964 by Pope Paul VI. In 1969 Pope Paul VI made a pilgrimage to Namugongo—the first-ever visit to the African continent by a pope.

A.A.S. 12 (1920), pp. 272-81; H. Streicher, *The Blessed Martyrs of Uganda* (1928); J. P. Thoonen, *Black Martyrs* (1941); A. E. Howell, *The Fires of Namugongo* (1948); J. F. Faupel, *African Holocaust* (1962); *Bibl.SS.*, 12, 476-8; *O.D.S.*, pp. 306-7.

St Cecilianus (? 248)

In St Jerome's *De Viris Illustribus* and in the Roman Martyrology, one Cecilius is commemorated as "a priest of Carthage who brought St Cyprian to the faith of Christ." Some commentators have identified him with the Cecilius whose conversion to Christianity is described in the *Octavius*, a treatise by Minucius Felix. This treatise describes a discussion in which Minucius himself and his friend Octavius argue with the pagan Cecilius and finally convince him of the truth of Christianity; but the Cecilius who was converted was probably Cecilius Natalis, chief magistrate of Cirta in North Africa in the year 210, not the priest of Carthage.

There is good evidence in the best manuscripts of the biography of Cyprian, bishop of Carthage, by his deacon Pontius that the name of the teacher who won over Cyprian by argument and example about the year 246 was Cecilianus, though some sources give his name as Cecilius. He seems to have been a man of advanced years when Cyprian met him. Cyprian probably lived in his teacher's house for some time after his conversion, and he reverenced him greatly as "the father of his new life." When the old teacher was dying, he commended his wife and children to Cyprian's care.

AA.SS., June, 1, pp. 264-5; *D.C.B.*, 1, pp. 366-7 (cf. 3, p. 924); *N.C.E.*, 3, pt. 2, pp. 245-9. The *N.C.E.* entry on Cyprian has some information about Cecilianus and a relevant bibliography.

SS Pergentius and Laurentinus, *Martyrs* (251)

The brothers Pergentius (or Pergentinus) and Laurentinus are said to have died in Arretium (Arezzo) in northern Italy during the persecutions of the emperor Decius. They are venerated as patrons of the city.

According to legend they were students attending the schools at Arezzo, and they were brought before the magistrate accused of being Christians and of converting others. They belonged to one of the leading families in Arezzo, and because of their youth and their noble connections the magistrate dismissed the charges, telling them to give up Christianity on pain of torture. The young men continued to proselytize until they were arrested again and beheaded.

Fr Delehaye and others think that this story is hagiographical fiction and that it probably arose out of the dedication on 3 June of a church at Arezzo in honour of St Laurence (10 Aug.), who was martyred in Rome in 258. It has been suggested that the name of Pergentius was supplied by one Expergenti, whose name occurs on the following day. The people of Arezzo may have felt the need of local saints and adopted the names from elsewhere. The story has been embellished with extravagant details: for instance, the Roman magistrate who examined the two is said to have rent his clothes on hearing them speak against the Roman gods; but the rending of garments was a sign of indignation among the Jews, not among the Romans.

The details may be a matter of later accretion, but their rejection does not necessarily invalidate the whole story. It is not unlikely that two students in Arezzo or somewhere else in northern Italy took this stand on their convictions and died for them, even if their real names are unknown.

AA.SS., June, 1, pp. 265-7; *C.M.H.*, p. 221; *B.H.L.*, 2, pp. 963-4; Quentin, p. 273; Dufourcq, 3, pp. 172-5; *B.G.*, June, p. 22.

SS Lucillian and Companions, *Martyrs* (273)

The story of Lucillian, four Christian youths whom he met in prison, and the Christian woman Paula, who visited them in prison, became a source of much devotion in Constantinople and took many forms. In one version Lucillian is a Christian priest; in another Paula is said to be his wife and the four young men their children; in a third they are described as martyrs of Egypt.

According to the Menology of the emperor Basil, Lucillian was a pagan priest of Nicomedia who became converted to Christianity at an advanced age. He was arrested during the reign of the emperor Aurelian and brought before a magistrate named Silvanus. After being tortured he was committed to prison, where he met the four young men, Claudius, Hypatius, Paul, and Dionysius, and strengthened their faith. Paula took them food in prison and tended their wounds, until she too was arrested.

Paula was tortured and finally beheaded. Lucillian and the young men were taken in chains to Byzantium, where he was crucified, and the others were beheaded.

It is now thought probable that Lucillian and his companions were martyred in Nicomedia and that their relics were later translated to Constantinople, where the cult developed.

AA.SS., June, 1, pp. 267-79, contains Greek and Latin texts of the passion. *Anal. Boll.* 31 (1912), pp. 187-92, gives another Greek text. See also the editor's comments in the same issue, pp. 232-5. *C.M.H.*, p. 222.

St Clotilda (545)

Clotilda, or Clothilde, was a daughter of the former Burgundian king Chilperic. She was a Catholic, though most of her family were Arians. When she married Clovis, king of the Franks, in 492 or 493, he was still a heathen. Clotilda exercised great influence over him and attempted to win this intemperate and tempestuous warrior to Christianity. Gregory of Tours tells how, when their first son was born, Clotilda insisted that he should be baptized, saying, "The gods whom ye worship are naught: they cannot aid themselves or others, seeing that they are images, carved out of wood or stone or metal." Though "the king's mind was nowhere moved to belief," he allowed her to present their son for Baptism; but the child died on the same day, still in his baptismal robes.

Clovis "was moved to bitter wrath, saying 'If the child had been dedicated in the name of my gods, he would have survived, but now, baptized in the name of thy God, he could not live a day.'" They had another son, and again Clotilda pleaded with Clovis that he should be baptized. Despite his own lack of faith, he finally agreed that this should be done, and there was consternation in the court when the child became very ill soon afterwards; but this son survived.

Clovis himself did not become a Christian until he was hard pressed in battle. He was fighting the German tribes, and his troops were giving way when he prayed to "Clotilda's God," promising that if he was granted victory he would become a Christian. The battle was won and he kept his word. The queen asked Bishop Remigius of Reims (1 Oct.) to come and instruct the king in the Faith. Remigius taught him personally and explained the events of Christ's passion. "Hah!" said Clovis, "Had I and my faithful Franks been there, the Jews had not dared to do it." In 496 Clovis was baptized in a magnificent ceremony in Reims cathedral. There were coloured banners in the streets, and the cathedral, draped in white, was illuminated with many perfumed tapers. Among clouds of incense, says Gregory of Tours, "like a new Constantine he moved forward to the water, to blot out the former leprosy, to wash away in this new stream the foul stains from old days." Three thousand Franks followed his example.

On his Baptism Clovis became the only Catholic sovereign in Christendom. The emperor Anastasius was thought to favour the Eutychian heresy, and the kings in Italy, France, Spain, and North Africa were all Arians. Clovis may have been influenced in his conversion by his need of the support of the Church in his planned conquest of Gaul; but, influenced by Remigius and Clotilda, he seems to have been sincere in his devotion to "this unarmed God who is not of the race of Thor or Odin."

Clovis died in 511. Clotilda lived for another thirty-four years, but her life was saddened by murderous family feuds. Gregory of Tours suggested that she incited her sons to avenge the murder of her parents, but his view is now thought to be unreliable. She and Clovis had three sons, Clodomir, Childebert, and Clotaire, and when Clovis died she had the property divided between them in the hope of preventing further bloodshed. Clodomir had his cousin Sigismund, king of Burgundy (1 May), executed but afterwards repented and put on a monk's habit (1 May). He was subsequently killed by Sigismund's brother. Clotilda adopted Clodomir's three sons, intending to bring them up as her own, but her younger sons Childebert and Clotaire seized them, and Childebert killed the elder two with his own hand. The youngest, Clodoald or Cloud (7 Sept.), survived and became a monk in the monastery near Paris, later named Saint-Cloud in his memory.

Clotilda left Paris and went to live at Tours, where she lived quietly, devoting her life to the relief of poverty and suffering. Gregory says: "She won the respect of all. She was never weary in almsgiving, or in prayer through the night watches; in chastity and in all virtue, she showed herself without stain ... humility bore her to grace."

When she heard that her two surviving sons were on the verge of a fratricidal battle, she is said to have spent the whole night at the tomb of St Martin of Tours (11 Nov.) praying that the conflict might be averted. A fierce hailstorm on the following day forced the armies to withdraw. A month later she died, "full of days and rich in good works," and her sons, united in grief, buried her with Clovis in the church of SS Peter and Paul, afterwards renamed St Geneviève.

Gregory of Tours, *History of the Franks*, trans. and intro. O. M. Dalton (1967), 2, pp. 67-9, 88, 102, 106. *AA.SS.*, June, 1, pp. 285-91; *C.M.H.*, p. 222; The best modern account is that of G. Kurth, *Sainte Clothilde* (Eng. trans., 1898), in the series Les saints. See also B.G., June, pp. 23-7; *N.C.E.*, 3, p. 962; A. Dumas, *Dict.Biog.Franc.*, 9, pp. 34-5; *Dict.Hag.*, p. 169. For background, see Edward James, *The Franks* (1988). The fifteen-hundredth anniversary of this occasion was celebrated by a papal Mass on 22 September 1996. The congregation would no longer fit into the cathedral, as some 200,000 worshippers attended, so the commemoration took place on an airfield near Reims.

SS Liphardus and Urbicius, *Abbots* (Sixth Century)

Liphardus (Lifard, or Liéfard) was a lawyer with a reputation for probity who rose to one of the highest judicial posts in Orleans before deciding to enter a religious Order. He went to the abbey of Saint-Mesmin at Micy; he may have been a brother of the abbot. After a time he and Urbicius retired to live as hermits in the ruins of an old castle near the present town of Meung-sur-Loire. They built themselves huts and lived very austerely. It is said that they took only bread and water, and that only every third day. Soon others came to join them, and their small community became the nucleus of a new monastery. The bishop of Orleans, who knew Liphardus from the time when he was a lawyer and had a great regard for him, ordained him priest and built a church for the community.

Liphardus became the abbot of Meung-sur-Loire, and the monastery flourished. When he died at the age of seventy-three, he nominated Urbicius as his successor. A cult developed soon after his death.

AA.SS., June, 1, pp. 291-301, includes accounts from Micy written no earlier than the ninth century. Mention in *C.M.H.*, p. 222, testifies to the early date of the cult. A. Poncelet, in "Les saints de Micy," *Anal.Boll.* 24 (1905), p. 1-97, suggests that the Micy biographies may be unreliable.

St Kevin, *Abbot* (? 618)

There is no written record of Kevin's life earlier than the tenth or eleventh century, but he is venerated chiefly as the founder of the celebrated abbey of Glendalough in County Wicklow. Oral tradition has preserved his memory and embellished it with many charming Irish legends. His family were Leinster nobility. At one time they were the ruling house, but they were forced to relinquish the kingship in the fifth century. Kevin, or Coemgen (his name means "the Fair-begotten"), was born in Leinster, baptized by St Cronan (28 Apr.), and educated in a monastery at Cell na Manach (now Kilmanach) near Dublin. According to tradition one of his teachers was St Petroc (15 June). After his ordination he withdrew to solitude in the upper reaches of Glendalough, the Valley of the Two Lakes, probably to the cave called "St Kevin's Bed" and to the *Teampull na Skellig* (the rock church), a Bronze-Age tomb which he may have used as an altar. There he lived alone for seven years, clad in skins, sleeping on the stones by the waterside, and eating nettles and wild sorrel. He sought out "the things which sick and morbid people have a desire for," such as blackberries and apples, which suggests a healing ministry.

He was discovered in his cave by a farmer named Dima, who induced him to leave his solitude. By this time, he must have been in very poor health, because he was brought down to Disert-Coemgen on a litter. There he gathered some disciples, and they made a settlement. According to legend a friendly otter brought them a fish in his mouth every day; but when one of the monks thought that the otter's skin would make fine gloves, the otter took fright and went away. Kevin moved his community to the upper lake and made a permanent settlement there. According to one of the Irish Lives he made a pilgrimage to Rome, and it is reported that "because of the holy relics and mould which he brought back, no single saint in Erin ever obtained more from God than Coemgen, save Patrick only."

Abbot Kevin is said to have gone to visit St Kieran (or Ciaran), abbot of Clonmacnoise (9 Sept.), when Kieran was dying. Kieran recovered sufficiently to talk to him and to make him a present of a bell. In his extreme old age Kevin contemplated making another journey to Rome, but he was told by a wise man that "birds do not hatch their eggs when they are on the wing." He is reputed to have lived to the age of 120.

Glendalough became one of the four main pilgrimage places in Ireland (seven visits to Glendalough being reckoned as equivalent to one pilgrimage to Rome). St Kevin is one of the principal patrons of Dublin, and his feast is kept all over Ireland.

Latin Lives in Plummer, *V.S.H.*, pp. 234-57, and Heist, *V.S.H.*, pp. 361-5. Plummer has a commentary on the Lives in his vol. 1, pp. liv-vi. See also *AA.SS.*, June, 1, pp. 303-15; *Anal.Boll.* 63 (1945), pp. 122-9; B.G., June, pp. 27-9; *Irish Saints*, pp. 79-83. For the pilgrimage sites, see Michael Rodgers and Marcus Losack, *Glendalough: A Celtic Pilgrimage* (1996).

St Genesius of Clermont, *Bishop* (*c.* 660)

Genesius (Genet, or Genès) was a much-loved bishop of Clermont, the twenty-first in line. He was born in the city of a senatorial family and became archdeacon. Reputed to be learned, generous, and virtuous, he was chosen unanimously as bishop by the clergy and people; but he would accept only after a three-day delay to test whether they would change their minds and elect someone else.

After five years as bishop he undertook a pilgrimage to Rome in the hope of obtaining leave to retire and live a life of solitude, but the people sent emissaries after him, insisting on his return. When he came near to Clermont the clergy came out to meet him, carrying candles and singing, and sick people were brought out for his blessing. He built a church dedicated to St Symphorian (22 Aug.), an early martyr at Autun, and a hospice near the gates of Clermont, and founded a monastery called Manlieu or Grandlieu. He died in his diocese and was buried in the church of St Symphorian, which afterwards bore his name.

His story has been confused with that of St Genesius of Arles (25 Aug.), who was martyred about the year 303—over three and a half centuries earlier. Only the similarity of names seems to be responsible; the difference in dates of death usually indicates two separate persons. Genesius of Arles was a notary, not a bishop, and was condemned for protesting when required to take evidence in court against Christians.

AA.SS., June, 1, pp. 322-4; Duchesne, *Fastes*, 2, p. 37; *D.C.B.*, 2, p. 627; Quentin, pp. 533-41; *N.C.E.*, 6, p. 331. B.G., June, confuses Genesius of Clermont and Genesius of Arles.

St Isaac of Córdoba, *Martyr* (852)

In the eighth century the Moors had surged into southern Spain, and some learned men such as Isaac were interested in their culture and their traditions of scholarship. Islamic scholarship was well advanced, and the Arabic culture must have been intriguing to Spanish intellectuals. They knew that Islam had much in common with Judaism and Christianity, since it was based on the Old Testament and recognized Christ as a prophet, and they hoped for a degree of common accord.

Isaac was a wealthy citizen of Córdoba and a devout Christian. He studied Arabic and became so proficient that he was appointed a notary under the Moorish government in Córdoba, the centre of Islamic rule in Spain, but he did not remain in post long. At close quarters, he found Islamic beliefs deeply alien to his own faith. He withdrew to a monastery where he lived for some years with his relative Abbot Martin.

The time came when he felt it his duty to go back to reason with the chief magistrate of Córdoba about the truth of Christianity as opposed to Islam. His biographer, Eulogius, makes it clear that he did this of his own volition. His invitation was accepted, but during the debate a panegyric on Mohammed led him into such an outspoken denunciation of Mohammed as a false prophet that he was arrested, tortured, and executed. After his death his body was impaled and set beside the river Guadalquivir as a warning to other Christians. In Spanish martyrologies he is given pride of place among the martyrs of Córdoba.

AA.SS., June, 1, pp. 317-9, contains the *Memoriale Sanctorum* of St Eulogius, who was Isaac's contemporary and fellow citizen and writes about him at some length. See also *D.H.G.E.,* 13, 846-7 (*s.v.* "Cordoue"); *D.H.E.E.*, 2, 886; *Anal.Boll.* 108 (1990), p. 210; *Bibl. SS.*, 7, 919-20; E. Colbert, *The Martyrs of Córdoba* (1962), pp. 201-6; K. B. Wolf, *Christian Martyrs in Muslim Spain* (1988), pp. 23-35. See also the entry on St Eulogius, 11 March, in the present work.

St Morand (*c*.1113)

The parents of St Morand were nobles who lived in the Rhine Valley near Worms, and he was educated in the cathedral school of that city. After his ordination to the priesthood he undertook a pilgrimage to Compostela. On the way he stayed at Cluny, and he was so deeply impressed with the life of the monks under the direction of their abbot, St Hugh (29 Apr.), that on his return from Compostela he entered the monastery. He spent his early years as a monk in one or other of the Cluniac houses in the Auvergne.

Early in the twelfth century Count Frederick Piers, the chief nobleman of Lower Alsace, rebuilt and restored the church of St Christopher, which his ancestors had built near the present town of Altkirch. He asked St Hugh for monks to serve the church and the neighbourhood, but though several were sent it soon became clear that they could not carry out missionary work in the area without a good knowledge of German. Morand was sent because German was his first language, though he was equally proficient in French.

The choice proved an excellent one. Regardless of the weather, he went out into the countryside, bareheaded and with a pilgrim's staff in his hand, to meet the people and bring them closer to God. He is said to have cured Count Frederick of facial paralysis and to have restored many sick people to health by his prayers. Every Friday he visited the shrine of Our Lady of Gildwiller, reputed to be the oldest sanctuary in Alsace. The people gave his name to a spring beside which he used to rest on his weekly pilgrimage. The cult of this popular priest is still observed in Alsace, and he is regarded locally as the patron saint of vinegrowers, perhaps because of a legend that he fasted through one Lent with only a bunch of grapes to sustain him.

AA.SS., June, 1, pp. 332-51, has the medieval Life of St Morand, written less than half a century after his death. See also J. Clauss, *Die Heiligen des Elsess* (1935); *N.C.E.*, 9, p. 1134.

Bd John "the Sinner" (1546-1600)

Juan Grande was born in Carmona in Andalusia. His father died when he was only fifteen, and he was sent to Seville to work with a relative engaged in the linen trade. When he had learned the trade he was set up in business in Carmona; but at the age of twenty-two he gave away all his possessions and retired to a hermitage near Marcena. Though he had apparently lived a blameless life since childhood, he had a deep and abiding sense of guilt and unworthiness. Perhaps his surname concerned him, for he thought he was the least of men. He styled himself *el grande pecador*, the great sinner, and it is as Juan Pecador that he is now honoured in Spain.

One day he saw two sick tramps lying by the roadside. He carried them to his hut, nursed them, and begged alms for them. Soon he saw other people in need and felt called to leave his solitary hermitage in order to minister to them. He went to Jerez and worked in the prison there ministering to the prisoners, who lived under appalling conditions. Though he bore insults, ingratitude, and even blows from some, he nursed them, begged for them, and cared for them, believing that no man was out of reach of the love of God.

After a time, he went to work in the neighbouring hospital, where he bore obstruction and insults from officials who resented his devotion to the sick—a standing reproach to their own negligence and callousness—but outside observers were impressed. One wealthy couple offered him a hospital of his own and built it for him. It soon filled with sick patients, and John recruited a group of young men eager to follow his own example in caring for them. To ensure the continuance of his work he affiliated it to the Order of Hospitallers, and he entered the Order himself. Its founder, St John of God (8 Mar.), had died at Seville when John Grande was a child of four.

John's sympathies spread beyond the hospital. He gathered orphans, fed them, and taught them. He collected money to give marriage portions to poor girls. He continued to take an interest in prisoners and when, after the storming of Cadiz by the English, three hundred fugitive Spanish soldiers came to Jerez, he nursed the wounded and provided them all with food and clothing—miraculously, as it seemed to them. He lived an intense prayer life, and if, after being rapt in prayer, he found himself surrounded by uncomprehending strangers, he would beg their pardon and go on his way quietly, with bowed head.

In 1600 there was an epidemic of plague in Jerez. Some three hundred people were dying each day, and John devoted himself to the care of the plague victims until he became a victim himself. He died at the age of fifty-four. He was beatified in 1853 by Pope Pius IX.

A.A.S. 23 (1931), pp. 18-9. An anonymous Life was published in Italian in Milan in 1727. The account in P.B., 6, pp. 434-8, is based on the *Vie abrégé de B Jean Grande*, published at the time of his beatification. *Dict.Hag.*, p. 366.

ST NORBERT (pp. 47-50)
Gold ciborium on black field.

4

St Petroc, *Abbot* (Sixth Century)

Many churches in Devon and several in Cornwall have dedications in honour of St Petroc, or Pedrog. His cult is ancient and well established, though the written sources for his life are fairly late and more inclined to legend than historical fact.

Petroc was reputedly the son of a Welsh king or chieftain. William Worcestre, who visited his shrine in the late fifteenth century, recorded that he was "once king of the Cumbrians." He moved south with some of his followers and settled at the monastery at Lanwethinoc, named for its founder Wethinoc. Later, when the cult of St Petroc developed, the place became known as Padristowe and ultimately Padstow. Little Petherick and Trebetheric also bear his name. According to the medieval Life written at Saint-Méen, which appears to be a copy of an earlier one from Bodmin Priory, Petroc and his companions studied in Ireland for twenty years. This is confirmed in the Life of St Kevin (3 June, above). Then they took ship to the estuary of the river Camel and settled at Lanwethinoc. Petroc lived a most austere life there for thirty years and then made a pilgrimage to Rome and Jerusalem.

Nicholas Roscarrock tells the story of how he returned from his pilgrimage and told his monks that the storms sweeping the area would end the next day. When the wind and the rain continued unabated he presumably thought that he had been arrogant in expecting the Holy Spirit to inspire him, because he went back to Jerusalem as a penance. On this second journey he reached the "East Ocean"—possibly the Gulf of Aqaba.

The older Life by John of Tynmouth, which the *Acta Sanctorum* classifies as a *vita suspecta*, says that he went to India, and there, as he stood by the seashore, he saw a shining bowl floating toward him. This bowl conveyed him to an island, where he spent seven years. Then he re-entered the bowl, floated back to India, and found a wolf guarding the staff and sheepskin he had left on the shore. There are parallels to this story in classical mythology.

After his return to Cornwall Petroc spent his time in prayer and in deeds of charity, and he developed a great reputation as a holy man. Several legends that appear to have originated in Cornish folklore are told of him: he is said to have healed many sick people, saved the life of a stag which was being hunted and then converted the hunter and his attendants, tamed a local monster, and prescribed for a dragon which came to him with a splinter in its eye.

Details of a more convincing nature come from a version of the Saint-Méen

Life made by a canon of Bodmin and included in a fourteenth-century manuscript found at Gotha in Germany in 1937. This is known as the Gotha Life. It describes how Petroc built a chapel and a mill at Little Petherick, where he established a second community. Later he withdrew to a remote place on Bodmin Moor, and again some of the brothers joined him. When he knew that his life was coming to an end, he went on a last visit to Little Petherick and Lanwithenoc. He was between the two places when his strength failed, and he died in the house of a man named Rovel. The present farmhouse of Treravel may mark the spot.

Petroc's feast is noted in several early West Country calendars as well as the Bosworth Psalter and the Missal of Robert of Jumièges. It eventually reached the Sarum calendar. Both Exeter and Glastonbury claimed relics.

Some time before the eleventh century the monks moved to Bodmin, and that became the centre of the cult; but the relics of Petroc were taken away by Martin, a canon of Bodmin Priory, who wrapped them in a cloth and took them to the abbey of Saint-Méen in Brittany. Relics were often moved from place to place in this way, those who lost them complaining that it was an act of theft, while those who received them maintained that it was an act of piety. The prior of Bodmin appealed to King Henry II, who ordered the return of Petroc's bones to Bodmin.

According to Roger de Hoveden, "the above-named prior of Bodmin, returning to England with joy, brought back the body of blessed Petroc in an ivory shrine." The bones were received by Walter of Coutances, the keeper of the Great Seal, at Winchester, and the king and all his court prostrated themselves in front of them. The shrine, of Sicilian-Islamic workmanship, may have been a gift from Count Walter. The annual "riding" custom at Bodmin is said to be a commemoration of the saint's return.

The reliquary was seen and much admired by William Worcestre. Some three centuries later, in the eighteenth century, the empty reliquary was discovered in the room above the south porch of Bodmin church, where it had been hidden during the Reformation. It remained in the parish church until 1970, when it was removed to the British Museum.

AA.SS., June, 1, pp. 391-4, contains the Life by John of Tynmouth; *N.L.A.*, 2, pp. 317-20; *B.H.L.*, 2, p. 965; William Worcestre, pp. 87, 103, 113; Roscarrock, pp. 101-4, 164-5; G. H. Doble, *St Petrock*, Cornish Saints Series 11 (3d ed., 1938); P. Grosjean, "Vie et miracles de S Petroc," *Anal. Boll.* 74 (1956), pp. 131-88; R. H. Pinder-Wilson and C. N. L. Brooke, "The Reliquary of St Petroc and the Ivories of Norman Sicily," *Archaeologia* 104 (1973), pp. 261-306; Stanton, pp. 254-5; *D.N.B.*, 15, pp. 651-2; *O.D.S.*, pp. 395-6; *Dict. Hag.*, p. 520. See also J. Stonor, "St Petroc's Cell on Bodmin Moor," *Downside Review* 66 (1948), pp. 64-74.

St Quirinus, *Bishop and Martyr* (308)

Siscia, now Sisak in Croatia, was one of the areas where the persecutions of the emperor Diocletian against Christians were carried out. We know nothing of the episcopate of Quirinus, but the story of his spirited defence of his faith at his trial and the manner of his death has been recorded by Jerome (30 Sept.), by Prudentius, and by Venantius Fortunatus (14 Dec.). No doubt the account of the trial has been somewhat amplified and interpolated by later copyists. It bears the marks of a familiar polemic, but commentators regard it as substantially genuine.

Quirinus, who was a venerable bishop, heard that orders were out for his arrest. He left the city but was pursued, captured, and brought before the magistrate Maximus. The following dialogue is recorded: Maximus asked why he had attempted to escape; Quirinus replied that he was only obeying the words of his master Jesus Christ, the true God, who had said, "When you are persecuted in one city, fly to another."

"Do you not know that the emperor's orders would find you anywhere?" asked the magistrate. "He whom you call the true God cannot help you when you are caught—as you must now realize to your cost."

"God is always with us and can help us," declared the bishop. "He was with me when I was taken, and he is with me now. He it is who strengthens me, and speaks through my lips."

"You talk a great deal," observed Maximus, "and by talking you postpone obeying the commands of our sovereign. Read the edicts, and do as they bid you!"

Quirinus protested that he could not consent to do what would be sacrilege. "The gods whom you serve are nothing! My God, whom I serve, is in heaven and earth and in the sea and everywhere, but he is higher than all, because he contains all things in himself: all things were created by him, and by him alone they subsist."

"You must be in your second childhood to believe such fables!" declared the magistrate. "See, they are offering you incense: sacrifice and you shall be well rewarded; refuse, and you will be tortured and put to a horrible death."

Quirinus replied that the threatened pains would be glory to him. Maximus ordered him to be beaten. Even while the sentence was being carried out, he was urged to sacrifice and was told that if he did he would be released and made a priest of Jupiter.

"I am exercising my priesthood here and now by offering myself up to God," Quirinus answered. "I am glad to be beaten. It does not hurt me. I would willingly endure far worse treatment to encourage those over whom I have presided to follow me by a short road to eternal life."

Since Maximus had no authority to pronounce a death sentence, Quirinus was sent to Amantius, the governor of Pennon Prima in the town of Sabre (now Szombathely in Hungary). Here he was brought before the governor, who, after reading the report of the previous trial, asked him if it was correct. Quirinus answered that it was and added, "I have confessed the true God at Siscia. I have never worshipped any other. Him I carry in my heart, and no man on earth shall succeed in separating me from him."

Amantius was unwilling to torture and order the execution of the old bishop and urged him again to fulfill the requirements of the edicts so that he could end his days in peace, but neither promises nor threats would move him, and eventually Amantius had no option but to condemn him.

Quirinus was thrown into the river Raab with a stone hung round his neck. He did not immediately sink, and was heard to call out prayers and exhortations as he was carried along by the water. His body was rescued by Christians. In the early fifth century his relics were carried to Rome by refugees driven from Pannonia by the barbarians. They rested in the catacomb of St Sebastian until 1140, when they were translated to the church of Santa Maria in Trastevere.

The text of the passion is printed in *AA.SS.*, June, 1, pp. 372-6, and also in Ruinart, pp. 522-5. The ancient Acts were seen by St Jerome (30 Sept.) and also by Prudentius, who composed his Hymn VII in honour of Quirinus. This is reproduced in *AA.SS.* See also *P.B.*, 6, pp. 442-4; *C.M.H.*, pp. 222-3; *B.H.L.*, 2, pp. 1023-4. Much interest has been taken in Quirinus since the research of Mgr de Waal in the Platonia and its surroundings revealed the existence of a fragment of a great inscription engraved there in his memory. See de Waal's monograph, *Die Apostelgruft "ad Catacumbas,"* printed as a supplement to the *Romische Quartalschrift* (1894), and L. Duchesne, "La Memoria Apostolorum de la Via Appia," in *Memorie della pontificia Accademia romana di Archaeol.*, 1 (1923), pp. 8-10.

St Metrophanes, *Bishop* (c. 325)

The holy life of Bishop Metrophanes is said to have been one of the major reasons why the emperor Constantine chose Byzantium for his new capital. According to the Greek Synaxaries he was the son of Dometius, brother of the emperor Probus. Dometius was converted to Christianity and took his family to live in Byzantium, then a small town, where he was a close friend of Titus, bishop of Heracles. Bishop Titus ordained him, and Dometius became bishop on Titus' death. He was succeeded first by his elder son, another Probus (named, presumably, for his uncle the emperor), and then by Metrophanes, the younger son. It is not clear whether the *cathedra* was moved from Heracles to Byzantium or whether the see was divided when the arrival of Constantine and his court transformed Byzantium into the capital of the empire. Metrophanes was certainly bishop of Byzantium and is ranked as its first bishop.

Old age and infirmity prevented Metrophanes from personally attending the Council of Nicaea, but he sent his chief presbyter, Alexander, to represent him and on Alexander's return designated him as his own successor.

A story preserved by Photius says that Constantine went to see Metrophanes shortly before his death. The old bishop told the emperor that Alexander was to be his successor and that a young reader named Paul, who was then in attendance, would follow Alexander. Athanasius (2 May), who was present as a junior deacon, said, "Behold the noble champion of Christ." Alexander became patriarch on the death of Metrophanes, and the boy reader subsequently became the patriarch Paul I of Constantinople (7 June) and a martyr. Metrophanes died seven days after Constantine's visit.

Metrophanes had a great reputation for sanctity throughout Eastern Christendom. A church was built in his honour soon after the death of Constantine, and it was restored in the sixth century by Justinian.

Metrophanes is commemorated in the Roman Martyrology, where he is described as *confessor insignis*. See also *B.H.G.*, p. 117; *AA.SS.*, June, 1, pp. 377-87; *C.M.H.*, p. 223; B.G., June, pp. 33-4; *Bibl.SS.*, 9, 396-7.

St Optatus of Milevis, *Bishop (c. 387)*

Although comparatively little known in Europe, Optatus was one of the outstanding Christian apologists of the Church in North Africa in the fourth century, and his writings have aroused fresh interest among scholars in recent years because he dealt with some of the fundamental issues concerning the nature of the Church. St Augustine of Hippo (28 Aug.), who was born in 354, writes of him as ranking with St Cyprian (16 Sept.) and St Hilary of Poitiers (13 Jan.), while St Fulgentius of Ruspe (1 Jan.), less than a hundred years later, considered him to be a saint and thought his influence as great as that of St Ambrose of Milan (7 Dec.) or St Augustine himself.

Optatus was bishop of Milevis in Numidia and a leader in the movement to refute the claims of the Donatists, a schismatic group who had divided the Church in North Africa. They repudiated the validity of ordination and the sacraments in the Roman Church, claiming that they alone were the true Church of Christ. The separatist movement arose through a disputed election for the bishop of Carthage in 311, when Donatus was the unsuccessful candidate, and others followed him in establishing a church of their own. One of their bishops, Parmesian, published a treatise setting out their claims. Though this has not survived, the reply made by Bishop Optatus is still extant. It is written in vigorous and spirited terms but in a spirit of conciliation. He was concerned not to condemn but to win over his opponents.

Optatus makes a distinction between heresy and schism. Heretics are "deserters or falsifiers of the creed," who can have no true sacraments or valid orders. Schismatics are separated Christians, still part of the Universal Church. The distinguishing mark of the Church is its universality, or catholicity, which the Donatists denied. Optatus asks how they can claim to be the one true Church when they represent only one corner of North Africa and one very small Roman colony.

The Universal Church, Optatus insists, owes allegiance to the papacy. "Peter sat first in this chair, and was succeeded by Linus." He then gives a list of popes (which is incorrect, but he was a long way from Rome) down to the reigning pontiff of his day, Siricius. He continues, "It was to Peter that Jesus Christ declared, 'I will give thee the keys of the kingdom of Heaven, and the gates of hell shall not prevail against thee.' By what right do you claim the keys—you who presume to contend against Peter's chair? You cannot deny that the episcopal chair was originally given to Peter in the city of Rome: that he sat there first as head of the Apostles. . . . The other apostles did not claim rival chairs, and only schismatics have ever ventured to do so."

In opposition to the teaching of the Donatists, who based their claim on the holiness of Donatus in comparison with his rival, Optatus laid down the doctrine that sacraments are holy in themselves and do not depend for their efficacy on the character of those who administer them. He also writes of original sin, and he describes in some detail the practices of the Church in North Africa in his day—the ceremonies used at Mass and at Baptism, the penances laid upon Christians, and the veneration paid to relics.

Optatus was still living in 384 and is thought to have died about 387, but we know nothing of his personal history.

AA.SS., June, 1, pp. 388-9; *N.C.E.*, 10, pp. 706-7; B.G., 6, pp. 444-8; R. Vassall-Philips, *The Work of St Optatus Against the Donatists* (1911); N. H. Baynes, "Optatus," and "Optatus: An Addendum," *Journal of Theological Studies* 26 (1924-5), pp. 37-44 and 404-6; C. H. Turner, "Adversaria Critica: Notes on the Anti-Donatist Dossier and on Optatus," *Journal of Theological Studies* 27 (1926), pp. 283-96.

St Francis Caracciolo, *Founder* (1563-1608)

The Caraccioli were a noble family in the south of Italy. Francis, who had been baptized Ascanio and who later took the name Francesco in religion, was related to St Thomas Aquinas (28 Jan.) through his mother and to the Neapolitan princes through his father. He led the usual life of a young nobleman, with a great love of hunting and other sports, until he was twenty-two years old, when he developed a virulent skin disease. At that time such conditions were often assumed to be leprosy, which was thought to be highly contagious and was much feared. The leper became a social outcast. In this crisis in his life Ascanio made a vow that if he recovered he would devote his life to God. The condition, which may have been due to an infection or a nervous condition, cleared up completely, and his recovery was thought to be miraculous.

In order to fulfill his vow, Ascanio went to Naples to study for the priesthood. After ordination he joined a confraternity called the Bianchi della Giustizia, which cared for prisoners, particularly those facing a sentence of death. He might have continued in that work, but when he was twenty-five a misdirected letter led him to a new field of service.

Giovanni Agostino Adorno of Genoa, a nobleman who had become a priest, was inspired to found an Order of priests pledged to a mixed vocation combining the active with the contemplative life. He consulted the dean of the collegiate church of Santa Maria Maggiore in Naples, Fabriccio Caracciolo, who recommended another kinsman, a distant relation also named Ascanio Caracciolo. Adorno's letter went to the wrong Ascanio; but when he received it, the future saint was so sure that he was being directed to join this Order that he at once associated himself with Adorno and became his colleague. The two made a forty-day retreat in the Camaldolese settlement, where, after a strict fast and much prayer, they drew up Rules for the new Order. When ten other priests had joined them, they went to Rome to obtain the approval of the pope. Sixtus V solemnly ratified their new society as the Order of the Minor Clerks Regular on 1 June 1588, and in the following April the two founders made their solemn profession. Ascanio took the name of Francis out of devotion to St Francis of Assisi (4 Oct.)

In addition to the usual three vows, members of the Order took a fourth: never to seek office either within the Order or outside it. They took it in turns to carry out continual penance: each day one brother fasted on bread and water, another took the discipline, and a third wore a hair shirt. At some stage, either while Adorno was superior or when he later succeeded him, Francis also proposed that everyone should spend an hour a day in adoration of the Blessed Sacrament.

The first house was in the environs of Naples. Once it had been established the two founders went to Spain, where the pope wished them to found another house, but they were not welcome at the court of Philip II or in the archdiocese of Toledo and were forced to return to Italy. On the way back they were shipwrecked near Genoa and finally came ashore half-dead from hunger and exhaustion. They managed to make their way along the coast and then to take a ship to Naples. They found that their house had prospered in their absence. Many more priests had come forward, and the dean of Santa Maria Maggiore had himself joined the Order. The church was offered to the Order and became the centre of their work. Some worked as missionaries, others ministered in hospitals and prisons, and there were hermitages for those who felt called to a solitary life.

Adorno died at the early age of forty. Francis, who had been seriously ill himself, was chosen to take his place, though he was reluctant to hold office. As superior he refused to take precedence over his brothers, insisting on taking his turn at sweeping rooms, making beds, and washing the dishes. He often slept on a table or on the altar steps. He was available every morning in the confessional, begged in the streets for the poor, and gave away most of his food and his outer clothes to any who needed them.

Francis made two more visits to Spain and succeeded in founding houses at Madrid, Valladolid, and Alcalá; but his main work was in Naples. He held the position of superior general for seven years, but he found it a severe strain. By temperament he found it repugnant to hold office, and his health was poor. Matters were made worse by opposition to the Order, sometimes supported by malicious and untrue rumours. At last he obtained permission from Pope Clement VIII to resign, and he became prior of Santa Maria Maggiore and novice-master. In 1607, when he was forty-four, he was relieved of all administrative duties and devoted himself to contemplation and preparation for death. He chose to live in a recess under the staircase of the house in Naples, and he was often to be found there with his arms stretched out in the form of a cross. The pope offered him bishoprics: he refused them.

Francis was not destined to die in Naples. St Philip Neri (26 May) had offered the Minor Clerks a house at Agnone, in the Abruzzi, for the novitiate, and it was decided that Francis should go and help with the new foundation. On the way there he visited Loreto and spent a night in prayer at the Holy House. While he was asking Our Lady's help, Adorno appeared to him in a dream and told him that he would soon die. Soon after this, he contracted a fever. He dictated a letter to the members of his Order urging them to remain faithful to the Rule, and he died soon after.

Francis was canonized in 1807. In art he is often depicted holding a monstrance, in reference to the perpetual adoration of the Sacrament laid down in his Rule. He is a patron saint of Naples. The Order of Minor Clerks Regular was for a time a very flourishing body but now has only a few small communities in Italy.

A considerable number of Lives of St Francis Caracciolo have been published in Italian: for example, those by I. Vives (1684); A. Cencelli (1769); A. Ferrante (1862); and G. Tagliatella (1908). G. Rossi (2d ed., 1926) has a bibliography of the Italian Lives to that date. See also A. B. Frassoni (1943), and *I felici* (Rome, 1959); *C.M.H.*, p. 222; *Anal.Boll.* 5 (1886), p. 151; *P.B.*, 6, pp. 448-55; *Saints in Italy*, pp. 181-2; *N.C.E.*, 3, pp. 96-7; *D.H.G.E.*, 18, 707-10; *Bibl.SS.*, 5, 1197-201.

ST BONIFACE
His emblem refers to his defence of the gospel, or the book he was reading
when he was killed—see p. 43. Gold book, sword with gold hilt
and silver blade, on red field.

5

ST BONIFACE, *Bishop and Martyr* (*c.* 675-754)

The Rhineland and Bavaria had become Christian before the time of Boniface, and isolated missionaries had penetrated into other parts of the country; but he was responsible for systematically evangelizing and civilizing the great central regions of Germany, for setting up an organized church, and for bringing it into relation with the Holy See. He is known as the apostle of Germany. His work in regenerating and reorganizing the Frankish church is less generally recognized.

Boniface was a Devon man. His baptismal name was Winfrid, and he was probably born at Crediton. He is said to have decided to become a monk when he was only five years old, after listening to some monastic visitors at his home. He went to school at a monastery near Exeter and then to the abbey of Nursling in the Winchester diocese, where he studied under the learned Abbot Winbert. He progressed so well that after completing his own studies he was made director of the school. He seems to have been an inspired teacher, popular with his students. He wrote the first Latin grammar known to have been compiled in England, and his lectures were so much appreciated that copies of lecture notes were made and circulated far beyond the monastery. When he was thirty he was ordained to the priesthood, and he then found further scope in writing sermons and instructions, all based on the Bible, which was his chief study and delight throughout his life.

Had he stayed in England, he would have been assured of preferment, but he felt called to work in Germany, where St Wilfrid (12 Oct.) and St Willibrord (7 Nov.) had been pioneers. His abbot reluctantly consented, and Winfrid set out with two companions in the spring of 716. However, the area of Friesland (now a northern province of the Netherlands) where they landed was occupied by warlike tribes. Radbod, the local chief, though at first prepared to be baptized, turned hostile and said that he was not prepared "to go to heaven with a handful of beggars." Winfrid withdrew and returned to Nursling. The other monks tried to keep him there, electing him as their new abbot; but he refused the charge and went instead to Rome to obtain a definite commission from Pope Gregory II. It may have been at this time that he changed his name to Boniface. He was sent to the more settled areas of Bavaria and Hesse; but when he heard that Radbod had died he went to help Willibrord, who was bishop of Utrecht. Willibrord would have made him his coadjutor and successor, but Boniface declined, saying that his commission had been a general one and not confined to one diocese.

The dialects of the Germanic tribes in north-western Europe seem to have been very close to the language spoken in England at that time. Boniface does not appear to have had any difficulty in making himself understood. His work prospered so much that in 722 Pope Gregory sent for him, and he was consecrated a regionary bishop with jurisdiction over Germany. He was also given a papal letter to the powerful Charles Martel, leader of the Franks, to afford him some protection on his travels. This he presented in person on his way back to Germany, and he received a sealed pledge of support from Charles Martel.

Armed in this way, he boldly challenged the traditions of the old Norse gods. A dramatic story is told of how he attacked the oak tree of Geismar on the summit of Mount Gudenberg, near Fritzlar, with an axe. This tree was a source of local superstition, and the crowds watched in awe, expecting the gods to strike back; but the first few blows split the oak into four parts, and it crashed to the ground. The wood was evidently not rotten, because Boniface used it to build a chapel of St Peter on the spot. This was accounted a miracle, and many conversions followed.

A monastery was established at Fritzlar and another at Amoneburg. From Bavaria and Hesse, Boniface moved on to Thuringia, where he established a monastery at Ordruf. On his accession in 732 Pope Gregory III sent him the *pallium*, making him archbishop with the power to consecrate bishops in Germany beyond the Rhine. He founded further monasteries at Erfurt, Wurzburg, and Eichstätt.

Wherever he went, he found people ready to listen. There was no shortage of converts: it was the teachers who were lacking, so he appealed to England in a famous letter to the English people, asking for their prayers and help in the mission to "those who are of one blood and bone with you." English monasteries responded with gifts of money, books, vestments, and relics; and parties of monks and nuns regularly crossed the sea to join him, some of them from the noble houses of Wessex. Some of these volunteer evangelists were also to be recognized as saints. Among them were his cousin Lull of Malmesbury (16 Oct.), who was to become his successor as archbishop of Mainz; Sturmi, later abbot of Fulda (17 Dec.); Burchard, later bishop of Wurzburg (2 Feb.); Wigbert, later abbot of Fritzlar (13 Aug.); his cousin Lioba, later abbess of Bischofstein (28 Sept.); and Thecla, later abbess of Kitzingen (12 Oct.).

In 738-9, Boniface made another visit to Rome, where he was appointed papal legate to Germany, and recruited two more outstanding missionaries for Germany, Willibald, later bishop of Eichstätt (7 June), and his brother Wynbald, who became abbot of Heidenheim (18 Dec.). Their sister Walburga (25 Feb.) came straight from England to join them and succeeded Wynbald as superior of the double monastery at Heidenheim. On his return to Germany, using his powers as legate, Boniface convened a synod for all the areas of Germany and established a hierarchy for Bavaria. Each of his new bishoprics was entrusted to one of his English followers capable of developing his tradition of true faith and learning.

In 741, when his work in Germany was well established, he was called to reorganize the Frankish Church. Though Charles Martel had given Boniface the protection that made the work in Germany possible, he had allowed the churches in his own territories to become very lax. Bishoprics were bought and sold, left vacant for long periods, or given to laymen without training or suitability for the task. The clergy were untaught and often unfit for office, and no general church council had been held for eighty-four years. When Charles Martel died his sons and successors, Carloman and Pepin, asked Boniface to reform the Church. He presided over five reforming councils or synods between 741 and 747 in which many abuses were remedied, and the Rule of St Benedict was established at all the Carolingian monasteries.

Carloman, Boniface's chief ally, himself entered a monastery, and Pepin was left as sole ruler. Boniface crowned him as king of the Franks at Soissons in 751. Pepin was somewhat less effective than his brother in controlling the Frankish chiefs, but Boniface's main work was finished. In the same year, he wrote to the pope to describe the last of his monastic foundations, Fulda:

> There is a wooded place in the midst of a vast wilderness situated among the peoples to whom I am preaching. There I have placed a group of monks living under the Rule of St Benedict, who are building a monastery. They are men of ascetic habits, who abstain from meat and wine and spirits, keeping no servants, but are content with the labour of their own hands. . . . Here I propose with your kind permission to rest my aged and worn body for a little time, and after my death to be buried here.

He was by this time nearly eighty years old. He resigned the leadership of the Frankish Church to Chrodegang of Metz (6 Mar.) and the diocese of Mainz to Lull, who became bishop in 754. Then he returned to his first love—the evangelization of the Friesians. At Utrecht he and his party were joined by Bishop Eoban (5 June), another of his English disciples. Many of the Friesians had lapsed, and there was fresh work to do.

A new and vigorous missionary effort was undertaken. This penetrated beyond the part of Friesland where Boniface had ministered many years earlier and led to a mission in an area where hostile tribes still roamed. Boniface was reading quietly in his tent, awaiting the arrival of some candidates for Confirmation, when a band of tribesmen suddenly attacked the camp. Others would have defended Boniface, but he would not allow this. He was one of the first to fall, and his companions were also killed.

Boniface's body was taken to Fulda, where it still rests. The monastery also treasures the book which he was reading and with which he is said to have warded off some of the first blows. It is dented with sword cuts, and the stains on its wooden cover are thought to be the marks of his blood.

Christopher Dawson's judgment is that Boniface "had a deeper influence on the history of Europe than any Englishman who ever lived." His tremendous power as a missionary preacher, his administrative ability, his teaching skills,

43

his capacity to inspire loyalty in his followers, and his courage are clear from the record of his life. He was a lovable man, simple, kindly, and holy, as his letters bear witness. Many of them are still extant, and he was clearly a very good correspondent. He wrote to popes, bishops, abbots, abbesses, and former pupils. He sought advice from many and offered it when asked. He requested books and vestments and prayers for his work, and his many friends in England and other parts of Europe answered his requests. He dealt with "false priests and hypocrites," with unlettered clergy who got the words of administration wrong in Baptism, with at least one adulterous king, and with a variety of human problems. He was above all a good pastor.

Soon after his death Archbishop Cuthbert of Canterbury wrote, "We in England lovingly count him as one of the best and greatest teachers of the true faith," and an English synod agreed that his feast would be celebrated every year as England's patron equally with St Gregory the Great (3 Sept.) and St Augustine of Canterbury (26 May). Like many Anglo-Saxon saints he suffered partial eclipse after the Norman Conquest. He never became a principal saint in England; the real centre of his cult is at Fulda, and he is still widely venerated in Germany and the Netherlands.

There has been a revival of interest in Boniface in the nineteenth and twentieth centuries, and several commentators suggest that he deserves to be better known and appreciated in England.

P.L., 89, 603-892, and *AA.SS.*, June, 1, pp. 445-96, contain several early Lives, and there are edited versions in *N.L.A.*, 1, pp. 122-30. A better edition is that of W. Levison, *Vitae sancti Bonifacii epis. Moguntini* (Eng. trans., 1916). It should be noted that the Life by Willibald is not by the saint of that name. See also G. F. Browne, *Boniface of Crediton* (1910); G. Kurth, *St Boniface* (1902; Eng. trans., 1935); G. W. Greenaway, *St Boniface* (1955); T. Reuter (ed.), *The Greatest Englishman* (1980); *O.D.S.*, pp. 59-60. Boniface's letters have been edited by M. Tangl in *M.G.H.*, *Epistolae Selectae*, and selected letters are available in English in C. H. Talbot, *Anglo-Saxon Missionaries in Germany* (1954). His works are available in many translations. For background see W. Levison, *England and the Continent in the Eighth Century* (1946); E. S. Duckett, *Anglo-Saxon Saints and Scholars* (1947); D. H. Farmer (ed.) *Benedict's Disciples* (1986, rp. 1995), particularly ch. 1, pp. 21-40, by Dom Aelred Sillem, and ch. 6, pp. 105-17, by Dom Frederick Hockey. The judgment by Christopher Dawson is in *The Making of Europe* (1946), p.166.

Bd Meinwerk of Paderborn, *Bishop* (1036)

Meinwerk was a Saxon nobleman from a very wealthy family. He trained for the priesthood first at Halberstadt and later at the cathedral church of Hildesheim. At Hildesheim he formed a lasting friendship with his kinsman, the future emperor Henry II (13 July). On the death of Ratherius, bishop of Paderborn, a city not far from Düsseldorf, Meinwerk was appointed to succeed him. He was consecrated by St Willigis, archbishop of Mainz (23 Feb.), on 13 March 1009.

The emperor's intention was that Meinwerk should spend his own great wealth on what was then a very poor diocese, and this he proceeded to do. Meinwerk did so much for his cathedral city that he has been called the second founder of Paderborn. He rebuilt the cathedral, which had been destroyed by fire, bringing in architects and goldsmiths from other parts of Germany. The new cathedral was consecrated in 1015. He founded a Cluniac monastery at Abdinghof and another monastery at Paderborn; he constructed the city walls, strengthened the fortifications, and restored buildings all over the diocese. He was a great patron of art and learning and made the cathedral school at Paderborn famous all over Germany. Apparently the discipline in the school was strict. Meinwerk's nephew, Bishop Imrad, wrote a letter in 1050 saying that the boys lived like little monks and were not allowed to speak in private even with their own fathers.

All these enterprises were expensive, and when Meinwerk had exhausted his own considerable resources he had no hesitation in asking for large sums of money from his friends, particularly the emperor. His visits for this purpose were so frequent and the demands so large that Henry II sometimes had to find ways of evading him, but he trusted Meinwerk as a friend and a wise counsellor. He summoned him to all his councils and frequently took him with the court when he travelled. These journeys enabled Meinwerk to satisfy a passion for collecting relics, particularly in Rome, where Pope Benedict VIII was generous.

The emperor Henry II died in 1024, to Meinwerk's great personal grief, but his successor, Conrad II, relied on him equally. Meinwerk's last major building project was the construction of a church on the pattern of the church of the Holy Sepulchre. This was to contain relics brought from Jerusalem. The completion of this church was hurried because Meinwerk felt that his own life was drawing to a close. The basilica was dedicated early in 1036, and he died at Whitsuntide.

AA.SS., June, 1, pp. 500-44, contains a twelfth-century Life written by a monk of Abdinghof and an account of the cult. The best text is that edited by F. Tenkhoff, *Vita Meinwerci* (1921). See also *N.C.E.*, 9, p. 623.

Bd Ferdinand of Portugal (1402-43)

Prince Ferdinand "the Constant" or "the Trusty" was half English: his father was King John I of Portugal, and his mother, Philippa, daughter of John of Gaunt. He is best known as the hero of Calderón's play, *El Príncipe Constante* ("The Constant Prince"), which was based on the chronicle kept by his secretary, João Alvarez. As a child he was delicate and often prostrated by illness, but he was very devout. It is said that from the age of fourteen he regularly recited the canonical Hours according to the Sarum use—a practice he must have learned from his English mother.

When his father died he was left very poorly provided for, and for a time he thought of settling in England, where he was assured of a welcome from his Lancastrian cousins; but his eldest brother, King Edward, conferred on him the grand-mastership of the Knights of Aviz, a military Order which had been formed to fight the Moors. The pope had granted a dispensation to the Portguese princes to allow them to hold this office, though it was primarily an ecclesiastical one. Ferdinand accepted with some reluctance; but when Pope Eugenius IV offered to create him a cardinal he refused, saying that he could not conscientiously take on this burden.

In 1437 King Edward sent an expedition against the Moors led by his two brothers, Ferdinand and Henry the Navigator. It was badly organized and destined to fail. Ferdinand was ill when the expedition left for North Africa but would not delay the party. They sailed for Ceuta with less than half the forces the king had ordered and would not wait for reinforcements. They attacked Tangier with reckless courage but disastrous results, and they were forced to accept humiliating terms, leaving Ferdinand as a hostage in the hands of the Moors. With twelve others, one of whom was his secretary and future biographer Alvarez, he was taken to Arzilla, where he was very ill for seven months. During this time he was treated comparatively well, but when the Portuguese refused to ratify a treaty which involved the surrender of Ceuta, the Moors turned their fury on their captives.

Ferdinand was taken to Fez, heavily chained, and forced to do heavy work in stables and gardens. He was frequently threatened with death, but he refused to consider escaping because it would mean leaving his fellow-prisoners to a worse fate. He was more concerned about the others than himself. He did not complain and he never spoke against the Moors.

His brothers made efforts to ransom him, but the Moors refused to free him unless Ceuta was surrendered, and to this they would not agree. Ferdinand remained a captive at Fez for over five years. In the last fifteen months of his life his treatment was even worse: he was separated from his attendants and incarcerated alone in a bare and airless dungeon. When it became evident that he had not long to live, a doctor, a priest, and a few other Christians were allowed to visit him. He died on 5 June 1443, and the Moors exposed his body, head downward, on the city wall. When Alvarez regained his freedom eight years later he brought Ferdinand's heart back to Portugal, and his bones were subsequently recovered, to be deposited in the church of our Lady at Batalha in the diocese of Leira.

Prince Ferdinand's cult was approved by Pope Paul II about the year 1470.

AA.SS., June, 1, pp. 552-84, contains a Latin version of Alvarez' *Chronica dos feitos, vida e morte do Iffante Fernando*. This includes illustrations of Ferdinand during his imprisonment. See also the biography by M. Gloning (1916) and A. Sánchez Moguel in the *Boletín de la real Academia de la Historia*, 20 (1892) pp. 332 ff.; *D.H.G.E.*, 16, 1043. Lives of Prince Henry the Navigator, for example, those by R. H. Major (1868) and J. P. Oliveira Martins (Eng. trans., 1914) have relevant material. Pedro Calderón de la Barca's play (1636) has been translated into English.

6

ST NORBERT, *Bishop and Founder* (1080-1134)

Xanten, in the duchy of Cleves, was Norbert's birthplace. He was the son of Herbert, count of Gennep, and Hedwig of Guise, related through his father to the emperor and through his mother to the counts of Lorraine. He received minor orders, as the sons of noblemen often did, and was appointed to a canonry in the church of St Victor at Xanten; but this was probably more a matter of having an official position on ceremonial occasions and a source of revenue than a testimony to his pastoral abilities. He was made a subdeacon but had no desire to become a priest. At the court of the emperor Henry V he was appointed almoner, and he joined in all the diversions of the young nobility.

His life was changed by a serious accident. One day, when he was riding near the village of Wreden in Westphalia, he was overtaken in open country by a violent thunderstorm. His horse, frightened by a flash of lightning, threw him, and he lay unconscious on the ground for some time. When he came round his first words were those of Saul on the road to Damascus: "Lord, what wilt thou have me to do?" An inner voice replied: "Turn away from evil, and do good. Seek peace, and pursue it."

This conversion was as sudden and complete as that of St Paul himself. Norbert returned to Xanten, where he spent much time in prayer, fasting, and a review of his past life. He made a retreat at the abbey of Siegberg, near Cologne, where he came under the influence of Abbot Conon. He then prepared himself for ordination as a priest, and in 1115 Archbishop Frederick of Cologne conferred on him the diaconate and the priesthood on the same day, which was canonically irregular. After another forty days in retreat he returned to Xanten determined to lead "an evangelical and apostolic life." It seems that the vigour of his exhortations and what was seen as eccentric behaviour for a man of his rank had made him enemies among the other canons. One even spat in his face. At the Council of Fritzlar in 1118 he was denounced to the papal legate as a hypocrite and an innovator and charged with preaching without a licence or a commission.

Norbert put an end to doubts about his sincerity. He sold his estates and gave away all that he had except forty marks in silver, a mule (which soon died), a missal, some vestments, and a chalice and paten. Then, accompanied by two attendants who refused to leave him, he travelled barefoot to Saint-Gilles in the Languedoc, where Pope Gelasius II was in exile. At the feet of the pope, he made a general confession of his misdeeds and the irregularity of his

47

ordination and offered himself for any penance that might be laid upon him. In response, the pope gave him leave to preach the gospel wherever he chose.

Armed with this permission, Norbert set out again in wintry weather, going barefoot in the snow. At Valenciennes his two companions fell ill and died. He was not alone long, for the archbishop of Cambrai and his young chaplain came to see him. The bishop was impressed by the change in one whom he had formerly known only as a frivolous courtier, and Hugh, the chaplain, asked why he showed such affection and respect for a poor mission priest. The bishop replied, "That man was once the gayest and most refined in the emperor's court. If he is now poor and despised, it is because he has refused wealth and honour. The bishopric of Cambrai was offered to him, but he would not take it." Hugh was so impressed that he decided to follow Norbert. He became his most trusted follower and eventually succeeded him as the head of his Order. He was beatified as Hugh of Fosse (10 Feb.).

Pope Gelasius II died in 1119 and was succeeded by Callistus II. Norbert went to Reims to see the new pope, hoping to obtain a renewal of his general mission to preach, but the new pope seems to have thought that it would be better to attach him to a diocese, and he was assigned to the bishop of Laon to help in the reform of the Canons Regular of St Martin's in Laon. The Canons proved obdurate and would not accept Norbert's strict regulations, so the bishop gave him permission to found a community of his own and gave him a choice of several locations. Norbert chose a lonely valley called Prémontré in the forest of Coucy. This valley had previously been the home of the monks of St Vincent at Laon, but they had abandoned it because of the poverty of the soil.

A beginning was made at Prémontré with thirteen disciples, some of whom came from the Canons Regular at Laon. Their numbers soon increased, and forty made their profession on Christmas Day 1121. They wore a white habit and kept the Rule of St Augustine with certain additional regulations. Their manner of life was extremely austere. The movement, whether regarded as a new Order or a reform of the existing one at Laon, soon spread to other countries. Both men and women came forward to join it, and many gifts of property were made for new foundations. Among the recruits were Bd Godfrey, count of Kappenberg (13 Jan.), who placed his castle at Norbert's disposal, built a convent for his wife and his two sisters, and himself joined the Order; St Evermod (17 Feb.), who was to become bishop of Ratzeburg and apostle to the Wends, and Bd Waltman (11 Apr.), who became abbot of St Michael's in Antwerp.

When the Order had eight abbeys and one or two nunneries, Norbert made a journey to Rome and asked Pope Honorius II for formal approval. This he obtained, and the canons of Laon, who had formerly refused his Rule, now voluntarily joined the Order.

Another nobleman, Count Theobald of Champagne, wanted to join the Order, but Norbert judged that he had no vocation and urged him to carry out his worldly responsibilities and to marry. At the same time he gave him a small white scapular to wear under his outer garments and prescribed certain rules and devotions for his use. This is the first known case of the affiliation of a layman living in the world to a recognized monastic Order as a tertiary.

When the count went to Germany to conclude a marriage treaty in 1126, Norbert accompanied him. On the way they visited Speyer, where the emperor Lothair was holding an assembly. At the same time a delegation arrived from Magdeburg asking the emperor to nominate a bishop to their vacant see. Lothair chose Norbert. The deputies led him back to Magdeburg, where he entered the city barefoot and so poorly clad that the porter at the episcopal palace refused to let him in, bidding him to go and join the other beggars. "But he is our bishop!" shouted the crowd. "Never mind, dear brother," said Norbert to the porter, "You judge me more truly than those who brought me here."

Norbert continued to practise the austerity of a monk; but though he was personally humble and required only the bare necessities of life, he was unflinching in his determination to assert the rights of the Church. Under the weak rule of his predecessors, much ecclesiastical property had been alienated. Norbert had no hesitation in taking action against the people responsible, for he regarded them as no better than robbers. He also undertook a major reform of the clergy of the diocese, many of whom were leading careless and sometimes scandalous lives and neglecting their parishes. Norbert reasoned with them first, but he was prepared to punish or dispossess them, and in some cases he brought in his own Premonstratensian Canons in their place.

Such wholehearted reforms invited opposition. Norbert found that his enemies united to discredit him and to raise resistance among the people. On two or three occasions he narrowly escaped assassination, and once the rabble broke into his cathedral while he was holding a service there. He took refuge in a tower, still in his ecclesiastical vestments. Two days later the mob in the courtyard below killed his chamberlain and advanced up the stairs of the tower. Norbert came out to the top of the stairs to confront them, wearing his mitre and chasuble. The leaders hesitated, and then the sound of troops was heard below. The count of Magdeburg had arrived with his men to relieve what remained of the garrison. Norbert went calmly into his church to say Mass, and since his clergy had fled, he read the Epistle and Gospel himself without a tremor.

The unrest in the city was such that Norbert finally decided to withdraw and leave the people to their own devices. This proved a wise decision. Faced with ecclesiastical censure and fearing the emperor's displeasure, they soon asked him to return. Before the end of his life he had carried through the greater part of his projected reforms. He was still directing the Premonstratensian houses with the help of his lieutenant, Hugh of Fosse, and he played an important part in the politics of the papacy and the empire.

After the death of Pope Honorius II in 1130 there was a schism. The anti-pope Anacletus II occupied Rome, while Pope Innocent II was exiled to France, where he was accepted as the lawful pontiff, largely through the efforts of St Bernard of Clairvaux (20 Aug.) and St Hugh of Grenoble (1 Apr.). Norbert attended a council that Pope Innocent held in Reims and worked for his cause, winning favour for it in Germany as St Bernard and St Hugh had done in France. When it became evident that, even with the support of France, Germany, England, and Spain, the pope could enter Rome only with the help of armed forces, it was largely through the influence of Norbert and Bernard that the emperor Lothair consented to head an army to support the pope. Both Bernard and Norbert went with him.

In recognition of his outstanding services to the papacy Norbert was invested with the *pallium* and constituted primate of all Germany. After their return from Italy the emperor insisted on making him his chancellor, but by this time Norbert's health was failing. In the twenty years since his ordination he had crowded in a lifetime of service. After he died his body was carried in turn to all the churches in Magdeburg and then laid in the church of his Order in that city. When Magdeburg became Lutheran the relics were translated in 1627 by Emperor Ferdinand II to the Premonstratensian abbey of Strabov in Bohemia. Norbert was canonized by Pope Gregory XIII in 1582.

Material in *P.L.*, 170, 1253-1360, and also in *AA.SS.*, June, 1, pp. 797-928, and appendix, pp. 26-58, is extensive but less reliable than a version edited by R. Williams in *M.G.H., Scriptores*, 12, pp. 663-706; *C.M.H.*, p. 226. The modern Lives are plentiful, especially in German and Flemish. The best is perhaps A. Zak, *Der heilige Norbert* (1930). There are biographies in French by E. Maire (1932) and G. Madelaine (3d ed., 1928). In English see C. J. Kirkfleet, *History of St Norbert* (1916); C. L. Smetana (ed.), *The Life of St Norbert by John Capgrave* (1977). See also P. Lefèvre in *R.H.E.* 56 (1961), pp. 813-26, and an important article on the origins of Prémontré by C. Dereine in *R.H.E.* 91, pp. 352 ff.; also *D.T.C.* (*s.v.* "Prémontrés"), 13, 1-34. Cf. H. M. Colvin, *The White Canons in England* (1951), pp. 1-25.

St Philip the Deacon (First Century)

All that is known about Philip the Deacon is to be found in the Acts of the Apostles. He was not the apostle Philip (1 May) but one of the deacons appointed by the apostles when the Greeks complained that preference was being given to the Hebrews in the daily distribution of food (Acts 6:1-6). He stands second to Stephen in the list of "seven men of good reputation, filled with the Spirit and with wisdom," who took over the task of ministering to the poor and needy, leaving the apostles free to concentrate on the ministry of the word. Like Stephen, he was probably a Greek, as his name suggests.

The work of the deacons soon developed beyond their original task, and Philip became an evangelist who "went from place to place spreading the good news" (Acts 8:4-13). He went into Samaria and converted many. He baptized Simon Magus, a local magician with a great reputation. After his baptism

Simon "went round constantly with Philip." When the apostles were told of Philip's work, Peter and John went into Samaria "and prayed for the Samaritans to receive the Holy Spirit. . . . Then they laid hands on them, and they received the Holy Spirit." They gave short shrift to Simon, who wanted to buy the Holy Spirit for silver. Peter said, "Thy silver perish with thee." There are traditions that he faced this antagonist again later in Rome.

Philip felt called to take the desert road that led south from Jerusalem to Gaza. On that road he met the chief treasurer of the *kandake* (queen) of Ethiopia, who had been on a pilgrimage to Jerusalem and was returning home. The official, who was probably an African convert to Judaism, sat in his chariot reading. Philip went up to him and saw that he was studying the writings of Isaiah and puzzling over Isaiah 53:7-8:

> Like a sheep that is led to the slaughterhouse,
> like a lamb that is dumb in front of its shearers,
> like these he never opens his mouth.
> He has been humiliated and has no one to defend him.
> Who will ever talk about his descendants,
> since his life on earth has been cut short?

Philip asked him if he understood what he was reading, and he replied that he needed a guide. Was the prophet speaking of himself, he asked, or of someone else? Philip got into the chariot, and explained that the prophecies had been fulfilled in the incarnation, death, and resurrection of Jesus Christ. They must have travelled together, talking over this revelation, and the official believed. When they came to water, he asked if he could be baptized. Then they went down to the water and Philip baptized him. They never met again, but the official "went on his way rejoicing" (Acts 8:26-40).

This is a key episode in the story of the Acts of the Apostles. Philip seems to have realized, even before the apostles, that the gospel had to be taken outside the confines of Israel, to other races in other lands. The official was a man of standing in an African court. He was probably black and possibly a eunuch, like most court officials in the Middle East and the Orient. Philip welcomed him into the Christian community—and this may have been the beginning of the Church in Ethiopia.

Philip "continued his journey proclaiming the good news in every town as far as Caesarea," which may have been his home. Much later, when St Paul and his companions had been to visit the Christians in Ephesus, they made their way home through Caesarea and stayed with Philip, clearly identified as "the evangelist, one of the Seven." This may have been his home town, because he had a family—four virgin daughters, who were "prophets" (Acts 21:8-9). The daughters, whose names are unknown, are sometimes listed as saints with Philip.

According to a later Greek tradition Philip afterwards became bishop of Tralles in Lydia, but no more is known for certain about his ministry.

AA.SS., June, 1, pp. 608-10; *P.B.*, 6, pp. 472-4; *O.D.S.*, pp. 397-8.

St Ceratius, *Bishop* (*c.* 455)

Accounts of the life of Bishop Ceratius (Cérase, in French) contain apparent conflicts, though there is definite evidence that he was bishop of Grenoble in the middle of the fifth century and that he was honoured in that city a century or so later on 6 June. It has been established that he was present at the Council of Orange in 441 and that, together with two other bishops in Gaul, he wrote to Pope Leo the Great (440-61; 10 Nov.) in 450. He is also mentioned in a letter written to Pope Leo by Eusebius of Milan.

Difficulty arises because a Cerasius or Ceratius is claimed in Gascony as the founder and first occupant of the see of Eauze, later the diocese of Auch. His relics are said to be preserved in the abbey of Simorre, near Lombes. It is not clear whether the two are the same. One suggestion is that Ceratius of Grenoble was driven away by the persecution of the Arians in Burgundy and migrated to Aquitaine to found a new see, but there is no historical evidence to support this theory.

The cult of Ceratius of Grenoble was confirmed in 1903, but without resolving the problem.

AA.SS., June, 1, pp. 697-8; Duchesne, *Fastes*, 1, p. 231.

St Eustorgius II, *Bishop* (518)

Two bishops of Milan have borne the name of Eustorgius. The second of these was of Greek origin and lived in Rome during the reigns of Popes Gelasius (21 Nov.), Symmachus (19 July), and Hormisdas (6 Aug.), which covered the years 492-523. He was consecrated in 512 and remained in Milan until his death over six years later. His episcopate appears to have been a peaceful one. He is said to have received into his own house, instructed, baptized, and ordained a young man from Pannonia named Florian, who was subsequently martyred, venerated in France under the name of St Laurien, and listed in Spanish martyrologies as bishop of Seville.

Eustorgius is described as a man of great virtue, an excellent shepherd of his people, and a defender of the patrimony of the Church. He ransomed many of his people who were taken prisoner in the wars between the north Italian duchies during his episcopate. Two documents from Cassiodorus show that King Theodore the Great regarded him with great respect. A letter to him from St Avitus of Vienne (5 Feb.) is extant, as are some short Breviary lessons which he composed. He was buried in the church of San Lorenzo in Milan, where his relics are still preserved.

The documents mentioned above are quoted in *AA.SS.*, June, 1, pp. 633-4. See also *M.G.H., Auctores antiquissimi*, 7, p. 271; *D.H.G.E.*, 16, 47.

St Jarlath, *Bishop* (*c*. 550)

The archdiocese of Tuam in Galway venerates Jarlath as its principal patron and as the founder of its ancient episcopal seat. He is not to be confused with an earlier Jarlath who became bishop of Armagh and whose feast is kept there on 11 February. Jarlath of Tuam is one of the Irish saints of the sixth century, and while definite information on his life is scarce, there is a very strong tradition to support him.

He is said to have been born in Galway, where his family dominated a large area of territory. The date of his birth is unknown. He was trained by a holy man, was ordained, and founded a monastery at Cluain Fois, near the present town of Tuam. He ruled over the community as abbot-bishop honoured for his piety and learning, and he opened a school which had a high reputation. Among his pupils were said to be Brendan of Clonfert (16 May) and Colman of Munster.

Jarlath died about the middle of the sixth century, and his feast is kept throughout Ireland. A silver or silver-gilt shrine was kept at a chapel, *Teampol na Scrine*, at Tuam until about 1830 but was then lost.

AA.SS., Nov., 4, pp. 147-86; John Colgan, *De sacris Hiberniae antiquitatibus* (1647), 1, pp. 307-8; *Irish Saints*, p. 199.

St Gudval of Brittany (? Sixth Century)

The most recent historical research, by Canon Doble in his Cornish Saints Series, identifies St Gudwal with Gurval of Brittany. His name in one form or the other figures prominently in the ancient Armorican litanies as one of the earliest missionaries to evangelize Brittany. In the Missal of Saint-Vougay he comes third in the list of pioneer saints, St Samson being first and St Malo second.

At the inland sea of Etel, between Vannes and Lorient in south Brittany, he founded the monastery of Plecit on the island which bears his name (Locoal is a corruption of Gurval), and this is still the centre of his cult. He made other settlements in the same area and a more distant one at Guer, between Vannes and Rennes. The chapel of St Stephen at Guer, described as the oldest religious monument in the district of Morbihan, is regarded by at least one modern archaeologist as his hermitage.

We know little of Gudval's activities. He is said to have died in one of his monasteries which stood in a wood, but his body was taken back to Locoal after his death. When the Norsemen invaded Brittany in the tenth century his relics were taken for safety to Picardy, and then to Ghent, to the abbey of St Peter.

Many years later a monk compiled a Latin Life; but oral and written tradition was scanty, and the account was supplemented by fictitious details. There is a late tradition that Gudval was bishop of Saint-Malo, but this is incorrect. It seems to have arisen from the fact that during the Middle Ages, though geographically part of Brittany, Guer was under the jurisdiction of the bishops of Saint-Malo.

There is a tradition that Gudval was British, possibly from Wales or Cornwall, but this is not substantiated. His cult came to England, possibly from Ghent. He is the patron of Finstall (Worcestershire), and Worcester celebrated his feast. He has been claimed as the patron of Gulval in Cornwall.

AA.SS., June, 1, pp. 715-36; *N.L.A.*, 1, pp. 501-4; G. H. Doble, *St Gurval*, Cornish Saints Series, no. 30 (*c.* 1932); Stanton, pp. 258-9; *D.H.G.E.*, fasc. 128, 645-6; *Dict.Hag.*, p. 316.

St Claud of Besançon, *Bishop* (*c.* 699)

Claud is said to have been born in Franche-Comté, the son of a local nobleman. He may have borne arms as a young man, but he renounced a worldly career at the age of twenty. He lived a very simple life, fasting often and denying himself sleep. He was ordained and was one of the clergy of Besançon for at least twelve years. After that there are two traditions: one says that he continued as a secular priest until his elevation to the episcopate in 685; the other is that he retired to the monastery of Condate, now called Saint-Claude, where he became abbot at the age of thirty-seven, introduced the Benedictine Rule, and restored the monastic buildings.

When he became bishop of Besançon he was already an old man, and he was unwilling to accept the responsibility of administering a diocese, but he ruled it well. He was assiduous at divine office, listened patiently to ecclesiastical causes, cared for his clergy and people, and carried out many works of charity. He is said to have been eighty-six when he finally laid down his burden and went (or went back) to Condate. He died there at a very advanced age and was buried without pomp in the monastery church. Some of the people of the area were convinced that demons lived in the dark valleys of the Jura Mountains, and Claud was often invoked for his protection. His cult became widespread in the twelfth century, and his burial place was for centuries a favourite place of pilgrimage.

There has been some confusion with Claudius, a bishop of Besançon who lived over a century earlier: Claudius attended the Council of Epson in 517 and that of Lyons in 529, but the late-seventh-century bishop and abbot of Condate is the saint.

AA.SS., June, 1, pp. 634-96, includes a medieval text of relatively late date. Duchesne, *Fastes*, 3, p. 212; *B.G.*, June, pp. 674-9.

7

ST WILLIBALD, *Bishop* (*c*. 700-786)

Willibald was the son of St Richard of the West Saxons (7 Feb.), whose wife, Winna, was sister to St Boniface (5 June). His brother and sister were St Wynbald (18 Dec.) and St Walburga (25 Feb.). As a small child he suffered a serious illness. No remedies improved his condition, and he was thought to be dying. His parents laid him at the foot of a great cross near their home and promised that if he recovered they would offer his life to God. He did recover and was educated in the monastery at Waltham in Hampshire, which he left in the year 720 to accompany his father and brother on a pilgrimage. According to one account, the pilgrimage was Willibald's idea. Richard died at Lucca, where he is still venerated. The two brothers pressed on to Rome, where they were both very ill, and Wynbald, whose health was delicate, had to stay there. Willibald went with two companions on "a great peregrination into the unknown country—the Holy Land itself."

Later he dictated an account of his travels to Hugebure, a nun of Heidenheim, and her *Hodoeporicon* is the earliest known travel book by an Anglo-Saxon writer. We can catch something of her sense of wonder at this venture into the lands held by the Saracens and his journey to the Holy Places in her account: "Willibald visited and saw these places with his own eyes, and trod with his feet in the footsteps of Him who was born into this world, suffered, and rose again for our sake."

They travelled down Italy to Reggio di Calabria, then to Sicily, and took a ship for Ephesus. There they saw the cave of the Seven Sleepers (27 July), which must have been of particular interest, because the Sleepers were reputed to have emerged from their long martyrdom alive a little over a century earlier. They saw the tomb of St John the Evangelist (27 Dec.). They went on into Syria, where they were twice arrested by the Saracens, who thought they were spies. On the first occasion the elderly magistrate had encountered Christian pilgrims elsewhere. He said, "I have often seen men of the parts of the earth whence these come travelling hither. They mean no harm, wishing but to fulfil their law." On the second, a friendly Spaniard explained to the magistrate, "These men come from the West, where the sun sets. We know nothing of their country except that beyond it lies nothing but water."

The travellers (there were seven in the party at this stage) went on to visit the Holy Places. They took the road from Damascus to Jerusalem and prayed in the church on the spot where St Paul was converted. They went to Galilee

55

"to the place where Gabriel first came to Our Lady and said 'Hail Mary.'"
They went to Cana of Galilee and drank wine from pots kept on an altar, said
to be those used at the wedding feast when Jesus turned the water into wine.
They went to Mount Tabor and meditated on the Transfiguration in a monastery. They went to Capernaum, to Nazareth, and they bathed at the spot on
the Jordan where Jesus received his baptism from John. They saw the Wilderness of the Temptation and finally came to Jerusalem.

Three crosses had been placed outside the Church of the Holy Sepulchre to
mark the place of the crucifixion, then covered only with a makeshift roof.
The walls of the city had been extended in the time of the empress Helena,
Constantine's mother, to bring the site of the crucifixion into Jerusalem itself.
They went on to Bethlehem, a few miles to the south, and saw the cave where
Jesus was born, in the crypt of the Church of the Nativity—"a house of great
beauty" embellished with Constantine's mosaics and Justinian's marble pillars,
which can still be seen today.

The old hospices on the pilgrim routes had fallen into disuse because of the
spread of the Muslim empire, so the journey was fairly hazardous, and since
they were begging their way, they often went short of food and were reduced
to a diet of bread and water. Willibald returned to Jerusalem several times. He
visited many famous monasteries and hermitages, including the Great *Laura* of
St Sabas, learning all that he could about Christian tradition and the religious
life. Eventually he sailed from Tyre to Constantinople and after a long stay in
that city, he reached Italy again in 730.

Willibald spent ten years in the monastery of Monte Cassino, which had
then recently been restored by Pope Gregory II (11 Feb.), and contributed
much to the restoration of the primitive Benedictine Rule there. His experiences in the East must have been of great interest to the monks, and Pope
Gregory III (10 Dec.), himself a Syrian, also wanted to hear of his travels.
About 740 the pope sent him to Germany to join the mission of his kinsman
Boniface (5 June). Boniface, who had asked the pope for recruits (and may well
have asked for Willibald personally, since Willibald was his sister's son), was
by that time metropolitan of Germany beyond the Rhine and papal legate.

Willibald joined Boniface in Thuringia, was ordained priest, and devoted all
his energies to evangelizing the people of Franconia, in the southern part of the
Rhine Valley. In 742 he was consecrated bishop of Eichstätt. One of his early
acts was the foundation of the double monastery at Heidenheim, with the same
Rule as that at Monte Cassino. His brother and sister came to join him, Wynbald
as abbot and Walburga as abbess. The evangelization and administration of the
diocese were conducted from this monastery, and Willibald found it a quiet
refuge from the cares of office. Despite his love of solitude he was active in
pastoral care, visiting all parts of his diocese and attending to his people's
spiritual needs. As Hugebure says, "The field which had been so arid and
barren flourished as a very vineyard of the Lord."

Willibald outlived both his brother and his sister and served as bishop of Eichstätt for forty-five years. His body was enshrined in Eichstätt cathedral, where his tomb can still be seen.

The materials on St Willibald are unusually full and reliable. The best text of the *Hodoeporicon* is that edited by Petz in *M.G.H., Scriptores*, 15 , which also includes several minor biographies and letters. The most important material is also to be found in *AA.SS.*, July, 2, pp. 485-519. There is an English translation of the *Hodoeporicon* in C. H. Talbot, *Anglo-Saxon Missionaries in Germany* (1954). See also *Anal.Boll.* 49 (1931), pp. 353-97; W. Levison, *England and the Continent in the Eighth Century* (1946), pp. 43-4 and references elsewhere; Stanton, pp. 321-2; *D.N.B.*, 21, pp. 483-4 (which cites Willibald as "bishop and traveller").

St Paul I of Constantinople, *Bishop and Martyr* (350 or 351)

The troubled history of Paul's episcopate and its tragic end tell us much about the divisions in the Church resulting from the Arian heresy. Arius, who died about the year 356, was a priest in Alexandria who taught that Christ was not co-eternal with God the Father but created by him. Arianism spread through the Church, was condemned at the Council of Nicaea in 325, and again at Constantinople in 351. Constans was emperor in the West, and a Catholic, but Constantius was emperor in the East, and an Arian. During the reign of Constantius Arianism was sufficiently strong in the Eastern Church for Paul to be three times exiled and ultimately killed in captivity.

Paul was a Greek from Thessalonika. According to the historians Socrates and Sozomen he was the young reader whom the patriarch Metrophanes (4 June) prophesied would follow Bishop Alexander as his successor. From his boyhood he had been secretary to Alexander, who had him made deacon. When Alexander was dying, probably in the year 336, he named Paul as his successor, and the electors endorsed his choice. Paul was validly consecrated by a number of orthodox bishops, but the Arians induced Constantius to call a council of Arian bishops. Paul was deposed by this council and banished, Eusebius of Nicomedia being consecrated by the Arian bishops in his place.

Paul took shelter in Trier, the imperial capital of the Western empire, where he was welcomed by Bishop Maximian (29 May) and the emperor Constans. Trier had become a place of refuge for clergy who were persecuted by the Arians in the Eastern empire. St Athanasius (2 May) stayed there for two years. Paul went to Rome and assisted at the great council called by Pope Julius I in 341, when the orthodoxy of Athanasius was proclaimed.

When Eusebius of Nicomedia died soon after, Paul returned to Constantinople bearing letters from the pope and the Western emperor insisting on his restoration. He was reinstated, with popular demonstrations of support. The Arians still refused to acknowledge him and set up a rival bishop, Macedonius. The result was open conflict and violence in the streets of Constantinople. The emperor Constantius ordered his general Hermogenes to drive Paul out of the city, but the infuriated crowds set fire to Hermogenes' house, killed him, and dragged his body through the streets.

This outrage brought Constantius himself to Constantinople. He pardoned the people but sent Paul once more into exile. In order to calm the situation he refused to sanction the election of Macedonius. Both Constans, the Western emperor, and Pope Julius I (12 Apr.) supported Paul, and at some stage he returned to the city. He is known to have been there in 344 and may have had some years of peaceful administration. He attended the Council of Sardica in 347—though the party which still supported Macedonius set up an opposing council and proceeded to decree the excommunication of Paul, Athanasius, and Pope Julius.

Constans had exerted a restraining influence over Constantius, but the death of Constans in 350 left Paul without protection. Constantius sent a praetorian prefect named Philip to Constantinople with instructions to expel him and install Macedonius in his place. This could not be done openly because of the degree of popular support for Paul in the city, so Philip resorted to trickery. He invited Paul to meet him at the public baths of Zeuxippus, and while crowds gathered outside, suspicious of the prefect's intentions, Paul was seized, taken by force through a side window, and removed from Constantinople by ship. He was evidently still a threat, even in exile. He was taken to Mesopotamia, then to Syria, and finally to Cucusa in Armenia. According to the account of Philagrius, an official stationed at Cucusa at the time, he was left in a dungeon for six days and nights without food and then strangled.

Paul was not listed as a martyr by Cardinal Baronius in the Roman Martyrology, but he is honoured as a martyr in the Eastern churches and is given the title in the *Acta Sanctorum*.

There are scattered references to Paul in Sozomen, *H.E.*, bk. 4, and Socrates, *H.E.*, ch. 26. See also *AA.SS.*, June, 2, pp. 13-24; *C.M.H.*, p. 227; *O.D.C.C.*, p. 1052; *D.C.B.*, 4, pp. 256-7, and 3, pp. 775-7 (*s.v.* "Macedonius"); W. Telfer, "Paul of Constantinople," *Harvard Theological Review* 43 (1950), pp. 31-92; *Oxford Dictionary of Byzantium* (1991), 3, p. 1695.

St Meriadoc (? Sixth Century)

The legend of Meriadoc, *Beunans Meriasek*, is the only complete miracle play still surviving that is founded on the story of a saint and written in the Cornish vernacular. In the play, Meriasek is the son of the duke of Brittany. He becomes a priest, goes to Cornwall, founds Camborne church, causes a miraculous spring to appear at a place known as Marazaak's Well, and heals the sick before going home to Brittany.

There are also popular biographies and other accounts of the saint, such as the Breviary lessons used by the diocese of Vannes, but no reliance can be placed on these. They were based on a twelfth-century Life which appears to have been written to glorify the Rohan family by inventing a "royal" descent from Meriadoc's family.

Such evidence as we have on Meriadoc's life comes not from written records but from topographical conjecture. His name is Welsh, which suggests a Welsh origin. He is associated with the parish of Camborne in Cornwall, and a neighbouring parish perpetuates the name of St Gwinear, another Welsh saint. The two seem to have carried out a mission in Cornwall and founded churches before going on to Brittany, where both their names are venerated in the three parishes of Pluvigny.

Meriadoc may have been a regionary bishop, but he was never bishop of Vannes, though his name appears in the official list.

The topographical material is the work of Canon G. H. Doble: no. 34 in the Cornish Saints Series (1935). A text and translation of *Beunans Meriasek* was published by Whitley Stokes (1872), and an extract by R. Morton Nance and A. S. D. Smith is available (1949). The play was revived at Redruth in 1924. The account in *AA.SS.*, July, 2, pp. 35-9, is based largely on the legendary materials compiled by Albert Le Grand and André du Saussay. *P.B.*, 6, adheres to the twelfth-century story of a royal French ancestry. See also Roscarrock, p. 87 and notes pp. 150-1; *O.D.S.*, pp. 337-8.

St Colman of Dromore, *Bishop* (Sixth Century)

There are about three hundred Irish saints named Colman, so their history easily becomes confused, and some of the later manuscripts relating to this Colman are full of anachronisms and extravagant legends; but he is one of the most widely venerated in Ireland, and there is a basis of fact behind the legends. He may have been born in Argyllshire or in Ulster: he is mentioned in the ancient calendars of both countries, and there was a considerable movement of missionaries from one to the other, probably travelling by the short sea route through the islands.

According to Irish tradition Colman was the son of Daire, of the royal blood of the kings of Cashel. He received his early training at Nendrum, or Mahee Island, and became a disciple of St Ailbhe of Emly (12 Sept.). Among his friends was St Macanisius (3 Sept.), and Colman asked him what he should do. Macanisius answered, "It is the will of God that you build a monastery within the bounds of Coba plain," and this Colman proceeded to do. The community was established by the river Lagan, which passes through Dromore (Druim Mór), probably about the year 514, and Colman is venerated as the first bishop. The most famous of his pupils was Finnian of Moville (10 Sept.).

Colman seems to have died about the middle of the sixth century or earlier, and he was probably interred at Dromore, though the *Aberdeen Breviary* gives Inchmacome as his place of burial.

AA.SS., June, 2, pp. 24-9, contains a Latin Life, mutilated at the end, from the *Codex Salmaticensis*. See also *Aberdeen Breviary Lessons*; *K.S.S.*, pp. 304-5; *B.G.F.*, 8, pp. 162-4; Heist, *V.S.H.*, pp. 357-60; *O.D.S.*, pp. 105-6.

St Vulflagius (645)

There is very little serious evidence for the life of Vulflagius, or Wulphy, but his relics are still venerated at Montreuil-sur-mer in northern France, and his story illustrates what must have been a fairly common situation at a time when the Church did not require secular priests to be celibate but valued celibacy highly.

It is said that Vulflagius married an accomplished and pious girl when he was young and settled down in his home town of Rue, near Abbeville in northern France. There he led so exemplary a life with his wife and three daughters that when their priest died, the people of Rue asked him to be their pastor. St Riquier (26 Apr.), the bishop of Amiens, examined him and agreed but stipulated that Vulflagius and his wife must live in continence. With his wife's consent, Vulflagius agreed; but they were very much attached to each other and failed to keep to the agreement. He regarded his failure as a great sin, and his penitential practices were extreme.

He undertook a pilgrimage to the Holy Land in expiation. When he returned he still regarded himself as unfit to undertake pastoral responsibilities, so he consulted Bishop Riquier and then withdrew to a lonely place called Regnière Ecluse to live as a hermit. There is no record of his wife's reactions, but his daughters also withdrew from the world and took monastic vows.

Many people came to Vulflagius for instruction and healing. Though he was very much tempted to give up this solitary life, he continued in it until his death. His relics were translated to Montreuil-sur-mer about the ninth century.

AA.SS., June, 2, pp. 29-34; *Anal.Boll.* 17 (1898), p. 307, and 21 (1902), p. 43; *P.B.*, 6, pp. 510-14, from the *Historia Abbavillana* (1480); B.G., June, pp. 71-2.

St Gottschalk (1066)

The *New Dictionary of Saints* (1993), following an earlier edition of the present work, says of Gottschalk that "there seems to be no solid reason for regarding him as either a saint or a martyr." This may be unduly dismissive: his life illustrates something of the battle raging between Christian and Norse beliefs in the early eleventh century and the way in which individuals were torn between the two. He carried out many Christian works, and he died as a Christian.

Gottschalk was a Wendish prince, one of a Slav race which had spread across Germany and settled in Saxony. Adam of Bremen calls him *Godeschalko, princeps Sclavorum*. He was brought up a Christian, but when he was studying at Luneberg his father, an Obotrite king, was murdered by a Christian Saxon. Gottschalk, who had lost his own territories, repudiated his allegiance to the Christian duke of Saxony with the intention of avenging his father's death. For a time he led a horde of Lyutitzi, the pagan tribes of north-east Germany, against the duchy and the archbishopric of Hamburg-Bremen. After a time he surrendered to Duke Bernard II of Savoy and joined the Christian forces again. Though the chroniclers represent his defection as a regression to paganism, it seems that it was more a matter of an extreme reaction to bereavement and filial devotion than of loss of faith.

Duke Bernard sent him to Denmark, where he fought in the service of Canute, who was a Christian. He came to England with Canute's son Sweyn and married Sweyn's daughter. He recovered his own territories in the Hamburg-Bremen archdiocese and protected the archdiocese against the Lyutitzi. He helped the Church to expand, establishing monasteries and churches and calling over missionary priests from England.

In 1066 Gottschalk was killed at Lenzen on the Elbe, being one of the first to fall in a revolt led by his brother-in-law in an anti-Christian and anti-Saxon revolt.

There is no medieval Life of Gottschalk, but he occurs in chronicles, notably that of Adam of Bremen: see *AA.SS.*, June, 2, pp. 39-42. He is mentioned in the *Cologne Breviary* of 1515. For his services to the Church, see E. Kreusch, *Kirchengeschichte der Wendenlande* (1902), and the *Cambridge Mediaeval History*, 3, pp. 305-6 (which calls him "Godescale"). See also B.G., June, pp. 73-5; *O.D.S.*, p. 131.

St Robert of Newminster, *Abbot* (1159)

Robert was born at Gargrave, in the Craven district of Yorkshire. He is said to have studied in Paris as a young man. Paris was already a centre of theological learning, though the establishment of a college by Louis IX's chaplain, Robert de Sorbon, was not made until 1257. Robert from Gargrave was ordained, returned home, and ministered for a time at Gargrave before taking the Benedictine habit at Whitby. Later he obtained his abbot's permission to join a band of monks from St Mary's Abbey in York who had Archbishop Thurston's permission to found a new abbey in Skeldale.

They moved in 1133, in the depth of winter, under conditions of extreme poverty, and founded Fountains Abbey—so called because of the local springs. At their own request the monks were allowed to adopt the Cistercian reforms, and Fountains became a centre of great religious devotion allied to hard manual work. According to the *Fountains Chronicle*, Robert was "modest of demeanour, gentle in companionship, merciful in judgement and exemplary in holy conversation."

Five years later Ralph de Merly, lord of Morpeth, visited Fountains and was so impressed that he decided to build a Cistercian monastery in his own territory. Twelve monks were sent from Fountains to found this abbey of Newminster, with Robert as abbot. He held that office until his death over twenty years later, and he was able to found three other houses, at Pipewell (Northamptonshire) in 1143, Sawley (South Yorkshire) in 1147, and Roche (North Yorkshire) in 1148.

Robert was known as a man of prayer and austerity. He wrote a commentary on the psalms, but this has not survived. In 1147 or 1148 he was slandered by some of his monks, who accused him of undue familiarity with a pious woman. He travelled to see St Bernard of Clairvaux (20 Aug.) in order to clear himself of the charge but was assured by him that no defence was necessary. During this visit Robert had an interview with Pope Eugenius III, then in exile, who had been one of Abbot Bernard's monks. The pope asked the bishop of Durham to give Newminster some land at Wolsingham in recognition of his appreciation of Robert's work.

One of Robert's close friends was the hermit St Godric (21 May), a former seafaring trader who lived at Finchale, in County Durham, for something like sixty years. Godric is said to have known of Robert's death on the night it occurred and to have seen his soul ascending to heaven "like a ball of fire."

Robert's tomb was a popular place of pilgrimage until the Reformation. He is sometimes confused with Bd Robert of Knaresborough (24 Sept.), a hermit born in York about the time of Abbot Robert's death.

A Life preserved in the British Library (Lansdowne Ms. 436) has been edited in *AA.SS.*, June, 2, pp. 46-8, and in *N.L.A.*, 2, pp. 340-5. See also *C.M.H.*, pp. 227-8; *Anal.Boll.* 56 (1938), pp. 334-60; W. Williams, "St Robert of Newminster," *Downside Review* 57 (1939), pp. 137-49; Stanton, pp. 260-1; *N.C.E.*, 12, p. 534; *O.D.S.*, pp. 419-20.

Bd Baptista Varani (1527)

Bd Mark of Montegallo (20 Mar.) was a former physician who became a Franciscan and a powerful preacher. Camilla Varani, who was to become Baptista as a Poor Clare, heard him preach on a Good Friday when she was only eight or ten years old. Writing to him many years later, she says that it will surprise him to learn that his sermon on that occasion was the foundation of her whole spiritual life. He had preached on the passion of Our Lord and concluded by asking his congregation to meditate every Friday on his sufferings.

Camilla kept this intention throughout her education, which included literature and Latin, and after her entry into society. She was the only daughter of the lord of Camerino, Prince Julius Caesar Varani, commander-in-chief of the pontifical army under Popes Nicholas V and Sixtus IV, and her mother was the daughter of Sigismund Malatesta, lord of Rimini. They expected Camilla to make a brilliant marriage, and she spent the first three years of her adult life in the kinds of pursuits expected of a nobly-born young lady—"music, dancing, driving, dress, and other worldly amusements." At this time she had a distinct aversion to monks and nuns and says that she "could not bear the sight of them." Then she heard a sermon by another Franciscan, Fr Francis of Urbino. She says that his words were "like flashes of lightning": "These heavenly inspirations were more bitter than gall, because they went right against my natural inclinations and my attachment to the world."

She wrote to Fr Urbino, not mentioning her own problems but commending other people to him. He replied, assuring her that he would give them pastoral care, and added: "As to you, my child, I entreat you to make great efforts to preserve the purity of your heart. . . . Guard yourself from the seduction of the world, and strive to overcome yourself."

Camilla made a general confession and began to think seriously about the religious life. Gradually she surrendered herself to the will of God, and she says in her own writing that "he who is the Flower of the field and the Lily of the valley" gave her "three lilies"—a hatred of the world, a sense of her own unworthiness, and a willingness to suffer. She had some kind of infirmity about this time and accepted it gladly as a gift she could offer to Christ.

Prince Varani was predictably opposed to the suggestion that his daughter should enter the religious life and even talked of imprisoning her to prevent her from taking this step. All the houses of the Franciscans and the Poor Clares felt his anger. It took more than two years to convince him that her vocation was a true one. At last, on 14 November 1481, she chose a life of poverty, chastity, and obedience—very different from that of her magnificent family— and received the habit at the convent of Poor Clares in Urbino. Soon after, at the suggestion of her superior, she began to write down her meditations, *The Sufferings of the Agonizing Heart of Jesus*. "During the two years I spent at Urbino," she writes, "a wonderful grace of the Holy Spirit led me into the depths of the heart of Jesus—an unfathomable sea of bitterness in which I should have been drowned had God not supported me."

After her profession Camilla (now Baptista in religion) was obliged to leave Urbino. Her father refused to lose her from the family, even if it meant accepting the Poor Clares in his own domain. He obtained the pope's approval for a convent for Poor Clares at Camerino, had it built at his own expense, and succeeded in having her transferred there together with several other Poor Clares of the Varani family. Baptista continued to live an intense spiritual life, in which periods of great peace and love were followed by periods of trial and total desolation.

Her writing continued. About 1488, she produced *I dolori mentali di Gesù*, which is concerned with the mental sufferings of Jesus. This small work has been published many times and must have done much to pave the way for an explicit recognition of devotion to the Sacred Heart. Baptista also wrote a history of her spiritual life in the form of a letter to Mark of Montegallo, whose preaching had so greatly inspired her in childhood, and later she drew up a series of instructions on how to seek spiritual perfection for a Spanish priest who looked to her for guidance. These instructions show the shrewd common sense and humour that often characterize the great mystics. Though written for a fifteenth-century monk, they would form an excellent rule of life for any Christian today.

Baptista lived on until 1527. To her great grief, her father and her three elder brothers were murdered in an insurrection provoked by Cesare Borgia.

63

Pope Julius II subsequently restored Camerino to her only surviving brother. The pope also commissioned Baptista to establish a new house of her Order at Fermo. She remained there for about a year but returned to Camerino and continued as superior until her death.

For Baptista's own writings and an Italian Life by Fr Pascucci (1689), both in Latin translation, see *AA.SS.*, May, 7, pp. 467-503. A large number of biographies or studies of her spiritual life have been published, including those by A. M. Marini (1882); M. Santini (1894); G. Jörgensen (1919); V. della Vergiliana (1926); D. Aringoli (1928); P. Luzzi (1983). Her works have been edited in the original Italian by Santoni, *Le opere spirituali della ba Battista Varani* (1891; new ed. by G. Boccanera, 1958). See also *Auréole Séraphique*, 2, pp. 315-48; B.G., June, pp. 396-405; *Dict.Sp.*, 1, 1240-2, and a more recent annotation in 16, 280-1. *F.B.S.*, pp. 392-4.

Bd Anne of St Bartholomew (1626)

In the writings of St Teresa of Avila (13 Oct.) there are repeated allusions to a young lay Sister, Ana de San Bartolomé, whom she made her special companion and whom she described as a great servant of God. Anne was the child of peasants living at Almendral, near Avila, and their family name was García. Her parents died when she was only ten, and she was brought up by her brothers. Until the age of twenty she worked as a shepherdess. Her brothers wanted her to marry but she was drawn to the religious life, and she was admitted to the Carmelite convent of St Joseph at Avila on 7 November 1570. On 15 August 1572 she was professed as the first lay Sister of the Reform. From 1575 to 1582 she was the close companion of Teresa and accompanied her on nearly all her journeys. Teresa said that she found her more useful than anyone else. On several occasions she suggested that Anne should become a choir Sister, but Anne always refused, thinking that she was not sufficiently well educated. Anne has left a graphic description of their final journey from Medina to Alba and of Teresa's death on 4 October 1582: "The day she died she could not speak. I changed all her linen, head-dress, and sleeves. She looked at herself quite satisfied to see herself so clean: then, turning her eyes on me, she looked at me smilingly, and showed her gratitude by signs."

Teresa died in Anne's arms. For six years after her death Anne remained quietly at Avila; then a great change came into her life. There was a movement to establish a house for the Discalced Carmelites in Paris, and Teresa's successor, Sister Anne of Jesus, set out with five companions, of whom Anne of St Bartholomew was one.

When they arrived in Paris the party was welcomed by the Princesse de Longueville and ladies of the court, but Anne slipped out to the kitchen to prepare a meal. Her superiors, however, had decided that Teresa's chosen companion should have an honoured part in their community and that she should be a choir nun. There is some mystery over her reluctance to be fully professed. Anne was a very humble person and perhaps very conscious of her peasant background. She would have been hesitant in taking equal status with nuns from noble and wealthy families. It was probably more difficult for a woman to cross the barriers between the social classes than for a man to do so. Some commentators have suggested that she was unable to read or write: she signed her profession with a simple cross, but according to the best authorities she had acted as Teresa's secretary, so she must have become literate. Later she wrote her autobiography.

The establishment of the Paris house met with various difficulties, and five of the Sisters went to the Netherlands. Anne, who remained in France, was appointed prioress, first at Pontoise and then at Tours. She was very distressed at being set to govern others, and in her prayers she pleaded her incompetence, comparing herself to a weak straw. The answer that came to her was, "It is with straws that I light my fire."

In 1611 Anne was sent to Mons, where she remained a year. In 1612 she made a foundation of her own at Antwerp. It was soon filled with the daughters of the noblest families, all wishing to learn from one who had worked so closely with Teresa and who was already regarded as a saint herself. On two occasions when Antwerp was besieged by the prince of Orange, Anne prayed all night, and when the city was saved she was acclaimed as its protectress. Her death in 1626 was the occasion for extraordinary demonstrations, as twenty thousand people came to view her body and touch it with rosaries and other religious objects. For many years afterwards the city of Antwerp continued to venerate her memory by an annual procession in which members of the municipality, bearing candles, led the way to her convent. Anne was beatified on 6 May 1917 by Pope Benedict XV.

Anne of St Bartholomew wrote an autobiography at the request of her superiors. The account is carried down to the first years of her residence in Antwerp, and the original document is preserved in the Carmelite convent there. An incomplete French translation published in 1646 is available in the public library at Liège (Ms. 9.389, 214). Fr M. Bouix makes use of this in his Life (2d ed., 1872). There is also a collection of documents in the Bibliothèque Nationale in Paris (H. 369A, 629-55). C. Henriques published a Life in Spanish in 1632, and there is a modern account by Florencio del Niño Jesús (1917). Silverio de Santa Teresa includes Anne in his *Historia de las Carmelitas Descalzas* (1937), ch. 17, pp. 318 ff. See also *N.C.E.*, 1, p. 558; *D.H.G.E.*, 3, 346-9; *Dict.Sp.* 1, 676-7; *A.A.S.* 9 (1917), pp. 139-42, 180-3, 257-61; *D.H.E.E.*, 1, pp. 60-1; *Bibl.SS.*, 1, 1307-9.

8

St Maximinus of Aix, *Bishop* (? Fifth Century)

The Church in Gaul had many medieval traditions in which the disciples and friends of Christ were said to have visited Gaul in person and died there. These combined devotion with local sentiment and provided opportunities for pilgrimages to the places where the relics were thought to be enshrined. One of the most persistent of these stories related to Lazarus of Bethany (17 Dec.) and his two sisters, Martha (29 July) and Mary (22 July). The story is that they were put into an oarless and rudderless boat with other disciples, including Mary of Cleophas (26 Aug.) and Maximinus, and drifted through the Mediterranean before landing in Provence.

The legends arising from this supposition seem to have been developed in the eleventh century. They include the Provençal legend of the *Trois Maries*, revived by the nineteenth-century French poet Frédéric Mistral in *Mireio* and *Mes Origines* and by the devotion to Lazarus in the abbey church of St Victor in Marseilles. Maximinus figures largely in these stories: he is supposed to have made his headquarters in Aix and to have become the first bishop. Mary Magdalene is identified in the accounts with Mary the sister of Lazarus, though this identification is now rejected by the Roman Calendar. She is said to have lived in a cave at La Sainte-Baume and to have been taken when she was dying to a place now called Le Saint-Pilou, where she was given the last sacraments by Maximinus. The church of Saint-Maximin is close to Le Saint-Pilou. It was built to replace an older church with the same dedication and to enshrine the reputed relics of the two saints.

Historical research has so far failed to reveal the true story of Maximinus. All we have to go on is the dedication of the church and a long-standing cult. He is commemorated in the Roman Martyrology, but even which century he lived in is uncertain.

AA.SS., June, 2, pp. 53-4; *C.M.H.*, pp. 228-9; H. Leclercq in *D.A.C.L.*, 10, 2798-820; Duchesne, *Fastes*, 1, pp. 321-62.

St Médard, *Bishop* (? 470-560)

St Médard (Mard) was a favourite saint among the peasants of northern France, and his cult goes back to his death in the sixth century. He is the patron of the corn harvest and the vintage. He was born at Salency in Picardy, his father being a Frankish nobleman and his mother a Gallo-Roman. He was educated at the place now called Saint-Quentin and remained a layman until the age of thirty-three. After he was ordained his preaching and missionary work were so outstanding that he was chosen to succeed Bishop Alomer. He is said to have been already an old man when he was consecrated by St Remigius (13 Jan.). Though he had a very large diocese, he worked with energy and commitment, spreading the Faith and opposing worship of the Roman gods and the pagan practices of the Frankish tribes. He received Queen Radegund (13 Aug.) when she became a deaconess at Poitiers. Radegund had left Clotaire, king of the Franks, after his murder of her brother, and Médard gave her much support. Gregory of Tours (17 Nov.) and Venantius Fortunatus (14 Dec.), writing not long after his death, testify that Médard was highly thought of and that his feast was kept with great solemnity.

So much is fact, but the story that he moved his see from Saint-Quentin to Noyon and was given charge also of the diocese of Tournai is highly suspect. This is given in a biography by Radbod, bishop of the united sees of Tournai and Noyon, written about 1080. Radbod maintained that the two dioceses had been united ever since Médard's time, that is, for nearly five hundred years; but if this had been the case Gregory of Tours, Venantius Fortunatus, and other contemporary writers would certainly have mentioned the fact. It seems that Radbod invented this story when he was faced by a strong movement to separate the two dioceses, using the respect and affection still felt for Médard to claim a precedent.

The legends are numerous. Médard, like the English St Swithin (15 July), is credited with power over the weather. It is said that if it rains on 8 June, his feast-day, it will rain for forty days thereafter; and conversely, if 8 June is fine, a spell of forty days of fine weather is to be expected. In his native town of Salency there is a traditional ceremony on that day, which it is claimed that he invented. He provided from his own estate a sum of money to be given, with a crown of roses, to the most virtuous girl in the village. The first girl to be crowned as a *Rosière* was his own sister, and they are represented together in a picture above the altar in the church of St Médard in Salency.

Medieval pictures of Médard often show him laughing, with his mouth wide open (*le ris de S Médard*). H. Leclerc suggests that this representation is really a grimace of pain, indicating that he had trouble with his teeth. Médard was often invoked to cure toothache, so there may be a lost legend relating to his own cure. In Italy, he is known as San Medardo, and there is a church dedicated to him at Arcevia, near Sassoferrato.

An early prose Life (*c.* 600), at one time attributed to Venantius Fortunatus, is thought to be reliable. This is included in *AA.SS.*, June, 2, pp. 72-104, together with a metrical Life, and is also in *M. G. H., Auctores Antiquissimi*, 4, pt. 2, pp. 67-73. Redbod's story is dealt with by H. Leclercq in *D.A.C.L.*, 11, 102-8, and by L. Duchesne in *Fastes Épiscopaux*, 3, p. 102. See also *B.H.L.*, 2, pp. 857-8; *O.D.S.*, p. 335; *Saints in Italy*, p. 311; *Bibl.SS.*, 9, 262-4.

St Clodulf, *Bishop* (692 or 696)

Clodulf (Clou, or Chloud) and his brother Ansegis were the sons of St Arnulf, bishop of Metz, and his wife, Doda, who became a nun when Arnulf became a priest. Like their father they both held high office at the court of the kings of Austrasia. Ansegis married Begga, daughter of Pepin of Landen, and became the ancestor of the Carlovingian kings of France. When Arnulf's successor died, Clodulf, who was then a layman living a devout and holy life, was chosen to be bishop of Metz. As a priest and bishop he ruled his diocese wisely for forty years, giving alms liberally and being widely respected.

He is thought to have written the life of his father, Arnulf, and to have lived to the age of ninety-one. In France he is known as Chodulfe, or Chloud, to distinguish him from St Clodoald, or Clou (7 Sept.).

The Life printed in *AA.SS.*, June, 2, pp. 125-31, was written long after Clodulf's time and is largely concerned with legendary material. There is a better Life by Paulus Diaconus in his *Gesta Episcoporum Metsensium*, ed. Pertz, in *M.G.H., Scriptores*, 2, pp. 219, 305. See also Duchesne, *Fastes*, 3, p. 56.

St William of York, *Bishop* (1154)

William Fitzherbert, sometimes called William of Thwayte, was treasurer of York Minster and was nominated by King Stephen as archbishop of York in 1140 on the death of Archbishop Thurston. The clergy of the York chapter were divided over whether they should ratify the king's nomination, and Archbishop Theobald of Canterbury refused to consecrate William. In 1143 the bishop of Winchester carried out the consecration without prior papal approval. Pope Innocent II died only two days later, and his successors refused to approve the consecration. After a long and bitter debate William was deposed in 1147 by Pope Eugenius III, and a new election was ordered.

The clergy of the chapter, caught between pope and king, could not agree on a successor. The pope ruled that Henry Murdac, the abbot of Fountains Abbey, should be archbishop and conducted the consecration himself; but it was five years before archbishop Murdac was able to enter England, and even then the people of York refused to admit him to the city. He had to administer such parts of his province as obeyed the pope from Fountains Abbey, nearly thirty miles away, rather than from his cathedral seat.

Meanwhile William, after spending some time with his relative King Roger of Sicily, went to Winchester. There he stayed for six years under the protection of the bishop until 1153, when Pope Eugenius II and Archbishop Henry Murdac died. He then went to Rome, where the new pope, Anastasius IV, conferred the *pallium* upon him. He returned to York in April 1154, to be greeted with enthusiasm by the citizens; but on Trinity Sunday he developed violent pains after celebrating the Eucharist, and he died on 8 June. The new archdeacon of York, Osbert, was alleged to have poisoned him. The case was remitted to Rome, but there is no record of any judgment resulting from it.

So much is a matter of national and local record, testified to by the chroniclers of the period. It is a puzzling story, comprehensible only in the light of two bitter sets of disputes in which William Fitzherbert and Henry Murdac became entangled—and for which they bore no personal responsibility. One was the struggle for the English throne between Stephen of Blois and Henry II's daughter Matilda: William was King Stephen's nephew and his nominee. The other dispute was the feud between St Bernard of Clairvaux (20 Aug.) and the powerful monks of Cluny. Bishop Henry of Winchester was Stephen's brother, William's uncle, and a monk of Cluny. He had great influence in Rome and consecrated his nephew without specific papal authority, but after the death of Pope Innocent II the support on which he had counted was no longer forthcoming. He ceased to be papal legate, and Cluniac influence in Rome was replaced by Cistercian influence. Fountains Abbey, where Henry Murdac was abbot, was Cistercian.

William was the son of Emma, half-sister to King Stephen and to Henry of Winchester, and of Count Herbert, treasurer to Stephen's predecessor, Henry I. Emma and Count Herbert had three sons, of whom the other two, Herbert and Stephen, became chamberlains in King Stephen's court. It was an age when nepotism was not merely acceptable but taken for granted. Powerful people looked after their own. Stephen and his brother Henry had a very strong sense of obligation to their parental house of Blois.

In Innocent II's time Bishop Henry was the papal legate, and his cathedral seat of Winchester was the royal capital. King Henry I had bequeathed the throne to his daughter Matilda, forcing the barons to swear on three occasions that they would support her as ruler; but on his death in 1135 Bishop Henry used his considerable influence to gain possession of the royal treasury and to have Stephen crowned in her place. When Matilda landed in England to claim her inheritance a civil war began which divided the barons and the clergy. People of conscience were genuinely perplexed—who was the rightful heir to the throne, and whom should they support? Matilda set up her headquarters at Gloucester, and her forces gathered strength in the west country. By 1140 Stephen could not rely on the support of Theobald, archbishop of Canterbury, who was turning to Matilda's camp, and gave her open support in the following year. Stephen needed ecclesiastical allies—above all, an archbishop of York whom he could trust. William Fitzherbert was his nephew and treasurer at York Minster. Archbishop Theobald opposed William's election to York, but the king was so determined to secure it that he sent William of Aumâle, earl of York, with a message ordering the dean to secure his election. The earl actually sat in the chapter house at York while the canons were deliberating; and the archdeacon, who voted against William, was seized on the way home, and imprisoned in the earl's castle at Bytham in Lincolnshire.

The city of York gave solid support to Stephen and thus to his nominee, but the Minster clergy were divided by the struggle between Cluny and Cîteaux and confused by reports from Rome of the changing attitudes of successive popes. Pope Innocent II had recognized Stephen as *de facto* king of England while reserving judgment on the legitimacy of his claim, but after Innocent's death in 1143 there were rapid changes in the papacy: Innocent was followed by Celestine II (1143-4), then by Lucius II (1144-5), and then by Eugenius III (1145-53). None of these popes renewed Henry of Winchester's appointment as legate. None of them formally recognized Stephen as king of England. None of them approved William's consecration. When Pope Eugenius took office the Cluniac influence which had been so helpful to the royal brothers was decisively ended. Eugenius himself had been a monk at Cîteaux under Abbot Bernard of Clairvaux, who, despite his sobriquet of "the honeysweet Doctor," was currently thundering against the laxity of the Rule at Cluny. His view of Bishop Henry was particularly vitriolic: he described him in a letter to Pope Lucius II as "the enemy . . . the man who walks before Satan, the man who disrupts all rights and laws."

Pope Eugenius and Henry Murdac had both been monks at Cîteaux when St Bernard was abbot. When William was first nominated as archbishop by his uncle the king, the chapter was bitterly divided, and the Cistercian abbots in particular opposed his election. There were allegations that he was an unsuitable candidate—that he was unchaste and lax in religious observance. Such allegations were often made by the supporters of St Bernard against monks of the Cluniac foundations, and we have no way of knowing whether they had substance in William's case. John of Hexham says that he delighted in sports and luxuries and rarely worked hard, but that he was kind-hearted, gave liberally to the poor, and was popular. During his years of exile in the shelter of the cathedral monastery at Winchester, William is said to have lived a penitential life of great simplicity.

He was restored to office by the new pope, Anastasius IV, in 1153. Eugenius II and Henry Murdac had both died in the previous year. When he entered York in 1154 the crowd that turned out to welcome him was so great that the Ouse bridge collapsed under the weight of people who had crowded upon it; but no one was hurt, and this was claimed by his supporters as a miracle.

During his brief period in York William seems to have behaved well. He showed no resentment toward his former adversaries. He visited Fountains Abbey and promised restitution for the damage which his violent relatives had inflicted on it; but his own death took place very soon after. The fact that he was taken ill at the high altar on Trinity Sunday and that the archdeacon, Osbert, was alleged to have given him a poisoned chalice, caused much local scandal. King Stephen died in October of the same year, and Matilda's son succeeded him as Henry II. Henry of Winchester went back to Cluny, so there was no one left to support the cause of the house of Blois. The matter was discreetly dropped. Though Osbert was charged with William's death, and the case was remitted to Rome, it lapsed, probably for lack of proof. Of the local

Yorkshire chroniclers, John of Hexham mentioned the charges but thought that they were unfounded; John of Salisbury thought Osbert was guilty; Gilbert Foliot thought he was innocent; and William of Newburgh (a local chronicler) thought that William died of a fever. Osbert went to the Continent, was laicized, and lived out his life as a minor baron.

William was canonized by Pope Honorius III in 1227 after an inquiry conducted by the Cistercian abbots of Fountains and Rievaulx. By that time, the bitter dynastic struggle between Stephen and Matilda and the equally bitter disputes between Cîteaux and Cluny were a matter of distant memory. Toward the end of the thirteenth century his shrine was erected on the site of the present high altar in York Minster, but by the middle of the sixteenth century it had been dismantled. Portions of it may be seen in the York Museum. A great window in the north choir transept of York Minster, an outstanding example of medieval glass dating from 1415 to 1420, celebrates the events of William's life and the miracles attributed to him in 110 separate panels. The altar in the chapel of St William in the crypt was a gift from the Catholic diocese of Leeds, and the sarcophagus is traditionally thought to hold his relics.

William of Newburgh, *Historia rerum Anglicarum* (R.S. 82), 1, pp. 47 and 71-2; John of Hexham, in Symeon of Durham, *Historia Ecclesiae Dunelmensis* (R.S. 75), pp. 315-21; *Annales Monasterii de Wintonia*, ed. H. R. Luard (1865), p. 53; *AA.SS.*, June, 2, pp. 134-44; *N.L.A.*, 2, pp. 455-9. For commentaries, see Frank Barlow, *The Feudal Kingdom of England, 1042-1216* (4th ed., 1992), pp. 226-7, 288; R. L. Poole, "The Appointment and Deprivation of St William, Archbishop of York," *E.H.R.* (1930), pp. 273-81; David Knowles, *The Monastic Order in England* (1940), pp. 255-7. The letter from Bernard of Clairvaux to Pope Lucius II (one of many to the papacy on the subject) is Letter no. 236 of October 1143.

ST COLUMBA OF IONA (pp. 74-7)
Blue Iona cross on white field.

9

ST EPHRAEM, *Doctor* (*c.* 300-73)

Famous in his own lifetime as a great orator, teacher, poet, commentator, and defender of the Faith, Ephraem (Efrem) is the only Syrian father who has been honoured with the title of Doctor of the Church. The Syrians, both Catholic and Orthodox, call him "the Harp of the Holy Ghost" and use his homilies and poems in their liturgies. Basil of Caesarea (2 Jan.) describes him as "one who is conversant with all that is true," and Jerome (30 Sept.) mentions him in a list of the great Christian writers: "Ephraem, deacon of the Church of Edessa, composed many works in Syriac, and became so distinguished that his writings are repeated publicly in some churches after the reading of the Scriptures. I once read in Greek a volume by him, *On the Holy Spirit*, which someone had translated from the Syriac, and recognized, even in translation, the incisive power of lofty genius." Though Cardinal Robert Bellarmine (17 Sept.), another great Doctor of the Church, thought him "more pious than learned," Ephraem's spiritual insights in his many writings have greatly enriched the whole Christian tradition.

He was born about the year 306 in Nisibia in Mesopotamia, which was then still under Roman rule. There are two accounts of his early years: one, in what purport to be his own words, states that he was the child of Christian parents and "the kindred of martyrs." The other says that his father and mother were opposed to Christianity and turned him out of the house. It is known that he was baptized at the age of eighteen and attached himself to Bishop James of Nisibia (19 July), whom he is said to have accompanied to the Council of Nicaea in 325. He became head of the cathedral school and worked in close association with Bishop James and his two successors. During this period the Persians three times laid siege to Nisibia. In some of his Nisibean hymns there are descriptions of the sieges and the final repulse of the enemy from the city in 350. Thirteen years later it was ceded to Persia as part of a negotiated peace with the emperor Jovian.

The Christians abandoned the city, and Ephraem retired to a cave on a cliff overlooking Edessa. Here he led a most austere life, sustained only by a little barley bread and a few vegetables; and here he wrote the greater part of his spiritual works. He is described as a small man, bald and beardless and with skin shrivelled and dried up like a potsherd. His gown was patched and the colour of dirt; he wept much and never laughed. Although the cave was his home, he was not a recluse. He exerted great influence in the city of Edessa.

He frequently preached there with great eloquence; when he treated of the second coming of Christ and of the last judgment, the loud weeping of the congregation nearly drowned his words.

His special concern was to oppose the doctrines of a Gnostic sect called the Bardesanes. Ironically, it was from them that he learned what was to be one of his greatest contributions to the Church. They spread their teachings by setting them to popular tunes, and Ephraem recognized the potential value of songs in public worship. He imitated the enemy's tactics, writing his own words to be sung to the same tunes; and he trained a choir of women to sing them in church. This seems to have been the origin of organized hymn singing as a regular part of worship and a means of instruction.

It was not until late in his life that Ephraem was raised to the diaconate. There is some doubt as to whether he was ever ordained priest, though some passages in his writings suggest that he was. About the year 370 he made a journey from Edessa to Caesarea in order to visit St Basil. This meeting is mentioned in his own writings and also in those of Basil's brother, Gregory of Nyssa (10 Jan.), who was much impressed by him.

The last time Ephraem took part in public affairs was in the winter of 372-3, shortly before his death. There was a famine in and around Edessa. Though there were wealthy men, some of them with full granaries, they refused to help the starving because they said that no one could be trusted to make a fair distribution. Ephraem offered to manage the supplies, and his offer was accepted. He administered very large sums of money and quantities of food. He also organized a relief service for the sick and was widely praised for his work. After this great effort, he returned to his cave, where he died only a month later. The date of his death is given by the Chronicle of Edessa and the best authorities as 373, though some writers have asserted that he lived until 378 or 379.

Ephraem was a very prolific writer. Of the works that have come down to us, some are in the original Syriac and some in Greek, Latin, and Armenian translations. Practically all except the commentaries are in metrical form. The most interesting of his poems are the Nisibian hymns, of which seventy-two out of seventy-seven are still extant, and the canticles for the seasons, which are still in use in the Syrian churches. His commentaries include nearly all the Old Testament and much of the New Testament. For the Gospels he used the only version then current in Syria, the Harmony called the *Diatesseron*, which now survives only in an Armenian translation. A small fragment in Greek has been discovered in Mesopotamia.

Although we know comparatively little about Ephraem's life, his writings reveal a remarkable spiritual insight into the great mysteries of Christ's sufferings and the redemption of the world through his crucifixion. For example, he writes of the upper room where the Last Supper took place: "O blessed spot! No man hath seen or shall see the things which thou hast seen. In thee, the

73

Lord himself became true altar, priest, and bread and chalice of salvation. He alone sufficeth, yet none for him sufficeth. Altar he is, and lamb, victim and sacrificer, priest as well as food."

In a meditation on Christ's scourging at the pillar, he contrasts the helplessness of the victim with the divine omnipotence:

> Let heaven and earth stand awe-struck to behold him who swayed the rod of fire, himself smitten with scourges; to behold him who spread all over the earth the veil of the skies and who set fast the foundations of the mountains, who poised the earth over the waters and sent down the blazing lightning-flash, now beaten by infamous wretches over a stone pillar that his own word had created. . . . The pillar of ignominy was embraced by him who sustains the heavens and earth in all their splendour. Savage dogs did bark at the Lord who with his thunder shakes the mountains, they sharpened their teeth against the Son of Glory.

In the document known as *The Testament of St Ephraem*, he speaks to his friends and disciples in language of profound humility of his own approaching death:

> As for me, escort me only with your prayers.
> Give ye your incense to God,
> And over me send up hymns.
> Instead of perfumes and spices
> Be mindful of me in your intercessions . . .
> For the dead truly derive succour
> From the sacrifices offered up by the living.

Ephraem's writing was not translated into Latin until the 1730s and has been slow to reach a Western readership. He was declared a Doctor of the Church by Pope Benedict XV in 1920.

Jerome, ch. 116, in N.P.N.F., 2d series, 3, p. 382. Lives by C. Emerau (1919); G. Ricciotti (1925); A. Vööbus (1958). See also *B.H.G.*, 1, p. 179; Bardenhewer, 4, pp. 342-75; *D.T.C.*, 5, pt. 1, 188-93; *Bibl.SS.*, 4, 944-9. Works in 6 vols. ed. J. S. Assemani (1732-46) with a translation in Latin are now said to be incomplete and inexact. Much new work is available in the *Corpus Scriptorum Ecclesiasticorum Orientalum* (1903-), listed in the *Encyclopaedia of the Early Church*, 1, 276-7. *Selected Metrical Hymns and Homilies of Ephraim Syrus*, trans. and ed. H. Burgess (1853); *Selection from the Hymns and Homilies of Ephraim the Syrian*, ed. J. Gwynn (1979); *The Harp of the Spirit: Eighteen Poems of St Ephrem*, ed. M. Roncaglia, trans. S. Brock (1983).

ST COLUMBA OF IONA, *Abbot* (*c.* 521-97)

Columba, the most famous of Scottish saints, was in fact an Irishman of the Uí Néill of the North and was born at Gartan in County Donegal. He came of two royal lines: his father was great-grandson to Niall of the Nine Hostages, overlord of Ireland, while his mother was descended from a king of Leinster. At his baptism he received the name Colm, Colum, or Columba. In later life he was commonly called Columcille. Bede calls him Columbkille and says that the name was compounded from Columba and cell, presumably in reference to the many cells or religious foundations he established. He went to study at Leinster under an aged bard named Master Gemman. The bards preserved records of Irish history and literature, and Columba himself was a poet of some note. His name is also traditionally associated with two famous monastic schools: those of St Finnian of Moville (10 Sept.) and St Finnian of Clonard (12 Dec.), who was called the tutor of Ireland's saints. The identification of his teachers is somewhat obscure. His chief biographer, Adomnán (23 Sept.), records only that he studied the sacred scriptures under a bishop whose name is variously given as Finnbarr or Finnio or Uiniau.

Columba was one of the distinguished band who are called the Twelve Apostles of Erin. He was probably ordained priest at Clonard. After his ordination his family gave him a fort at Daire Calgaich, which became the centre of his first monastery. This place was known for nearly a thousand years as Daire Choluimcille. The English conquerors called it Londonderry, but to the Irish it is still Daire or Derry.

Columba is said to have been a giant of a man, with a voice "so loud that it could be heard a mile off." He spent fifteen years going about Ireland preaching and founding monasteries, of which the chief were those at Derry, Durrow, and Kells. He loved learning and went to much trouble to obtain manuscripts. Among the many precious books which Finnian of Clonard had brought back from Rome was the first copy of St Jerome's Psalter to reach Ireland. Columba borrowed it and made a copy for his own use. When Finnian heard, he laid claim to the transcript. Columba refused to give it up, and the case was laid before King Diarmaid, overlord of Ireland. The judgment was: "To every cow her calf, and to every book its son-book." Columba had to hand the copy back.

Columba soon had a much more serious reason for opposing King Diarmaid. When a man named Curnan of Connaught fatally injured an opponent in a hurling match, he took refuge with Columba. Diarmaid's men tore him from Columba's protecting arms and killed him, thus violating the rights of sanctuary. War broke out between Columba's clan and Diarmaid's followers, and three thousand men were killed at the battle of Cuil Dremne. Most of the Irish Lives hold Columba responsible for this slaughter. The synod of Telltown in Meath passed a vote of censure upon him, and this would have resulted in excommunication had it not been for the intervention of St Brendan (16 May).

The traditional account of why Columba decided to leave Ireland is that his conscience was uneasy, and he determined to expiate his offence by going into exile and converting as many people as had perished at Cuil Dremne. Not all his biographers subscribe to it; but for whatever reason he and twelve companions, all of them blood relations, set sail in a wicker coracle covered with hide in the year 561. Columba was about forty years of age. They landed on the island later known as *I-Colm-Kill* (the island of Colum of the churches), which lies off the coast of Mull, at Pentecost. There they set about building the monastery which was to be Columba's home for the rest of his life and which would become famous throughout Christendom. The land was made over to him by his kinsman Conall, king of Scottish Dalriada, who may have invited him to Scotland. The island was flat and low, with poor soil and pastures. Columba is said to have mourned over his exile, choosing for his cell a place where he could no longer see the coast of Ireland.

He spent about two years teaching the people of Scottish Dalriada, who had some knowledge of Christianity and were of Irish descent. Then he turned to the more difficult task of evangelizing the Picts of the north, who had a Druidic form of worship based on the natural world. Accompanied by St Comgall and St Canice (both 11 May), he made his way to the castle of King Brude at Inverness. The king had given orders that the party was not to be admitted, but when Columba raised a great arm and made the sign of the cross, bolts were withdrawn and gates opened, and they passed into the castle unhindered. Brude listened to them and ever after held Columba in high esteem. He confirmed the saint's possession of Iona and gave him leave to preach. We know from Adomnán that he crossed the mountain range which divides west Scotland from the east two or three times and that he undertook missions to Ardnamurchan, to Skye, to Kintyre, to Loch Ness, and to Lochaber. He is often credited with having evangelized Aberdeenshire and the whole of Pictland; but when the kings of Dalriada became kings of Scotland they may have exaggerated his achievements, crediting him with missionary endeavours carried out by others.

Columba never lost touch with Ireland. In 575 he was at the Synod of Drumceat in Meath, where he defended the status and privileges of his Dalriada kin and vetoed a proposal to abolish the order of bards. He was in Ireland again ten years later; but he made his headquarters at Iona, where many people came to him for spiritual or bodily help. He lived very austerely. In his younger days, he was as hard on other people as he was on himself; but Adomnán paints an attractive picture of him in his old age—gentle, peaceful, and a lover of man and beast.

As his strength began to fail he spent much time in writing poetry and transcribing books. Some of his poetry survives, including a narrative poem in which he deals with the nature of the triune God, the fall of Satan, the creation of the world, the fall of man, the torment of hell, the delights of paradise, and the final judgment. It is said that he transcribed three hundred copies of the Gospels. On the day before his death, he was copying the Psalter. He had written, "They that love the Lord shall lack no good thing," when he paused and said, "Here I must stop: let Baithin do the rest." Baithin was his cousin, whom he had nominated as his successor. That night, when the monks came to the church for Matins, they found their abbot lying before the altar. He made a feeble effort to bless them and then died.

Adomnán did not know Columba personally: he was born some thirty years after his death; but as his kinsman and eventually a successor as abbot, he must have met some people who had known him well and many who had followed in his tradition. He writes of him:

He had the face of an angel; he was of an excellent nature, polished in speech, holy in deed, great in counsel. He never let a single hour pass without engaging in prayer, reading or writing or some other occupation. He endured the hardships of fasting and vigils without intermission by day and night, the burden of a single one of his labours would seem beyond the powers of man. And in the midst of all his toils, he appeared loving unto all, serene and holy, rejoicing in the joy of the Holy Spirit in his inmost heart.

Columba's influence lasted after his death and dominated the churches of Scotland, Ireland, and Northumbria for some years. Celtic Christians in these lands upheld Columban traditions in matters of order and ritual against the practices brought from Rome by St Augustine of Canterbury (27 May). Augustine landed in Kent in the year of Columba's death, but even after the Synod of Whitby, sixty-six years later, differences remained. Bede says that the monks of Iona were "distinguished for their purity of life, their love of God, and their loyalty to the monastic Rule," and notes that they "held on to their own manner of keeping Easter for another 150 years." The Rule which Columba had drawn up for his monks was used by many monasteries in western Europe until it was superseded by the milder Rule of St Benedict, and his last blessing for the Isle of Iona came true:

Unto this place, small and mean though it be, great homage shall yet be paid, not only by the kings and peoples of the Scots, but by the rulers of barbarians and distant nations with their peoples. The saints, also, of other churches shall regard it with no common reverence.

Adomnán's Life is the most valuable source on Columba, and this is available in *P.L.*, 88, 725-9, and several other editions: ed. W. Reeves (1857); J. T. Fowler (1929); A. O. Anderson and M. O. Anderson (1961, rp. 1990); and most recently R. Sharpe (1995), which has a good commentary. See also Bede, *H.E.*, 3, 4 and 25; 5, 9; *AA.SS.*, June, 2, pp. 180-233. *C.M.H.*, pp. 230-1; *N.L.A.*, 1, pp. 122-6; Heist, *V.S.H.*, pp. 366-78; *D.N.B.*, 4, pp. 865-9; Pertz in *D.A.C.L.*, 7, 1425-61 (*s.v.* "Iona"); *Irish Saints*, pp. 93-105; G. T. Stokes, *Ireland and the Celtic Church* (2d ed., 1938), pp. 99-180. W. D. Simpson's controversial *The Historical St Columba* (1927) and *The Celtic Church in Scotland* (1935) drew replies by P. Grosjean in *Anal.Boll.* 46 (1928), pp. 197-9, and *Anal.Boll.* 54 (1936), pp. 408-12. There are more recent accounts in K. Hughes, *Early Christian Ireland* (1972) and *Early Christianity in Pictland* (Jarrow Lecture, 1970); N. Chadwick, *The Age of the Saints in the Early Celtic Church* (1961); Máire Herbert, *Iona, Kells and Derry* (1988). For Columba's poems, see the *Irish Liber Hymnorum* (1898), 1, pp. 62-89; 2, pp. 23-8 and 140-57.

SS Primus and Felician, *Martyrs* (*c.* 297)

Primus and Felician were brothers, two elderly Roman patricians who devoted their lives to charity and especially to the relief of Christians who had been imprisoned for their faith. They escaped persecution for many years, but about the year 297, in the reign of the emperors Diocletian and Maximian, they were arrested. When they refused to sacrifice to the Roman gods they were imprisoned and scourged. They were then conveyed to Nomentum, about twelve miles outside Rome, where they were tried by a magistrate named Promotus, tortured, and sentenced to be beheaded.

The magistrate tried to break down Felician's resistance by telling him that his brother had given in, but Felician refused to believe this. He said, "I am four-score years old, and thirty of those years have I spent in the service of Christ, and I am ready to die for him." Then Primus was brought out of prison and told that Felician had obeyed the emperors and sacrificed to the gods. He answered boldly, "In vain do you attempt to deceive me. I know that my brother has not renounced his Lord and God to adore vain idols."

The style of this exchange suggests that, as the Bollandists put it, the dialogue was "composed out of his own imagination by the author," but it is probably true that each refused to believe that the other had broken under pressure. They were both beheaded. Their bodies were laid in a catacomb on the via Nomentana, and a church was built over the burial place. In 640 Pope Theodosius had their relics translated to San Stefano Rotundo, and a mosaic, still in existence, was set up behind the spot where they were venerated. This shows them both beneath a figure of Christ. Though the account of their passion has been considerably embroidered, there is no doubt that they were put to death and that they were buried by their fellow-Christians at this place.

AA.SS., June, 2, pp. 148-53; *C.M.H.*, p. 230; *B.H.L.*, 2, p. 1008; B.G., June, pp. 87-9; *Saints in Italy*, p. 367; *Bibl.SS.*, 10, 1104.

St Andrew of Spello (1234)

This priest was a secular, a man of means who served in the Spoleto diocese. When he was about twenty-nine his mother and sister died. Freed of family responsibilities, he gave his property to the Church and to the poor, resigned his living, and received the habit from St Francis of Assisi (4 Oct.). As one of the seventy-two disciples of St Francis, Andrew was privileged to be at his death-bed and to receive his blessing.

Andrew served in Spain for a time, then returned to Italy, where he worked as a missioner in Lombardy. Later he was involved with the Zelanti, or "Spirituals," who insisted on a very strict interpretation of the Rule of St Francis and came into conflict with Church authorities. He was subjected on two occasions to imprisonment.

When he was placed in charge of the Poor Clares of Spello, he was instrumental in securing them a new abbess—St Clare's aunt, Bd Pacifica Guelfoccio, who made this into one of the most spiritual and effective communities in the Order. His body was buried in the convent, and his relics are still preserved there.

Andrew of Spello is the subject of Longfellow's popular poem "The Vision." This relates how he was praying in his cell when he received a vision of Christ. The insistent sound of the chapel bell broke in on his ecstasy. The monk was in a dilemma: should he obey the Rule and lose the vision or stay with the vision and disobey the Rule? He obeyed the bell. When he returned, the vision was still there. According to the early Life preserved at Spello, *Jesus dixit "Bene fecisti, Andreas: et si aliter fecisses hic me non invenisses."* In Longfellow's version, which takes some poetic liberties with the story, this becomes, "Hadst thou stayed, I must have fled."

AA.SS., June, 1, pp. 356-62, includes a valuable summary made from the early Life of Andrew preserved at Spello. Wadding, 4, pp. 262-3, contains errors, some of which are repeated in Leon's *Auréole Séraphique*, 2, pp. 349-51. *D.H.G.E.*, 2, 1647-8; *F.B.S.*, pp. 417-9.

BB Diana, Cecilia, and Amata (1236 and 1290)

When St Dominic (8 Aug.) began to develop the work of his Order in Italy, he chose Bologna as a centre because he thought its famous university would provide the kind of recruits he wanted. A suitable site for a priory was found, but there was strong opposition from the powerful d'Andalo family, who were the landowners. They finally gave way to the wishes of Andalo's only daughter, Diana, who had been much impressed by the preaching of the friars. Dominic privately received Diana's vow of virginity and a solemn promise that she would enter the religious life as soon as possible.

Diana had hoped to persuade her father to found a convent for Dominican nuns which she could enter, but he absolutely refused to consider the proposal or to allow her to become a religious. She then went to the Augustinian canonesses at Ronzano and took the veil there.

When this became known, her father and brothers went in force to fetch her back and treated her with such violence that one of her ribs was broken in the scuffle. She was taken home and kept in close confinement, but when she had recovered she managed to escape, and returned to Ronzano. Bd Jordan of Saxony (15 Feb.), who was then the Dominican provincial of Lombardy, talked to Andalo and his sons and managed to convince them that Diana had a true vocation. They were so completely won over that they helped him found a small convent for Dominican nuns near their palace, and there Diana and four companions were installed in 1222. As the new nuns were quite inexperienced in the religious life, four Sisters were sent from the convent of San Sisto in Rome. Two of these Sisters, Cecilia and Amata, are always associated with Diana d'Andalo.

79

Jordan of Saxony stayed in touch with the new community and kept up an active correspondence with Diana. His one fear was that the nuns might become too austere and overtax their strength. Diana led an intense and mystical prayer life and was a "soul-friend" of Lutgardis of Aywières (16 June), with whom she corresponded. She died in 1236 at the age of thirty-five.

Nothing further is known of Amata; but Cecilia Cesarini survived for many years. She was a member of a noble Roman family, a woman of great initiative and commitment to the Dominican movement. When she was only seventeen, in the convent of Trastevere before it moved to San Sisto, she had been the first to respond to Dominic's proposals for reform and she had persuaded the abbess and the other Sisters to accept his Rule. It is said that she was the first woman to receive the Dominican habit, and she became abbess of the new convent at Bologna. In her old age she dictated her reminiscences of Jordan, including a simple and graphic pen-portrait.

Diana, Cecilia, and Amata were beatified by Pope Leo XIII in 1891.

AA.SS., June, 2, pp. 357-62. There is a Latin biography of Diana in H. M. Cormier, *La bse Diane d'Andalo* (1892), and a Life in Italian by N. Malvezzi (1894). Jordan's letters to Diana were re-edited by B. Altaner in *Die Briefe Jordan von Sachsen* (1925). See also M. C. de Ganay, *Les Bienheureuses Dominicaines* (Paris, 1913), pp. 23-47; Procter, pp. 168-70; N. Georges, *Bd Diana and Bd Jordan* (1933); E. I. Watkin, *Neglected Saints* (1955), pp. 109-40.

Bd Silvester of Valdiseve (1288-1348)

Silvester, whose baptismal name was Ventura, was born near Florence and worked as a carder and bleacher of wool. He was forty when he entered the Camaldolese monastery of St Mary in Florence as a lay brother. He was totally uneducated, but the monks greatly respected his forthright and sensible advice. He became the monastery's cook, and even the prior would consult him on many matters. He was often asked for his counsel by learned men, notably by the Austin friar Simon of Cascia (2 Feb.), who said that Silvester had enlightened him on more than a hundred abstruse theological points. (Simon's *De gesti Domini Salvatoris* was later said to express some rather incautious views, which were picked up by Martin Luther, also an Austin friar; but we have no way of knowing whether these originated in Silvester's kitchen.)

Silvester tried to dissuade the monks from prolonged and harsh penitential practices, which he said tended to encourage the sin of pride. When one monk told him that he was troubled by carnal thoughts, he made light of it and said that was only to be expected: temptation was not the same as sin. He never learned to read, but he had a great devotion to the divine office and said that he wondered how the hearts of men could remain unbroken at the sound of words so sweet and so sublime. He died at the age of seventy.

AA.SS., June, 2, pp. 252-7, contains a short Life translated from the Italian of Fr Zenobius and a poem in the original Italian on Silvester's life and history. *Saints in Italy*, p. 416.

Bd Pacifico of Cerano (1424-82)

Pacifico Ramota was born at Novara, in Piedmont. His parents died when he was very young, and he was educated in the Benedictine abbey in Novara. He entered the Order of the Friars Minor of the Observance when he was about twenty-one and became one of the most learned clerics of his time. After his ordination he preached in many parts of Italy, conducting many successful missions between 1452 and 1471. Then he was sent on a mission to Sardinia by Pope Sixtus IV to set right certain irregularities and problems in the Church there. He wrote a treatise on moral theology which was widely circulated; this was published in Milan in 1475, and for many years it was regarded as the standard work on the subject. It was entitled *Sommetta di Pacifica Coscienza*, commonly known as the *Somma Pacifica*. He resumed his mission work, chiefly in the north of Italy, using as his headquarters the convent of Vigevano, which he had founded in the diocese of Novara.

In 1480 Pacifico was sent again to Sardinia, this time as visitor and commissary for the convents of the Strict Observance and also as apostolic commissary, charged by Pope Sixtus IV to proclaim a crusade against the Muslim ruler, Mohammed II. He was already ill, and before he left he asked that his body might be brought back to Cerano, where he was preaching at the time. He died soon after reaching Sardinia, and his request was carried out: his body was taken back to Cerano, and a church was built in his honour there. Pacifico's cult was confirmed in 1754 by Pope Benedict XIV.

AA.SS., June, 1, pp. 406-7 and 789-90; *Auréole Séraphique*, 2, pp. 352-5; *F.B.S.*, pp. 422-4.

Bd Joseph de Anchieta (1534-97)

"A tireless and genial missionary," according to the decree of his beatification, José de Anchieta was born in San Cristóbal de la Laguna, on Tenerife in the Canary Islands. At the age of seventeen he made a vow before the statue of Our Lady in Coïmbra, Portugal, consecrating himself to God's service. He entered the Society of Jesus and in 1553 he was sent to Brazil, where he served in the remote mission of Quisininga with the people of the rain forests.

He was much attached to his people, learning their customs, taking part in their daily activities, and respecting their way of life. He composed a catechism for his "Brazilian brothers" adapted to their understanding, which was widely used in missionary work, and he defended them against the exploitative commercial interests which invaded their homeland in the wake of the Portuguese explorers. He undertook many trips into the interior, covering great distances without regard to danger or discomfort.

At the ceremony which marked his beatification on 22 June 1980 Pope John Paul II called him "this great son of Ignatius." He was a man of great charity, constant prayer, and devotion to the Blessed Virgin, in whose honour he composed a long poem in elegant Latin. He became known as "the apostle of Brazil."

N.S.B., 1, p. 160; *Osservatore Romano*, 30 June 1980.

Bd Anne Mary Taigi (1769-1837)

Anna Maria Gesualda learned about poverty early and lived in poverty all her life. She was born in Siena, where her father was an apothecary; but he lost his livelihood, and the family went to Rome, where both her parents became domestic servants. Anne was sent to a school for poor children, and at the age of thirteen she had to earn her living. She worked for some time in factories and then became a housemaid in the household of a noble lady, where she was much attracted by fashion and the worldly life led by her employer. In 1790 she married Domenico Taigi, a servant in the great Chigi Palace. They had seven children, two of whom died in infancy, and they also cared for Anne's parents.

Fairly early in this hard and busy life she felt the need for spiritual direction. She approached a priest, but he sent her away without help or advice. Then she met a Servite friar, Fr Angelo, who remained her confessor for many years. She dated her conversion from the time when she first met him. She renounced all worldly interests, wearing the plainest of clothes and devoting herself to prayer while still fulfilling all her many domestic duties. She undertook sewing—a very badly paid home industry—to supplement Domenico's wages, and she managed to find money or food to help those who were poorer than she was. Every morning she gathered her household together for prayers. Those who could do so attended Mass and in the evening they all met again for spiritual reading and night prayers.

Her spiritual life was of a very high order. She was much concerned with the dangers that threatened the Church and with the burden of evil in the world. Fr Angelo introduced her to Cardinal Pedicini, who shared with him the responsibility of her spiritual direction for thirty years. The cardinal wrote a memoir after her death, which describes the agonies of mind that she went through and the great consolations she found in the Faith. It was probably through him that she became known as a wise woman who could help others on their spiritual path, and many people came to her for guidance and intercession. Her husband, who made a deposition in the process for her beatification when he himself was ninety-two years old, left a touching picture of her work and her care for him:

> It often happened that on my return home, I found the house full of people. At once she would leave anyone who was there—a great lady, maybe, or a prelate—and would hasten to wait upon me affectionately and attentively. One could see that she did it with all her heart: she would have taken off my shoes if I would have allowed it. In short, she was my comfort and the consolation of

all. . . . The servant of God knew how to keep everyone in his place and she did it with a graciousness that I cannot describe. I often came home tired, moody, and cross, but she always succeeded in soothing and cheering me.

Anne died on 9 June 1837, after seven months of acute suffering and many spiritual trials, at the age of sixty-eight. She was beatified by Pope Benedict XV in 1920. Her shrine is in the church of St Chrysogonus, belonging to the Trinitarians, of which Order she was a tertiary member.

A.A.S., 12 (1920), pp. 240-5, contains the depositions at Anne's beatification, which are particularly interesting and valuable as biographical material. There are many Lives, of which Mgr C. Salotti's *La Vénérable Servant de Dieu, Anna-Maria Taigi* (1865, rp. 1922) is the fullest. See also *D.H.G.E.*, 3, 355; *Bibl.SS.*, 11, 99-101.

ST ANTONY OF PADUA (pp. 101-3)
Gold book, silver lilies with green stems, on brown field.

10

St Ithamar of Rochester, Bishop (c. 656)

Ithamar, or Ythamar, was the first Anglo-Saxon to become a bishop in the English Church. Honorius, archbishop of Canterbury (30 Sept.), consecrated him to the see of Rochester after the death of Paulinus (10 Oct). Bede says that he was "a man of Kent" and "as worthy and learned as his predecessors." On the death of Honorius in 653 the archbishopric of Canterbury was vacant for eighteen months; and after Deusdedit (14 July), a South Saxon, was elected, Ithamar consecrated him as the sixth archbishop in 655.

St Augustine of Canterbury (27 May) and his party from Rome arrived in England in 597, so the consecration of English bishops in the south of England less than sixty years later marks an important stage in the development of the English Church.

The exact date of Ithamar's death is unknown, but he was buried at Rochester. His relics were enshrined in 1100 by Gundulf, bishop of Rochester, and several churches were dedicated in his honour.

Bede, *H.E.*, 3, 14 and 20; *AA.SS.*, June, 2, pp. 291-2; *N.L.A.*, 2, pp. 83-6; *B.H.L.*, 1, p. 667; Stanton, pp. 264-5; B.G., June, p. 133.

St Landericus of Paris, Bishop (c. 660)

Landericus (Landry) became bishop of Paris in 650 during the reign of Clovis II. He is especially remembered for his care of the poor and sick people of the city. During a great famine in 651 he sold not only his own personal possessions but also some of the vessels and furniture of the church in order to relieve their sufferings.

Before his time the only provision for the sick poor consisted of a few small hostels without endowments, dependent for their upkeep from day to day on casual alms. Bishop Landericus founded the city's first real hospital, near Notre Dame, which was dedicated under the name of St Christopher. This developed into the institution later known as the Hotel-Dieu, which is still one of the major hospitals of Paris.

In 653 Landericus signed an order exempting the newly-established abbey of Saint-Denis from episcopal jurisdiction. Though this order has been lost, it is mentioned in a document of Clovis, dated 22 June 654. The date of Landericus' death is uncertain, but it cannot have been earlier than 660. In that year a monk named Marculf dedicated to him a collection of ecclesiastical formulae compiled under his instructions.

AA.SS., June, 2, pp. 289-91; Duchesne, *Fastes*, 2, p. 472; *N.C.E.*, 8, pp. 360-1.

St Bogumilus, *Bishop* (1092)

Little was known about Bishop Bogumilus until the fifteenth century, though there was a long-standing cult in the village of Dobrova in Poland. Archbishop Mathias (1641-52) initiated an inquiry in order to obtain confirmation of the cult from Rome. This turned out to be a very lengthy process.

Bogumilus and Boguphalus are said to have been the twin sons of noble Polish parents. They were well educated and completed their studies in Paris. Boguphalus then entered a Cistercian monastery; and Bogumilus, whose name means "friend of God" or "beloved of God," like the Latin Amadeus and the Greek Theophilus, built a church at Dobrov, their birthplace, which was dedicated to the Holy Trinity.

After being ordained priest he took charge of the parish himself. His uncle John, who was archbishop of Gniezno, appointed him as his chancellor and nominated him as his own successor. When John died in 1167, Bogumilus was consecrated, and he administered the diocese for nearly five years. He founded the Cistercian monastery of Coronowa and endowed it with some of his family estates. Though he was reputed to be a wise and zealous bishop, he was apparently unable to impose discipline on his clergy or to remedy abuses of which he greatly disapproved. He asked for permission to resign his office, and when this was granted, he entered the Camaldolese Order.

He spent the rest of his life in a Camaldolese hermitage at Uniow. After his death his body was taken back to the church at Dobrov which he had founded. Bogumilus is mentioned in the *Annales des chapîtres de Cracowie*, a manuscript dating from 1122, as having died in 1092. His cult was confirmed by Pope Pius XI in 1925.

AA.SS., June, 2, pp. 336-57, contains an edited form of a Latin Life by Stephen Damalewicz, published in Warsaw in 1649. *A.A.S.* 17 (1925), pp. 384-7; *D.H.G.E.*, 9, 417-8; *N.C.E.*, 2, p. 635. *D.T.C.*, 9, 415-7, lists a number of sources in Polish.

Bd Henry of Treviso (1315)

Enrico, known as "San Rigo" in the Trentino region of northern Italy, was born in Bolzano to a life of poverty and apparent obscurity. As a young man he went to Treviso. Some accounts say that he married there and that his wife and child died young. After that he had no interest in secular life. He worked as a day labourer, giving away whatever he could spare from his meagre wages. He never learned to read or write, but his whole life was devoted to the service of God. He made his confession and heard Mass daily, frequently made his Communion, and spent all his spare time in prayer and devotion. He is said to have been a small, thick-set man with sunken eyes, a long nose, and a crooked mouth. People, especially children, sometimes mocked this shabby and unattractive figure in the streets, but he never replied to their taunts: his only response was to pray for them.

When he was too old to work a citizen of Treviso gave him a room and occasionally food; but he lived largely on alms, sharing what he was given with beggars and never holding food or money back from one day to the next. Age and increasing infirmity did not keep him from performing his religious duties, and he continued to visit all the churches within walking distance.

Henry's humble and austere life and his sweetness of temperament eventually made an impression on the people of Treviso. When he died his only possessions were found to be a hair shirt, a wooden log that served him as a pillow, and some straw for a bed. His room was soon filled with people wishing to venerate him and to take away some fragment belonging to him. His body was removed to the cathedral in order to protect it, but the crowd broke into the cathedral at night, so that the bishop and the authorities had to put a wooden palisade around the bier. His interment was followed by an enthusiastic and often near-hysterical popular cult in which many miracles were attributed to his relics. Notaries appointed by the magistrates listed 276 such miracles within a few days of his death.

His cult was confirmed by Pope Benedict XIV.

AA.SS., June, 2, pp. 363-70, has a Life by a contemporary, Pierdomenico de Baone, later bishop of Treviso, written in 1381. See also R. degli Azzoni Avogaro, *Memorie del Beato Enrico* (2 vols., 1760); A. Tschöll (1887); a Life published in Treviso (1915); *Saints in Italy*, p. 313; *N.C.E.*, 6, p. 1034; *Anal. Boll.* 45 (1927), p. 443.

Bd Bonaventure Baduario, *Cardinal* (1386)

Bonaventure Baduario was born at Peraga, near Padua, a member of one of the leading families of the city. He became an Augustinian friar as a young man and was sent to the University of Paris. When Pope Innocent VI established a theological faculty in the university, he became an outstanding scholar and teacher. He wrote a number of theological treatises and commentaries and had a wide knowledge of literature. One of his friends was the poet Petrarch, whose funeral oration he preached.

In 1377 Bonaventure was chosen as prior general of his Order, and in the following year he was created cardinal of St Cecilia. On several occasions he acted for Pope Urban VI. He always strongly defended the rights of the Church, and this brought him into conflict with his kinsman Francis, prince of Carrara, who was the ruler of Padua. Bonaventure was crossing the Tiber in order to visit the Vatican when he was struck by an arrow and killed. Though his killer was never identified, it was generally believed that the prince of Carrara was responsible.

The Augustinian Order venerated Cardinal Bonaventure as a martyr for some time after his death, but the facts have never been fully established.

The account in *AA.SS.*, June, 2, pp. 386-8, is largely based on T. de Ferrera's *Alphabetum Augustinianum*. There is a short Life in Italian by D. A. Perini (1912).

Bd John Dominici, *Bishop and Cardinal* (1376-1419)

Young men who wished to enter the Order of Preachers in the fourteenth century were usually well born and well educated. Giovanni Dominici was neither: he came from a humble family in Florence and had little formal education. Worse still, he stammered; but he was earnest and persistent, and he received the habit at the age of eighteen in the priory of Santa Maria Novella. Once accepted, he managed to overcome the stammer, which may have been due to anxiety. He studied at the university of Paris, becoming one of the leading theologians of his day and an eloquent preacher. He wrote commentaries on the scriptures, and *laudi*, or hymns in the vernacular.

For twelve years after the completion of his studies he taught and preached in Venice, and he became prior of Santa Maria Novella. He founded new houses for his Order at Fiesole and Venice and the convent of Corpus Christi for nuns in Venice. He contributed much to the reform of the Order in northern Italy, introducing or restoring the strict Rule of St Dominic in several priories with the approval of the master general, Bd Raymund of Capua (5 Oct.).

At this time the revival of classical art and learning associated with the Renaissance was sweeping Italy. In their early stages, the revolt against the formalities of the medieval schoolmen and the rediscovery of the culture of classical Greece and Rome had their dangers: they could have led to a rejection of theology in favour of humanism and a resurgence of pre-Christian forms of worship. John Dominici was acutely aware of these dangers and did much by preaching and writing to expose and resist them. At the same time, he appreciated art and was something of an artist himself. He illustrated the choral books of his convent with exquisite miniatures. He wrote two important educational treatises, *Lucula Noctis* and *Regola del governo di cura familiare*, and an ascetical work, *Il Libro d'amore del carità*.

In 1406 he attended the conclave which elected Pope Gregory XII, and he later became the pope's confessor and adviser. He was created archbishop of Ragusa and cardinal of San Santo. During the Great Schism he was instrumental in inducing Pope Gregory to resign when this proved to be the only means of inducing the antipopes to forgo their claims; and it was he who conveyed the pope's resignation to the Council of Constance.

Clearly he had a very high reputation as a diplomat and a negotiator to supplement his theological learning; but the next pope, Martin V, gave him an impossible task: he appointed him legate to Bohemia, charged with the task of countering the influence of the Hussites, an evangelical group with views similar to those of the followers of John Wyclif in England.

He arrived in Prague soon after John Huss was burned at the stake in 1414. The city was in a state of turmoil, and Huss was a national hero. The university of Prague had declared Huss a martyr, and his followers were arming themselves in readiness to make war on the emperor. Cardinal Dominici tried to introduce measures to suppress the Hussites, but King Wenceslaus of Bohemia refused to accept them, and the legate was forced to leave the country. He went on to Hungary but caught a fever soon after his arrival and died at Buda on 10 June 1419. His cult was confirmed in 1832 by Pope Gregory XIV.

There are near-contemporary records: a short biography written by Archbishop Antoninus of Florence (10 May), which is included in *AA.SS.*, June, 2, pp. 388-412, and a portrait by Fra Angelico on the walls of San Marco in Venice. Both the biographer and the painter were received by Cardinal Dominici into the Dominican Order. *Lucula Noctis* has been republished with a useful preface by Fr Couthon (1908); also by E. Hunt (1940). See also Mortier, 3, pp. 551-96 and 604-84; 4, pp. 5-97; Procter pp. 171-4; I. Taurisano, *Catalogus Hagiographicus O. P.* (1918), pp. 35-6; Hefele-Leclercq, 7, pt. 1, pp. 171ff.

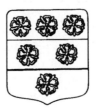

ST BARNABAS
His feast-day was formerly celebrated by young men
bedecked with roses.
Top and bottom rows: silver roses on red field; centre: red on silver.

11

ST BARNABAS, *Apostle* (First Century)

Barnabas was not one of the original twelve apostles, but he was styled an apostle by St Luke and by the early Fathers because of his apostolic work and the special commission he received to carry the mission of the Church beyond Jerusalem.

Barnabas was a Levite of Cypriot origin. His original name was Joseph, and the apostles surnamed him Barnabas, "son of encouragement," which suggests a cheerful and outgoing temperament (Acts 4:36). He owned a piece of land, and when the small Christian community decided to have all things in common, he sold it and gave the money to the common fund. His conduct is contrasted with that of Ananias and Sapphira, who sold their land but kept part of the proceeds for themselves (Acts 4:37–5:11).

After the death of Stephen (26 Dec.) the story of Stephen's stand before the Sanhedrin and his martyrdom was spread abroad by disciples. It reached Antioch, and the Church in Jerusalem heard that a body of Christians was coming together in that city. Somebody had to be sent to confirm and instruct them, and Barnabas was chosen—"a good man, filled with the Holy Spirit and with faith." Barnabas went to Tarsus to meet Paul, and the two went back to Antioch together. It was the beginning of a notable partnership, in which Barnabas was the leader. Since Paul, before his conversion, had been a party to Stephen's death, Barnabas showed a remarkable trust and openmindedness in accepting him as a companion. Perhaps Paul's presence was necessary to bring home to the Christians of Antioch the full impact of the story he had to tell. The two instructed large numbers of people, and it was at Antioch that the disciples were first called "Christians" (Acts 11:22-30).

They stayed in Antioch for a whole year. Then the Christians in Antioch, which was a wealthy city, heard that there was a famine in Judaea and raised money for the relief of their fellow-Christians. Barnabas and Paul were sent back to Jerusalem with the money, and it was there that they met John Mark, who was to join them in their mission (Acts 12:25). The three returned to Antioch and then set out by sea on a mission to Cyprus. They landed at the great Graeco-Roman city of Salamis, in the extreme north-east, and then travelled over the whole island. In Paphos they confronted the false prophet Bar-Jesus and converted Sergius Paulus, the Roman proconsul (Acts 13:4-12).

John Mark went back to Jerusalem, but Paul and Barnabas continued their work together in Asia Minor. Their usual practice was to go to a city and preach in the synagogue—and they must have been very well aware that they might suffer Stephen's fate for this head-on confrontation with orthodox Judaism. At Lystra they were mistaken for Greek gods. Barnabas must have been the leader of the two, for he was taken to be Jupiter, while Paul was assigned the role of Mercury. They were highly successful at first and gained many supporters, then they nearly did suffer Stephen's fate, because the opposing Jews gathered together to stone them. Paul was severely wounded, and they had to leave the city in haste. The pattern was repeated in other cities where the Christian message brought dissension and conflict, but the converts stood firm. When Paul and Barnabas had reached Derbe, where they had made many converts, they retraced their steps, confirming and ordaining presbyters. Then, "full of joy and the Holy Spirit," they returned to Antioch (Acts 14).

They went to Jerusalem to take part with the apostles in the great debate about whether Gentiles should be circumcised and instructed in the Mosaic Law. They had planned a second great missionary journey, but this issue divided them. Paul, as in his confrontation with Peter at Antioch, was determined to free the faith he preached from the trammels of Jewish legal observance. A disagreement, or, as the *New Jerusalem Bible* translates the phrase, "a violent quarrel," broke out between them. They were also divided over whether John Mark should accompany them on their next journey. Barnabas was willing to take him, but since he had deserted his colleagues in Pamphilia on the first journey, Paul was not. Eventually they decided to separate: Paul took Silas as his companion; Barnabas took John Mark (Acts 15:36-40). Given the hazardous nature of these early missionary journeys, it was important to have a reliable colleague. Evidently Barnabas was prepared to trust John Mark, just as he had earlier trusted Paul.

After that, we hear little more about Barnabas. It seems clear from Paul's allusions in 1 Corinthians 9:5-6 that Barnabas was still living and working in the year 56 or 57 and that the two were reconciled. "Are Barnabas and I the only two who are never allowed to stop working?" he demands of the Christians of Corinth. When Paul was a prisoner in Rome in 60 or 61, he asked John Mark to go to him, which suggests that Barnabas may have been dead by that time. He is thought to have been stoned to death in Salamis on another mission to Cyprus.

He was buried by the Christians near Salamis, and his body was reputedly found much later with a copy of St Matthew's Gospel lying on his chest. His remains were taken to Constantinople, where a church was built in his honour.

Barnabas is often found in Venetian paintings because he was related to St Mark (Col. 4:10), and Mark is the patron saint of Venice. His church in Venice has a painting of him robed as a bishop above the high altar.

The only reliable source for Barnabas is the Acts of the Apostles. There is a considerable apocryphal literature, including the *Acts of Barnabas*. The text of the Acts is included in *AA.SS.*, June, 2, pp. 415-54, together with the references available at the beginning of the eighteenth century. This text provides a full history of Barnabas, an account of his later work in Cyprus, his martyrdom at Salamis, and his cult; but it dates only from the fifth century, though it is claimed that it was written by John Mark. There is also a work, at one time current in Muslim scholastic circles, called the *Gospel of Barnabas*. On this, see W. Axon, *Journal of Theological Studies* 3 (April 1902), pp. 441-51. See also *O.D.S.*, pp. 38-9.

St Rembert, *Bishop* (888)

Rembert (Rimbert) was born near Bruges and became a monk at the neighbouring monastery of Torhout. From there he was called by Anskar, archbishop of Hamburg, to assist in his difficult mission to Scandinavia and northern Germany.

Anskar said, "Rembert is more worthy to be archbishop than I am to be his deacon." In 848, work began to unite the see of Bremen, then under the jurisdiction of the archdiocese of Cologne, with Hamburg. Anskar became archbishop of Hamburg and Bremen with superintendence of the churches in Scandinavia, and papal approval was given by Pope Nicholas I in 864. Anskar died in the following year, and Rembert was elected his successor.

The Swedish mission collapsed during Rembert's time as archbishop, but he promoted missions in southern Norway and in Schleswig. He also carried out a mission to the Slavs of the north. He sold sacred vessels to redeem captives from the Norsemen and on one occasion gave the horse he was riding for the ransom of a girl captured by the Slavs. He wrote a Life of Anskar, said to be remarkable for its accuracy and style, and an eloquent letter to Walburga, abbess of Nienheerse.

Rembert died on 11 June 888. His feast was formerly commemorated on 4 February, the date on which he was chosen archbishop.

P.L., 136, 99-1010; *AA.SS.*, Feb., 1, pp. 564-71; G. Waitz in *M.G.H., Scriptores*, 11, pp. 683-723, edits the Life with Rembert's *Vita Anskarii*. Eng. trans. of the latter by C. H. Robinson (1921). *Bibl.SS.*, 11, 99-101. For background see C. J. A. Opperman, *English Missionaries in Sweden and Finland* (1937).

St Mary Rose Molas y Vallvé, *Foundress* (1815-76)

Rosa Molas was born in Reus, near Tarragona in north-eastern Spain, where her parents kept a small shop. Her mother died of cholera when she was seventeen, and she wanted to enter the religious life, but her father refused his consent. It was not until she was twenty-six that she left home and joined a group of nuns working in the hospital and the almshouse at Reus. She received the habit, with the name María Rosa (Mary Rose). After eight years she was sent as superior to a House of Mercy in the suburbs of Tortosa, further south on the Mediterranean coast. There she found three hundred inmates living in squalor and disorder—old and sick, children and babies. She worked unremittingly to improve their living conditions and to bring order out of chaos.

She had been at Tortosa for a further eight years when she discovered that the Order she had joined was irregularly constituted. After much agonizing discussion she and twelve of her colleagues placed themselves under the jurisdiction of the bishop of the diocese and became the nucleus of a new Congregation, the Sisters of Our Lady of Consolation. She chose the name to indicate a concern for education, health care, and any other means of helping people, particularly children, in need. Today the Sisters have a special commitment to the Third World, working in Europe, South America, and parts of Africa and Asia.

Mother Mary Rose died at Tortosa on Trinity Sunday, 11 June 1876. She was beatified by Pope Paul VI in May 1977 and canonized by Pope John Paul II on 11 December 1988.

A.A.S. 80 (1988), pp. 1058, 1094; *N.S.B.*, 1, pp. 142-3; *D.N.H.*, pp. 311-14; *Osservatore Romano*, 12 Dec. 1988.

St Paula Frassinetti, *Foundress* (1809-82)

Paula was born in Genoa and grew up in that city in the troubled circumstances of the early nineteenth century, a time of political uncertainty for all and great misery for many. Her brother was the parish priest of Quinto, and she joined him in order to teach the poor children of the parish. Other women came forward, and she founded an Institute, the Sisters of St Dorothy, devoted to teaching. She encountered many obstacles in her work, but the intensity of her prayer life and her wisdom in dealing with human problems became widely known, and after a period in which she was very short of resources the movement attracted support and prospered.

Branches were founded in other Italian cities, in Portugal, and in Brazil, and the Institute was formally approved by the Holy See in 1863. Paula was beatified in 1930 and canonized in 1984 by Pope John Paul II.

A.A.S. 22 (1930), pp. 316-9. Lives by A. Capacelatro (1901); J. Umfreville (*c.* 1904).

Bd Mary Schinina, *Foundress* (1844-1910)

Maria Schinina was born in Ragusa of a noble Sicilian family. She was sixteen when their traditional way of life was overturned by the Risorgimento and the beginning of the struggle for the unification of Italy. She saw that the poor were suffering from war and famine and determined to devote her life to serving the casualties of political and social upheaval.

Given the social rigidity of their traditions, it is perhaps understandable that the local nobility were horrified at what they regarded as desertion from their ranks. They did all they could to dissuade her; but the archbishop of Syracuse supported her, and with five companions she founded the Sisters of the Sacred Heart of Jesus, working with prisoners of war and peasants. Their own money and property went into the venture. Their motherhouse became a home for the first Carmelites who went to establish a monastery in Ragusa, and was later a shelter for the people of Messina and Reggio di Calabria who were left homeless after an earthquake. Many secular priests and religious learned there how to serve Christ in works of mercy.

Mary spent her whole life working in Ragusa and died there on 6 June 1910. She was beatified by Pope John Paul II on 4 November 1990.

A.A.S. 84 (1992), pt. 1, pp. 111-3; *D.N. H.*, pp. 235-6; *Osservatore Romano*, 5 Nov. 1990

12

St Antonina, *Martyr* (? 304)

The Antonina or Antonia whose feast falls on this day appears to be the saint who was also commemorated in the previous Roman Martyrology on 1 March and 4 April. There are three separate traditions of her martyrdom, all different and all describing cruel forms of torture; and three different places called Cea claim her: the Greek *Menaion* claims her as a martyr of Nicaea (Cea) in Asia Minor, the Aegean islanders commemorate her as belonging to the island of Cea, and in Spain she is venerated at Ceja in Galicia.

These stories seem to be the result of an oral tradition which travelled by sea along the length of the Mediterranean. Though the details are now obscure, the events which inspired it must have been unusual and much discussed on ships and in ports. Her memory endured: the tradition became attached to different places, and different stories developed in each locality. Commentators agree that she was a genuine martyr who died, probably in Nicaea or Nicomedia, in the time of the governor Priscillian, as the Greek Synaxaries state.

AA.SS., Mar., 1, pp. 26-8, and May, 1, pp. 379-82; *C.M.H.*, pp. 81, 170, 234. The June entry in p. 234 is unusually long, and the problems are discussed by Delehaye. See also *Anal.Boll.* 30 (1911), p. 165; *Synax.Const.*, pp. 500 and 746.

St Onuphrius (? *c.* 400)

Onuphrius is one of the Egyptian desert hermits of the fourth or fifth century, and his story was recounted by Paphnutius, an abbot in Lower Egypt, who went to visit some of the hermits of the Thebaïd. It seems to have been written down by one or more of the monks to whom Paphnutius told it; there are now several versions, which may have become more colourful in the telling.

Paphnutius undertook his pilgrimage in order to study the hermits' way of life and to find out whether he himself was called to it. He wandered in the desert for sixteen days, meeting with one or two strange adventures, and on the seventeenth day he was startled by the appearance of a curious apparition who appeared to be very aged. His hair and beard reached to the ground, his body was covered with hair that looked like fur, and he wore only a loincloth of leaves. Paphnutius was so alarmed that he ran up the side of a mountain, but the figure called after him, "Come down to me, man of God, for I am a man also, dwelling in the desert for the love of God."

94

Paphnutius turned back and fell at the old hermit's feet, and the hermit said, "Arise, my son, for thou also, I perceive, art a father of the saints." When they began to talk, he said that his name was Onuphrius and that he had once been a monk in a large monastery in the Thebaïd, but he felt called to the solitary life and had been a hermit for seventy years. In the manner of the Desert Fathers he had endured hunger and thirst, extremes of temperature, and violent temptations; but God had given him consolation, and a palm tree near his cave provided him with a few dates. He took Paphnutius to his cell, and they remained deep in spiritual conversation until sunset, when bread and water miraculously appeared before them.

They spent the night together in prayer, but in the morning Paphnutius was distressed to find that Onuphrius was dying. Onuphrius said, "Fear not, brother Paphnutius, for the Lord in his infinite mercy has sent you here to bury me." Paphnutius asked if he should stay and occupy the cell himself, but Onuphrius told him that God willed it otherwise: "That may not be, thy work is in Egypt with thy brethren." There follows a conversation which, even if it is not exact reportage, illustrates the commitment of the Desert Fathers to the intercession and the communion of saints. Onuphrius said:

> Do thou, my brother, when thou returnest to Egypt, call for a memorial of me like incense, in the midst of the brethren and of the whole Christian people. For if anyone in my name, and in memorial of me, shall offer anything to the Lord our God, he shall be numbered among the elect, and shall be released from temptation. This is what I have besought of the Lord. And if anyone shall give food to one of the brethren, or to a beggar, in my name, I will be mindful of that man before our God in the day of judgment, and he will enter into eternal life.

Paphnutius asked what a poor man might do who had nothing to give and could not afford incense. Was he to be denied the hermit's benediction? But Onuphrius replied, "If there be any too poor to offer incense or to make any oblation, then let him arise and pour forth his prayer to the Almighty God, and let him recite the holy Creed in memorial of me, and I will pray for him, that he may inherit eternal blessedness."

Then the old man blessed Paphnutius and died.

It was a barren and rocky place, so Paphnutius could not dig a grave. He tore his own cloak in half to provide a shroud and left the body of the old hermit in a cleft in the rocks, weighted down with stones to protect it from wild beasts. When he had done this, we are told, the cave which had been Onuphrius' cell crumbled and the date palm drooped and died, clearly indicating that Paphnutius should not stay in that place.

Paphnutius was a fairly common name among the monks of the Upper Thebaïd. It is now thought that the teller of this remarkable story was Paphnutius of Scetis, a fourth-century abbot in lower Egypt, and not Paphnutius the Great (11 Sept.); but Paphnutius the Great also had a number of stories to tell of visions and miraculous happenings in the desert, some of them in much the same vein as the story of Onuphrius.

There are frescoes of the legend of Onuphrius in the Campo Santo at Pisa. A church was erected in his honour on the Janiculan Hill at Rome in the fifteenth century. In art he appears as a wild figure covered with hair and wearing a girdle of leaves.

AA.SS., June, 3, pp. 16-30; *C.M.H.*, pp. 234-5; *B.H.L.*, 2, pp. 155-8, has a long citation; *B.H.O.*, p. 179, lists ancient Lives in several languages; C. A. Williams, *Oriental Affinities of the Legend of the Hairy Anchorite*, Illinois Studies 10 (1925), pp. 195-242, and 11 (1926), pp. 427-507: cf. *Anal. Boll.* 47 (1929), pp. 138-41. B.G., June, pp. 150-4; *P.B.*, 6, pp. 588-91; *Saints in Italy*, p. 330; Tim Vivian, *Paphnutius: Histories of the Monks of Upper Egypt and the Life of Onnophrius* (1993).

St Ternan, *Bishop* (Fifth or Sixth Century)

It is fairly certain that Ternan was engaged in the conversion of the Picts and became one of their earliest bishops, but there are conflicting accounts of his life. According to one he was a monk of Culross for many years. The Aberdeen Breviary states that he was baptized by Palladius (7 July) and became his disciple. He may have been consecrated by Palladius as successor to Ninian (16 Sept.) in 432 or have been commissioned directly from Rome, which he is said to have visited. He appears to have had his headquarters at Abernethy, the capital of the Pictish kings, and to have died there. His body was buried at Liconium, or Banchory Ternan, as it came to be called. About the year 1530 the compiler of the *Aberdeen Breviary* saw his skull at Banchory.

Some of Ternan's relics were venerated in Aberdeen Cathedral, which is thought to have been originally dedicated to him. Several churches in that part of Scotland bear, or once bore, his name. His cult spread to Ireland, and his name occurs in several old Irish calendars, but there is no reliable evidence that he ever visited Ireland.

AA.SS., June, 3, pp. 30-2, contains some limited source material. See also *K.S.S.*, pp. 450-1; three pamphlets by W. Douglas Simpson: *The Origins of Christianity in Aberdeenshire* (1925); *The Historical St Columba* (1927); *On Certain Saints and Professor Watson* (1928).

St Odulf (855)

In the early ninth century the Church had made some penetration into Friesland, in the northern part of the Low Countries, but much remained to be done. Bishop Frederick of Utrecht (18 July) sent Odulf, a priest born in North Brabant, to develop the work in the area. Odulf built a church and a monastery at Stavoren.

After his death his cult grew, and a number of churches were dedicated to him in the Low Countries. His connection with England resulted from the supposed theft of his relics by Viking pirates in the early eleventh century.

They brought the relics to London, where the bishop of London, Aelfward, bought them for a hundred marks and gave them to Evesham abbey. However, the relics were stolen from Stavoren, and there is a strong tradition that Odulf was buried at Utrecht, so the Evesham relics may have been spurious; but the Life of Odulf comes from Evesham and is thought to be the work of Prior Dominic.

The Chronicles of Evesham (R.S., 29), pp. 319-20, and see preface by W. D. Macray, p. xi. *AA.SS.*, June, 3, pp. 87-92; *N.L.A.*, 2, pp. 229-30; Stanton, pp. 265-7; *O.D.S.*, p. 363; J. C. Jennings, "The Writings of Prior Dominic of Evesham," *E.H.R.* 77 (1962), pp. 298-304.

St Eskil, *Bishop and Martyr* (*c.* 1080)

King Ethelred "the Unready" sent Sigfrid (15 Feb.), a monk of Glastonbury, to Norway at the request of the Viking king, Olaf Trygvasson. Eskil, who was a relative of Sigfrid's, went with him. They were both probably raised in England, though their names suggest that they had Viking blood.

The people of Scandinavia had been Christianized by Anskar, the indefatigable archbishop of Bremen (3 Feb.), but after Anskar's death in 865 they were lapsing into the worship of the old Norse gods, and a new mission was necessary. Sigfrid became bishop of Vaxjo. Eskil worked in Sweden, mainly in Södermanland, and was consecrated bishop at Strängnäs, inland from what is now the Stockholm area. Though some accounts refer to him as the first diocesan bishop, he was probably a regionary bishop.

He received much support from King Inge; but Inge was murdered, and under his successor, Sweyn the Bloody, there was a violent reaction against the Christians. A great festival glorifying the Norse gods was held at Strängnäs. A pagan altar was set up, and sacrifices were prepared. Eskil, seeing that many professed Christians were taking part, confronted them and made a public appeal to them to renounce their pagan practices. When they ignored him he appealed to God to give a visible sign that he alone was the true God. There was a violent hailstorm which destroyed the altar and the sacrifices and left Eskil and his attendants untouched.

Sweyn ascribed this to magic and ordered Eskil to be killed. The crowd turned on him and stoned him to death. The place where his body was buried in 1082 is called after him, Eskilstüna.

AA.SS., June, 3, pp. 94-6; *B.H.L.*, 1, p. 394; C. J. A. Oppermann, *English Missionaries in Sweden* (1937), pp. 103-11: cf. *Anal. Boll.* 57 (1939), pp. 162-4; Stanton, pp. 287-8; *O.D.S.*, p. 162.

St John of Sahagún (1430-79)

This saint derives his distinctive surname from an early Spanish martyr, St Facundus or San Fagún, at whose shrine a Benedictine abbey was founded. John was educated there and ordained priest in 1445, apparently at the age of fifteen. Since his family was wealthy and influential, he acquired four small livings. He was only twenty when the bishop of Burgos presented him with a canonry in his cathedral. Pluralities were commonplace at that time, though they were forbidden by Church ordinances. The excuse was that clerical stipends were small; but John had an unusually sharp conscience and he resigned all his benefices except the chapel of St Agnes in Burgos. There he celebrated Mass daily, instructed his people, and led a life of extreme asceticism and poverty. After a time he felt the need for a sounder theological basis to his work and obtained permission to study at the University of Salamanca, where he remained for four years.

When he had completed his studies he took the parish of St Sebastian, Salamanca, and combined it with a chaplaincy (probably unpaid) in the College of St Bartholomew. He won a considerable reputation as a preacher and spiritual director and worked there for nine years. Then he was faced with an operation for gallstones, which at that time was extremely painful and often fatal. He vowed that if he survived he would join a religious Order. When he had recovered he said, "God alone knows what has passed between God and my soul." As soon as he was able to walk he went to the local community of Augustinian friars and asked to be admitted. He was professed in 1464. He had already absorbed the spirit of the Rule and was highly regarded for his wisdom and his capacity to reconcile opposing factions.

John was a person of great spirituality. He took so long to say Mass that his superior forbade him to celebrate until, with great reluctance, he revealed the depth of his worship and the visions he received while celebrating. The prohibition was immediately lifted. He became novice-master, definitor, and eventually prior of the Augustinian house at Salamanca. He taught many of the feuding nobles of Salamanca, who were his penitents, to forgive injuries, real or fancied, and to live in peace with one another. He was no respecter of persons, and though he would hear the confessions of all who came to him, he would be firm in refusing or deferring absolution to those who were not truly penitent.

His keen conscience inevitably brought him into conflict with people who resented his denunciation of their way of life. When he preached against rich landlords who oppressed their poor tenants, the duke of Alba sent two assassins to kill him; but the assassins, face to face with their victim, were stricken with remorse and confessed to him, asking his forgiveness. On another occasion his preaching against prostitution led to his being stoned by a group of enraged women, and he was saved only by the arrival on the scene of a company of archers. A prominent man in Salamanca had an open association with a mistress which was causing a public scandal. John persuaded him to give up the connection, and the woman vowed vengeance on him. It was afterwards alleged that she caused his death by poisoning him, but given his frugal eating habits, this seems unlikely. The contemporary account by John of Seville, written in 1498 and based on information from John of Sahagún's brother and others who knew him, makes no mention of this allegation.

John was venerated both inside and outside his Order, and many miracles were attributed to him. In paintings he is represented holding a chalice surrounded by a halo or rays of light. He was canonized in 1690.

AA.SS., June, 2, pp. 112-57, contains a Latin translation of letters from John of Seville to Duke Gonsalvo of Córdoba, giving an account of John of Sahagún's life and other material. A summary written about a hundred years after his death by his fellow Augustinian, Bd Alphonsus d'Orozco (19 Sept.), preacher at the court of Philip II, is printed in M. Vidal, *Agustinos de Salamanca* (1751), 1, pp. 51 ff. There is a modern Life in Spanish by T. Camara (1891). See also *C.M.H.*, p. 234; *Bibl.SS.*, 6, 899-901.

Bd Stephen Bandelli (1369-1450)

This Dominican friar was one of the most successful preachers in northern Italy in the first part of the fifteenth century. He was a man of learning, holding a doctorate in canon law and a professorship in the university of Pavia. His preaching drew great crowds, and he was noted as a confessor and spiritual director. He died at the age of eighty-one at Saluzzo, in the Turin diocese, and was much honoured in the locality.

Thirty-seven years later, when Saluzzo was under siege by hostile forces, strange forms seen in the sky were held to be those of Our Lady and Friar Stephen. In gratitude the people of Saluzzo instituted an annual procession in his honour on his feast day.

The ancient cult was confirmed by Pope Pius IX in 1856.

Procter, pp. 174-5; Taurisano, *Catalogus Hagiographicus O.P.* (Rome, 1918), pp. 37-8.

St Caspar Bertoni, *Founder* (1777-1853)

Gaspare Bertoni was born at Verona, the son of a notary. The family was a prosperous one, but he suffered a number of tragic experiences in his childhood, including the death of his only sister. He studied at the local municipal school, where some of his teachers were Jesuits who continued to teach although the Society of Jesus had been suppressed. Among them was Fr Louis Fortis, who later became the first Jesuit superior general when the Society was restored.

The men of the Bertoni family usually entered the legal profession, but Caspar had a vocation to the priesthood. He was in the first year of his training at the diocesan seminary when the French invaded northern Italy in 1796. This was the beginning of twenty years of suffering under foreign occupation for the people of Verona, and Caspar joined the Gospel Fraternity for Hospitals, working with the sick and wounded under the direction of Fr Peter Leonardi.

He was ordained to the priesthood in 1800 at the age of twenty-three and for the next twelve years served as a parish priest. These were years of great difficulty, in which any kind of religious work was severely restricted by the French occupation of northern and central Italy. Pope Pius VII was for a time a prisoner in the Vatican, and Fr Bertoni rallied his fellow priests and his parishioners to support the pope as head of the Church and the successor to St Peter. During this period of trial he developed a deep spirituality with a special devotion to the stigmata, or five wounds of Christ, and acted as counsellor and spiritual director to many religious, both men and women, who worked for the renewal of the Church.

In 1816, when Napoleonic forces had finally been defeated, he founded a religious group in a house adjacent to the church of the Stigmatics of St Francis, which had been suppressed. He was a gifted preacher and started a series of parish missions to which crowds flocked, but the area was now under Austrian occupation, and the Austrian government, suspicious of large gatherings, forbade the missions. He had to find other ways of renewing the Church, and the group devoted its efforts to education, opening a tuition-free school and fostering religious vocations.

In 1812 Fr Bertoni had suffered an attack of "military fever," probably yellow fever, and though he made a recovery his health deteriorated steadily. Not long after the foundation of the "Stigmatines," as his group was called, he became confined to a sick-bed, from where he carried on a remarkable ministry for many years. He accepted abandonment to the will of God through considerable suffering, including more than three hundred operations on his right leg. Many people came to him for spiritual direction and derived inspiration from his faith and endurance. He died on Sunday 12 June 1853.

The Congregation of the Holy Stigmatics of Our Lord Jesus Christ did not receive its official title until a decree of papal approval in 1890, but its work developed steadily beyond the confines of Verona. The Order has several hundred priests in seventy-eight houses established in Europe, North and South America, parts of Africa, Thailand, and the Philippines, and was a forerunner of Catholic Action.

Fr Bertoni was beatified on All Saints Day 1975 by Pope Paul VI and canonized exactly fourteen years later, on All Saints Day 1989, by Pope John Paul II.

D.N.H., pp. 320-2; *Osservatore Romano*, 6 Nov. 1989.

13

ST ANTONY OF PADUA, *Doctor* (1195-1231)

The popularity of Antony of Padua, reflected in church dedications, paintings, statues, and frequent appeals to him as the patron saint of lost possessions, is so great that we are in danger of losing the saint in the legends. He was a Portuguese from a noble family in Lisbon, and his baptismal name was Fernando. His family name is variously rendered as Bulhon, Bouillon, and de Buglione. He was educated by the cathedral clergy of that city and became an Augustinian friar at the age of fifteen or sixteen. After two years he asked if he might be transferred to the priory of the Holy Cross at Coïmbra to avoid the distractions caused by visits from his friends. He stayed at Coïmbra for eight years, concentrating on prayer and study and acquiring the remarkable knowledge of the Bible that was later to be a feature of his preaching.

About the year 1220 Don Pedro of Portugal brought from Morocco the relics of Franciscan friars who had been martyred by the Moors. Antony felt a vocation to a similar missionary life and perhaps to a similar martyrdom. This was not possible as a Canon Regular, so after discussions with some Franciscans who visited the priory he was permitted to join their Order, and he was sent to Morocco to preach to the Moors; but soon after his arrival he suffered from a serious and incapacitating fever, and eventually he was sent home. The ship on which he sailed for Portugal was blown badly off course, and he landed at Messina in Sicily. He learned from the Franciscans there that a general chapter was about to be held in Assisi, so he made his way north in order to attend. This was the Great Chapter of 1221, the last chapter open to all members of the Order. St Francis (4 Oct.) was still living then. The chapter was presided over by Brother Elias as vicar general, and Francis, who remained a deacon, sat at his feet.

Antony was deeply impressed by Francis and showed a similar humility. At the close of the chapter he was sent to a hermitage near Forli, and there he devoted himself to prayer and solitude, serving the other friars and doing household tasks. It is not clear whether he was already a priest at this time, but it seems that no one knew of his scholastic record or his preaching gifts until an ordination was held at the Minorite house at Forli. Both Franciscans and Dominicans were present, and through some misunderstanding, no one had been asked to give the customary address at the ceremony. Since the Franciscans were the hosts, the Dominicans expected them to provide a preacher. Since the Dominicans were the Order of Preachers, the Franciscans, who were not a learned Order, had assumed that their visitors would do so. Antony was asked to speak at short notice. He protested that his work was washing dishes and sweeping floors, and that he was fit for nothing better, but his superior overrode his objections. Facing the bishop and the critical Dominicans unprepared, he began simply, haltingly, and in familiar language. Then he became animated and, as the *Vita Anonyma* says, "as if in spite of himself, he poured forth brilliant and burning words, a flood of divine eloquence." He preached a sermon that was so inspired, so eloquent, and so learned that it astonished them all.

The Franciscans realized that he had a special gift. He was recalled from his retreat and sent to preach in different parts of Lombardy. Antony had a beautiful and compelling voice and the ability to make theological issues real and vital to ordinary people. Crowds gathered to hear him. Men left their shops and other places of work, women rose early or sat in church all night to keep a place where they might hear him speak. Soon the churches were not big enough, and he moved into the squares and the marketplaces. We are told that sometimes there were as many as thirty thousand people crowded into a piazza, though this is likely to be an exaggeration, as few Italian piazzas would have held half that number. The crowds heard him in "the most religious silence." It was said that he could bring sinners to their knees and soften the hearts of hardened criminals.

We do not know what he looked like. While some accounts emphasize his "fine-drawn austerity" and his "long delicate hands," others describe him as short and stout. We know that he was always in poor health, but none of this mattered: the power of his preaching, developed in the years of study and contemplation, was overwhelming. He was, in the original sense of the term, a charismatic personality.

In addition to his commission as a preacher he was appointed lector in theology to the friars in Bologna and Padua. Francis himself confirmed this appointment in a letter generally regarded as authentic: "To my dearest brother Antony, brother Francis sends greetings in Jesus Christ. I am well pleased that you should read sacred theology to the friars, provided that such study does not quench the spirit of holy prayer and devotion according to our Rule."

Antony became a favourite disciple and friend of Francis. He was sent to the south of France to preach against the Albigensians. He preached at Montpellier, Toulouse, and Arles, where he was described as "the hammer of the heretics." When Francis died in 1226, he was recalled to Italy, probably to be the provincial of Emilia or Romagna. Dissensions arose among the Franciscans when Brother Elias and other superiors contravened the ideals and practice of their founder, relaxing the Rule on extreme poverty. At one time it was thought that Antony headed the opposition to Brother Elias and to any departures from the original Rule, but it is now thought that he acted as a mediator, taking the problems of the chapter to Pope Gregory IX for decision. Pope Gregory deposed Elias from the generalship. He had a very high opinion of Antony and once called him "the Ark of the Testament" because of his knowledge of scripture. He dispensed him from office so that he could concentrate on preaching.

Antony returned to Padua, where he continued to draw great crowds to listen to his preaching and had a remarkable effect on the life of the whole city. Quarrelsome nobles became reconciled, prisoners were freed from private dungeons, and those who had stolen or cheated came to lay their ill-gotten gains at Antony's feet, often in public. He denounced the practice of usury and was instrumental in getting a local law passed to the effect that debtors who were willing to sell their possessions to pay their creditors should not be imprisoned—an early version of bankruptcy.

In the spring of 1231, when he was only thirty-six, his limited strength gave out. It was clear that he had not long to live, and he retired for a time with two other friars to a hermitage at Camposanpiero. Then he asked to be taken back to Padua, but he died on the outskirts of the city. There were extraordinary scenes of veneration at his funeral, and his body was enshrined in the friars' church of Our Lady in Padua.

Antony was canonized within a year of his death. On that occasion, Pope Gregory IX intoned the anthem *O doctor optime*, but he was not formally named as a Doctor of the Church until 1946, when Pope Pius XII proclaimed the title. Legends have focussed on his devotion to the Christ-Child and his love of the natural world. He was of a gentle and affectionate nature, sharing St Francis' love of trees and flowers, animals, birds, and fish. He is often shown in art holding an open book with the Christ-Child sitting on it. He is also shown holding a lily (an emblem of purity), sitting in a nut tree (a symbol of solitude), preaching to the fishes, and showing a consecrated Host to a mule, which ignores a bale of hay to kneel in reverence. In most Franciscan churches he is represented wearing the robe of his Order.

The idea that Antony could be invoked to find lost articles seems to have originated in an incident when a novice ran away, taking with him a valuable Psalter which Antony was using and which may have been of his own transcribing. Antony prayed for its recovery. On his journey, the novice had to cross a river. He saw an alarming apparition on the opposite bank, which commanded him to take the book back, and he did so.

Antony's devotion to poverty and the poor is marked by the comparatively recent institution of "St Antony's Bread," a charity devoted to the relief of hunger, which still operates, particularly in the Third World.

The *Vita Anonyma*, known from its first word as the *Assidua*, is best studied in the edition of W. C. Van Dyk, *L'Assidua: la vie de saint Antoine racontée par un contemporain* (1984). *AA.SS.*, June, 3, pp. 196-269; *Auréole Séraphique*, 2, pp. 382-421; *Bibl.SS.*, 2, 156-88; *H.S.S.C.*, 6, pp. 69-79; *Saints in Italy*, pp 35-7; *F.B.S.*, pp. 427-31. Modern Lives by C. M. Antony (1911); E. Gilliat Smith (1926); R. Maloney (1931); R. M. Huber (1949); A. Curtayne (1950); A. Masseron (1956); sermons edited by A. Locatelli and others (1895-1913). In 1946 the Conventual Friars of Padua issued a commemorative volume of studies.

St Felicula, *Martyr* (Late First Century)

Felicula is thought to have been the foster-sister of Petronilla (31 May), who, probably on account of her name, was mistakenly listed in the Roman Martyrology as the daughter of St Peter (29 June). Her martyrdom is associated with that of Nereus and Achilleus (12 May). With these two, we are on somewhat firmer ground, because an inscription dating from the pontificate of Pope Damasus (366-84; 11 Dec.) commemorates the fact that they were Roman soldiers who became Christians, left the Roman army, and were martyred for their faith.

The acts attributed to all these martyrs are probably legendary. The story is that after the death of Petronilla her rejected suitor, Count Flaccus, offered Felicula the choice of marrying him or sacrificing to the Roman gods. She refused to do either and was imprisoned without food for seven days. Her jailer tried to persuade her into marriage, pointing out that the count was noble, young, rich, elegant, and a friend of the emperor. When that failed, she was sent to the vestal virgins, but nothing could induce her to change her mind. Eventually she was tortured and killed. Her body was rescued by a priest named Nicomedes (15 Sept.) and buried on the via Ardeantina at the seventh milestone.

Several Roman churches, including those of St Praxedes and St Laurence in Lucina, claim to posess her relics, and it is uncertain where they actually lie. Similar claims are made by the church of St Paul in Parma, and there are said to be relics in Pavia and at Fulda. There were other saints called Felicula in Rome, and it may be that their remains have been ascribed to their more famous namesake, the companion of Petronilla.

AA.SS., June, 3, pp. 10-11, has an account of the acts of Nereus and Achilleus, to which an account of Felicula forms a supplement. *C.M.H.*, p. 235; *B.H.L.*, 1, p. 430.

St Triphyllius, *Bishop* (*c.* 370)

While he was still young Triphyllius attached himself to Spiridion, bishop of Tremithos (14 Dec.), in the northern part of Cyprus. Spiridion was a former shepherd with little formal education, but Triphyllius was well educated and had been destined for a legal career. The two worked well together, and Triphyllius became Spiridion's constant companion and devoted disciple. They attended the Council of Sardica together in 347, and both firmly opposed the Arian heresy. Triphyllius became bishop of Ledra (Nicosia) and was renowned as a preacher, teacher, and writer. St Jerome (30 Sept.) wrote of him as "the most eloquent of his age, and the most celebrated during the reign of King Constantius," but Jerome's dating is often somewhat haphazard, and Constantius, successively tetrarch, Caesar, and Augustus, died in 306.

Jerome also writes of "Triphyllius the Cretan, who so filled his books with the doctrines and maxims of the philosophers that you did not know which to admire more—his secular erudition or his knowledge of the scriptures." There is no other evidence that Triphyllius came from Crete, and Jerome may have been confusing Cyprus with Crete.

Triphyllius also composed poetry and is said to have recorded the miracles of St Spiridion in iambics.

His relics are venerated in the Hodigitria church in Nicosia.

AA.SS., June, 3, pp. 174-8, has a text from a late ms. of the *Synax. Const.*; but cf. Delehaye's ed. of this *Synaxary*, p. 173; *C.M.H.*, p. 235.

Bd Gerard of Clairvaux (1138)

Gerard was an older and favourite brother of Bernard of Clairvaux (20 Aug.). He was not one of the group of young relatives and friends who entered Cîteaux with Bernard in 1112. Evidently more extrovert than Bernard, he preferred a career as a soldier, but he was badly wounded in the siege of Grancy and suffered a long spell of imprisonment. This gave him time for reflection, and when he was finally released he went to Cîteaux to take the habit under Bernard's Rule. He accompanied Bernard to Clairvaux, where he was appointed cellarer, and managed the domestic affairs of the abbey with great efficiency. He was said to have developed such a degree of skill in manual occupations that builders, smiths, shoemakers, weavers, and labourers all turned to him for instruction.

Gerard was on his way to Rome in 1137 when he fell ill at Viterbo and appeared to be on the point of death. He recovered sufficiently to return to Clairvaux but died in the following year. Bernard was preaching on the Canticle when he was told of his brother's death. He broke off his address and poured out his grief in an eloquent and touching tribute:

> My sons, be well assured my grief is just, my wound is to be pitied. Ye see how my faithful comrade has deserted me in the way we were treading together. . . . A brother by blood, he was more than a brother in religion. I was infirm in body, and he held me up; feeble-hearted, and he cheered me; slothful, and he stimulated me; forgetful, and he reminded me. . . . We loved each other in life, how is it that we are parted by death? . . .
>
> I mourn for my own loss, and for that of this house. I mourn for the necessities of the poor, to whom Gerard was a father. I mourn for our whole Order, which derived no little strength from thy zeal, counsel, and example, Gerard. I mourn—no, not over thee, but for thee, for I love thee very dearly.

The sermon casts light on the personalities of both brothers—Gerard, who was so often overshadowed by the more brilliant Bernard, and Bernard, whose often astringent and austere character was on this occasion softened by a deep personal affection.

AA.SS., June, 3, pp. 192-5, has extracts from the *Cistercian Magnum Exordium*. B.G., June, pp. 638-9, from the *Vie des saints du diocèse de Dijon*, includes Bernard's sermon. See also *Dict.Hag.*, p. 293, and Lives of St Bernard: Watkin Williams (1953); J. Leclercq (1966). Letters of St Bernard, ed. B. S. James (1953; rp. 1997).

14

St Dogmael (? Sixth Century)

Research on the Welsh or Breton saints has little to tell us about Dogmael (Dogfael, Dogwel). While he is listed in a number of publications, the details of his life are largely unknown. It has been established that he was a Welshman who lived in the late fifth or early sixth century. He is called the son of Ithel son of Ceredic son of Cunedda Wledig. This distinguishes him from another Dogmael, his great-uncle, the son of Cunedda Wledig. He must have had considerable influence in Pembrokeshire (now Dyfed, in south Wales). Place names and dedications indicate that the greater part of his ministry was in that area, and one church is dedicated under his name in Anglesey. His name was perpetuated in St Dogmael's abbey, near Cardigan, of which Caldey was a cell.

It is likely that he moved to Brittany, where St Dogmael, or Toël, has had a considerable cult, especially in the diocese of Tréguier, where he was traditionally invoked to help children to learn to walk.

AA.SS., June, 3, pp. 436-7; Giraldus Cambrensis (R.S., 21), 2, p. 216, mentions him briefly; B.G.F., 2, pp. 349-51; *O.D.S.*, p. 133; *Bibl.SS.*, 4, 673. The *Archaeologia Cambrensis*, 6th series, 5 (1905), p. 166, has a short account of "St Dogmael's stone."

St Methodius of Constantinople, *Patriarch* (847)

The Greeks regard Methodius with great veneration because of the courageous part he played in the final overthrow of Iconoclasm, and his endurance in prison. He is often called "The Confessor" and "The Great." He was born in Sicily and received a good education in Syracuse. He went to Constantinople with the object of securing a post at court, but he was influenced by a monk, and entered the monastery of Chenolakkos. Later he built a monastery on the Aegean island of Khios or Chios, and he was called from there to Constantinople by the patriarch Nicephorus (13 Mar.).

Iconoclasm, the movement to destroy all holy images and the veneration of saints in the time of the Eastern emperor Leo the Isaurian (717-40), had been strongly contested and defeated in the eighth century (*see* St John Damascene; 4 Dec.), but in the early ninth century it was revived by the emperor Leo V the Armenian. The pressure in the Eastern Church came from the growth of Islam, which forbade any representation of images or sacred objects. Some Christians feared that images might be put to superstitious uses, but Methodius, like John Damascene before him, argued that statues and pictures were an aid to devotion and an inheritance of Church tradition. He stood out boldly against this new attack. After the deposition and exile of the patriarch Nicephorus he went to Rome, apparently charged by his fellow bishops to inform Pope Paschal I (11 Feb.) of the situation. He remained in Rome until Leo's death. Then the pope sent a letter to the new emperor, Michael the Stammerer, requesting his reinstatement, and Methodius returned to Constantinople; but the controversy was still raging, and on arrival he was accused of having incited the pope to write the letter. He was thrown into prison and remained there for seven years, according to some accounts, or nine according to others.

The conditions of his imprisonment were appalling. He is thought to have been incarcerated in a cave or a tomb. He was confined with two thieves, one of whom died and was left to rot where he lay. When Methodius was released he was scarcely recognizable. He was reduced to a skeleton, he was bald, his skin was blanched from years of living in darkness, and he wore filthy rags; but his spirit was unbroken. When another emperor, Theophilus, recommenced the persecution of sacred images, he boldly attacked the veneration of imperial images, saying, "If an image is so worthless in your eyes, how is it that when you condemn the images of Christ, you do not also condemn the veneration paid to representations of yourself?"

Theophilus had him flogged and thrown into prison, and his jaw was broken. His supporters managed to free him during the night. Theophilus died soon after. Power passed to the hands of his widow, the empress Theodora, as regent for her infant son, Michael III, and she reversed the work of the Iconoclasts. Persecution stopped, the exiled clergy were recalled, and within thirty days the sacred images had been replaced in the churches of Constantinople. The Iconoclast patriarch was deposed, and Methodius was installed in his place, still wearing a bandage to sustain his broken jaw.

His patriarchate lasted four years. During that time he convened a synod in Constantinople at which the lawfulness of venerating religious images was reaffirmed. He had the relics of his predecessor, the patriarch Nicephorus, who had died in exile, brought back to Constantinople and saw that due honour was paid to him. He instituted an annual Festival of Orthodoxy, which is still observed in Orthodox churches on the first Sunday in Lent, and wrote the *Synodicon*, a statement on the true Faith, to be read on that occasion. Unfortunately, he inherited from Nicephorus a dispute with the Studite monks. They had previously been among his strongest supporters, but relationships became acrimonious when he condemned some of the writings of their famous abbot, Theodore the Studite (11 Nov.).

Methodius was a prolific writer, though many of the poetic, theological, and other works, some of them controversial, that have been attributed to him, are now not considered authentic. He is now thought to be the author of certain hagiographical writings, including a Life of St Theophanes the Chronicler (12 Mar.).

P.G., 100, 1243-6; *AA.SS.*, June, 3, pp. 439-47; *Regestes des Patriarches de Constantinople*, 1935, folio 2; *B.H.G.*, pp. 116-7; Bardenhewer, 2, pp. 291-304; *Anal.Boll.* 18 (1899), pp. 211-59; V. Laurent in *D.T.C.*, 10 (1928), 1597-606, has a full and discerning bibliography; *Dict.Hag.*, p. 472; *Oxford Dictionary of Byzantium* (1991), 2, p. 1355; *Bibl.SS.*, 9, 382-93. *P.G.*, 120, 724-36, contains the *Synodicon*. For background, see F. Dvornik, *The Photian Schism* (1948), especially pp. 13-18.

15

SS Vitus, Modestus, and Crescentia, *Martyrs* (? *c.* 300)

Of these three saints, St Vitus is by far the best known and has the most ancient cult, going back to the original *Hieronymianum* of Jerome (30 Sept.). He is mentioned alone in the martyrology of Bede and in the Old English martyrology. According to tradition he was the son of a Sicilian senator, and Modestus and Crescentia were his tutor and his nurse respectively. They brought him up as a Christian. When this was discovered, Vitus' father and the administrator of Sicily, Valerian, did their best to shake the boy's faith; but he remained firm and did not betray the other two. The three escaped together by boat to Lucania in southern Italy. They subsequently went to Rome, where Vitus cured the emperor Diocletian's son of devil possession, but Diocletian believed their invocations to be sorcery, and all three were tortured and condemned to death.

The later stages of the story are medieval fictions: they include repeated escapes from attempts to execute the three and their final liberation by an angel who took them back to Lucania. It is now thought probable that two traditions have been conflated and that there was a cult of St Vitus in Lucania which pre-dated the cult of the three saints in Sicily. Nothing is known of their true history or of the circumstances of their martyrdom, but it seems certain that they were Christians who were martyred for their faith, probably in the time of Diocletian.

The cult of St Vitus spread among the Slavs and the Germans as well as in Rome, Sicily, and Sardinia. Churches have been dedicated to him since the fifth century. His reputed relics were conveyed to Saint-Denis in Paris in 775 and then to Corvey in Saxony in 836. So great was the devotion to him in Germany that he is named as one of the Fourteen Holy Helpers, who were collectively venerated in the Rhineland from the fourteenth century. There are several artistic representations of this group, including one by Cranach now at Hampton Court near London. Though the cult was discouraged by the Council of Trent (1545-63), it continued in some of the abbeys of Bavaria and Swabia.

"St Vitus' dance" is the popular name for Sydenham's chorea, which derives its medical name from the physician who first described it. In the Middle Ages the popular term was used for a variety of conditions causing convulsive and involuntary movements. In Norman Sicily it was observed among the soldiers of King Roger II's army, who are now thought to have been suffering from bites from a poisonous local tarantula. The "dancing mania" which occurred in medieval epidemics may have been a form of mass hysteria; but toxicity induced by rabies, snake bite, insect stings, or food poisoning could cause similar symptoms, as could epilepsy and many neurological conditions. St Vitus thus became the patron saint of people suffering from all these conditions, and by extension, the patron saint of dancers and actors.

AA.SS., June, 3, pp. 491-519; *C.M.H.*, p. 238; *B.H.G.*, 315-6; *P.B.*, 6, pp. 26-30; B.G., June, pp. 207-8; *Golden Legend*, 1, pp. 322-3; *N.C.E.*, 14, p. 730; *Bibl.SS.*, 12, 1244-8.

St Orsiesius, *Abbot* (*c.* 380)

When St Pachomius (14 May) was ruling the great communities he had established at Tabbenisi, he had two younger monks whom he regarded as being of exceptional promise. One was Orsiesius, the other was Theodore (28 Dec.). Pachomius took them as companions on visitations to the other monasteries and eventually placed Orsiesius in charge of the monastery of Khenoboski and Theodore in charge of Tabbenisi, while he himself retired to a hermitage; but when he came toward the end of his life, he could not bear to name either of them as his own successor. Theodore was actually disgraced for having admitted that he had thought of possibly taking the responsibility one day. Though Pachomius had prophesied that Orsiesius would one day diffuse the splendour of a golden lamp over the house of God, he found him no more acceptable. Eventually, pressed by the monks in his last hours in 346, Pachomius designated a monk named Petronius as the next abbot, but Petronius died only thirteen days after Pachomius.

The monks then elected Orsiesius. The desert monk St Antony (17 Jan.) and St Athanasius (2 May) both praised the choice, but though he was a holy man and strict in his own observance, Orsiesius did not have the ability to manage so large and scattered a monastic system. He was humble enough to recognize this, and when opposition increased in the more distant monasteries, he resigned in favour of Theodore.

The resolution of this difficult situation was satisfactory to all concerned; for Theodore, after his disgrace at the hands of Pachomius, accepted only with great reluctance and continued to regard Orsiesius as his superior, consulting him constantly. The two were deeply attached to each other and agreed to take it in turns to visit the outlying monasteries. So they worked in harmony until Theodore's death in 368, when Orsiesius took sole charge for some twelve years.

He was the author of a treatise on the Rules and maxims of the religious life, which was later translated by Jerome into Latin.

AA.SS., June, 3, pp. 531-4; Rule and Letters of Pachomius translated by Jerome in *P.L.*, 23, 61-99; *Anal.Boll.* 47 (1929), pp. 376-7; Bardenhewer, 3, pp. 85-6; D. L. O'Leary, *The Saints of Egypt* (1937), pp. 156-7; L. T. Lefort, *Les vies coptes de saint Pachôme et de ses premiers successeurs* (1943); A Boon, *Pachomiana Latina* (1932); T. H. Lefort, *Oeuvres de S Pachôme et ses disciples* (1965); P. Rousseau, *Pachomius: The Making of a Community in Fourth-Century Egypt* (1985).

St Landelinus, *Abbot (c. 686)*

Landelinus (Landelin) made a bad start in life. He was born about 625 at Vaux, near Bapaume, of Frankish parents and entrusted to the care of Aubert, bishop of Arras-Cambrai (13 Dec.), to study for the priesthood. At the age of eighteen he broke away and went off with a group of wild young men to commit robbery and other crimes. He was brought to a realization of what he had done when one of his companions died suddenly. He returned to Aubert, who had been praying fervently for him and helped him to repentance. Then, with Aubert's approval, he went away to Lobbes, a wild and lonely place and the scene of his former crimes, to atone for his sins.

Like many other hermits he was soon surrounded by other young men who wanted to emulate his way of life, and from this small group developed the great abbey of Lobbes. Landelinus thought himself quite unfit to rule a community and appointed his follower St Ursmar (19 April) as abbot. He himself went away—in turn to Hainault, to Wallens, to Crespin in the forest that lies between Mons and Valenciennes. At each place new communities sprang up. Finally, he stayed to govern the monastery at Crespin, though he spent much of his time in solitude away from the community.

P.L., 203, 1348-9; *AA.SS.*, June, 3, pp. 538-44; *M.G.H., Scriptores rerum Merov.*, 6, pp. 433-44, contains a Life written by Folcwin of Lobbes about a century after the death of Landelinus; *P.B.*, 7, p. 61; the account of St Aubert in *P.B.*, 14, pp 247-51, deals with his conversion; *Bibl.SS.*, 7, 1090.

St Edburga of Winchester (960)

Several Anglo-Saxon princesses named Edburga or Eadburh are included in the calendars of the saints, including Edburga of Minster (12 Dec.) and Edburga of Bicester (18 July). Edburga of Winchester was a daughter of Edward the Elder, king of Wessex (900-25), and his third wife, Eadgifu, and was a granddaughter of King Alfred. She was destined for the religious life from an early age. There is a story that when she was three years old her father asked her to choose between a chalice with a book of the Gospels and a pile of trinkets and that she chose the sacred objects.

She went to the abbey of Nunnaminster, which her grandmother, King Alfred's wife, had founded at Winchester. It appears that she never became abbess. She was a gentle creature, much loved for her humility and her works of charity. Osbert of Clare says that she would rise at night and clean the other nuns' sandals, replacing them quietly beside their beds, and William of Malmesbury records that she washed their socks. Far from being appreciated, this service earned her a public rebuke, according to Osbert. She was told by her superior that it was "unseemly for a royal child to bow her neck to such humble service" and that to set about the work of a common slave was "harmful to the dignity of her illustrious birth."

When her royal father came to visit, the superior told him of this incident in hesitant tones. She seems to have been afraid that the king would blame her for his daughter's vulgar behaviour, but the king, far from disapproving, supported his daughter and assured the nuns that he thoroughly approved of her humility.

Later, Edburga asked her father for an endowment for the abbey. Women religious at this time were strictly enclosed and unable to take part in any activity which would assist their own support. They were entirely dependent on dowries and gifts from wealthy patrons and could often suffer real hardship if these were not forthcoming. She pleaded eloquently for her Sisters:

> There are some, established in the wilderness, who on account of the grief of their pilgrimage and their ardent desire to contemplate the face of God, are prevented neither by the pains of hunger nor by thirst from divine contemplation. These, because they have risen above the sufferings of the flesh, abhor the pleasures of the flesh. And while they seek to provide for the spirit, they easily deny themselves the delights of corporal food. But the weaker multitude and the inferior sex are not endowed with that fortitude: for them, it is impossible to live without bodily sustenance.

Perhaps she exaggerated a little, for the nuns of Nunnaminster were allowed to keep their own money and property, such as it was, and Edburga used her own for the care of the poor of the district; but the king came to the abbey, and she sang for him. Greatly moved, he endowed the abbey with an estate known as Canaga (All Cannings in Wiltshire).

Edburga died at the age of forty or earlier. Osbert of Clare says that the gentle princess was much lamented: "The daughters of Syon wept for the daughter of Juda."

There was a cult in the monasteries of Wessex, particularly in Winchester and in Pershore Abbey, which possessed some relics of Edburga. This survived the Norman Conquest, when the cults of many Anglo-Saxon saints were abruptly terminated. Edburga was also venerated at Westminster.

William of Malmesbury, *Gesta Regum* (R.S., 90), 1, pp. 268-9, and *De Gestis Pontificum* (R.S., 52), pp. 174, 298. Part of the twelfth-century Life by Osbert of Clare (Laud Misc. 114, folios 85-20, in the Bodleian Library, Oxford) has been edited by Susan J. Ridyard as an appendix to *The Royal Saints of Anglo-Saxon England* (1988), pp. 253-310: see also editor's comments, *op.cit.*, pp. 96-103 and elsewhere. *N.L.A.*, pp. 308-11; William Worcestre, pp. 147, 151 and n.; Stanton, pp. 269-70.

St Bardo, *Bishop* (? 982-1053)

Bardo was born at Oppershofen, on the right bank of the Rhine, a member of the imperial family. He was educated at the abbey of Fulda, where he received the habit. He was apparently very studious. When his fellow students found him poring over St Gregory's *Regula Pastoralis* on the duties of a bishop, he explained rather diffidently that some king might be foolish enough to make him a bishop if no one else could be found for the task, and he thought it best to learn how it should be done. In view of his royal blood his later preferment was probably not unexpected. The emperor Conrad II nominated him abbot of Kaiserswerth about the year 1029, and later he became superior of Horsfeld. In 1031 he was chosen as archbishop of Mainz.

The emperor attended Mass on Christmas Day, and Bardo preached. It was a very poor sermon, and the emperor complained loudly: "What a man is that Bardo for an archbishop? He is a stick, he can't preach." His courtiers fostered his irritation, saying "Why did your majesty appoint a boorish monk?" On St Stephen's Day Bardo (who had probably pitched his Christmas sermon at too low a level, not knowing what level of theology the emperor and the court were capable of understanding) preached again. This time it was a powerful and erudite sermon. The emperor, delighted, declared that Bardo had restored his appetite and said, "It is Christmas Day to me now."

Bardo's early studies helped him to be a good metropolitan. He managed to combine the personal austerity expected of a monk with an openhanded hospitality, particularly to the poor and needy. He was charitable and merciful and seemed not to notice slights or insults. On one occasion, while he was speaking at his own table, he saw a young man mocking him. He stopped speaking, looked at the offender, and instead of rebuking him directed that a special dish of food should be presented to him.

Bardo had an extraordinarily kind heart. He loved animals and kept an aviary of rare birds, which would feed from his hand. When he died Jews as well as Christians lamented his passing.

AA.SS., June, 2, pp. 296-315; *M.G.H., Scriptores*, 11, pp. 317-21, includes a short Life by Fulcold, who was chaplain to Bardo's successor as archbishop of Mainz. See also F. Schneider, *Der hl. Bardo* (1871); *B.G.*, June, pp. 133-5; *N.C.E.*, 2, pp. 296-315; *Bibl.SS.*, 2, 781-3.

St Aleydis (1250)

The Life of Aleydis, or Alice, was written by a contemporary who was probably a Cistercian monk and confessor to her community. It is very simple but written with great sincerity. Aleydis was a delicate and gentle child, born at Scharembeke near Brussels. At the age of seven she was committed to the care of Cistercian nuns in the convent of Camera Sanctae Mariae, just outside the city. She was still very young when she contracted leprosy and, to the sorrow of the other Sisters, had to be segregated. Leprosy had come to Europe at the time of the Crusades and was greatly feared.

Aleydis accepted the sickness and the segregation in her usual humble and retiring way, with total resignation to the will of God; but her one comfort was to receive the Sacrament, and she was allowed to take only the Host, for fear of contagion if she received the chalice. Communion in one kind or by intinction does not seem to have been practised at Scharembeke, and she was greatly distressed at the deprivation until it was revealed to her in prayer that nothing was lacking in her Communion. "Where there is part," she came to understand, "there is also the whole."

On the feast of St Barnabas 1249 she suddenly became very ill. She received the Last Rites but prophesied that she would live for another year. During that time she suffered greatly and lost her sight in both eyes; but she prayed incessantly, offering her suffering to Christ for the souls in purgatory, and was greatly sustained by revelations and visions. She died, as she had foretold, on the feast of St Barnabas in the year 1250. Her feast is kept by the Cistercian Order and in the diocese of Malines on 15 June.

Her cult was confirmed in 1907 by Pope Pius X.

The Life is printed in *AA.SS.*, June, 2, pp. 471-7. See also C. Henriques, *Quinque prudentes virgines* (1630), which includes a biography; B.G., June, pp. 147-8.

Bd Jolenta of Hungary (1299)

Jolenta (Helen, or Yolanda) was one of four sisters who were honoured with the title of Blessed. They were the daughters of Bela IV, king of Hungary, the nieces of St Elizabeth of Hungary (17 Nov.), the great-nieces of St Hedwig of Poland (16 Oct.), and lineal descendants of the Hungarian kings St Stephen (16 Aug.) and St Ladislaus (27 June). When Jolenta was five years old, she was committed to the care of her sister Cunegund (24 July), who had married Boleslaus II, king of Poland. She grew up in their court and married Duke Boleslaus of Kalisz.

This was a very happy marriage, in which duke and duchess carried out many good works and made a number of religious foundations. When Boleslaus died, Jolenta settled two of her daughters and then entered a convent of Poor Clares at Stary Sacz with her sister Cunegund and her own third daughter. Cunegund had founded this convent. Later, Jolenta moved to a convent at Gniezno, which she herself had founded, and remained there for the rest of her life.

Acta Sanctorum Hungariae, 2, appendix, pp. 54-5; *N.C.E.*, 7, p. 1091; *F.B.S.*, pp. 421-5.

BB Peter Snow and Ralph Grimston, *Martyrs* (1598)

The religious upheavals of Tudor England culminated in the Elizabethan Settlement and a complete break with the papacy. Fr Peter Snow was one of the priests who volunteered for the English mission—an attempt to bring England back into conformity with Rome. The mission began from Douai in 1579 with the blessing of Pope Gregory XIII. Three Jesuit priests, Edmund Campion, Ralph Sherwin, and Alexander Briant (all 1 Dec.), were in the first party, and all three met their death at Tyburn in 1581. They were followed by many others, some of whom are commemorated among the Forty Martyrs of England and Wales canonized by Pope Paul VI on 25 October 1970.

Peter Snow was not among this representative group. He came from Chester, according to the Douai Catalogue, or from Ripon in Yorkshire, according to other sources. He studied at Reims, was ordained as a secular priest on 17 April 1591, and was sent on the mission in May of the same year. Like other missioners, he must have been well aware of the dangers. He carried out his ministry for seven years—moving from place to place and frequently hiding when search parties came to seek out the recusants. He was apprehended at Ripon "about the feast of St Philip and St James" (3 May).

Ralph Grimston was a gentleman of Nidd, a few miles from Ripon, who was with Fr Snow when he was arrested. He was arrested on a charge of felony, in that he had "lifted up his weapon" to defend Fr Snow, and they were both subsequently tried for treason. They were hanged at York on 15 June 1598. Their beatification by Pope John Paul II took place on 22 November 1987.

A.A.S., 1987, pt. 2, p. 608; *M.M.P.*, p. 233; Anstruther, 1, p. 324.

St Germaine of Pibrac (*c.* 1579-1601)

Germaine Cousin was a poor and sickly child, born with many disadvantages, and she died young; yet the apostolic brief for her beatification described her as one who "shone like a star not only in her native France, but throughout the Catholic Church."

The family lived in the village of Pibrac, near Toulouse. Germaine's father was an agricultural labourer. Her mother died when she was very young. The child had a paralyzed right arm and suffered from scrofula, or the "King's Evil," a condition no longer medically recognized as a specific syndrome. This caused ugly swellings in the neck, which in Germaine's case may have been tuberculous in origin. Her step-mother treated her harshly, keeping her away from her healthier step-brothers and step-sisters. She was fed on scraps, made to sleep in the stable or under the stairs, and sent out as soon as she was old enough to mind the sheep in the fields.

Germaine accepted this treatment without complaint. Out in the fields she learned to talk directly to God and to live in his presence. The adults of the village tended at first to accept her family's estimate of her as useless and diseased and to treat her with contempt and ridicule. She never mixed with girls of her own age, but she spoke to the younger children, gathering them round her and giving them simple religious teaching. She went to Mass as often as she could and shared her meagre scraps of food with beggars.

Gradually village opinion changed, and strange stories began to circulate about her: how she left her sheep to go to Mass, but they never strayed or fell prey to wolves; how she forded a stream in torrent to get to Mass: some said that the waters parted like the Red Sea before Moses; how two neighbours saw her step-mother pursue her with a stick, saying that she had stolen bread, and when she let fall her apron, summer flowers fell to the ground. Such stories were indicative of pity and affection for the sickly girl and of growing veneration. The people of Pibrac decided that they had a saint among them. Even her father and step-mother relented and would have taken her into the house, but Germaine continued to live as before until, at the age of twenty-two, she was found lying dead on her pallet under the stairs.

Her body was buried in the church at Pibrac, and a considerable local cult developed, with reports of many miracles and healings. Germaine was first beatified and then later canonized during the pontificate of Pius IX (1846-78). An annual pilgrimage takes place to Pibrac church, where her relics still rest. She is represented in art with a distaff and spindle, sometimes with a sheep at her side and sometimes with roses in her apron.

There is a Life by Louis Veuillot, revised by his nephew François Veuillot in the series Les saints. See also H. Bartolini, *La Bergère au pays des loups* (1923); *P.B.*, 7, pp. 43-59; B.G., June, pp. 216-8; *Dict.Hag.*, p. 299.

16

SS Ferreolus and Ferrutio, *Martyrs* (*c.* 212)

These two saints were a priest and a deacon ordained by St Irenaeus, bishop of Lyons (28 June), and sent as missionaries to the area around Besançon in Gaul. They may have been Greeks, but it is more probable that they were natives of Gaul who had studied in Asia Minor and come under Christian influence. Trading links between the Rhône Valley and the Middle East had existed for centuries, and Lyons was a centre of Christian activity. Their legendary acts say that the two were converted by St Polycarp, bishop of Smyrna (23 Feb.), who died in 155 or 156.

Ferreolus and Ferrutio ministered in the Besançon area for some thirty years. At this early stage in the Christian era worshipping communities were small and liable to be persecuted. Rumours still circulated that Christians practised black magic and ate children. At the time of the great pagan festivals the Christians had to go into hiding, and near Besançon there is a deep cleft in the rocks, which is reputed to have been their place of shelter.

In an outbreak of persecution about the year 212 Ferreolus and Ferrutio were apprehended, tortured, and beheaded. Their relics are said to have been discovered in a cave near Besançon in 370 by a military tribune whose dog was chasing a fox, and they were then enshrined by Bishop Anianus.

The two saints were greatly venerated in the late sixth century. Gregory of Tours mentions them, and the *Missale Gothicum*, compiled about 700, contains a full "proper" of the Mass in their honour.

AA.SS., June, 4, pp. 4-13; *C.M.H.*, pp. 239-40; *B.H.L.*, 1, pp. 438-9; Duchesne, *Fastes*, 1, pp. 48-62; Ruinart, pp. 489-91; *P.B.*, 7, pp. 66-72; Quentin, p. 74n.

SS Cyricus and Julitta, *Martyrs* (*c.* 304)

The name of Cyricus appears in the records in a number of different forms: the Roman Martyrology calls him Quiricus, and in France he is known as Cyr or Cirgues. He is the St Cyr of the French military academy (originally the site of a Benedictine abbey). Four churches in the Ile de France alone are dedicated to him. He is celebrated in place names, church dedications, and artistic representations in many countries of Europe and the Near East, and he was widely venerated in the Middle Ages.

In fact he was not French. The *Hieronymianum* states that he came from Antioch, but there is no evidence that this was the case. The belief may have arisen because some relics were brought back to Gaul from that city by Amator, a fourth-century bishop of Auxerre. If the many legends about him have any foundation, he was a very young martyr: he is said to have been only three years old at the time of his death.

The tradition is that Julitta, the child's mother, was forced to flee with him from Iconium, where she was a member of a noble family with great possessions, during the persecutions of Diocletian. She was apprehended in Tarsus and stood her trial with the child at her side. She replied to all questions by saying that she was a Christian and was condemned to be racked and scourged. When attendants tried to separate the child from his mother, he cried and screamed, and the governor, Alexander, took him on his knee in an attempt to pacify him. When Julitta, taken to the rack, called out again, "I am a Christian," Cyricus cried, "I am a Christian, too!" Struggling to release himself, he kicked Alexander, scratched his face, and bit his shoulder. Alexander, in fury, hurled him down the steps and fractured his skull, killing him immediately. Julitta, instead of showing grief, thanked God that her child was safe and had died a martyr. She was tortured and executed.

The story of this spirited child and his equally spirited mother caught the popular imagination. They were said to have been secretly buried by two maids. When Constantine brought peace to the Church, crowds came to the place where they were buried to venerate them.

How much truth there is in this story is not known. The "Acts of Cyricus and Julitta" were proscribed in the decree of Pseudo-Gelasius regarding written records which ought not to be accepted, but they were restored by Pope Gregory XIII (1572-85). Fr Delehaye thinks that Cyricus was the real martyr and that the mother-and-child story was fabricated on the basis of a genuine martyrdom.

There is a story, reproduced in the *Golden Legend* of Jacob de Voragine, that Charlemagne had a dream in which he was saved from a wild boar by a child who promised to protect him if he would give him clothes to cover himself. The bishop of Nevers ingeniously interpreted this as meaning that Charlemagne was being guided to repair the roof of his cathedral, which was dedicated to St Cyr. From this derives the representation of St Cyr as a naked child riding on a wild boar. English dedications to him include Newton St Cyres (Devon). He is the patron saint of Nevers.

P.L., 132, 852-8, and 203, 1303-6; *AA.SS.*, June, 4, 13-31; *C.M.H.*, p. 240; *B.H.L.*, 1, p. 271; *Origines du culte*, pp. 139, 208; *Golden Legend*, 1, pp. 323-4; Ruinart, pp. 503-4; B.G., June, pp. 219-21; *P.B.*, 7, pp. 72-6, from the *Hagiologie Nivernaise* and the *Actes des Martyrs*.

St Tychon of Amathus, *Bishop* (? Fifth Century)

Amathus is the ancient name for Limassol, in Cyprus. Tychon, who was an early bishop, has been greatly venerated in southern Cyprus as the patron saint of vinegrowers. He came of a poor family and is said to have been a baker's son.

One story relating to him is that he owned a small vineyard but had no means to stock it. He took a cutting which other vinegrowers had thrown away as dead and planted it with a prayer that he be granted four favours: the sap should rise again in the cutting; it should produce an abundance of fruit; the fruit should be sweet; and it should ripen early. Ever afterwards the grapes in this vineyard ripened long before all the others, and that is the reason why St Tychon's feast and the blessing of the grape harvest take place on 16 June, long before the other grapes in the district are ready for picking. Part of the ceremonial consists of squeezing the juice of a bunch of partially-ripened grapes into a chalice.

St Tychon's tomb was a famous shrine, and during the ninth century St Joseph the Hymnographer composed an office in his honour. His Life was written by John the Almsgiver, patriarch of Alexandria, who was born at Amathus and died there at the beginning of the sixth century. The German editor of this work suggested that Tychon might be identified with the Greek fertility god Priapus, but it can be accepted that he was a real person and a Christian bishop.

B.H.G., 2, pp. 309-10; *AA.SS.*, June, 4, pp. 79-83; the German edition (ed. H. Usener) is *Der heilige Tychon* (1907). This was reviewed in *Anal.Boll.* 26 (1907), pp. 229-32, and 28 (1909), pp. 119-22. See also *C.M.H.*, p. 240.

St Aurelian, *Bishop* (551)

Aurelian became bishop of Arles in 551 and received the *pallium* from Pope Vigilius together with appointment as papal vicar for Gaul. He founded monasteries for both men and women at Arles and wrote a Rule for them, which was stricter than the Benedictine Rule.

He is chiefly remembered for his intervention in the affair of the Three Chapters. The pope had been pressed by the emperor Justinian to condemn the work of Theodore of Mopsuestia, Theodoret of Cyr, and Ibas of Edessa. In the year of Aurelian's consecration the emperor himself issued thirteen anathemas against these theological writers, chiefly on the advice of Cyril, patriarch of Alexandria (27 June). The pope issued a qualified condemnation at the emperor's request, but Aurelian and other bishops in the West were apprehensive that this reflected on the validity of the Council of Chalcedon. Aurelian acted as the bishops' spokesman, writing to Vigilius in the interests of sound doctrine and the freedom of the Church from imperial interference. The pope, caught between the emperor and the bishops, wrote a letter of reassurance, couched in somewhat vague terms.

Aurelian died in Lyons, where his grave was discovered in 1308 in the church of St Nizier de Lyon.

AA.SS., June, 4, pp. 91-194; Hefele-Leclercq, 3, pp. 1-67; *P.B.*, 7, pp. 102-3, from *La France pontifical*; Duchesne, *Fastes*, 1, pp. 258-9; *N.C.E.*, 1, p. 1079; *D.H.G.E.*, 4, 236. For the Three Chapters, see *N.C.E.*, 14, pp. 144-5.

St Benno of Meissen, *Bishop* (*c.* 1010-1106)

General chronicles and archives record something of the chequered public career of Bishop Benno. He was born at Hildesheim, the second son of Frederick, count of Bultenberg. He was educated in the care of his kinsman Bernward, bishop of Gildesheim, and stayed with the old bishop until he died. After that he became a monk at Hildesheim. The emperor Henry III brought him to Goslar and made him master of the canons attached to the imperial collegiate. In 1066 he was made bishop of Meissen. Thereafter he was caught up in the struggle between the emperor and successive popes over the investiture question for about thirty years. He gave encouragement to the Saxon nobles in their conflict against the emperor Henry IV, who oppressed Saxony with heavy taxes and forced labour. Though he took no active part in the struggle, he was imprisoned for a year. After his release he identified himself with the supporters of Pope Gregory VII against the emperor and was deposed by the German prelates in 1085 at the Synod of Mainz. He spent his exile in missionary work, preaching to the Slavs and the Wends. He regained his see with the help of the antipope Guibert, but Guibert's good offices did not last long. In 1097 Benno finally made his submission to the powerful Pope Urban II (1087-99), and he seems to have spent his last nine years in comparative political peace.

Later writers have given a much more picturesque and sympathetic account of Benno's career. As a bishop he did even more than was expected of him. He watched diligently over his people, enforced discipline on his clergy, made regular visitations, gave liberally to the poor, led an ascetic life, restored the public singing of the divine offices, and introduced chants that he had learned at Hildesheim. He opposed simony because the buying and selling of ecclesiastical preferment was an attempt to exert secular control over the life of the Church. In the struggle between Pope Gregory VII and the emperor Henry IV over the investiture question, he strongly supported the pope—a very unpopular policy in Germany where the issue was fought out with great bitterness and the emperor was powerful. At the Synod of Worms in 1076 the assembled prelates, in response to pressure by the emperor, declared the deposition of the pope. Benno attended, but when he found that opposition was useless, he escaped and went to Rome, where he was warmly received by Pope Gregory.

According to legend, he foresaw that the emperor would press for the deposition of the pope and that the pope would excommunicate the emperor in retaliation. He sent a message to the canons of Meissen telling them that if this happened and the city was besieged by the imperial forces they were to lock the cathedral and throw the keys into the Elbe. This they did, and it is said that after Benno's subsequent restoration to his diocese the keys were miraculously discovered inside a fish which a fisherman had brought to the bishop's kitchen.

Another story about Benno suggests a nice mixture of piety and a sense of humour. Apparently he was walking in the fields when his musical ear was offended by the croaking of frogs, and he told them to be silent. Then he thought of the words of the *Benedicite*: "Ye whales and all that move in the waters, bless ye the Lord," so he addressed the frogs again and told them to praise God in their own way. As Fr Delehaye points out, this story is also told of other saints, including Anthony of Padua (13 June) and Hervé (17 June); but it indicates a popular affection for Benno.

Benno died about 1106 and was canonized in 1523, when he again became the centre of controversy. The canonization drew a virulent political treatise from Martin Luther entitled, "Against the New Idol and the Old Devil About To Be Set Up at Meissen." Fifty years later Meissen had become a Protestant stronghold, so Benno's relics were translated to Munich, of which city he remains the principal patron.

AA.SS., June, 4, pp. 121-86, contains a long life by Jeremy Emsner, written early in the sixteenth century, which claims to be based on earlier sources, but these are not quoted. The most careful investigation of Benno's life is that of O. Langer in the *Mitteilungen des Vereins f. Gesichte Meissens*: see 1, pt. 3 (1884), pp. 70-95; 1, pt. 5 (1886), pp. 1038; 2, pt. 2 (1888), pp. 99-104. See also H. Delehaye, *The Legends of the Saints* (Eng. trans. of *Les légendes hagiographiques*, 1962), pp. 24-5.

Bd Guy of Cortona (? 1245)

Guido Vignotelli was a young man with a small fortune. He was living very simply in Cortona when Francis of Assisi (4 Oct.) visited the town with a companion. Guy, who was noted for his charity, gave them both hospitality, and at the end of a meal he asked Francis to receive him as a disciple. Francis embraced him, saying, "By the grace of God, this young man will be one of us from this day forth, and he will sanctify himself in this town." Then Francis told him that he must first abandon all his possessions, so he went out and did so, and the proceeds were immediately distributed in alms. On the following day Francis formally clothed him with the habit in the parish church in the presence of a large assembly. A small friary named Cella was founded in or near Cortona, and Guy went there for his training. When this was completed he was given permission to live as an anchorite, provided that he joined his brothers at the choir offices. He occupied a separate cell near a bridge. Because he was an educated man, it was thought desirable that he should be ordained, and so he became a priest.

On a subsequent visit to Cortona Francis spoke in high terms of Guy, who was much revered for his sanctity, his gifts of healing, and his eloquence as a preacher. On one occasion Francis sent him to preach in Assisi. Guy died in either 1245 or 1250.

AA.SS., June, 3, pp. 97-102, includes a Life by a contemporary. Wadding, 3, pp. 601-7; *Auréole Séraphique*, 2, pp. 379-81; *F.B.S.*, pp. 467-70.

St Lutgardis (1182-1246)

Lutgardis, or Lutgard, is one of the group of medieval women mystics who had a special affinity with the earthly life of Christ. Though she did not compose music, like Hildegard of Bingen (17 Sept.), or write, like Julian of Norwich (13 May), her spiritual experience bears comparison with theirs. It bears out the contention that mystics are not esoteric personalities with a taste for the fantastic but people who live closer to reality than most Christians are able to do.

Lutgardis was born at Tongeren, between Brussels and Maastricht. She was placed in the Benedictine monastery of St Catherine's for women at the age of twelve, for the simple reason that her father had lost the money intended for her marriage portion in a business speculation. He gave twenty marks to a merchant to increase her dowry, but the merchant returned from a trip to England with only one mark left. Without a dowry, Lutgardis could not find a suitable husband, so she was sent to the monastery. She gave no signs of a religious vocation, liked pretty clothes and amusements as most girls of her age did, and was regarded by the nuns as a boarder rather than a future nun. One day, while she was entertaining a friend, Christ appeared to her, showed her his wounds, and told her to follow him. From that time she renounced all worldly concerns. The nuns, observing her sudden fervour, thought that it was only a passing phase, but she lived close to Christ, speaking to him familiarly in her prayers, and had visions of Our Lady and St John the Evangelist, whom she saw in the form of an eagle. In her meditations on Christ's passion she appeared actually to share his sufferings, and her sympathy went out to all who were in bodily pain or grief.

She stayed at St Catherine's for twelve years and then, seeking a stricter Rule, moved to the Cistercian house at Aywières, south of Liège, on the advice of her confessor. Her own language was a form of Low German, but only French was spoken at Aywières, and she never mastered this strange tongue. Her inability to converse fluently became a form of mortification. She lived in an alien culture with great humility, undertaking long fasts and deprecating her lack of response to the graces she received from God.

In spite of her broken French she became an outstanding spiritual counsellor and healer, with an insight into the scriptures born of long meditation and prayer. In 1235, eleven years before her death, she lost her sight, and she welcomed this affliction as a God-sent means of detaching her from the physical world. When she knew that death was approaching, she felt that she was bidden to approach it in three ways: to praise God for the blessings she had received; to pray unremittingly for the conversion of sinners; and to rely in all things on God alone, waiting patiently for the time when she would go to him for ever. She died on the Saturday after the feast of the Holy Trinity, just as the night office for Sunday was beginning.

During the French Revolution the abbey at Aywières was destroyed, and the nuns were forced to wander from place to place, taking Lutgardis' relics with them. The relics were given for safekeeping to the parish of Ittré in 1804.

AA.SS., June, 4, pp. 187-210, contains the Life of Lutgardis, written by Thomas of Cantimpré, who died in 1270 and was therefore a near-contemporary: Eng. trans. Margot H. King (1987). Unfortunately Thomas' other writings show him to have been a very credulous person with a taste for the supernatural. Modern accounts of Lutgardis, which may be closer to her experience, are given in H. Nimal, *Vies de quelques-unes de nos grandes saintes au pays de Liège* (1898); A. Janssen (1921); Thomas Merton, *What Are These Wounds?* (1950). See also *C.M.H.*, p. 241; *B.H.L.*, 2, pp. 735-6; *P.B.*, 7, pp. 79-86; *Dict.Sp.*, 9, 1201-4.

ST ALBAN (pp. 141-5)
Gold saltire on blue field.

17

St Bessarion (Fourth Century)

The name Bessarion is frequently encountered in records of the Eastern Church and has often been given in baptism. Josef Stalin's father was called Vissarion, a Russian form of the same name. Several Bessarions are listed as saints. The fourth-century Bessarion was an Egyptian anchorite, and he may be the one for whom all the others were named. He was reputed to be a disciple of St Antony, the patriarch of the Desert Fathers (17 Jan.). We are told that having heard the call to perfection he wandered about "like a bird," refusing to stay under a roof, observing silence, and fasting mightily. On one occasion he is said to have gone for forty days without food, standing in prayer in a thicket of brambles.

Legends clustered around his solitary figure. He was reputed to have made salt water fresh, brought rain during a drought, walked on the Nile, and wrestled with demons. All the possessions he owned were a tunic, a cloak, and a book of the Gospels. One day, it is said, he found a dead beggar. He clothed the body in his tunic and buried it. Then he met a naked man, to whom he gave his cloak, so that he had only the Gospels left. A few days later he sold the Gospels to redeem a prisoner who was about to be sent into slavery.

Like many of the other Desert Fathers, Bessarion lived to a great age. His reputation for holiness was so great that he was compared with Moses, Joshua, Elias, and John the Baptist.

Anal.Boll. 65 (1947), pp. 107-38, contains a Life by the anchorite's namesake, Cardinal Bessarion, drawn from the Greek synaxaries. See also *AA.SS.*, June, 4, pp. 240-3; *C.M.H.*, pp. 242-3; *N.C.E.*, 2, p. 366. *D.H.G.E.*, 8, 1180-1, lists five saints named Bessarion, of whom the first two are early Christian martyrs and the fifth is a patriarch of Constantinople. Bessarion the anchorite is no. 3 and may also be no. 4, the Thaumaturge, or wonderworker.

St Hypatius, *Abbot* (? 446)

A deserted monastery in a suburb of Chalcedon, in Bithynia, had acquired a reputation as a haunt of evil spirits. A holy ascetic named Hypatius came across it when he was travelling with two companions, Timotheus and Moschion, in search of a retreat. Disciples joined them, and a great community developed.

The Life of Abbot Hypatius was written by Callinicus, one of his monks, who records that his master was born in Phrygia and educated by his father, a learned scholar who was determined that his son should follow him in a similar career and who beat him when he failed to come up to his expectations. Hypatius ran away from home at the age of eighteen and went to Thrace, where he found occupation as a shepherd. A priest who heard him singing to his flock taught him the Psalter and the chant, and Hypatius joined an ex-soldier named Jonas in the solitary life. They lived very austerely, abstaining from food and drink for long periods. Here Hypatius was discovered by his father, and a reconciliation took place.

Jonas seems to have stayed in Constantinople, which the two visited together, but Hypatius returned to Asia Minor with Timotheus and Moschion and founded his monastery. As abbot he was a powerful champion of orthodoxy. He followed Bishop Eulalius of Chalcedon in denouncing the Nestorian heresy (which maintained that the human and divine persons in Christ were separate and not combined), and he gave shelter and hospitality to Abbot Alexander Akimetes (23 Feb.) and his monks when they were driven out of Constantinople by the patriarch Nestorius. Hypatius challenged Eulalius when there was a proposal to reintroduce the Olympic Games at Chalcedon, and Eulalius made no objection, defeating the proposal by the vehemence of his objection to the restoration of pagan practices.

Commentators have thrown some doubt on this narrative by Callinicus, partly because of his credulity and his liking for the supernatural and partly because there is no record of a Bishop Eulalius at Chalcedon. However, there is a record of a Bishop Eleutherius, who was in office in 451: given the difficulties of translation and transliteration, there seems no good reason to doubt that this is the same person. Hypatius is said to have died about the middle of the fifth century. For centuries he was invoked in the Greek Church as a protector against harmful beasts.

AA.SS., June, 4, pp. 240-82. This includes the long Greek Life by Callinicus on pp. 240-3, but the text is incomplete. The Life has been edited critically, and perhaps over-critically (1895), from another manuscript by the pupils of H. Usener. See also *C.M.H.*, p. 242; *N.C.E.*, 7, p. 304.

St Nectan (? Sixth Century)

Nectan is said to have been the eldest of the twenty-four children of the Welsh king Brychan, whose name survives in the place name of Brechnock. An alternative interpretation is that he was the leader of a group of Cornish and north Devon saints known as "the children of Brychan." Nectan came to England, followed by his many companions, and lived in solitude, meeting them only on the last day of each year. He founded churches in Devon and Cornwall and died at the hands of robbers. William Worcestre tells us that "the venerable man Nectan, while he was making his way through certain woody districts in order to explore the country, was found by these robbers in the place which to this day is called New Town [*i.e.* New Stoke] and there a church is built in his honour." Worcestre says that Nectan was murdered "on the fifteenth day before the kalends of July."

125

A. P. Graves argues that Worcestre was working from a Life of Nectan which has now been lost, because he says that Nectan was slain by "these robbers," and he has made no previous mention of robbers. The existence of a lost Life is confirmed by Nicholas Roscarrock, who records that his friend Mr Camden consulted a Life "written att the end of a booke . . . in the library of Martine Colledge Oxford" (Merton College); but when he asked for a copy of it, Mr Camden went back to the library to discover that it was "imbazzled, being cutt out of the booke and carried away."

Nectan's tomb at Hartland in Devon became the centre of a cult, and according to Worcestre, the town once bore his name. Bishop Lyling of Crediton (1021-46) at first refused to translate his body but later approved the shrine, providing bells and lead for the roof of Hartland church and a sculptured reliquary. Nectan's staff was decorated with gold and silver, and the church was provided with landed property. Benefactors to the church are said to have included King Hardicanute and Earl and Countess Godwin, the parents of King Harold. In the early twelfth century the Augustinian Canons restored the church and the shrine and became its custodians until the Reformation. Nectan was also venerated in Cornwall, where the annual Nectan Fair took place at Launceston on his feast-day. In the neighbourhood of Lostwithiel and Newlyn, chapels were dedicated in his honour under the name of St Nighton, and "St Nighton's Kieve" (*i.e.* vat) is near Tintagel. In Brittany, Lanneizant and Kerneizen are thought to bear his name.

William Worcestre, p. 89; Roscarrock, pp. 93-4 and notes, pp. 157-60. Richard Pearse Chope's *A Book of Hartland*, ed. I. D. Thornley (1940), contains the Life, but the best account in English is in G. H. Doble's *St Nectan, St Keyne, and the Children of Brychan*, Cornish Saints Series, 8, 2d ed. (1939). See also *D.C.B.*, 4, pp. 10-11; *B.G.F.*, 4, pp. 1-2; *Anal.Boll.* 71 (1953), pp. 359-414. Stanton, p. 273; *O.D.S.*, p. 351; A. P. Graves, *Lives of the British and Irish Saints* (1931), pp. 163-5.

St Hervé, *Abbot* (Sixth Century)

The story of Hervé (or Harvey), as set out in a thirteenth-century Life, is as follows: his father was a British minstrel called Hyvarnion, who was driven from his own country by the Saxons and went to Paris to the court of King Childebert of the Franks. He was popular there because of his music, but he had no taste for courtly life, and after two or three years he retired to Brittany. There he married Rivanon, an orphan girl, and they had a child who was born blind. They named him Hervé, which means "bitterness." When the child cried his mother sang to him, and he grew up with a great love of music and poetry.

Hyvarnion died young, and Rivanon put the child in the care of a holy man named Arthian. Later Hervé joined his uncle, who had a small monastic school at Plouvien, working on the farm and doing odd jobs. There is a legend that one day when he was working in the fields, a wolf came and devoured the ass

126

that was drawing the plough. A young boy, Gutharan, who was acting as Hervé's guide, cried out to warn him of the danger he could not see. Hervé prayed for help, and the wolf meekly accepted the harness and finished the ploughing.

When his uncle could no longer manage the monastic school, he entrusted it to Hervé, who had a group of monks and scholars to assist him. After a time he felt inspired to change the school's location. With his companions he went to Léon, where the bishop would have ordained him priest had Hervé's humility not caused him to refuse. From Léon the party went west, and beside the road to Lesneven is the spring of St Hervé, which he is said to have caused to flow when his companions were thirsty. They reached their final destination at Lanhouarneau, where Hervé founded a monastery. The blind abbot remained there for the rest of his life, becoming greatly venerated for his holiness and his powerful preaching. He was much in demand as an exorcist in the neighbourhood.

Hervé is the patron saint of those with eye trouble. He is usually represented with the wolf and with Gutharan, his child guide. He is one of the most popular saints in Brittany and figures largely in Breton ballads and folklore. His cult originally centred on Lanhouarneau, but his relics were distributed widely in 1002 when the cult became general throughout the area. His shrine was said to be preserved at Finisterre until the time of the French Revolution. Solemn oaths were taken over his relics until 1610, when the *parlement* made it obligatory for all legal declarations to be sworn over the Gospels.

Hervé is second only to Yves as the most popular boy's name in Brittany. Canon Doble says that there is no cult of St Hervé in Britain. The name seems to have come to England after the Norman Conquest, and its Anglicized form, Harvey, is now more often encountered as a family name than a Christian name. The Latin form is Huvarno or Hervaeo.

In art Hervé is sometimes represented with a wolf leading him and sometimes, like Antony of Padua (13 June) or Benno of Meissen (16 June), silencing the frogs. The frog story has a special meaning in Brittany. The early Breton Christians called the Druid bards "the frogs," and there is an ancient Breton poem called "The Dialogue of the Frogs and the Christians" containing a debate between the bards and the clergy.

AA.SS., June, 4, pp. 295-306; B.G., June, pp. 239-46; *Dict.Hag.*, p. 333.

St Botulf, *Abbot* (680)

Botulf (Botolph or Botwulf) seems to have been held in great veneration in Anglo-Saxon England; but like many Anglo-Saxon saints, he suffered something of an eclipse after the Norman Conquest. There is a Life written by Folcard, abbot of Thorney, in 1068; but this describes the Saxons as Christians before they invaded Britain and may be unreliable in other respects. Botulf and his brother Adulf were the sons of noble Saxon parents. They were educated in Germany or Belgian Gaul and received the habit there. Adulf is said to have stayed there and to have become bishop of either Utrecht or Maastricht— probably a regionary bishop, since his name does not appear in the records of diocesans.

Botulf returned to England and looked for a place to build a monastery. He found a barren spot in the Fen District surrounded by marshland and inhabited only by wildfowl. Its name was Icanhoh, or Ikanhoe, and it is usually identified with Boston (Botulf's stone) in Lincolnshire but is more probably Iken in Suffolk. Folcard says that it was "just the sort of God-forsaken devil-possessed spot he was in search of."

He was granted land in this dismal place by a king of the southern Angles. The *Anglo-Saxon Chronicle* states that he began to build an abbey in 654 and that he soon gathered a band of disciples. He was said to have suffered some molestation from evil spirits who had formerly haunted the district, but he defeated these, establishing his foundation and living there peacefully until his death in 680. It is recorded of Abbot Ceolfrid of Wearmouth (25 Sept.) that he "once journeyed to the East Angles that he might see the foundation of Abbot Botulf, who fame had proclaimed far and wide as a man of remarkable life and learning, full of the grace of the Holy Spirit." After instruction he returned to Wearmouth "so well grounded that no one could be found better versed than he, either in ecclesiastical or in monastic traditions."

Icanhoh and its church were destroyed in one of the Danish invasions, but the relics of Botulf and his brother Adulf, who had been buried with him, were distributed to the abbeys of Thorney and Ely, and to the king's own oratory, in the time of King Edgar. No less than sixty-four English churches had dedications in honour of St Botulf. Three of those rebuilt by Wren in the city of London are known as St Botolph's.

AA.SS., June, 4, pp. 324-30; *AA.SS.OSB.*, 3, pp. 1-7. *N.L.A.*, 1, pp. 130-3; Stanton, pp. 271-3; *D.N.B.*, 2, p. 908; *D.C.B.*, 1, p. 382; *O.D.S.*, p. 66.

St Moling, *Bishop* (697)

The cult of Moling (Mulling, Mlingus, Daircheall) goes back to an early date and has been widespread all over Ireland. Giraldus Cambrensis mentions him with SS Patrick (17 Mar.) and Columba (9 June) as one of the prophets of Ireland and says that Moling's books were extant in his time in the Irish language. The *Book of Mulling* is a ninth-century Gospel book, probably copied from Moling's own manuscript. It is now kept in a jewelled shrine in Trinity College Library, Dublin.

We can only arrive at a conjectural outline of Moling's life through tradition and place names. He is said to have been born in the district of Kinsellagh in County Wexford of a family related to the kings of Leinster. After spending some years in the monastery of Glendalough, where he received the habit, he founded an abbey at Achad Cainigh, which was named Tech Moling after him. There is a plan of the abbey in the Book of Mulling. He is said to have lived in a hollow tree, to have kept a pet fox (or a pack of foxes), and to have fasted every day in his later life except when he was entertaining guests.

He was credited with great feats of strength and endurance. A well-known story tells how he cut a millstream for the monastery's mill without any assistance, refusing to drink from the stream or to wash in it until the work was completed. The stream was said to be a mile long.

Moling succeeded St Aidan (31 Jan.) as bishop of Ferns and was instrumental in settling a long-standing dispute in the kingdom of Leinster. This related to the so-called cattle tribute, by which the king demanded a heavy tribute of oxen, and had caused many local wars. In 693 King Finacta (Finnachta the Festive) was induced to remit the tribute in the cause of peace.

Bishop Moling resigned his see several years before his death, which occurred in 697. He was interred in his own monastery of Tech Moling, a site now covered by the town of Saint Mullins in Co. Carlow. Wading the millstream against the current became part of the ceremony of a pilgrimage to his shrine. He is reputed to have started the ferry service across the river Barrow, which continues to the present time.

AA.SS., June, 4, pp. 331-4; Plummer, *V.S.H.*, 2, pp. 190-205, and notes in preface, 1, pp. lxxxi-iii; Heist, *V.S.H.*, pp. 353-6; *B.H.L.*, 2. pp. 873-4; H. J. Lawlor, *Chapters on the Book of Mulling* (1897); *Irish Saints*, pp. 252-7; *Anal. Boll.* 46 (1928), p. 110; *O.D.S.*, pp. 242-3.

St Rainerius of Pisa (1117-c.61)

The relics of Rainerius (Raniero), who is Pisa's principal patron saint, lie in his chapel at the end of the south transept in Pisa Cathedral, and scenes from his life appear among the celebrated fourteenth-century frescoes in the ancient Campo Santo. One of the bells in the campanile is named after him. His life was written soon after his death by Canon Benincasa, a personal friend and disciple. Rainerius, who came of a well-to-do family, the Scaccieri, seems to have spent his youth in frivolity and dissipation. Through the influence of a relative he came into contact with a religious from the monastery of San Vito, Alberto Leccapecore, who led him to penitence. His regret for his past behaviour was so overwhelming that he wept continually and refused to eat—to the distress of his parents, who thought he was losing his reason. At the end of three days of this extreme repentance he went blind for a time, like St Paul (29 June; Conversion 25 Jan.; see Acts 9:8-18).

When he had recovered his sight he tried to continue his life as a merchant, and business took him to Palestine. There, as he followed in the footsteps of Christ, his spiritual life developed. One day he had an experience in which his jewelled money pouch, instead of being filled with coins, seemed to contain burning pitch and sulphur, and he extinguished the flames with water. The meaning of the vision was explained to him by an inner voice saying, "The purse is your body: fire, pitch, and sulphur are inordinate desires which water alone can wash away." From that time on he became a barefoot beggar and visited the Holy Sites. We are told that on Mount Tabor he tamed wild hyenas by making the sign of the cross.

When Rainerius returned to Pisa the whole city, led by the archbishop, came out to meet him. He made his home with the canons of Santa Maria. He never joined an Order, but he lived a more or less cloistered life, first in the abbey of St Andrew and later in the monastery of San Vito, where he died. He was probably not ordained priest. His reputation derives from his preaching and from his reputation as a healer. From the use he made of holy water he was called Rainerius "de Acqua." His attribute in art is the symbol of his city, the Leaning Tower of Pisa.

AA.SS., June, 4, pp. 343-84, contains a Life which seems to have been written by a contemporary. Many books about him have been published in Pisa: see especially G. M. Sanminiatelli, *Vita di S Ranieri* (1704 and later editions); G. Sainati, *Vita di S Ranieri Scaccieri* (1890). See also *C.M.H.*, p. 243; *Saints in Italy*, pp. 374-5; *O.D.S.*, pp 412-3.

Bd Peter of Pisa, *Founder* (1355-1435)

Pietro (Peter) Gambacorta was the founder of the Hermits, or Poor Brothers, of St Jerome. When he was a young man, Pisa was a republic, and Peter's father, who bore the same name, was its ruler. At the age of twenty-five the younger Peter left the court secretly, disguised as a penitent, and went to live in the solitude of Monte Bello, subsisting on alms from the nearest village. There he found the means to build an oratory and cells for a dozen companions (popular tradition says that they were highwaymen whom he had converted). He chose St Jerome (30 Sept.) as patron of the new Congregation and drew up his Rule to include some observances derived from Jerome's writings. His monks kept four Lents in the year, fasted on all Mondays, Wednesdays, and Fridays, and continued in prayer every night for two hours after Matins.

In 1393 his father and his brothers were assassinated by a political opponent. All his familial instincts prompted him to leave his retreat and pursue a vendetta, but like his sister Bd Clare Gambacorta (17 Apr.), he found it possible to forgive the murderer. His Congregation, approved by Pope Martin V in 1421, was soon established in other parts of Italy. At one time there were forty-six houses in the provinces of Ancona and Treviso alone. Small groups of hermits and tertiaries became affiliated to them, and in 1668 Pope Clement IX united the Order with that of St Jerome of Fiesole. The combined Order continued in operation until 1933.

AA.SS., June, 4, pp. 436-51; *F.B.S.*, pp. 441-3.

18

St Amandus of Bordeaux, *Bishop* (c. 431)

What we know of the life of Bishop Amandus comes from the letters of Paulinus of Nola (22 June). Paulinus was initially brought to Christianity by his Spanish wife. Amandus instructed him and prepared him for baptism, and this led to a lifelong friendship. Paulinus wrote many letters to Amandus, and it is evident from those which survive that he had the highest admiration for his instructor's holiness and wisdom.

Paulinus says that Amandus had a Christian upbringing, that he was well instructed in the scriptures, and that he lived a chaste and sober life untroubled by worldly considerations. He was ordained by Delphinus, bishop of Bordeaux, who kept him to minister in his own church, where he worked with great zeal. On the death of Delphinus Amandus was elected bishop. He served for some years and was becoming increasingly frail when, according to Gregory of Tours (17 Nov.), he had a vision in which the Lord appeared to him and said, "Go and meet my servant Severinus. Honour him just as the Holy Scriptures say that a friend of the Divine is to be honoured. For he is a better man than you, and more distinguished, because of his merits." Amandus may have thought that the diocese needed a younger man. He went out to meet Severinus (23 Oct.) and treated him with honour, advising the people to elect him as bishop. After Severinus was elected, the old bishop welcomed him to Bordeaux and helped him to assume his pastoral responsibilities; but before long Severinus died, and Amandus took over the burdens of administering the diocese again.

Gregory of Tours quotes Paulinus as writing that Amandus was a bishop "worthy of God." Amandus was at one time credited with having preserved the correspondence of Paulinus, but it now seems that this was not his work.

P.L., 121, 928-82; *M.G.H.*, *Scriptores*, 14, pp. 210-11; *AA.SS.*, June, 4, pp. 484-5; Gregory of Tours, *De gloria confessorum*, Eng. trans. R. Van Dam (1988), pp. 55-6; *C.M.H.*, p. 244; Duchesne, *Fastes*, 2, p. 59; *P.B.*, 7, pp. 139-40; *D.H.G.E.*, 11, 938; *Histoire littéraire*, 2, pp. 173-9.

St Gregory Barbarigo, *Bishop and Cardinal* (1625-97)

Gregory, who came of an ancient and noble Venetian family, was educated in his native city. In 1648, when he was still in his early twenties, he was chosen by the Venetian government to accompany its ambassador, Luigi Contarini, to the Congress of Münster, where the Treaty of Westphalia was signed between Germany, France, and Sweden, ending the Thirty Years' War. At Münster he met the apostolic nuncio, Fabio Chigi, who was much impressed by him. The nuncio became Pope Alexander VII in 1655. It was during his pontificate that Gregory Barbarigo became bishop of Bergamo and later of Padua and that he was created a cardinal.

Gregory was a very rich man. He devoted his wealth to charity and to the promotion of learning. His gifts to charities are known to have amounted to some 800,000 crowns. He founded a college and a seminary for young priests, and both had a high reputation. Thanks to his generosity, the college had its own printing press. He also founded a fine theological library and worked earnestly for the reconciliation of the Byzantine Church with Rome.

C. Bellinati, *San Gregorio Barbarigo* (1960); *Pensiere e massime di S Gregorio Barbarigo* (1962); *N.C.E.*, 2, p. 88; *D.H.G.E.*, 21, 1482-3, lists many unpublished materials. Nine studies for a more extended Life were published in Italian by Professor S. Serena of Venice between 1929 and 1940.

ST ROMUALD
Gold ladder on black field, referring to his spiritual ascent.

19

St Romuald, *Abbot and Founder* (*c.* 950-1027)

Romuald was a member of the family of the Onesti, dukes of Ravenna. Though he grew up to become a worldly young man, he was appalled when he witnessed his father kill a relative in a duel after a quarrel about property. He fled to the Cluniac monastery at San Apollinare-in-Classe, the old Roman port of Ravenna. There his behaviour was so fervent and so austere that he irritated some of the other monks. He anticipated Bernard of Clairvaux (20 Aug.) in wanting to reform Cluniac practice in the direction of greater austerity, but he was too young and too junior in the religious life to carry out major reforms himself. He placed himself under the direction of a hermit named Marinus near Venice and then wandered about northern Italy, setting up hermitages.

Romuald longed for martyrdom and at one point obtained the pope's licence to carry out a mission to Hungary, but as soon as he entered the country he became seriously ill, and the sickness returned every time he tried to proceed. He concluded that it was not God's will that he should continue the mission and returned to Italy, though some of his associates continued to work among the Magyars.

After studying the writings of the Desert Fathers, he came to the conclusion that the monastic life, particularly the life of a solitary, was the way to salvation. Dom David Knowles points out that the eremitic tradition had never completely died out in Italy and was still quite strong in the south, which in Romuald's time was still part of the Byzantine Empire. The Italian terrain, with many "wild but habitable mountain districts," was suitable for the solitary and penitential life. Romuald's achievement was to revive the spiritual legacy of the East in northern Italy and to do so within the framework of the Benedictine Rule. St Benedict (11 July) had esteemed the solitary life, though he rejected it for his own community.

Among Romuald's disciples was Peter Damian (21 Feb.), later bishop and cardinal. Together they virtually refounded a monastery at Fonte Avellana and founded another at Camaldoli in 1012. The latter lay in an isolated valley beyond a mountain near Arezzo and derived its name, originally Campus Maldoli, from that of the lord of the district, Maldolo. Here they built a monastery, and Romuald gave it a new Rule founded on a stricter form of the Benedictine Rule and providing for a new form of monastic life. Silence was "all but perpetual," and fasts were of great severity. The hermits came together for liturgical worship and certain meals but otherwise lived in isolation.

The cells at Camaldoli are built of stone. Each has a small walled garden and its own chapel in which the occupant may celebrate Mass. Romuald himself lived in a small hermitage about two miles from the main settlement, set on the mountainside against a wood of fir trees and with seven clear mountain springs.

After some years at Camaldoli Romuald began to travel again, and he died alone in his cell at the monastery of Val-di-Castro on 19 June 1027. The Camaldolese became a separate Congregation after his death and still exist as an independent branch of the Benedictines. Their observance influenced Bruno (6 Oct.) in the foundation of the Carthusian Order.

The two descriptions most frequently attached to Romuald are "harsh" and "restless," but hermits are seldom sociable characters, and his self-appointed mission drove him from monastery to monastery. He attracted many disciples during his life, and his work had a lasting influence on monasticism. In art he is shown in the white robe of his Order with his finger on his lips, enjoining silence.

P.L., 144, 953-1008, and *AA.SS.*, Feb., 2, pp. 102-45, contain the Life by Peter Damien. *C.M.H.*, p. 246; see also A. Fortuna, *De origine ordinis Camaldulensis* (1592); modern Lives by C. Ciampelli (1927) and A. Pagnani (1967); *Anal. Boll.* 31 (1912), pp. 376-7; *Saints in Italy*, pp. 385-6; David Knowles, *The Monastic Order in England* (2d ed., 1963) pp. 192-6; *O.D.S.*, p. 422.

There is a picture of the saints of the Order by Taddeo Gaddi in the National Gallery in London. Andreas Sacchi's *The Vision of Romuald* is in the Vatican Gallery.

SS Gervase and Protase, *Martyrs* (? Second Century)

Nothing is known of the lives of these two saints, but the story of the discovery of their relics by St Ambrose of Milan (7 Dec.) in the presence of St Paulinus of Nola (22 June) and St Augustine of Hippo (28 Aug.) must rank as one of the most dramatic and best attested of such events in the fourth-century Church.

Ambrose had built his great cathedral in Milan. He describes in a letter to his sister Marcella how he prepared for its dedication and was pressed to make this a great occasion, comparable with the ceremony in which he had dedicated another church containing relics of the apostles. He had a "presentiment" (Augustine calls it a vision) that there were relics of early Christian martyrs buried in the cemetery church of SS Nabor and Felix. Excavations revealed the bodies of two very tall men with their heads severed from their bodies. Inquiries identified them as SS Gervase and Protase, of whom nothing was remembered some two centuries later except their names and the fact that they had been martyred. When their relics were being carried through the streets, a blind butcher named Severus had his sight restored by touching the fringe of the pall which covered them. Ambrose, Paulinus, who was then his secretary, and Augustine, who was in Milan at the time, all mention the case of the butcher, and Paulinus tells us that Severus was still working in Milan when he wrote the Life of Ambrose in 411.

Much controversy has arisen over the two proto-martyrs. Dr J. R. Harris made a bold attempt to claim that they were mythical figures, identifying them with the Dioscuri (Castor and Pollux, sons of Zeus). The trail is confused by a spurious letter purporting to have been written by St Ambrose. This provided life histories for Gervase and Protase, claiming that they were martyred in the time of Nero; but most modern hagiographers regard them as genuine martyrs whose history is not accessible to us but who died in the reign of the emperor Antoninus or even earlier.

Ambrose, Paulinus, and Augustine are three remarkably good witnesses. Ambrose was a man of excellent judgment—he was governor of the provinces of Aemilia and Liguria before he became a bishop—and undoubted integrity. The saint who confronted an emperor was hardly likely to accept dubious relics for his cathedral. He was so convinced of the truth of the martyrdom of Gervase and Protase that he directed that his own remains should lie with theirs in his cathedral when he died. In the ninth century the then bishop of Milan, Angilbert II, had the relics of all three placed in a sarcophagus of porphyry. There they have remained undisturbed, and they are now in a special crypt in Sant'Ambrogio.

According to German accounts, some relics were said to have been taken away from Milan by the emperor Frederick Barbarossa, but the supposed relics held in some German churches and at Soissons are now thought to be spurious.

In the pictures of the Assumption of the Blessed Virgin by Borgognone in the Brera in Milan, Gervase and Protase appear as attendant saints. The church of San Trovaso in Venice is dedicated in their honour, the title being an elision of their names in the Venetian dialect.

AA.SS., June, 4, pp. 680-704, contains the relevant passages from the works of Paulinus and Augustine, as well as the pseudo-Ambrosian letter. See also *C.M.H.*, pp. 245; *B.H.L.*, 1, pp. 524-5; Delehaye's *Origines du culte* contains many scattered references to the two saints. J. R. Harris, in *The Dioscuri in the Christian Legend* (1903), ch. 3, pp. 42-51, advances the claim that Gervase and Protase are classical figures, "displacements" of ancient Greek gods, but cf. *Anal.Boll.* 23 (1904), pp. 427-32, and 49 (1931), pp. 30-5; *O.D.S.*, pp 202-3.

St Deodatus of Nevers, *Bishop* (? 679)

Deodatus (Dié, Didier, or Dieudonné) became bishop of Nevers about 655. In 657 he attended the Synod of Sens together with Eligius of Noyon (1 Dec.), Audoenus of Rouen (24 Aug.), and other leading bishops. After some three years in office he retired to the Forest of Hagenau in the Vosges mountains as a solitary; but apparently he incurred some hostility from the local people, so he withdrew to an island near Strasbourg where a few other solitaries were leading an eremitical life. He became their leader and, with the help of King Childeric II, who gave him land, built the abbey of SS Peter and Paul there.

The growing community was the nucleus from which the abbey of Ebersheim

135

developed; but Deodatus still needed solitude, so he withdrew and tried to find a place where he could live alone with God without being persecuted. This proved difficult. Eventually he returned to the Vosges and settled there in what is now called the Val Saint-Didier. Disciples gathered round him again, and for them he may have founded the monastery that was called Jointures because it stood at the confluence of two rivers, the Rothbach and the Meurthe. This place is now known as Saint-Dié.

Not far away another retired bishop, Hidulf of Trier (11 July), was ruling another community of hermits. The two became close friends, though they limited their visits to each other to one a year, when they would spend the night in prayer and praising God. It was to Hidulf that Deodatus commended his monastery before his death. Hidulf was with him when he died and conducted his funeral.

The town of Saint-Dié grew up around the abbey of SS Peter and Paul. The bishopric was suppressed in 1801 but re-established in 1817. The abbey church was destroyed in 1944, but the remaining relics were salvaged, placed in a casket, and solemnly re-interred in 1950.

The Life written in the tenth century and printed in *AA.SS.*, June, 4, pp. 725-37, is of limited historical value, and the part of Deodatus in the founding of Jointures is now thought to be doubtful. See also *M.G.H.*, *Scriptores*, 25, pp. 276-7; Duchesne, *Fastes*, 2, p. 484; *P.B.*, 7, pp. 150-5, drawn from the *Hagiologie Nivernaise* and the *Saints d'Alsace*; *Anal.Boll.* 6 (1887), pp. 151-60, and 11 (1892), pp. 75-99; *Bibl.SS.*, 4, 572.

St Boniface of Querfurt, *Bishop and Martyr* (? 974-1009)

This saint was baptized Bruno but took the name of Boniface in religion. Because he was known by both names, some commentators, including Cardinal Baronius in the Roman Martyrology, have regarded Bruno of Querfurt and Boniface of Querfurt as two different people; but his history is sufficiently distinctive to make it clear that they are the same.

Querfurt lies to the west of Leipzig. In Bruno's day it was within the Holy Roman Empire, a border fortress against the unconverted tribes who roamed outside and preyed on travellers. Bruno came of a noble Saxon family in that city. After being educated at Magdeburg he went to the court of the emperor Otto III, who regarded him with much confidence and affection and made him a court chaplain. He accompanied the emperor on a journey to Italy in 998, and there he came under the influence of St Romuald (19 June, above). He received the monastic habit and the name of Boniface and set himself to write a Life of St Adalbert of Prague (23 Apr.), who had been martyred while preaching to the Prussian tribes. He had an increasing conviction that he was called to continue St Adalbert's work. The emperor approved his scheme for a mission, and two monks were sent in advance to Poland to learn Slavonic. The two, Benedict and John, were murdered with three others by robbers in November

1003 near Gniezno before he could join them. These were the Five Martyred Brothers, whose biography Boniface subsequently wrote.

Bearing Pope Silvester II's authorization for his expedition, Boniface set out in the depth of a winter so severe that his boots sometimes froze to his stirrups. At Merseberg he was consecrated as a missionary bishop by the archbishop of Magdeburg—or possibly as a missionary archbishop, since the pope had given him the *pallium*. It seems that he may have been intended to be a metropolitan for eastern Poland.

Owing to political difficulties he had to work among the Magyars of the lower Danube for a time, and he went on to Kiev where he preached under the protection of the prince, Vladimir (15 July), himself a Christian though most of his people were not. From Kiev, he moved into the territories of another Christian prince, Boleslaus the Brave, and tried to Christianize the people on the borders of his lands with those of the Prussian tribes. He encountered violent opposition but disregarded all warnings in his attempt to convert the tribes, and he was killed with eighteen companions on 14 March 1009. He was only thirty-five years old.

Boniface was a young man of great courage and great faith. He had plans for evangelizing as far north as Sweden and had already sent two monks to Sweden when he died. His body was purchased by Boleslaus, who returned it to Poland, and the Prussians subsequently honoured his memory by giving his original name to the town of Braunsberg, on the reputed site of his martyrdom.

AA.SS., June, 4, pp. 758-60, and appendix, pp. 35-42, make it clear that Bruno and Boniface are the same person. H. G. Voigt's *Bruno von Querfurt* . . . (1907) includes a late document apparently based on an earlier one. See also Voigt's *Bruno als Missioner des Ostens* (1909); F. Dvornik, *The Making of Central and Eastern Europe* (1940), pp. 196-204.

Bd Odo of Cambrai, *Bishop* (1113)

Of the distinguished scholars who taught in the great French schools of the eleventh century, Odo, later bishop of Cambrai, was among the most learned and influential. He came from Orleans and taught for several years at Toul before the canons of Tournai appointed him *scholasticus*—in effect director—of their cathedral school. He taught philosophy, rhetoric, dialectics, and astronomy, and he was often to be seen on a clear night sitting on the cathedral steps and demonstrating to his pupils the position and movements of the stars and planets. He had a skill in teaching and disputation that drew students to him from as far away as Normandy, Saxony, and Italy.

Most of Odo's teaching was in the classical Graeco-Roman tradition. His masters were Plato and Aristotle, and he had little time to spare for theology or patristic texts. He had been at Tournai for five years when, in preparing for a lecture on the great Roman philosopher Boethius, he had to look up a quotation from St Augustine on the doctrine of free will. A scholar had brought him a work of St Augustine, which he had bought and then thrown aside some two months before. When he looked at it again, it caught his attention, and he studied it all that day and the next. He came to the passage where St Augustine likens the sinful soul, labouring without profit or pleasure, to a slave emptying the cesspits of a palace. Philosophy suddenly seemed stale and unsatisfying, and he went to church, weeping for his own spiritual blindness.

He had experienced a sudden and complete conversion. He restricted his teaching time, gave away all his money to the poor, spent long hours in church, and undertook fasts and penances that soon reduced him to a walking skeleton. The bishop of Tournai, anxious to keep him in the city, gave him the disused abbey of St Martin, and the citizens of the town were so impressed that they offered to pay for his keep and that of his former pupils who joined him. They were led to the abbey by the bishop and canons in procession.

After three years, on the advice of Bishop Aimeric of Anchin, the new community adopted the Benedictine Rule. They lived very simply. It is said that when Odo was offered a silver cross and costly altar vessels for his church he refused them. He set all his monks to work—some on the farm and some in the *scriptorium*, where they copied sacred manuscripts and created the nucleus of the great library of Saint Martin at Tournai. The community grew into a double monastery of about sixty monks and sixty nuns.

Odo had been abbot of St Martin's for thirteen years when, in 1105, he was chosen bishop of Cambrai. It was a difficult appointment. His predecessor, Gaucher, or Gautier, had been deposed and excommunicated by Pope Paschal II for simony and for having accepted investiture from the emperor Henry IV; but a strong party at Cambrai supported Gaucher, and it was not until a year later, when Henry IV died, that Odo was able even to enter his see. Relations with Henry V were no better. Within a short time Odo was driven from office because he refused to accept his symbols of office from the emperor's hands. He took refuge with his old friend Aimeric of Anchin and occupied the last seven years of his life in writing books. He seems to have returned to Cambrai for a short period toward the end, but he died and was buried at Anchin.

Among his many writings are an exposition of the Canon of the Mass, a treatise on original sin, another on the coming of the Messiah, a harmony of the Gospels, and a Psalter in four languages.

AA.SS., June, 4, pp. 761-6; *M.G.H.*, *Scriptores*, 14, pp. 210-11, and 15, pp. 942-5, contain short contemporary accounts of Odo's career by Amand de Castello, prior of Anchin, and (by attribution) Herman of Tournai; cf. 14, pp. 274-318. See also *P.B.*, 7, pp. 156-62, from the *Vie des saints de Cambrai et d'Arras*; B.G., June, pp. 260-7.

St Juliana Falconieri, *Foundress* (1270-1341)

Juliana was the second member of the Falconieri family to be commemorated in the Order of the Servites of Mary: her uncle, Alexis Falconieri (17 Feb.), was one of the Seven Founders of the movement. Juliana's parents, who were very wealthy, had built the magnificent church of the Annunciation in Florence, and her father was elderly when she was born, the only child of the marriage. After his death, Alexis Falconieri shared the upbringing of the child with her mother. She grew up with a determination to consecrate her life to God, and at the age of fifteen, after instruction by her uncle, she was invested with the Servite habit by Philip Benizi (23 Aug.). A year later she became a tertiary in the Order. The ritual employed on this occasion appears to have been identical with that used in the profession of a Servite Brother. Juliana continued to live according to the Servite Rule in her own home. Her mother, who had once urged the girl to prepare for marriage, was so impressed by the holiness of her life that she finally placed herself under her daughter's direction.

While living at home Juliana collected a group of the ladies of Florence and installed them in the Palazzo Grifoni, near the church of the Annunciation. When her mother died, she was thirty-four years of age. She went to the Palazzo Grifoni and asked to be admitted as a servant, but the others soon insisted that she should be their abbess. There was a sense in which they were all servants. They were commonly called *mantellate* by the people of Florence because their habits had short sleeves, giving the appearance of a mantle and leaving their hands free for work. This term was later applied to Servite tertiaries in general. In time the group at the Palazzo Grifoni were recognized as full Servite nuns. Juliana drew up a Rule which was formally recognized for her successors by Pope Martin V over a hundred years later. Just as Philip Benizi is regarded as the founder of the Servite Order because he drew up their Constitution, so Juliana is regarded as the foundress by all the women religious of the Order, though she was not the first to be admitted.

Her contemporaries describe her as a very conscientious and hardworking superior, austere but full of charity and eager to give whatever help she could to others. Her many penances and fasts seriously impaired her health, but she lived to the age of seventy-one. She was buried below the altar in the church of the Annunciation in Florence. Some convent churches in England are dedicated to her.

AA.SS., June, 4, pp. 762-3; Lives by M. Conrayville (1915) and A. M. Rossi (1954); *C.M.H.*, p. 245; *B.H.L.*, 1, p. 670; *Bibl. SS.*, 6, 1184-8; *O.D.S.*, p. 274.

Bd Thomas Woodhouse, *Martyr* (1573)

Queen Mary Tudor reigned for only five years, from 1553 to 1588. During that time she reversed the Protestant policies of Henry VIII and Edward VI in an attempt to bring England into conformity with Rome. Links with the papacy were re-established, and Protestant bishops were replaced with Catholic bishops. Archbishop Cranmer and Bishops Latimer and Ridley went to the stake. Any young man who received his theological training during those five years must have been deeply committed to the re-establishment of Catholicism and to the belief that England's breach with Rome was only a temporary aberration.

Thomas Woodhouse had been ordained toward the end of Mary's reign. He became rector of a small parish in Lincolnshire, but he had been there less than a year when the queen died. Under her successor, Elizabeth I, contact with the papacy was once more severed, and the Acts of Supremacy and Uniformity of Henry VIII were reinstated. Thomas lost his benefice. He taught for a time in Wales but was arrested in 1561 while saying Mass and committed to the Fleet prison. He remained there for twelve years.

Tyrrell, the warden of the Fleet, was in sympathy with the Catholics and gave them a considerable amount of freedom. During the early part of his imprisonment Thomas was allowed to say his office daily, to celebrate Mass in his cell, and even to try to make converts by discussions with his fellow-prisoners. He took to writing messages for passers-by, which he wrapped round stones and threw out of the window. When plague broke out in London in 1563, he and the other Catholics in the prison were removed to Tyrrell's country house for safety.

About the year 1572, after negotiations with the provincial in Paris, Thomas was admitted by letter to the Society of Jesus. The papal Bull of 1570, which excommunicated and deposed Queen Elizabeth, must have been much discussed in the confines of the prison. The Act of Parliament (13 Eliz. c.1) which declared that it was high treason to say that she was not, or ought not to be, queen was probably less discussed, for most of Thomas' companions were recusants. In the first fervour of his reception the newly-admitted Jesuit wrote a letter to Lord Burleigh urging him to persuade the queen to submit to the pope. To Burleigh this was in itself evidence of high treason. He saw Thomas Woodhouse personally and had him examined by the council, who were amazed at his outspoken defence of the papal position and classed him as a dangerous fanatic. At his trial in the Guildhall he challenged the authority of the judges and denied the right of a secular court to try a priest for his religious views. After so long in prison and with little contact with the outside world, he may not have fully understood the political context in which he was being judged; but he defended his beliefs with courage. He was condemned, and he died at Tyburn, still demanding that the queen should submit to the pope.

L.E.M., 2, pp. 186-203; *D.N.B.*, 21, p. 403; J. H. Pollen, *English Catholics in the Reign of Elizabeth* (1920), p. 72n.

20

ST ALBAN, *Martyr* (Early Third Century)

Alban is the proto-martyr of Britain. His death is the earliest recorded case of execution on a charge of being a Christian in this country, and much has been written about him over the centuries, though the ascertainable facts that have come down to us are limited.

There is an account by the Welsh abbot Gildas (29 Jan.), written about 540, and a fuller one from the Venerable Bede (25 May), written about 731. According to Bede, Alban suffered in the persecutions of Diocletian in the year 301. He was a pagan, but he gave shelter to a Christian who was being hunted by the imperial forces. He was so much impressed by this man's "unbroken activity of prayer and vigil" that he became converted and received instruction from him. Then "it came to the ears of the evil ruler that Christ's holy confessor, whose time for martyrdom had not yet come, lay hidden in Alban's house. Accordingly he gave orders to his soldiers to make a thorough search, and when they arrived at the martyr's house, holy Alban, wearing the priest's long cloak, at once surrendered himself in the place of his guest and teacher, and was led bound before the judge."

When it was discovered that he was not the priest, the magistrate was angry and demanded to know his name. He replied, "My name is Alban, and I worship and adore the living God, who created all things." He would not talk about his family. He confessed himself a Christian and refused to offer sacrifice to the Roman gods. The magistrate had him flogged, hoping that this would lead him to recant. When he did not, he was sentenced to be immediately beheaded.

Led out to execution, "the saint came to a river which flowed swiftly between the wall of the town and the arena where he was to die." A huge crowd had collected. We are told that "so many people had come out from the city that the judge was left unattended." The river dried up in its course so that the saint could cross. The executioner was so moved by this miracle that he refused to carry out the execution and "changed from a persecutor to a companion in the true Faith." Then Alban, accompanied by the crowd, ascended a gently-sloping hill covered with many kinds of flowers, about five hundred paces beyond the river, where he asked God to give him water, and a spring bubbled up at his feet: "a sign to all present that it was at the martyr's prayer that the river also had dried up in its course. For it was not likely that the martyr who had dried up the waters of the river should lack water on a hill-top

141

unless he so willed it. But the river, having performed its due service, gave proof of its obedience, and returned to its natural course."

There on the hilltop Alban and the soldier who had refused to carry out his execution were both beheaded. The executioner's eyes dropped out as Alban's head fell; and the judge, "astonished by these many strange miracles," called a halt to the persecution. Bede is precise about the month and the place: "St Alban suffered on the twenty-second day of June near the city of Verulamium, which the English now call Verlamcestir or Vaeclingacaestir."

Gildas and Bede wrote after the Roman power in Britain had crumbled under the attacks of the Angles and Saxons, and centuries after Alban. Gildas probably wrote his account while living as a solitary in the Bristol Channel, and Bede was a monk of Jarrow in Northumbria, so neither of them would have had any local knowledge of an area some twenty-five miles north of London. The similarity between the two accounts has long exercised scholars and led to the conclusion that both were based on an earlier manuscript, now lost. The discovery of some earlier records, identified and published by Professor Meyer of Göttingen in 1904, has settled some questions but raised others. These records are illiterate and unsatisfactory copies made in the eighth and ninth centuries from an original dating from about the year 500 and written in Gaul. They are now preserved in Turin and Paris.

Discussion has centred on four main issues: the date of the martyrdom, the place, the identity of Alban, and the identity of the priest whose place he took. Gildas and Bede both date the event to the persecutions of Diocletian. Bede tells us that the persecutions of Diocletian in the East and Heraclitus in the West were "carried out without any respite for ten years, with the burning of churches, the outlawing of innocent people, and the slaughter of martyrs," and that this was the tenth period of persecution since the time of Nero. We now know that Bede was mistaken: the period of persecution under Diocletian was much shorter—from 303 to 305—and it was largely confined to his eastern empire. In the western empire, Maximian ruled Italy and North Africa, and Constantius ruled Spain, Gaul, and Britain. Constantius had a Christian wife, Helena, and Constantine was their son. There was no persecution in Britain during this period. Eusebius of Caesarea, who died in 340, writes in his *Ecclesiastical History* that there were no persecutions at all under Constantius: "He stood apart from the war against us, and protected the pious who were under him from harm and insult, and did not pull down the houses of the churches or devise any other evil against us."

This is confirmed by other contemporaries, but there were earlier persecutions of Christians in Britain in the time of Decius (*c.* 254) and Septimus Severus (*c.* 209). The Turin manuscript mentions Severus and says that Alban was questioned and condemned by "Caesar." Severus was in Britain from the summer of 208 until his death in 211. His wife and his two sons, Antoninus Augustus and Geta Caesar, accompanied him. During the summer of 209 Severus and

Antoninus went north to campaign against the Caledonians, leaving Geta Caesar in charge of the civilian administration in the south. Alban's judge is called "Caesar." Geta is reported to have ordered the cessation of the persecution on the grounds that it only increased the fervour of the Christians, which accords with Bede's account of the judge's reaction after Alban's execution. Some scholars find this an acceptable solution to the problem, dating the martyrdom precisely to the year 209; but Charles Thomas, writing in 1981, thinks it has "failed to overcome scholastic doubts." His view is that Wilhelm Levison, who published an important paper on the Turin manuscript, was right in thinking that the problem was insoluble but that "the middle of the third century is still the least improbable period." More recent excavations, still in progress, have supported this view, which means that the martyrdom would have occurred in the persecutions of Decius or Valerian I.

Where did the martyrdom take place? It has been argued that it occurred in what Bede calls "the City of Legions," possibly Caerleon on Usk, where he tells us that two other Christians, Aaron and Julian, were martyred in the same persecution; but the topography given in the Turin manuscript and copied by Bede is so precise that it can apply only to Verulamium: the remains of the city, the river Ver, the site of the amphitheatre, and the hill on which St Albans Abbey now stands are clearly identifiable. There is only one discrepancy: the Ver is more of a stream than a river and was always easily forded, so there would have been no need for a miraculous crossing—particularly in June, which tends to be a dry month.

Alban must have been a prominent citizen of Verulamium, perhaps of Romano-British extraction. He had a house large enough to conceal his Christian visitor for some time. He was a Roman citizen: he was accorded the dignity of a trial before Caesar, and he was beheaded rather than being thrown to the wild beasts in the arena. The whole city turned out to watch the execution, leaving Caesar unattended—and executions were not rare events in Roman Britain. A more modern belief has grown up that he was a Roman soldier, perhaps an officer in the Roman army; but in that case, he would have been court-martialled and executed within the walls of the city, not publicly tried and executed. Although he is often represented as carrying arms, any Romano-British citizen of some standing would have done so. A French source suggests that he was a young Roman nobleman who may have fled from persecutions on the Continent, thinking that Britain was farther from Rome and therefore safer. It has also been suggested that since his name is an unusual one for a Romano-British citizen, he may have come from the Albanus region of Italy, south-east of Rome.

In some accounts the name of the confessor whom Alban tried to save and who was subsequently captured and martyred is given as Amphibalus. John Morris, writing in 1968, provides an interesting if involved derivation. Antoninus, the son with whom the emperor Severus went campaigning in

Scotland, had done service with the Rhine army and ostentatiously wore a kind of greatcoat called a *caracalla*, which was popular with the officers of that army. This led to him being nicknamed "Caracalla." It seems that an early manuscript may have borne a marginal emendation "et Caracalla," meaning that Antoninus accompanied his father on the Scottish campaign. Much later, a copyist who knew that a *caracalla* was a greatcoat but not that it was the nickname of an emperor's son, attached it to the name of Alban, two lines below. In later versions, when the term *caracalla* was no longer in current use, copyists replaced it with the later term *amphibalon*. Thus instead of Severus and his attendant son, manuscripts referred to Alban and his attendant confessor. In the twelfth century Abbot Simon of St Albans Abbey excavated bones (probably those of a Saxon invader) at Redbourn, four miles away, and declared them to be those of St Amphibalus. The lively but often inaccurate chronicler Geoffrey of Monmouth (*c.* 1136) recorded this event, and so "St Overcoat" came into existence. This ingenious line of reasoning, if accepted, would incidentally support the dating of the martyrdom to the reign of Severus.

The relics were venerated until the dissolution of the monasteries in Henry VIII's reign, when they were scattered; but the present shrine of St Amphibalus in St Albans Abbey commemorates Alban's Christian teacher, whatever his real name.

The abbey and the town of Saint Albans developed on the site of Alban's execution. His tomb is thought to have been on the hill on which the abbey now stands. The hill was a Roman cemetery until the fourth century. In 1257 the monks discovered a mausoleum under the eastern end of the abbey church and concluded that it was the tomb of St Alban himself. The early martyrs' tombs were often used as the sites of churches, and the church then bore a dedication for the martyr rather than for a biblical saint.

The story of Alban survived the collapse of the Roman Empire: this was probably due to Constantius of Lyons, whose *Vita S. Germani*, written about 480, mentions the visit of St Germanus of Auxerre (3 Aug.) to Saint Albans in 429. Germanus, who had come with a fellow-bishop to assist in putting down the Pelagian heresy, had a very rough crossing on his way to England. Constantius attributes the calm seas of their return journey to the intercession of Alban the Martyr. By the time of Bede, Alban's story was well known beyond the shores of Britain as that of the first British martyr, and a particularly illustrious one. Bede notes that Venantius Fortunatus (14 Dec.), in Poitiers, had celebrated it in his poem *In Praise of Virgins*: "In fertile Britain's land / Was noble Alban born."

There were many church dedications to Alban in Gaul and in the Rhineland. Odensee, in Denmark, once claimed his relics. Nine English churches had dedications to him. There are several paintings of his execution in the *St Albans Psalter* (*c.* 1119-23), and he appears in a number of medieval windows in English churches. In St Albans Abbey he was carved in stone in classical robes on the pedestal to his shrine, which dates from 1308. This was lost on 5 December 1549, when the abbey was dissolved and the buildings destroyed, but most of it was discovered among rubble during rebuilding in 1872. The shrine pedestal was restored and returned to the abbey in 1991-3.

The idea that Alban was a soldier seems to have originated in stained-glass windows of the nineteenth century, when several new churches were dedicated to him. After World War I he was represented as a young soldier in St Albans Abbey by Sir Ninian Comper as a memorial to those who died in the war, and there are similar representations in war memorial windows in Exeter and Coventry; but though we are fairly certain that he was not a soldier, he would have done military service according to Roman law, so this is not inappropriate.

Alban's feast was traditionally on the anniversary of his death but has been moved in the Roman Calendar to give him greater prominence.

Gildas, *De excidio Brittaniae*, chs. 10-11; Bede, *H.E.*, 1, 7 and 17-21; Matthew Paris, *Gesta Abbatum S Albani*, 1, 12-18 , 94, and *Chronica Majora*, 2, 306-8; Geoffrey of Monmouth, *History of the Kings of Britain*, 5, 5. *AA.SS.*, June, 5, pp. 146-70, commemorates Alban, Amphibalus, and two thousand companions for whom there is no historical evidence. T. D. Hardy, *Catalogue of Materials, History of Great Britain and Ireland* (R.S., 26), 1, pp. 3-30, lists and comments on eighty-six manuscript Lives of Alban. The full account of the finding of the Turin and Paris documents is in the *Abhandlungen der Königlichen Gesellschaft der Wissenschaften zu Göttingen*, Phil. Hist. Klasse, N. F. VIII, 1 (1904), pp. 3-81. A more accessible version is that of W. Levison, "St Alban and St Albans," *Antiquity* 15 (1941), pp. 337-59. R. M. Wilson in *The Lost Literature of Modern England* (1952), pp. 92-3, considers the possibility of a lost (and even earlier) Life of St Alban "written in the English or British language." John Morris, "The Date of Saint Alban," *Hertfordshire Archaeology* 1 (1968), pp. 1-7, argues for the *Caracalla* theory and for 209 as the date of the martyrdom; Charles Thomas, *Christianity in Roman Britain* (1981), pp. 48-50, argues for a later date. O. Pächt, C. R. Dodwell, and F. Wormald (eds.), *The St Albans Psalter* (1960).

St Silverius, *Pope and Martyr* (537)

One of the major theological controversies in the sixth-century Church was the debate with the Monophysites, who held that the human element in the person of Christ was totally subordinate to the divine. Pope Hormisdas (6 Aug.), whose pontificate lasted from 514 to 523, is credited with having secured a rejection of this view by the Formula of Hormisdas, accepted at Constantinople in 519. The Monophysites were far from reconciled, and in the pontificate of Hormisdas' son, Silverius, the conflict reflected the growing schism between the papacy and the imperial court at Constantinople.

Agapitus I (22 Apr.) was pope for only eleven months. He was at Constantinople when he died in 536. At this time the emperor Justinian and his general Belisarius were planning to recover Italy from the Goths. The empress Theodora, who was herself a Monophysite, wanted a Byzantine candidate of Monophysite beliefs to replace Pope Agapitus II; but the Ostrogothic king of Italy, Theodehad, proposed Silverius, and though the clergy of Rome were at first dubious (for he was only a subdeacon) they agreed to accept him in order to block Theodora's nominee. It was his misfortune to be propelled into office at a time of great political instability and Byzantine intrigue.

Justinian was very much influenced by his wife, Theodora, a former dancing-girl of great beauty and considerable force of character. Theodora's closest ally and confidante was Antonina, wife of General Belisarius. Ravenna was the first Italian stronghold captured by Belisarius, and in the mosaics of San Vitale the figure next to that of the bejewelled and powerful empress is traditionally said to be that of Antonina. Theodora wrote to Silverius demanding that he recognize the Monophysites Anthimus of Constantinople and Severus of Antioch as patriarchs. He refused and is said to have commented that he knew he was signing his own death-warrant. Theodora found her opportunity to depose him when suburban Rome was devastated by an Ostrogothic general named Vitiges, and pope and senate were forced to open the gates to Belisarius in order to save the city.

Belisarius sent for Silverius. According to the *Liber Pontificalis*, when the pope arrived he found the general sitting at his wife's feet. Antonina accused Silverius of betraying the city to the Goths. His *pallium* was ripped off, and he was forced to wear a plain monk's habit instead of his papal robes. Attempts were made to arraign him for conspiracy with the Goths on the strength of forged letters. When that attempt failed, he was kidnapped and taken to Patara in Asia Minor. In his place Belisarius proclaimed a deacon named Vigilius as pope.

It appears that Justinian had been kept in ignorance of events in Rome. The bishop of Patara went to inform him that Silverius was being held prisoner in his diocese and added pointedly that there were many kings in the world but only one pope. Justinian gave orders that Silverius should be returned to Italy. Accounts differ as to whether the emperor intended him to be released or to stand trial.

When Silverius landed in Italy he was taken prisoner. A charge of treason was trumped up against him, and he was taken under escort to the island of Palmarola in the Tyrrhenian sea, off Naples. There, or on the neighbouring island of Ponza, he died as a result of ill treatment. One account was that he starved to death; another that he was murdered at the instigation of Antonina by one of her servants.

This was a very low point in the history of the papacy. It is not clear how the appointment of Vigilius to the papal see came to be regularized. He was pope for twenty-eight years, from 537 to 555; but he did not respond further to the intrigues of the empress. Belatedly, the emperor supported the pope, and he was able to refuse to appoint Monophysite bishops.

In the eighteenth century a commission set up by Pope Benedict XIV proposed to remove the feast of Silverius from the general Roman Calendar, but this proposal was not carried out. The stand he made against the Monophysite doctrine in his brief and tragic pontificate kept the Church of Rome on the path of orthodoxy, though Monophysitism survives in the Coptic Church and some of the Eastern Churches.

Silverius is shown in art carrying a model of a church to commemorate his stand against imperial intervention in ecclesiastical affairs.

AA.SS., June, 5, pp. 11-6; *P.L.*, 66, 79-87; Jaffé, 1, pp. 115-6; *Lib. Pont.*, 1, pp. 290-5. In his introduction to the *Lib.Pont.* (pp. xxxvi-xxxviii), Duchesne notes a curious difference of tone between the earlier and later parts of this notice. He concludes that the entry was compiled by two different writers, one hostile to Silverius, and the other friendly to him. See also *D.C.B.*, 4, pp. 670-6; *D.T.C.* (*s.v.* "Silvère"), 14, pt. 2, 2065-7; *O.D.P.*, pp. 59-60.

St Adalbert of Magdeburg, *Bishop* (981)

Many attempts were made from the eastern boundaries of the Holy Roman Empire to carry out missions to the tribes who lived beyond its borders and harassed the frontier cities. In 997 Adalbert of Prague (23 Apr.) was martyred by the Prussians, and in 1009 Boniface of Querfurt (19 June, above) was to suffer the same fate. Adalbert of Magdeburg was called in 961 to lead a mission to the Slavs.

He was a monk of Saint-Maximin at Trier. The call came from Princess Olga of Russia (11 July), a Scandinavian who had married Igor, grand duke of Kiev. She had been converted to Christianity in Constantinople at the age of seventy, and she asked the emperor Otto the Great to send missionaries to convert her subjects. Otto was married to the English princess Edith, granddaughter of Alfred the Great and sister of King Athelstan. For both political and religious reasons he wanted to evangelize the Slavs, the Prussians, and the Magyars at his borders, and the mission was set up. Olga's protection should have ensured their safety, but by the time Adalbert and his companions arrived she had been forced to hand over power to her son Svyatoslav, who was hostile to the mission. Some of the missionaries were massacred, but Adalbert managed to escape and return to his own country. He remained at the imperial court at Mainz for four years and was then made abbot of Weissenberg, where he did much to foster learning. He continued the chronicle of Reginald von Prüm, which covers the years between 907 and 967, and later handed this task on to one of his monks.

By this time Magdeburg had become an important city, strongly fortified to deter the neighbouring Slavs. Otto, from both political and religious motives, wished it to become the centre of an archdiocese. After much opposition from the archbishop of Mainz and others the request received papal sanction, and Adalbert was nominated as the first archbishop of Magdeburg, with general jurisdiction over the Slavs. He laboured hard to achieve the conversion of the Wends, who were on the opposite bank of the river Elbe, and was strict in enforcing discipline in religious houses.

When Otto died in 973 he was buried in Adalbert's church, which had now

147

become Magdeburg Cathedral, beside his English empress. Adalbert continued as archbishop for a further eight years and died while making a visitation in the diocese of Merseburg.

AA.SS., June, 5, pp. 1028-33; *M.G.H.*, *Scriptores*, 1, pp. 613-29, and 14, pp. 381-6, contain passages from Thietmar's *Chronicle* and the *Gesta Episcoporum Magdeburgensium* relating to Adalbert; *B.H.L.*, 1, p. 7. See also F. Dvornik, *The Making of Central and Eastern Europe* (1949), pp. 60 and 68-70.

Bd Osanna of Mantua (1449-1505)

Osanna was the daughter of a nobleman, Nicholas Andreasi, and his wife, Louisa Gonzaga, who was related to the reigning dukes of Mantua. She was the eldest child of a large family, some of whom were to be her constant care throughout her life. When she was only five she had a religious experience in which she understood that "life and death consist in loving God," and she resolved to surrender her whole life to God, doing what he asked of her day by day.

She spent long hours in prayer and penance and often went into a state of trance, which caused her parents to be concerned that she suffered from epilepsy. They were certainly not looking for miracles. She asked to be taught to read and write but her father refused, arguing that learning was dangerous to women. The fact that she did become literate may be due to the fact that she learned from her brothers. When she was fourteen, she asked her father for permission to join the Third Order of St Dominic, but he refused again because he wished her to marry. He did allow her to wear the habit for a time, as a thanksgiving for recovery from a serious illness, but he was angry when she announced that she had committed herself for life.

Perhaps because of this parental opposition and her family responsibilities after the death of her parents, Osanna did not make her profession as a tertiary for another thirty-seven years. She remained a novice and always occupied the lowest place at tertiary meetings. She continued to live in the Andreasi palace and to care for her brothers and their families. Her devotions were conducted as privately as possible in a spirit of great reticence and humility.

When she was eighteen she had a vision in which Our Lady made her a Bride of Christ, and Christ placed a ring on her finger. She said that she could always feel it, though it remained invisible to others. Between 1476 and 1484, she had a series of experiences in which she was able to share the pain of Christ's passion. She had a repeated vision of him as a crucified child. At other times she saw a heavenly vision, so sublime and unfathomable that she could not find words to describe it. Her fellow-tertiaries thought she was shamming or even possessed by devils, and for a time she suffered something like persecution from them. She tried to conceal her religious experiences from the others, but the visions occurred without warning and often at inconvenient times, such as when she was in the garden or out in the rain.

Duke Frederick of Mantua had a high regard for Osanna. When he was leaving to conduct a campaign in Tuscany, he sent for her and asked her to care for the duchess and their six children in his absence. She continued to live in the Andreasi palace and to care for her own family but spent much time in the ducal palace. She seems to have acted as the duke's lieutenant rather than simply as a housekeeper or nanny, and she made many wise decisions, in spite of her youth and inexperience, through simple trust in God. When the duke returned, he consulted her often. Once, when she had gone to Milan under pressure from her Dominican superiors, he wrote imploring her to return. The whole of the ducal family regarded her as their closest friend and adviser, and when Francis II succeeded his father he and his bride Isabella D'Este carried on the tradition.

Osanna lived quietly, asking nothing for herself but frequently interceding for some person in distress—a prisoner or a victim of injustice. She entertained beggars and distributed loaves in the street during a famine. Many people came to her for advice and help, and she did not refuse them. Her letters, which are still extant, tell of her holy life, as structured as that of any nun; of her prayers and austerities; and of her fears for the world outside her restricted circle. She was appalled at the corruption in the Church of her day, and this may account for her reluctance to become more closely identified with it.

She prayed earnestly for the salvation of individuals and nations. Italy at the time was in a state of religious ferment and political turbulence, and the papacy had fallen into disrepute. We know from her disciple Girolamo da Monte Oliveto that she read Savonarola's *The Triumph of the Cross* in hours snatched from sleep, and her judgment on Church and society was not far from his. She told Girolamo that she had prayed three times for the salvation of the pope, Alexander VI (Alexander Borgia). On the first two occasions, God seemed disposed to show mercy to him, but on the third, she received no reply. Then she asked help from Our Lady and all the apostles, "and all prayed that mercy might be shown him. Alas, wretched sinner that I am! God ever kept motionless, with aspect and countenance of wrath; and he gave no reply to anyone who prayed; not to the Madonna, not to the Apostles, nor to my soul."

At last, in 1501, Osanna made her full profession as a Dominican tertiary. When she died four years later Duke Francis and his duchess were with her. She was given a magnificent funeral, and the Andreasi family was exempted from all taxes for twenty years in recognition of her services to the ducal household.

Osanna received many revelations. They placed an obligation on her which she felt she could fulfill only by continual and direct reliance on God rather than in the structures of the Church. If her spiritual experience needs any validation, it is to be found in her life of service to others.

AA.SS. has a long entry: June, 4, pp. 552-664. A Latin biography, written by her confessor Francis Silvestri, was printed a few months after Osanna's death. The Olivetan monk Dom

Girolamo published his notes of their discussions and her letters in 1507. The best materials for her history are to be found in G. Bagolini and L. Ferretti, *La Beata Osanna Andreasi da Mantova* (1905). This incorporates the earlier material mentioned above and a considerable collection of her original letters. See also M. C. de Ganay, *Les Bienheureuses Dominicaines* (1924), pp. 369-412; P.B., 7, pp. 136-8; Procter, pp. 175-8; I. Taurisano, *Catalogus Hagiographicus O.P.* (1918), pp. 50-1; *Dict.Sp.*, 11, 1008-9.

The English Martyrs of the Titus Oates "Plot" (1678-80)

On this date are commemorated five priests of the Society of Jesus, Thomas Whitebread, John Fenwick, William Harcourt, John Gavan, and Antony Turner, who died as a result of Titus Oates' allegations of a "Popish plot." Fr Whitebread was the provincial superior of the Order. In all, some forty-five Catholics were executed on fabricated evidence. Public fury was directed particularly against the Jesuits, and there were plenty of malcontents ready to support Titus Oates—people who had prospered under Cromwell's régime, had become impoverished after the restoration of Charles II in 1660, and were ready to act as informers for money. As public panic mounted and scurrilous broadsheets circulated, it became impossible for the accused to receive a fair trial.

Fr Whitebread, Fr Harcourt, and Fr Fenwick were in prison for months before their trial. They were originally charged with others for an alleged conspiracy to kill the king, said to have been planned in Fr Harcourt's rooms; but their trial had been put back, perhaps for lack of evidence that would stand up in court. When they finally came to trial with Fr Gavan and Fr Turner, they knew that the prisoners with whom they had originally been arraigned had already been condemned and executed and that the charge was high treason.

The evidence against them all was muddled and contradictory. Fr Whitebread conducted a brilliant defence in which he pointed out that of the three witnesses against the Jesuits, Oates himself was a man of ill repute who had been expelled from school and from a Jesuit College, the second witness had an equally unsavoury background, and the third had contradicted himself so clearly that he must be guilty of perjury. An onlooker was heard to remark, "If there had been a jury of Turks, the prisoners would have been acquitted."

The judge was Lord Chief Justice Scroggs, a man of extremely harsh views who virtually directed the jury to bring in a verdict of guilty of high treason. All five were condemned to death. The chaplain of Newgate Gaol attempted to convert them to Protestantism and found them "very obstinate," but he was much impressed by Fr Whitebread's calm and modesty of spirit. He records that when they finally parted Fr Whitebread "put off his hat" to him—a small gesture of courtesy, but in the circumstances a telling one.

On the scaffold, with the ropes about their necks, the five were offered a free pardon if they would reveal what they knew about the conspiracy; but since they knew of no conspiracy they could reveal nothing, and they were executed.

Their bodies were delivered to their friends, who buried them in the churchyard of St Giles in the Fields.

Lord Chief Justice Scroggs belatedly became suspicious that evidence was being manufactured for the courts. In later trials he exposed the falsity of some of the testimony and was himself attacked for doing so. Titus Oates, who had been maintained at the public expense and fêted in the days of his success, was tried for perjury, unfrocked, flogged, and sentenced to prison for life in the brief reign of James II.

For other martyrs of the Oates "plot," see William Ireland and John Grove (24 Jan.), Thomas Pickering (9 May), Richard Langhorne (14 July), Oliver Plunket (11 July), John Plesington (19 July), Thomas Thwing (23 Oct.), John Kemble (25 Oct.), Edward Coleman (3 Dec.), and William Howard (29 Dec.). They were all beatified by Pope Pius XI in 1929.

M.M.P., pp. 525-37; *R.P.S.J.*, 5, pp. 1-66; *Cobbett's State Trials*, 7, 311-418, has a complete transcript of these martyrs' trials, followed by the chaplain's comments, 543-70, in the same volume. See also Sir George Clark, *The Later Stuarts*, Oxford History of England (2d ed., 1936), pp. 92-5.

ST ALOYSIUS GONZAGA (over page)
Symbol of the Society of Jesus.

21

ST ALOYSIUS GONZAGA (1568-91)

The life of Aloysius Gonzaga has long been regarded as an example of piety and total dedication to the religious life—though his spiritual director, the future cardinal Robert Bellarmine (17 Sept.), said that his example was so extreme that other people should not be encouraged to follow it.

Aloysius devoted himself to prayer and mortification from the early age of seven, fought a titanic battle with his family to be allowed to enter the Society of Jesus, volunteered to nurse plague victims, and died of plague at the age of twenty-three with the name of Jesus on his lips. Fr Bellarmine and three other confessors were of the opinion that he never committed a mortal sin in his whole life. He was canonized in 1726 by Pope Benedict XIII and named patron of Catholic youth in 1729, an honour confirmed by Pope Pius XI in 1926.

There are fashions in holiness: in recent years the kind of sanctity Aloysius is often assumed to represent has not attracted the same approval. It may, of course, have been exaggerated by his contemporaries; but we are told that as a novice he irritated the other novices by stopping to say a "Hail Mary" on every step when going up or downstairs, and one called him "the Censor" because of his disapproval of any lightness or frivolity. Even his superiors said that he prayed too much and advised him to relax. His mortification of the flesh was savage and masochistic. He refused to look at women, including his own mother. He kept his eyes persistently downcast in their presence and said that he would not recognize any of his female relatives because he had never looked at them. He had a strong and often-repeated desire for an early death. Such behaviour suggests religiosity rather than true religion. He has been described as "priggish," "naïve," "angular," and "unattractive." Pictorial representations, such as those in the *Acta Sanctorum*, are often extremely sentimental, showing a rather effeminate youth yearning after heaven.

Both the early adulation and the later reaction may miss the mark. We can only begin to understand Aloysius by realizing that he was himself in reaction against a remarkable background. He was born to a great position, being the eldest son of Ferrante Gonzaga, marquis of Castiglione delle Stivieri in Lombardy and prince of the Holy Roman Empire. His mother, Donna Marta Tana Santena, was the daughter of a baron of Piedmont, a member of the Della Rovere family. Between them they were related to many of the noble families of Italy and to the nobility of Spain, France, and Germany as well. Dukes, marquises, cardinals, and bishops were their kinsmen. Donna Marta's family

152

had produced two popes—Sixtus IV and Julius II. The couple met when Don Ferrante was in attendance at the Spanish court of Philip II, and his bride was a lady of honour to the queen. They were married with great ceremony, and King Philip gave them estates in Milan and Naples. The Spanish connection must have been long-standing, for Ferrante's father was named Aloysio—not Luis, the Spanish form of the name which had been borne by his ancestors. The first child was baptized Aloysio after his grandfather, and the duke of Mantua was one of his sponsors.

Perhaps Aloysius would have been more at home in Madrid, where Philip II lived an almost monastic life of passionate austerity; but he grew up in Lombardy, where the ducal courts were luxurious and vicious, centres of intrigue and frequently of murder. He was the heir to his father's extensive estates, a future prince of the empire, and putative heir to Solferino and Castelgoffredo, held by uncles who had no sons. The marquis took it for granted that his eldest son would have a military career: the Gonzagas spent most of their lives in fighting the petty wars of the ducal states. When the child was only four, he was given a set of miniature guns and mortars, and at five, his father took him to stay at a camp where three thousand Spanish soldiers were in training for an expedition against the Moors in Tunis. For a time the small Aloysius delighted in taking part in parades, walking at the head of a platoon with a pike over his shoulder. On one occasion he loaded and fired a cannon while the camp was at rest—to general consternation. He also picked up a soldier's vocabulary—and was told by his tutor on his return home that such language was not only vulgar but blasphemous. The child was overcome with shame and seems never to have forgotten what he regarded as a great sin.

At seven he had already rejected the worldly life of the Italian courts and led a devotional life of his own. He recited the Office of Our Lady daily, followed by the seven penitential psalms and other devotions, kneeling on the floor without a cushion. At nine he and his younger brother Ridolfo were sent to the court of their relative the grand duke Francis at Florence. Fr C. C. Martindale, who gives a sympathetic and imaginative account of the conflicts Aloysius faced, describes vividly how he was appalled by this society of "fraud, the dagger, poison, and lust." His reaction was to lead a life of personal mortification.

Before he was twelve he and Ridolfo were sent to the great Gonzaga palace in Mantua, to the court of his godfather the duke. The palace is a virtual town, said to have sixteen separate courtyards, and it was the centre of a very sophisticated and dissolute court life. There Aloysius became very ill. A painful attack of a condition diagnosed as kidney disease gave him an excuse for not appearing at court. It is possible that the origins of this illness were psychological rather than physical. His digestion never recovered. For the rest of his life he had difficulty in assimilating ordinary food. He spent his time in prayer and reading the Lives of the Saints in the version by Surius. It was Surius' account of the life of St Louis of Anjou (19 Aug.) that inspired his refusal to look at women. Two other books particularly caught his attention: one was a work by Peter Canisius (21 Dec.), who has been called "the first literary Jesuit"; the other was an account of the work of the Society of Jesus in India. Ignatius Loyola (31 July) had founded his company of "soldiers of Christ" in 1534, only forty-six years earlier, and the new movement was full of zeal and self-sacrifice.

By this time Aloysius had determined to cede his hereditary right to the marquisate of Castiglione to Ridolfo, although he had already been invested as a prince of the empire by the emperor. He began to practise more extreme austerities, scourging himself with a dog whip till the blood ran, fasting three days a week, rising at midnight to pray, kneeling on the stone floor of his room, and refusing to have a fire even in bitter weather.

In 1581, when he was thirteen, he and his brother had to accompany their father in escorting the empress Maria of Austria on a journey from Bohemia to Madrid. On arrival at court, the two boys were appointed pages to the young prince of the Asturias, Don Diego. Aloysius shared the *infante*'s studies and pursuits, but he was so grave and circumspect in his behaviour that even the stiff and reserved Spanish courtiers concluded that he was not made of flesh and blood like other people. It was at Philip II's court that his resolve to join the Society of Jesus finally formed.

His father, predictably, was appalled at the prospect and flatly refused to consider it. His mother pleaded his cause but was accused of trying to cheat Aloysius out of his heritage in order to pass it to Ridolfo. The argument was still raging when the family returned to Italy two years later. Gonzagas and Medicis, Della Roveres and D'Estes were all horrified at this abdication of family responsibility. Priests were sent to argue with him. His godfather, the duke of Mantua, tried to change his mind and then in desperation suggested that he should become a secular cleric, hinting that a bishopric might be arranged. But Aloysius had no desire for high office in the Church. His mind was set on a life of poverty and renunciation. A bishop was sent to argue with him, but failed to convince him—and was thankful for it, for he came to the conclusion that the young man's vocation was genuine. Francis Gonzaga, general of the Franciscans of the Observance and a kinsman, interviewed him and took a similar view. The Jesuits (with whom he seems to have had no family connections) were prepared to receive him, but Don Ferrante was still unconvinced. He stormed and wept and stormed again. He gave Aloysius permission to leave, then retracted it; and when sheer parental fury failed, he tried more devious methods. Aloysius was sent on a tour of the courts of northern Italy, Ferrara, Mantua, Turin, Florence, Parma, perhaps in the hope that something—a new activity, an offer of preferment, a bride—would attract him to court life. Nothing had the slightest effect. Aloysius returned home and was locked in his room. Don Ferrante was told by servants that he should see for himself what his son was doing there. Old and suffering from gout, he had himself carried to the room, looked through a hole in the door, and saw Aloysius holding a crucifix and beating himself with a whip. He finally confessed defeat.

An imperial commission transferred the succession to Ridolfo, and Aloysius set out for Rome. There, he made the rounds of several cardinals with famous names—Farnese, Alessandrino, D'Este and Medici—as his position demanded and had an audience with Pope Sixtus V. The pope examined the young nobleman, asked him if he realized how wearisome the religious life was, and dismissed him with a blessing. Aloysius entered the Jesuit novitiate on the following day, 25 November 1585, at the age of seventeen.

He had rejected his heritage to find God in religious life; but religious life was not what he had expected. His superiors told him that his previous mortifications had been too extreme. He was directed to take recreation, to eat more, and not to pray or meditate except at stated times. This cost him a struggle. He was eager to forsake his wealthy and aristocratic background, and he begged to be allowed to wash the dishes, serve in the kitchen, and do the most menial tasks. Eventually he was given the solitary task of sweeping the cobwebs off the ceilings. He was not popular with the other novices: he did not know how to talk to them. He went through a period of depression and exhaustion.

He was sent to Naples for six months, where he suffered from headaches, insomnia, and erysipelas—a painful and contagious skin infection. Then in May 1587 he was sent to Rome to study metaphysics and to begin his theological training. Learning was no pleasure to him: he had no imagination and no talent for speculation. He was so determined to lead a life of poverty that he would keep only two books, the *Summa theologica* and the Bible. When he found that his room mate had a copy of the *Summa theologica* he gave his own away. He spent most of his time in contemplation in his dark attic room.

In February and March 1588 he was admitted to minor orders in St John Lateran in Rome, and he continued his studies. A year later there was an outbreak of the plague in Rome. Aloysius' biographer and associate, Fr Virgilio Cepari, describes it vividly: "Verily it was a horrible thing to see the dying creeping to the Hospitals, stinking and loathsome, and sometimes to behold them giving up their last breath in corners, or falling down dead at the foote of some payre of staires."

The Jesuits opened a hospital, where the father general and members of the Order cared for the patients. Aloysius asked to be allowed to join them. He nursed and instructed the plague sufferers, begged food for them in the city, and performed the lowliest offices for them. Several of the Fathers succumbed to the plague, and it was not long before Aloysius also became a victim. He believed that he was dying and welcomed the prospect with joy and relief. Then he felt that this impatience to reach heaven was sinful and redoubled his prayers.

He received the Last Rites, but he recovered for a time, only to develop a fever in the humid Roman summer. Though very weak, he would struggle out of bed to pray before his crucifix, kiss his sacred pictures, going from one to another, and kneel in prayer, propped up between the bed and the wall. He asked Fr Bellarmine if it was possible to go straight to heaven without passing through purgatory, and that wise and learned priest soothed him by saying that he thought it was possible.

He believed that he would die on the Octave of Corpus Christi and daily recited a *Te Deum* in thanksgiving. He received the viaticum again; but the octave passed, and he seemed to be improving in health. The rector thought that he might be sent to Frascati to recuperate, but he refused to accept the possibility of recovery. When the provincial came to visit him, he said, "We are going, father, we are going." "Where?" inquired the provincial. "To heaven." "Just listen to that young man," exclaimed the provincial, "he talks of going to heaven as we talk of going to Frascati!" At Aloysius' request, Fr Bellarmine recited the prayers for the departing, and he lay murmuring "Into thy hands." About midnight, between 21 and 22 June, he died.

The recurrent kidney trouble and the years of fasting and mortification had weakened his constitution, and he did not have the will to live. He had rejected from an early age the privileges and responsibilities to which he had been born, schooling himself for what he believed was the life of a religious; but when he finally entered the Society of Jesus, it was to find that his spiritual directors thought his devotional practices too extreme and counselled a life more like that of other novices. Did he volunteer to nurse plague victims because it was a way to the early death that alone could resolve his problems?

Aloysius was a devout and troubled young man, but he was something more. Fr Martindale makes the point that he was anything but effeminate. He was "by nature a hard man; uncompromising; going through life with his teeth clenched." Like his father, he was a tough character with a strong will: in the end, it was the father who broke. Aloysius concentrated all the fury, the passion, the courage, and the capacity for endurance that the Gonzagas were accustomed to expend on warfare and internecine feuds on opposing his family's ambitions for him and practising his faith. From an early age he saw the society into which he had been born with a terrible clarity. With all the power at his command he fought the evils of his day. God in Christ was his only reality, heaven or hell his only choice.

The Life by Fr Virgilio Cepari, Aloysius' contemporary and associate, was being written while Aloysius was still alive. It was subsequently checked and revised by a number of trustworthy critics, including Cardinal Bellarmine, and first published in 1606. It has since been published in many editions and translations, including *E.R.L.*, 201 (1974). The account in *AA.SS.*, June, 5, pp. 726-1026, is based on Cepari and on the documents for the processes of beatification and canonization. See also C. C. Martindale's illuminating study, *The Vocation of Aloysius Gonzaga* (1927); *N.C.E.*, 1, pp. 332-3; *O.D.S.*, p. 209; *Saints in Italy*, p. 14. The letters and spiritual writings of Aloysius have been edited by E. Rosa (1926).

St Eusebius of Samosata, *Bishop* (379)

Eusebius had the difficult and dangerous task of defending the doctrine of the Incarnation as defined in the Nicene Creed in the face of determined attacks by the Arians, who were in the majority in the Eastern Church. Nothing is known of his origin and early history. In 359, as bishop of Samosata, he attended a synod convened to select a successor to Bishop Eudoxus of Antioch. It was partly through his influence that the electors, many of whom were Arians, elected Meletius (12 Feb.).

Eusebius delivered his first sermon in the presence of the emperor Constantius, who was himself an Arian, and infuriated the Arians by setting out the Nicene doctrine of the Person of Christ—that he was "of one substance with the Father," rather than created by the Father for the salvation of the world. Attempts were at once made to secure his deposition, and Constantius sent an official to demand from Eusebius the synodical documents of the election, which had been entrusted to his keeping. Eusebius refused to hand them over without the authorization of all the signatories. Threatened by the emperor with the loss of his right hand, he held out both hands, saying that he would rather lose them both than betray his trust. The emperor admired his courage and let him go.

For some time Eusebius continued to attend councils and synods in order to maintain the Nicene doctrine, but he ceased to do so after the Council of Antioch in 363, believing that this constant controversy was not good for the Church. Nine years passed before he intervened again, at the request of Gregory the Elder, father of Gregory Nazanzien (2 Jan.). He was asked to go to Cappadocia and exert his influence on behalf of the younger Gregory's friend and colleague, Basil (2 Jan.), in the election to the see of Caesarea. He did so, and his contribution to the synod on this occasion was so outstanding that Gregory Nazanzien described him in a letter as "the pillar of truth, the light of the world, the instrument of the favours of God towards his people, and the support and glory of all orthodox." A warm friendship developed between Eusebius and Basil of Caesarea.

After this, perhaps encouraged by the renewal of his influence, Eusebius made several hazardous trips into Syria and Palestine in disguise to strengthen Catholics in their faith, to ordain priests, and to assist bishops in electing others who would make a stand against Arianism. This inevitably roused the animosity of the Arian party, and in 374 the emperor Valens issued an edict banishing Eusebius to Thrace. Concerned for the safety of the official who came to carry out the order, Eusebius warned him that his life might be in danger if the nature of his errand became public. He agreed to leave, said his night office, and made his way to the Euphrates quietly with only one servant, there boarding the vessel which was to take him to banishment. Some of the people of Samosata followed and begged him not to leave, but he said that the emperor's orders must be obeyed, and that they must trust in God. In his absence they proved staunchly loyal and refused to have any dealings with the two Arian bishops who were put in his place.

Valens died in 378, and Eusebius was free to return to his see. He continued to work for Catholic unity, and through his efforts a number of Catholic bishops were elected. He was on his way to install a bishop at Dolikha when he was struck on the head by a tile thrown by an Arian woman. The injury was a mortal one, and he died several days later, after making his friends promise that they would not seek out or punish the woman.

The turbulent life of Eusebius gives us a vivid insight into the passions roused by the Arian controversy and the dangers faced by those who resisted the Arian formulation.

AA.SS., June, 5, pp. 204-8, contains chapters from the writings of the historian Theodoret. There is a Syriac Life in Bedjan, *Acta Martyrum et Sanctorum*, 6, pp. 335-77. See also *D.C.B.*, 2, pp. 369-72, and Bardenhewer, 4, p. 388.

St Méen, *Abbot* (Sixth Century)

Méen (Mewan, Main, or Mevennus) is one of the sixth-century Celtic monks who travelled from Wales to Cornwall and Brittany and whose journeys and life history can now be conjectured only through tradition and place names. He is said to have been born in Gwent and to have been related to St Samson of Dol (28 July). Samson was at one time an abbot, perhaps of Caldey, and Méen entered his monastery. He went with Samson, or followed him, on his missionary journeys to Cornwall and Brittany. The seventh-century Life of St Samson mentions a deacon "as yet in the flower of the age of youth," who accompanied the saint on his journeys, but it does not name him.

Méen was given land at Gaël in the forest of Brocéliande and founded a great mission centre there. Later he made another foundation, which developed into the great abbey of Saint-Méen. Among his friends and disciples was his godson, Austol, also later venerated as a saint. The parishes of St Mewan and St Austell in Cornwall are only a few miles apart. A number of places in Brittany and some in Normandy still bear Méen's name in some form.

His relics are venerated at Saint-Méen in Brittany. He was renowned in the Middle Ages and later as a healer of skin diseases, including one particular form of ulceration known as St Méen's Evil. Cures were usually attributed to the water of wells and springs dedicated in his name, of which the most famous was the spring near his monastery at Gaël. Pilgrims used to come in the thousands to this spot every year. In Upper Brittany a wild flower which is a variety of scabious is still known as *l'herbe de S Main*.

Welsh accounts say that Méen returned to Wales in his old age and died there. A cross in the churchyard of Lantwit Major commemorates him.

AA.SS., June, 5, pp. 87-91; *B.H.L.*, 2, pp. 867-8; *Anal.Boll.* 3 (1884), pp. 141-58;

Roscarrock, pp. 103, 157, 164; G. H. Doble, *St Mewan and St Austol,* Cornish Saints Series 8 (1925, rp. 1939); *P.B.*, 7, p. 205; Thomas Taylor (ed.), *The Life of St Samson of Dol* (1925), pp. 30-3, 37.

St Engelmund, *Abbot* (720)

St Willibrord (7 Nov.), the apostle of Friesland, was followed to the Low Countries by many monks who were eager to help in his work of evangelization. One of them was Engelmund, an English abbot who had a particular advantage: he had lived in Friesland as a young man when his family migrated there. The places were familiar to him, he spoke the language, and he knew the people. Though he had been born and educated in England, entered an English monastery, been ordained in England, and acquired a reputation for learning there, he felt that he was called to the mission field. We do not know when he went back to Friesland or how old he was at the time, but since he was already an abbot, he was probably in his forties or fifties.

His offer was accepted, and he made his headquarters at Velsen, north of the present city of Haarlem. There he laboured for the rest of his life—apparently with great success, because after he died he was venerated as a saint. He was buried at Velsen, but his remains were later translated to the cathedral at Utrecht. When the shrine was desecrated by the Gueux, the scattered bones were carefully collected, and they are still preserved at Haarlem.

AA.SS., June, 5, pp. 100-1; *B.H.L.*, 1, p. 383; Stanton, p. 279.

St Leutfridus, *Abbot* (738)

Leutfridus (Leufroy) came of a Christian family near Evreux and studied in that city before going on to Condat and to the cathedral school at Chartres, where he was distinguished for his learning. After a short time spent in teaching he returned home and then decided to abandon the world. He slipped away secretly one night, gave his fine clothes to a beggar, and made his way to Cailly, where he lived under the direction of a hermit. He then moved on to Rouen, where he placed himself under the direction of another holy man and received the religious habit. Archbishop Ansbert (9 Feb.) was said to have a great regard for him.

After a time, Leutfridus went back to his own part of the country. He settled two miles from Evreux at a spot on the river Eure where Ansbert's predecessor, St Audoenus or Ouen (24 Aug.), had set up a cross—supposedly in response to a vision. There Leutfridus built an oratory, which he dedicated to the Holy Cross. It was first called La Croix-Saint-Ouen, but a monastery was built and after Leutfridus' death it was renamed in his memory, La Croix-Saint-Leufroy. Many disciples gathered around him, and he ruled as abbot for about forty-eight years.

On one occasion a monk died and three pieces of silver were found among his possessions. Leutfridus was much distressed, because this meant that the monk had violated his vow of poverty. When the funeral was over, he threw the three pieces of silver on the grave, saying, like St Peter to Simon Magus, "May your money perish with you!" But then he thought that the monk had died penitent and that God would have mercy upon him, so he fasted for forty days, praying and weeping continually, and asking that the monk might be spared the flames of purgatory. After that he had the monk's body reinterred in the monastery cemetery so that he might be among his brothers on the day of resurrection.

AA.SS., June, 5, pp. 91-100, has a Life written a century or more after Leutfridus' death. A critical text by W. Levison is available in *M.G.H., Scriptores rerum Merov.*, 7, pp. 1-18. See also *P.B.*, 7, pp. 186-91, and commentary in *Anal. Boll.* 41 (1923), pp. 445-6.

St Ralph of Bourges, *Bishop* (866)

Ralph (Raoul, Radulf, or Radulphus), was the son of Count Raoul of Cahors. It is not known whether he ever received the habit, but he derived a great love of the monastic life from his tutor, Abbot Bertrand of Solignac. He held several abbacies, including that of Saint-Médard in Soissons, to which his parents had given many gifts and privileges.

In 849 Ralph became archbishop of Bourges, and he began to take a prominent part in ecclesiastical affairs. He was regarded as one of the most learned priests of his day and was frequently consulted at synods. A rich man, he used his wealth to make religious foundations for both men and women. The chief of these were the abbeys of Dèvres in Berry, of Beaulieu-sur-Mémoire and Vegennes in the Limousin, and of Sarrazac in the Quercy. He died on 21 June 866 and was buried in the church of St Ursinus at Bourges.

One of his services to the Church was the preparation of a book of pastoral instruction for his clergy, based mainly on the capitularies of Theodulf, bishop of Orleans. His main object was to revive traditional customs and to correct abuses. Precise directions were given with regard to penitential practice: at this time, some extreme practices were being wrongly attributed to respected holy men and teachers. This book was forgotten and was not rediscovered until the beginning of the seventeenth century. It shows Archbishop Ralph to have been well versed in the writings of the early Fathers of the Church and in the decrees of the councils. He wrote a number of letters to Pope Nicholas I asking for clarification on various points of church discipline, but these have not survived.

AA.SS., June, 5, pp. 101-8, has an account of his life compiled from fragmentary sources, including Breviary lessons. See also *P.B.*, 7, pp. 205-6; *Histoire littéraire*, 5, pp. 321-4 ; Duchesne, *Fastes*, 2, pp. 20 and 22.

St John Rigby, *Martyr* (1600)

The life and death of John Rigby, a Catholic layman who refused to accept the Elizabethan Settlement, illustrate the strong and contradictory pressures on Catholics at this time. The pope told the faithful that the queen was an excommunicated and deposed heretic and that attendance at the established forms of worship was a sin. The queen and Parliament told them that refusal to attend church was a crime and that loyalty to the pope was treason.

John Rigby was the son of an impoverished recusant family and was forced to enter into service in an Anglican household. For a time he went to church occasionally, conforming outwardly as many others did. Then he made his confession to a Catholic priest imprisoned in the Clink prison and resolved that he must make his stand. He would not attend the church of the Elizabethan Settlement again. He moved to the household of Sir Edmund Huddlestone of Sawston Hall in Cambridgeshire. The Huddlestone family were also recusants, so life was easier for John for a time. Then the family sent him to court to plead on behalf of Sir Edmund's daughter, Mrs Fontaine. She had failed to attend church, and John Rigby was instructed to say that she was ill; but at the sessions house of the Old Bailey he was interrogated about his own position. He replied bluntly that he was a Catholic, that he would not go to church, and that he did not acknowledge the queen's supremacy. He was summarily committed to Newgate.

Outward conformity would have been enough: the authorities were not interested in his personal beliefs but only in a profession of loyalty to the Crown. Some of the judges would have liked to release him, and he was told quite clearly that if he would agree to attend church the case would be dropped. He refused, saying, "If that be all the offence I have committed, as I know it is, and if there be no other way but going to church to help it, I would not wish your Lordships to think that I have (as I hope) risen this many steps towards heaven and now will wilfully let my foot slip and fall into the bottomless pit of hell. . . . Let your law take its course."

There was a long discussion among the judges, but given the state of the law, they had no alternative to finding him guilty. Mr Justice Gaudy, who had visited him in prison, had urged him to make a formal submission. John Rigby recorded their conversation: "'Good Rigby,' said he, 'think not that I seek your death. Will you not go to church?' 'No, my lord.' 'Why then,' said he, 'judgment must pass.' 'With a good will, my lord,' said I."

Gaudy was deeply affected when he had to pass the death sentence; but John Rigby heard the sentence with composure. On 21 June, when he was told that he was to die that day, he said *"Deo gratias!* It is the best tidings that ever were brought to me since I was born." Even when he was being dragged to the scaffold on a hurdle attempts were made to induce him to "do as the queen would have him and conform." The authorities did not want a death: they wanted a recantation; but he refused to recant, gave the executioner a gold piece, and forgave him for what he had to do. According to John Gerard, "The people going away complained very much of the barbarity of the execution, and generally all sorts bewailed his death."

He was beatified in 1929 and canonized by Pope Paul VI in 1970.

John Rigby wrote his own account of the circumstances of his imprisonment and trial. This subsequently came into the hands of Thomas Worthington, president of Douai College, and was printed in a small book entitled *A Relation of Sixteen Martyrs Glorified in England in Twelve Months* (1601). Rigby's text, with an introduction and notes, is given in C. A. Newdigate (ed.), *A Lancashire Man: The Martyrdom of John Rigby at Southwark* (1928). See also John Gerard, *The Autobiography of an Elizabethan* (1609, ed. Philip Caraman 1951), pp. 80-1 and 232-3; *M.M.P.*, pp. 238-45; *O.D.S.*, p. 417.

22

ST JOHN FISHER, *Bishop, Cardinal, and Martyr* (1469-1535)

John Fisher was one of the "new men" of Tudor England—a draper's son born in Beverley in Yorkshire. He so distinguished himself in his studies and his work as a priest that the highest offices were open to him. He went to Cambridge at the age of fourteen, was elected a fellow of Michaelhouse (since merged into Trinity), and was ordained by special permission at the age of twenty-two. He proved to be an outstanding academic, becoming successively senior proctor, doctor of divinity, master of Michaelhouse, and vice-chancellor of the university. In 1502 he resigned his college headship to become chaplain to Lady Margaret Beaufort, countess of Richmond and Derby and mother of King Henry VII. She was a woman of considerable learning and great wealth who had survived many political intrigues. After the death of her third husband she decided to devote the rest of her life to God under the direction of Dr Fisher, whose learning and sanctity had greatly impressed her.

Lady Margaret was probably the greatest benefactress Cambridge has ever known. She founded Christ's College and St John's College to replace earlier and decaying institutions; she instituted Lady Margaret Chairs of Divinity in both Oxford and Cambridge; and she made many other benefactions to the two universities. Dr Fisher administered these innovations in Cambridge and did much on his own initiative to develop learning and academic life. When he first went to Cambridge, no Greek or Hebrew was taught there, the library had no more than three hundred books, and the new waves of humanist thought went unrecognized. He instituted scholarships in Greek and Hebrew, built up the library, and brought Erasmus, the most famous Christian humanist scholar of his day, over from the Netherlands to teach and lecture. Erasmus, impatient with rich monasteries, worldly bishops, and accretions to the Faith, wanted to get back to the early Fathers of the Church through the study of Greek.

In 1504, when he was still only thirty-five, John Fisher was made chancellor of the university, a post he continued to hold until his death. Later that same year King Henry VII nominated him bishop of Rochester. He accepted this appointment with reluctance because he was happier in the world of learning, but he fulfilled his pastoral responsibilities with great thoroughness. He held visitations, took Confirmations, supervised his clergy, visited sick and poor people in their homes, distributed alms, and exercised generous hospitality. The sermons he preached at the funerals of Henry VII and of Lady Margaret, both of whom died in 1509, are still preserved and are recognized as English classics of the period. The sermon on the king is particularly remarkable as a sincere tribute that bears little mark of the exaggerated and adulatory language usually employed for monarchs.

His studies did not suffer from his episcopal duties. He began to learn Greek at the age of forty-eight and Hebrew at fifty-one. He lived a very austere private life, limiting his sleep to four hours a night and eating very little. He kept a skull on the table at mealtimes to remind him of death. Books were his one earthly pleasure, and he built up one of the finest libraries in Europe with a view to bequeathing it to the University of Cambridge. He had no personal ambition. When offered wealthier sees than Rochester he refused them. The emperor Charles V's ambassador called him "the paragon of Christian bishops for learning and holiness," and King Henry VIII boasted that no other prince or kingdom had so distinguished a prelate.

In the intellectual ferment caused by the first stages in the Reformation Bishop Fisher was regarded as a defender of the Church and a bulwark against the new doctrines. He was selected to preach against Lutheranism in the universities and in London. He wrote four weighty volumes against Luther, which were the first serious refutation in England of the new movement. He was a reformer: at a synod called by Cardinal Wolsey in 1518 he boldly protested against the worldliness, the laxity, and the vanity of the higher clergy; but he wanted the abuses of the Church, which he saw very clearly, to be reformed from within to preserve the unity of Western Christendom.

His eminence and his royal connections made it almost inevitable that he should be involved in the king's nullity suit against Catherine of Aragon. His integrity demanded that he should take the queen's side. He was chosen to be one of the queen's counsellors in the suit before Cardinal Campeggio at Blackfriars in 1529, and he proved to be her ablest champion. Shortly afterwards the case was remitted to Rome, and his immediate connection with it ceased. His arguments were sent to the king, and Henry VIII's furious reply, with Fisher's marginal comments, is preserved in the Public Record Office.

When the king's suit failed in Rome and his measures to make himself supreme governor of the Church were debated in Convocation and Parliament, Fisher became the leader of the protest movement, making eloquent and powerful speeches to prevent the split. He was not inflexible: to him was due the addition of the words "so far as the law of Christ allows" to the form of assent which members of Convocation were required to make to the king's supremacy; but though this quieted other consciences, it was not sufficient to quiet his.

On 23 March 1534 the pope gave his decision in favour of Queen Catherine. By that time John Fisher was in danger and subject to many forms of persecution. He had twice been imprisoned, an attempt had been made to poison him, and a shot fired from across the river had shattered his library window. Thomas Cromwell had attempted to involve him in the affair of Elizabeth Barton, the Maid of Kent, a deranged woman who prophesied that if the king put away

Catherine and took another wife, he would cease to be king within a month and die within six months. The Maid of Kent and her chief supporters were executed at Tyburn on 20 April. By that time Fisher also was in prison. On 30 March the Act of Succession required the king's subjects to take an oath recognizing the offspring of Henry and Anne Boleyn as successors to the throne. To this were added a requirement for agreement to a statement that his marriage to Catherine of Aragon had not been valid and a repudiation of the authority of "any foreign authority, prince, or potentate." On 13 April Fisher was summoned to Lambeth to take the oath. He knew that he could not do so. He was arrested on a charge of treason and conveyed to the Tower of London.

By that time he was wasted by persecution and ill health. A contemporary said that his frail body could scarcely bear the weight of his clothes. Three years earlier Cardinal Pole had thought him a dying man. Now he lingered on in prison for months. Pope Paul III sent him a cardinal's hat, which so infuriated the king that he swore Fisher should not have a head to set it on. His trial was a farce, for the king's word was law. He was condemned to death on 17 June 1535. Five days later he was roused at five o'clock in the morning to be told that he was to be executed that day. He was very weak and had to be conveyed to the place of execution in a chair. Then he walked up Tower Hill, mounted the steps to the scaffold unassisted, pardoned his executioner, and addressed the crowd. Tall, thin, and emaciated, he told them in a clear voice that he was dying for the faith of Christ's holy Catholic Church, and he asked the people to pray that he might be steadfast to the end. After he had recited the *Te Deum* and the psalm *In te Domine speravi*, he was blindfolded. He knelt, and the axe fell.

Henry VIII's vindictive spirit pursued Fisher even after his death. His head was impaled for fourteen days on London Bridge and removed only to make room for that of his friend and fellow-martyr, Thomas More. The two were canonized together by Pope Pius XI in 1935, and their joint feast is celebrated on the anniversary of the first to die.

If Fisher has attracted less attention than More since his death, this may be because of the great clarity and simplicity of his life. He was a scholar and a churchman. He was loyal to the Faith. His writing was learned and soundly based but not witty or imaginative. He inspired no anecdotes and apparently had no eccentricities (apart, perhaps, from the skull on his desk). He endured with courage, and he died with honour.

The Letters and Papers, Foreign and Domestic, of the Reign of Henry VIII published by the Public Record Office, provide excellent primary materials for the Life of St John Fisher. There is also an important biography written sometime after 1567, probably by Dr John Young, who was vice-chancellor of the University of Cambridge in Mary Tudor's reign. The author was for many years thought to be Richard Hall: he was responsible for the Latin version. This Life is available in *Anal. Boll.* 10, pp. 119-365, and 12, pp. 97-287, edited by Fr van Ortroy. Other editions are those of the English Text Society (1913) and ed. Philip Hughes (1935). This last is in modern English, with a commentary. See also Lives by T.

Bridgett (3d ed., 1902); E. A. Benians (1935); N. M. Wilby (1929); E. E. Reynolds (1955); M. Macklem (1967); L. Surtz (1967) and R. L. Smith's *John Fisher and Thomas More* (1933). *Bishop Fisher's English Works*, pt. 1, ed. J. E. B. Mayor (1876), pt. 2, ed. R. Bayne (1915), are published by the Early English Text Society. See also *A Spiritual Consolation and other Treatises*, ed. D. O'Connor (1935).

ST THOMAS MORE, *Martyr* (1478-1535)

John Fisher was a great cleric and scholar. Thomas More was a statesman and adviser to the king. Both died because they stood in the way of the dynastic ambitions of an absolute monarch determined to force lesser men into submission by the example of their death.

Thomas More was the only surviving son of Sir John More, barrister, of Cheapside in London. He was always a Londoner. He went to school in Threadneedle Street and at the age of thirteen was placed in the household of Archbishop Morton, who was both archbishop of Canterbury and lord chancellor of England. Morton had become very unpopular through collecting benevolences for King Henry VII. He was the originator of "Morton's fork," a particularly heartless form of taxation; but he kept a great household. Thomas was "a merry boy," and the archbishop liked him, prophesying that he would grow up to be "a marvellous man." At fourteen Thomas went to Canterbury Hall, Oxford, later absorbed into Christ Church. His father kept him short of money and, disapproving of his enthusiasm for Greek and the new humanist ideas, took him away after two years. He set him to study law in London, probably thinking that the aridities of legal study would have a steadying influence, but the new ideas were circulating in London, too. Thomas became a lecturer in law and developed a reputation in the humanist movement. He lectured on St Augustine's *De Civitate Dei* at St Lawrence Jewry. Dean Colet of St Paul's was his spiritual director; Linacre was his medical adviser; and in 1497 he met Erasmus. Together they discussed theology, read Greek, and tried to reconcile the traditions and learning of the Church with the newly-discovered insights of classical Greek scholarship.

Erasmus was a monk who chafed at the cloister. More was a layman who was attracted to monastic life. For some time, he lived near the Charterhouse, taking part daily in the spiritual exercises of the Carthusians, wearing a hair shirt, and allowing himself only four or five hours' sleep a night; but his father insisted that he should marry and pursue a secular career. He married Jane Colt of Netherhall in Essex. According to William Roper, he was more attracted to her younger sister, but thought it would be "great grief and some shame" if the elder were left unmarried. This suggests a kindly man of great sensitivity but with a fairly prosaic attitude to marriage. Jane died after four years, leaving him with four children, and he remarried within a month. His second wife was Alice Middleton, a good plain woman seven years older than himself, and without education—a mother for the children and a competent housekeeper. If this was another prosaic choice, it does not imply that he thought women incapable of scholarship. He educated his daughters as well as his son because it was "a reasonable thing recommended by the prudent and holy ancients such as St Jerome and St Augustine." His house was a centre of learning and hospitality and prayer. Linacre, Colet, and John Fisher were frequent visitors. Erasmus came to stay. More often invited his poorer neighbours to dine but rarely invited the rich and noble. The household, with servants, met daily for prayers, and at meals one of the children would read from the scriptures. There was a chapel in his house, and he would serve at the altar even when he was lord chancellor. He slept on the floor with a log for a pillow and spent all Friday in prayer.

His secular career flourished. In 1510, with the new king Henry VIII on the throne, he was elected a reader of Lincoln's Inn and appointed under-sheriff of London. He was given a knighthood and appointed to other public offices. There was never enough time for learning and writing, but in 1515, at the age of thirty-five, this busy, preoccupied man was given a sabbatical. Cardinal Wolsey sent him to the Netherlands as part of a trade delegation. The negotiations hung fire, and he spent six months in the house of a humanist friend, Peter Gilles, the town clerk of Antwerp. It was there that he wrote the second part of *Utopia*, dealing with his imaginary country.

Utopia (no place) has been called a defence of Catholicism, an essay in socialism, a defence of the bourgeoisie when medieval feudalism was crumbling, and much more. The book, written in Latin, is full of puns, jokes, and literary conceits that often defy sober twentieth-century analysts. Like Plato's *Republic*, it is a social fantasy. In the Utopian social system there is no money, no private property, no family life, no personal privacy. People live communally and share the menial work. All this sounds very much like monastic life; but there is also religious tolerance and democratic government, neither of which existed in sixteenth-century England. Nobody starves, divorce is possible (once), there are women priests, and euthanasia is allowed. More, temporarily released from his many domestic, public, and social obligations, was speculating, thinking the unthinkable to stimulate discussion. He had learned much from his Greek studies of paradox, wit, and epigram, and he gave full rein to his imagination.

The second part of *Utopia* is a learned frolic; but More was certainly serious when he came back to London and wrote the introductory first part, which consists of searing social criticism of the state of the criminal law (about which he knew a great deal) and the evils of the enclosure movement. The book was greeted at once by his learned friends as a major contribution to the Christian humanist movement.

"That great expert in the art of government, his Invincible Majesty, King Henry the Eighth of England," as More called him in *Utopia*, probably enjoyed it. He was still young and not unlearned himself. More became his friend, and both the king and Wolsey were determined to have him at court.

He found himself rapidly promoted until in 1529 he became lord chancellor of England. During these years he worked in the legal profession, first as counsel and then as judge, with great integrity and scrupulous fairness. He was notably tolerant toward heretics, saying that of all those he had dealt with he had "never any stripe or stroke given them, so much as a fillip on the forehead." He spent what spare time he had in writing against Protestantism, particularly in opposition to William Tyndale. He was strongly opposed to the free circulation of the Bible in the vernacular. He had written *Utopia* in Latin so that the unlearned should not come to harm by reading it without understanding.

When King Henry VIII imposed on the clergy the acknowledgment of himself as "Protector and Supreme Head of the Church" (with Bishop Fisher's amendment "so far as the law of Christ allows"), More wished to resign his office, but he was persuaded to retain it. Perhaps he still hoped to be able to urge moderation on the king; but the king was past moderation. More defended the validity of Henry's marriage to Catherine of Aragon, but he was cautious. In March 1531, when he had to explain the state of the case to the Houses of Parliament, he was asked for his own opinion and refused to give it. But thereafter he found himself increasingly obliged to oppose the king's wishes in regard to his plan to marry Anne Boleyn. Eventually the king, greatly angered, accepted his resignation. He had held office as lord chancellor for a little less than three years.

The loss of his salary reduced More and his household to poverty. For eighteen months he lived very quietly, and he refused to attend the coronation of Anne Boleyn. Like Bishop Fisher he was subject to persecution, and an attempt was made to implicate him in the case of the Maid of Kent; but More was a lawyer: he knew (or thought he knew) what the law could do and how far he could go in opposing the wishes of the king. Like Bishop Fisher, he was summoned to Lambeth to take the oath following the Act of Succession, on 13 April 1534. He also refused, though he would not say why, believing that he was safe as long as he said nothing that could be construed as treasonable. He was committed to the custody of the abbot of Westminster and, when he refused again, to the Tower of London.

During the fifteen months that More was in the Tower, two things stand out—his quiet serenity at so unjust a captivity, and his love for his eldest daughter, Margaret. The two are seen together in his letters to her and in the conversations recorded by her husband, William Roper. The efforts of his family to induce him to come to terms with the king were fruitless. It was not that he would not: in conscience he could not, even when his family was reduced to such penury that Dame Alice had to sell her clothes to buy necessities. At his trial he said to the jury, "Ye must understand that, in things touching conscience, every true and good subject is more bound to have respect to his said conscience and to his soul than to any other thing in all the world beside."

168

The trial took place in Westminster Hall on 1 July 1535. He still refused to say why he would not take the oath, but he was found guilty on false evidence and condemned to death. Then at last he spoke, denying categorically that "a temporal lord could or ought to be head of the spirituality." He ended characteristically by saying that as St Paul had persecuted St Stephen, "and yet they be now both twain holy saints in heaven, and shall continue there friends for ever, so I verily trust, and shall therefore right heartily pray, that though your lordships have now here on earth been judges of my condemnation, we may yet hereafter in heaven merrily all meet together in everlasting salvation."

Four days later More was told that he was to die that day. He put on his best clothes, walked quietly to Tower Hill, speaking to various people on the way, and mounted the scaffold with a jest for the lieutenant in charge of the execution party. He asked for the prayers of the people and said that he died for the Holy Catholic Church. He was "the king's good servant—but God's first." He said the *Miserere*, comforted the executioner, and covered his own eyes before being beheaded. He was fifty-seven years old.

His body was buried somewhere in the church of St Peter ad Vincula within the Tower. After his head had been exposed on London Bridge, Margaret Roper begged it and laid it in the Roper vault in the church of St Dunstan, outside the west gate of Canterbury.

His stand on conscience has not been forgotten. It has been the subject of many books and, more recently, of the play and film *A Man for All Seasons*, which includes dialogue drawn from William Roper's account of his father-in-law and the transcript of the trial. He was from first to last a holy man, living in the spirit of his own prayer:

> Give me, good Lord, a longing to be with thee: not for the avoiding of the calamities of this wicked world, nor of the pains of hell neither, nor so much for attaining the joys of heaven . . . as even for a very love of thee.

More's canonization with St John Fisher took place in 1935, and their joint feast is celebrated throughout England and Wales. From the time of Hans Holbein (1497-1543), who was More's contemporary and sketched and painted him from life, he has been a compelling subject for artists, who have sought in his features the clue to a complex and attractive character. There are famous portraits in the Royal Collection at Windsor, in the National Portrait Gallery in London, in the Frick Collection in New York, and elsewhere, including many in private collections.

William Roper's *The Mirror of Vertue in Worldly Greatness, or the Life of Sir Thomas More* was probably first published in London during the reign of Mary Tudor. There is an edition ed. E. V. Hitchcock (1935). Other early Lives include one by Thomas Stapleton in *Tres Thomae* (1588), trans. P. E. Hallett, ed. E. E. Reynolds (1966). Among modern biographies the standard work is that by R. W. Chambers (1935): see review in *Anal. Boll.* 54 (1936), p. 245. For more recent biographies, see C. Hollis (1961); David Knowles (1970); J. A. Guy (1980); Antony Kenny (1983); Richard Maines (1984); Frank Barlow

(1986); Louis Martz (1990). Thomas More is claimed as a Franciscan tertiary: see *F.B.S.* pp. 453-6. There is an account of the trial by E. E. Reynolds (1953). More's correspondence has been edited by E. F. Rogers (Princeton, 1947). *Utopia* is available in many editions. A Yale University edition of the complete works commenced in 1963. *The Likeness of Thomas More*, a survey by Stanley Morison and Nicolas Barker (1965), provides a detailed study of portraits and engravings over three centuries.

ST PAULINUS OF NOLA, *Bishop* (*c.* 354-431)

Pontius Meropius Anicius Paulinus was born in Bordeaux into a patrician family which owned lands in Italy, Aquitaine, and Spain. His father was prefect of Gaul at the time; and the young Paulinus, under the tutorship of the great poet Ausonius and others, made a name for himself as an advocate. Jerome (30 Sept.) records that "everyone admired the purity and elegance of his diction, the delicacy and loftiness of his sentiments, the strength and sweetness of his style, and the vividness of his imagination." It was almost inevitable that he should follow his father into public service, and he seems to have held office in Campania and to have been prefect of New Epirus.

He travelled extensively and had friends in Italy, Gaul, and Spain. He married a Spanish lady named Theresia, and after some years he resigned his offices and led a cultured life in Aquitaine, managing his own estates. There he came into contact with Bishop Delphinus of Bordeaux. He was baptized (Theresia may already have been a Christian), and they went to live on their Spanish estates, near Barcelona. After years of childlessness they had a son, but the child died within a week. This seems to have been a turning-point in their lives, for they decided to live austerely and to dispose of much of their wealth to the poor of the area. The result may have been unexpected: the people of Barcelona clamoured for Paulinus to become a priest, and on Christmas Day, about the year 393, the bishop of Barcelona ordained him.

If the people of Barcelona had expected to keep the couple with them they were disappointed, for Paulinus still had some of his Italian estates, and they moved to Italy. They were warmly welcomed in Milan by Ambrose (7 Dec.) but had a chilly reception from Pope Siricius (26 Nov.) and the Rome clergy. This may have been because of the uncanonical nature of Paulinus' ordination or because of his friendship with St Jerome, who had stood as a candidate for the papacy against Siricius.

Paulinus and Theresia went south from Rome to settle in Nola, a small town near Naples, where they had estates. There they disposed of more wealth to religious and philanthropic schemes. They built a church for Fondi, provided an acqueduct for Nola, and supported a large number of poor debtors, tramps, and other people in need. Paulinus retired to a cell near the tomb of St Felix of Nola (14 Jan.), and Theresia had a separate cell. They both lived as hermits, coming out of seclusion only to say their daily Office with friends. There was a garden and a guest house where visitors could stay. Nicetas of Remesiana (below) left his wild and mountainous region twice to stay there; Melania the Elder, a patrician lady of great wealth, came there, and so did her granddaughter, Melania the Younger, with her husband, Pinian (both 31 Dec.). Many friends remonstrated with Paulinus, telling him that he was wasting his talent for public and ecclesiastical affairs; but he continued to live as a recluse until about 409, when the bishop of Nola died, and he was chosen to take his place. He is said to have ruled with wisdom and liberality, and he devoted himself to learning. He went to Rome only once a year for the feast of SS Peter and Paul (29 June) and otherwise never left Nola. He kept in touch with leading churchmen such as Jerome and Augustine of Hippo (28 Aug.) by correspondence and often consulted these two on subjects such as the meaning of obscure passages of the Bible.

When Paulinus went to Nola there were already three little basilicas and a chapel grouped about the tomb of St Felix, and he added another, adorned with mosaics, of which he has left a description in verse. The mosaics included the crossing of the Red Sea, Joshua with the Ark of the Covenant, and Naomi with her two daughters-in-law—Orpha, who went back to her own family, and Ruth, who said, "Thy people shall be my people." Paulinus commented that the two daughters-in-law were like the human race in relation to God—some deserting their faith while others remained loyal to it. Every year he wrote a poem for the festival of St Felix, and fourteen or fifteen of these poems are still extant.

Paulinus died at Nola and was buried in the church he had built in honour of St Felix. His relics were translated to Rome but were restored to Nola by order of Pope Pius X (26 Aug.) in 1909.

Of the writings of Paulinus, which seem to have been numerous, only thirty-two poems, fifty-one letters, and a few short fragments have come down to us; but he is esteemed the best Christian poet of his time after Prudentius, though Jerome said rather dismissively that he "composed many short works in verse."

P.L., 99, 18-152; Jerome, ch. 99, in N.P.N.F., 3, p. 394. *AA.SS.*, June, 5, pp. 167-204, has biographical material drawn from the letters of Paulinus and references by contemporaries. Another useful source is E. A. Clark's *The Life of Melania the Younger* (1984), which has an extensive bibliography. Modern biographies of Paulinus by A. Baudrillart (1903) and P. Fabré (1948-9). See also *D.C.B.*, 4, pp. 234-45; *D.T.C.*, 12, 68-71; *Histoire littéraire*, 2, pp. 178-99.

St Nicetas of Remesiana, *Bishop* (414)

The Roman Martyrology has an entry "In Dacia, of St Nicetas, Bishop, who by his preaching made nations mild and gentle that before were barbarous and savage." This describes Nicetas of Remesiana, who was a close friend of Paulinus of Nola (see above). Remesiana has been identified with a place named Bela Palenka in Serbia.

Paulinus wrote of how Nicetas had tamed the wild peoples in what he regarded as a savage region of snow and ice—the climate in Nola, in southern Italy, was much more clement. The Bessi in particular were a race of marauders, but in one of his poems Paulinus congratulates his friend for having brought them "like sheep into Christ's fold." Jerome (30 Sept.) also speaks appreciatively of the missionary work of Nicetas, but there is no information on the details of his missionary journeys, how he came to be promoted to the episcopate, or the date of his death.

The entry in the (1956) Roman Martyrology is under 7 January. It seems that Cardinal Baronius wrongly identified Nicetas of Remesiana with Niceas of Aquileia and thus transferred his feast from 22 June to the feast-day for Niceas.

There has been much interest by late nineteenth- and early twentieth-century scholars in the writings of Nicetas, some of which were previously attributed to Niceas of Aquileia and others. Dom Germain Morin and A. E. Burn have argued that he, rather than St Ambrose (7 Dec.), is the author of the great hymn of thanksgiving the *Te Deum*, though this view has not found universal acceptance.

AA.SS., June, 5, pp. 209-12; A. E. Burn, *Niceta of Remesiana, his Life and Works* (1905) and *The Hymn* Te Deum *and its Authors* (pamphlet, 1926); Dom Germain Morin, *Rev. Bén.* 7 (1890), pp. 151 ff., 11 (1894), p. 49, and 15 (1898), p. 99; Bardenhewer, 3, pp. 598-605; *D.T.C.*, 11, 477-9; *N.C.E.*, p. 440. For Nicetas' writings, see "De vigilis," *Journal of Theological Studies* 22 (1920-1), pp. 306-20, and "De utilitate," *Journal of Theological Studies* 24 (1922-3), pp. 225-52, both trans. C. H. Turner; also translations by G. G. Walsh, (1950).

St Eberhard of Salzburg, *Bishop* (1164)

Eberhard was born in or near Nuremberg some time between 1085 and 1090 and educated by the Benedictines. As a member of a noble family he received a canonry in Bamberg cathedral, but he soon resigned this to enter the local abbey of Mount St Michael. The bishop and the chapter would not allow him to remain there, presumably because they wanted him to be prepared for high ecclesiastical office, and he was sent to Paris to take a master's degree. He completed his studies with distinction, but his desire for the religious life was as strong as ever, and he was finally allowed to enter the monastery at Prüfening, near Regensburg. There he found a spiritual guide in Abbot Erbo, and he remained at Prüfening until he was called to become the superior of a new abbey which his two brothers and his sister had founded at Biburg, between Ingoldstein and Regensburg.

Under his rule the new abbey prospered, increasing rapidly in numbers and developing a fervent spiritual life. His ability and wisdom were so highly valued that in 1146 he was chosen to be archbishop of Salzburg. He was an excellent mediator. He began by settling a dispute between the chapter and two abbeys, and thereafter he was constantly in demand to reconcile contending parties. He had a care for both clergy and laity and remedied many abuses in the archdiocese.

Eberhard held two synods, at which he expressed his devotion to the Virgin Mary by enacting that her greater festivals should be honoured with octaves of prayer and commemoration. In the struggle between Frederick Barbarossa and Pope Alexander III, he was one of the few clergy who refused to take the emperor's side and recognize the antipope Victor IV. He was an important figure in the political world of his day. His last recorded act was to undertake a journey in order to make peace between Henry, duke of Austria, and his brother Conrad, bishop of Passau. He completed his task, but his strength gave out on the homeward journey, and he died at the Cistercian abbey of Rein.

The cause of Eberhard's canonization was urgently pressed by Archbishop Buckland in 1469, but no formal pronouncement was ever made, though he is commonly known as "saint."

AA.SS., June, 5, pp. 223-31, and *M.G.H.*, *Scriptores*, 9, pp. 97-103, both contain a Life of Eberhard written about the year 1180. The *M.G.H.* version is more accurately edited. *D.T.C.*, 14, 1293-5; *N.D.B.*, 4, pp. 231-2.

Bd Innocent V, *Pope* (1277)

This pope was baptized Pierre and for much of his life was known as Pierre de Tarentaise, from the name of his birthplace, Tarentaise-en-Forez, in the Loire region. He was a Dominican, and it is necessary to distinguish him from the Cistercian abbot and bishop of a century earlier, St Peter of Tarentaise (8 May).

The Dominican Peter entered the Order when he was very young and became one of the most eminent theological scholars of his age. After obtaining his master's degree he taught in the Sorbonne, where a fellow-teacher and fellow-Dominican was Thomas Aquinas (28 Jan.). In 1259 he was associated with Aquinas and three other members of the Order in drawing up a curriculum of study for the schools, which still remains the basis of Dominican teaching. His commentaries on the Pauline Epistles and on the *Sentences* of Peter Lombard were highly esteemed by his contemporaries. The Chartulary of the University of Paris lists the charges made by booksellers to loan books to students, and the works of Peter "de Tarentasia" are listed immediately under those of Thomas "de Aquino."

Peter had administrative gifts as well as scholarship, and at the age of thirty-seven he was appointed prior provincial of his Order for all France. He filled this office from 1264 to 1267 and 1269 to 1272. Visiting the houses under his control involved much travelling, all of which he did on foot, carrying out his visitations with much thoroughness. When Thomas Aquinas was summoned to Rome by the pope, Peter went back to teach in Paris. In 1272 he was appointed archbishop of Lyons by Pope Gregory X (10 Jan.), one of his former students; in the following year he was also made cardinal bishop of Ostia.

He was at Lyons for the ecumenical council summoned in 1274 by the pope and took a leading part in its deliberations. The purpose of the council was to heal the schism with the Greek bishops, and it was largely through Cardinal Peter's clear and scholarly enunciation of Catholic doctrine that the Greek delegates were able to accept it—though the healing of the breach proved to be short-lived. The council was still in session when his colleague Cardinal Bonaventure, bishop of Albano (15 July), died. At the funeral Cardinal Peter preached a moving sermon on the life of the great Franciscan, taking the text "I grieve for thee, my brother Jonathan."

With the appointment of a new archbishop of Lyons Peter's work in France ended, and he was free to return to Italy with the pope and the other cardinals. He was with Pope Gregory when he died, shortly after their arrival at Arezzo in January 1276.

In the election that followed Peter was a unanimous choice. He took the name of Innocent V and embarked on an energetic policy of making peace among the warring Italian states. He was anxious to implement the reunion with the Byzantine Church agreed on at Lyons and arranged to send envoys to Constantinople, but the envoys never left Italy. Though the new pope had a strong constitution and an excellent physique, he fell victim to the fever that struck Rome in the summer months, and he died only five months after taking office, in June 1277. He was fifty-one years old. This brought an end to the hope of reunion with Constantinople.

The cult of Bd Innocent was confirmed in 1898 by Pope Leo XIII, and his name was added to the Roman Martyrology as one who "laboured for concord among Christians." There is a thirteenth-century statue of him at prayer in the basilica of St John Lateran in Rome, where he was interred.

The definitive study is by M. H. Laurent, "Le B Innocent V et son temps," *Studi e Testi* (1947). Mann, 14, pp. 1-22, has a full account with a list of sources. See also Procter, pp. 179-81; Mortier, 2, pp. 143-5; I. Taurisano, *Catalogus Hagiographicus O.P.* (1918), p. 20; *O.D.P.*, pp. 198-9.

ST ETHELDREDA
Three gold crowns on red field.

23

St Etheldreda, *Abbess* (679)

Etheldreda (Aethelthryth or, more popularly, Audrey) was one of the best-known Saxon women saints, as many church dedications testify. She was the daughter of King Anna of East Anglia and the sister of three other saints: Sexburga (6 July), Ethelburga (7 July), and Withburga (8 July). Sexburga married a Kentish king and chose the religious life after his death; Ethelburga became a nun; and Withburga was a solitary. Etheldreda was twice married but is said to have remained a virgin.

As a girl she obeyed the wishes of her parents and married Tonbert, who was a prince in the Fen country. He may have been a sick man, for he died "shortly after the wedding," according to Bede. Etheldreda then retired to the Isle of Ely, which was surrounded by swamps and marshland. Ely had been a wedding gift to her from Tonbert. There she lived a secluded life of prayer for five years; but her relatives pressed her to marry again, and she was married to King Oswy's son Egfrid, a boy of fifteen. Egfrid was at first quite content that they should live in continence; but when he grew older and became a king, he wanted her to live with him as his wife. Etheldreda said that she had vowed her virginity to God, and both parties appealed to Bishop Wilfrid of York (12 Oct.). Egfrid tried to bribe Wilfrid, but Wilfrid decided that Etheldreda should be allowed to enter a convent. She went to Coldingham, where her aunt St Ebba (25 Aug.) was the abbess, and there she received the veil from Wilfrid. Egfrid must have resented the decision, for he subsequently encouraged Theodore of Canterbury (19 Sept.) to divide the huge northern diocese and banished Wilfrid, who had to go into exile for a time.

A year later Etheldreda went back to Ely. Bishop Wilfrid installed her as abbess, and she built a double monastery over which she ruled until her death. She may have used the Rule of St Benedict as a basis for monastic life. Her own way of life was very austere: except on great festivals or when she was ill she ate only once a day, and she wore the rough woollen clothing of the poor rather than the fine linen usually worn by great ladies, even in monasteries and convents. After the singing of Matins at midnight she would often remain in the church in prayer until sunrise. She died in 679. In accordance with her instructions she was buried in a simple wooden coffin.

The shrine of St Etheldreda became a great centre of devotion in the Middle Ages. Her remains have long since disappeared, but the empty shrine is still shown in Ely cathedral, where incidents from her life are carved round the

Lantern Tower. The word "tawdry," a corruption of St Audrey, was applied to the cheap necklaces and other showy goods for sale at her great annual fair.

Bede, *H.E.*, 4, 19-20; *Liber Eliensis*, ed. E. O. Blake (1962); Eddi, *Life of Wilfrid*, Eng. trans. ed. B. M. Colgrave (1927); *B.H.L.*, 1, p. 396; *N.L.A.*, 1, pp. 424-9; Dame Etheldreda Hession, "St Hilda and St Etheldreda," in *Benedict's Disciples*, ed. D. H. Farmer (1980; new ed., 1995), pp. 70-85; *D.N.B.*, 6, pp. 883-4 (a very unsympathetic account); *D.C.B.*, 2, pp. 220-2. *O.D.S.*, pp. 164-5.

St Lietbertus, *Bishop* (1076)

Lietbertus (Libert, or Liébert) came from Brabant and was the nephew of Gerard I de Florines, bishop of Cambrai. He was educated by Gerard and served under him as a deacon in various capacities. When Gerard died in 1051, he was elected as his successor. He was ordained priest at Châlon, and consecrated by his metropolitan at Reims. The emperor Henry V ratified his appointment and invested him with the temporalities of the see, but his installation had to be postponed. While he was away from Cambrai, a castellan named John of Arras had installed his family in the episcopal palace, driven the clergy out of the church of Notre Dame, and emptied the treasury. Lietbertus had to wait for some time before Baldwin V, count of Flanders, drove the castellan out.

Rudolphus, a monk of the Holy Sepulchre who compiled a biography of Lietbertus, writes: "He was an example to his flock. He avoided all luxury in dress, all devotion to frivolous pastimes, long sleep and inactivity. He had a horror of jealousy, detraction, envy and pride. Avarice he regarded as poison ... showing himself considerate towards all, giving to the poor and indigent all that he could spare, and acting with holy boldness and evangelical liberty towards the great and mighty of this world."

In 1054 Lietbertus set out with a company of three thousand pilgrims from Picardy and Flanders on a journey to Jerusalem. This was ill judged and turned out to be a disaster. In Hungary warring parties were disputing the throne. Rudolphus describes how, in "the deserts of Bulgaria," they were preyed upon by bands of robbers "on horseback, half-naked, their heads adorned with floating ribands, and wearing long cloaks and high boots." "These savages live like animals," he adds, "They have neither laws nor cities, and they live by rape and pillage."

Disease, famine, and hostile attacks reduced the numbers of the pilgrims, and when the remainder reached the sea and embarked for the Holy Land, they were shipwrecked. Less than a thousand reached Laodicea, only to learn that the Saracens had closed the Holy Sepulchre in Jerusalem to Christians and that it was dangerous for them to travel to any farther. Many of the pilgrims turned back, but Lietbertus and his immediate entourage were still resolved to reach Jerusalem. They took a ship, but contrary winds drove it to Cyprus and the ship's master insisted on sailing back to Laodicea for fear of pirates and Saracens. The party never saw the Holy Land and were compelled to return home. Failed pilgrimages of this kind were fairly common in the eleventh century and more destructive of human life than wars. The First Crusade (1096-9) was undertaken to free the Holy Places from Saracen control and to keep the pilgrimage routes open.

After his return to Cambrai Bishop Lietbertus built a monastery and a church to which he gave the name of the Holy Sepulchre. He often went there barefoot at night to pray for his people, and he devoted himself to their welfare. He opposed Hugh, the tyrannous son of John of Arras, and excommunicated him for his evil conduct. On one occasion he was seized on Hugh's orders and imprisoned in the castle of Oisy. He was rescued by Arnulf, count of Flanders, and shortly afterwards Hugh was driven out of Cambrai, to the great relief of the citizens.

His episcopate lasted for twenty years. When he was dying, he was able to render his people one last service. The city was about to be attacked by raiders under Robert the Friesian, who threatened to destroy it by fire and sword. Lietbertus had himself carried on a litter into the enemy's camp and by his eloquence and his threats of damnation succeeded in inducing them to withdraw without striking a blow.

The monk Rudolphus elaborated a biography of Lietbertus from the *Gesta episcoporum Cameracensium* soon after the bishop died. See *P.L.*, 146, 1449-84; *AA.SS.*, June, 5, pp. 498-516; *M.G.H., Scriptores*, 7, pp. 489-97 and 528-38. See also *B.H.L.*, 2, p. 732; *P.B.*, 7, pp. 239-51, from the *Vie des saints des diocèses de Cambrai et Arras*.

Bd Peter of Jully (1136)

This Peter was an Englishman, but he is associated with Jully or Juilly in Champagne, where his last years were spent. He studied theology in England until the death of his parents and then went to France, probably to continue his studies in Paris or in one of the great provincial schools. There he met Stephen Harding (17 Apr.), who was later to become abbot of Cîteaux. They both wished to dedicate themselves to God, and they made a pilgrimage to Rome together. On the way back they stopped at the Cistercian abbey of Molesme in Burgundy, and Stephen Harding was so impressed by its simplicity and austerity that he decided to remain there. Peter went away for a time but returned and was admitted to the Order.

Not far from the monastery at Jully-les-Nonnains was a convent which was subject to Molesme. The prioress was Humbeline or Humbelina (12 Feb.), only sister to Bernard of Clairvaux (20 Aug.) and Gerard (13 June). When their chaplain died the nuns asked if Peter might replace him, and the abbot consented. Peter and Prioress Humbeline worked together in the care and spiritual direction of the community, and he was with her when she died.

Peter's cult seems to have lapsed in the sixteenth century but was revived in the diocese of Sens in 1884.

AA.SS., June, 5, pp. 517-23, has a Latin biography written about a century after Peter's death; *N.C.E.*, 11, p. 220.

Bd Lanfranc of Pavia, *Bishop* (1194)

Lanfranc was possibly named for Lanfranc of Canterbury (24 May), who had been born in Pavia about a century earlier. The second Lanfranc, or Lanfranco, was born in Grupello, a village near Pavia, and became bishop of that city. Though he was a man of peace, he was forced to spend much of his fifteen years' episcopate in defending Church revenues and property from the rulers of Pavia. Northern Italy was lawless and unstable, and the rulers wanted money to build fortifications. Lanfranc absolutely refused to allow Church resources to be misappropriated for this purpose and was impervious to threats. At one time these became so menacing that he took sanctuary in the Vallombrosan monastery of San Sepulcro. After that there was peace for a time, but the demands were renewed, and the decision was taken to starve him out: it became a penal offence to bake the bishop's bread or to supply him with food.

Lanfranc went to Rome and laid his case before Pope Clement III, who threatened the rulers of Pavia with his censure but advised Lanfranc to return to his see. The appointment of a chief magistrate who was sympathetic to the Church made things easier for a time, but when the old claims were revived Lanfranc decided to resign and enter the Vallombrosan Order; before he could carry out this intention, he died.

His shrine in the church of San Lanfranco at Pavia is decorated with reliefs by Amadeo.

AA.SS., June, 5, pp. 532-42, has a Life written by Bernardo Balbi, Lanfranc's successor as bishop of Pavia and a famous canonist. *Saints in Italy*, p. 268; *Bibl.SS.*, 7, 1106.

Bd Mary of Oignies (*c.* 1175-1213)

In the twelfth and thirteenth centuries a number of holy women in the Low Countries seem to have anticipated the simplicity and austerity of the Franciscan movement. Mary of Oignies was one of them. Her life was written by the future cardinal Jacques de Vitry, who was her friend, her disciple, and probably at one time her confessor. He praises her virtues but warns his readers that her spiritual practices were extreme.

She was the daughter of wealthy parents who lived at Nivelles in Brabant—a serious child who never joined in games with other children. She could not bear having her hair curled or being made to wear fashionable clothes, and she told her parents that she wished to enter the religious life. They were annoyed by her refusal to behave like other girls, laughed at her, and married her off at fourteen to a young man of good position. She must have been a very strong-minded girl, for she persuaded him to live with her in continence and to turn their house into a hospital for lepers. The young couple nursed their patients with their own hands, sometimes sitting up with them all night, and distributed alms so indiscriminately that their relatives became alarmed. They slept on boards and faced mockery and insults. Mary practised great austerities, wearing a rough rope girdle, fasting and denying herself sleep in order to bring her body into submission. In one bitter winter she spent every night in a church from Martinmas to Easter, lying on the bare ground without wraps or blankets.

She had what was then called "the gift of tears," frequently weeping while she prayed or meditated on divine matters. While this might now be regarded as a physical reaction to the strains of an abnormal life, her biographer and many others at the time regarded tears as a spiritual grace. The Roman Missal had a set of collects *pro petitione lacrymarum*. St Ignatius Loyola (31 July), according to a fragment preserved from his diary, regarded the days on which he did not shed tears during Mass as a time of desolation, when God, so to speak, averted his face. Mary wept so copiously that, de Vitry says, "her steps might be traced in the church she was walking in by her tears on the pavement." She often fainted when she looked at a crucifix, or spoke of Christ's passion, or heard others speak of it; and she had a devotion to the Real Presence, often spending many hours in church adoring the Sacrament.

Mary's fame attracted many visitors who came to her for counsel or inspiration. A few years before her death she felt the need for solitude, and with her husband's consent she went to occupy a cell close to the Austin Canons' monastery at Oignies. There she remained in prayer and meditation. Fr de Vitry visited her frequently during the last five years of her life and afterwards spoke of her as his "spiritual mother." She prayed for him continually and gave him much spiritual help. Mary said that he had been sent in answer to her prayers. As a woman she could not teach the faithful and bring them to God, but he would be her deputy and her special "preacher." Fr de Vitry considered himself to be highly honoured by this charge. He retained his devotion to her all his life and wrote her Life soon after her death at the age of thirty-eight, before he became a cardinal.

Mary also had an influence on the founding of the Canons Regular of the Holy Cross (Croisiers) by Theodore of Celles at Clair-Lieu, near Huy, in 1211.

AA.SS., June, 5, pp. 542-88, contains de Vitry's Life and some supplementary material from Thomas de Cantimpré, who also knew Mary of Oignies. Eng. trans. by Margot H. King and Hugh Feiss (1993). The Life is translated in the Oratorian series of the Lives of the Saints and appended to the second volume of the Life of St Jane Frances de Chantal (1852). See also *P.B.*, 7, pp. 252-7; H. Thurston in *The Month*, June 1922, pp. 526-37; and a study by R. Hanon de Louvet reviewed in *Anal. Boll.* 71 (1953), pp. 481-5.

St Thomas Garnet, *Martyr* (1574-1608)

Thomas Garnet was born into a staunchly Catholic family, and his uncle was the distinguished Jesuit Fr Henry Garnet. After serving as a page to the earl of Arundel, Thomas was sent to the newly-opened college at Saint-Omer in 1594. In March 1596 he and a group of other students went to the English Jesuit College at Valladolid. After completing his theological course he was ordained priest and sent on the English Mission with Bd Mark Barkworth (27 Feb.) in August 1599. He spent six years, like other members of the Mission, in hiding and moving from place to place to carry out his ministry. During this time he was admitted to the Society of Jesus by Fr Garnet.

In the wave of arrests that followed the Gunpowder Plot in 1605 Thomas was arrested near Warwick and imprisoned, first in the Gatehouse and then in Newgate. He had been staying in the house of Ambrose Rookwood, who was implicated in the conspiracy, and it was hoped that important information could be extracted from him because of his close relationship with Fr Garnet; but repeated cross-examinations and threats of the rack failed to elicit any incriminating admissions. Thomas spent eight or nine months in a damp cell before he was deported to Flanders in 1606 with some forty-six other priests.

He went to Louvain for his Jesuit novitiate and was sent back to England in the following year to continue his ministry. It was only six weeks before he was re-arrested and sent to Newgate Prison. At the Old Bailey he was charged with treason in that he had been made a priest by authority derived from Rome and that he had returned to England in defiance of the law. Like others in similar circumstances, he made no answer to the charge of being a priest but firmly refused to take the Oath of Supremacy. He was convicted on the evidence of three witnesses who testified that while he was in the Tower he had signed himself Thomas Garnet, Priest. The earl of Essex and others tried until the end to persuade him to take the oath and save his life, "alleging that several priests had taken it, and many more looked on it as a disputable matter. He replied 'My lord, if the case be so doubtful and disputable, how can I in conscience swear to what is doubtful as if it were certain? No, I will not take the oath, though I might live a thousand lives.'"

Attempts were made to give him opportunities to escape, but he refused to take them. He said that a voice within him said *Noli fugere*—Don't run away.

In face of his steadfast refusals Fr Garnet was hanged. He was the first martyr from Saint-Omer and was thirty-four years old. He was beatified in 1929 and canonized as one of the Forty Martyrs of England and Wales by Pope Paul VI on 25 October 1970.

R.P.S.J., 2, pt. 2, pp. 475-505; J. H. Pollen, *Acts of the English Martyrs* (1891), p. 176; *M.M.P.*, pp. 296-9; Anstruther, 1, p. 127.

St Joseph Cafasso (1811-60)

It is often assumed that Giuseppe Cafasso was a member of the Salesian Congregation, but this is not the case. He was the spiritual director and close friend of the founder, St John Bosco (31 Jan.), but he remained a secular priest. The Salesian Congregation was not founded until 1854, six years before Don Cafasso's death.

Both were born in the small town of Castelnuovo d'Asti in the Piedmont. Joseph's parents were peasants in good circumstances, and he was the third of four children. He went to school in Chieri, near Turin, and then to a new seminary opened by the archbishop of Turin in the same town. He was the best student of his year, and when he was ordained priest he required a special dispensation because he was below the minimum age. He took very modest lodgings in Turin in order to pursue further theological studies. He did not find the teaching at the metropolitan seminary or in the university helpful, and he found a more congenial environment in the Convitto Ecclesiastico, the institute attached to the church of St Francis of Assisi. There he passed the diocesan examination with high distinction and was immediately engaged as a lecturer by the rector, the theologian Luigi Guala.

When Don Guala asked his assistant whom he should choose as a lecturer, the answer was, "Take the little one," meaning Joseph Cafasso. He was a small man with a twisted spine, and in a society which looked down on people with physical disabilities his physique was a grave handicap; but he had a beautiful and sonorous voice and a serenity (Don Bosco was to call it "undisturbed tranquillity") that impressed those who heard him. He proved to be a born teacher. He was not content to instruct without educating: he aimed not only to "teach things" but to enlighten and direct the understanding of his students. It soon became known that the Institute of St Francis in Turin had a remarkable new lecturer, and he was equally impressive as a preacher. He told Don Bosco, "Jesus Christ, the Infinite Wisdom, used the words and idioms that were in use among those whom he addressed. Do you the same." This gift for simple and colloquial preaching was used to encourage hope and a humble confidence in God, in contrast to the bleak Jansenist tenets then widespread in northern Italy. The Jansenists taught that the slightest fault was a grave sin, likely to lead to eternal damnation. Don Cafasso wrote later, "When we hear confessions, our Lord wants us to be loving and pitiful, to be fatherly to all who come to us, without reference to who they are or what they have done. If we repel anybody, if any soul is lost through our fault, we shall be held to account."

In 1848 Don Guala died, and Don Cafasso was appointed to succeed him as rector of the church of St Francis and the Institute. The task was not an easy one, for he took over the supervision of some sixty young priests from several dioceses, of varied education and cultural background and with differing political views. 1848 was a turbulent year in European politics, when one country after another experienced revolution and political unrest; and there was more unrest ahead for Italy until unification was eventually achieved in 1861. Don Cafasso's scholarship, his serene faith, and his care for individuals brought the Institute through a troubled period in which it had its detractors, both secular and clerical. His love and care for young and inexperienced priests and his insistence that their worst enemy was a spirit of worldliness had a marked influence on the clergy of Piedmont, and his ministry reached out to many others—nuns and laypeople of all walks of life. He had a remarkable intuition in dealing with penitents, and many came to his confessional.

He was also well known at the sanctuary of St Ignatius at Lanzo, in the hills north of Turin. When the Society of Jesus was suppressed, this sanctuary came into the hands of the archdiocese of Turin, and Don Luigi Guala was appointed as administrator. After his death, Don Cafasso took over this responsibility in addition to the church and Institute of St Francis. He continued his predecessor's work there of preaching to pilgrims and conducting retreats for both clergy and laity. The accommodation was enlarged, and the pilgrims' route to the sanctuary, begun by Don Guala, was completed during his period of administration.

Of all Don Cafasso's work, his ministry to prisoners most impressed the general public. In the prisons of Turin convicted men were herded together in barbarous and degrading conditions. Don Cafasso visited them, cared for them, and heard their confessions. Executions still took place in public, and he accompanied over sixty men, including a notorious brigand and a revolutionary general, to their execution. He called them his "hanged saints."

John Bosco first met Joseph Cafasso on a Sunday in the autumn of 1827, when he was still a lively boy and Don Cafasso already a priest. "I've seen him! I've talked to him!" announced John when he got home. "Seen who?" asked his mother. "Joseph Cafasso. And I tell you, he's a saint." Fourteen years later, Don Bosco celebrated his first Mass at the church of St Francis in Turin. After that, he joined the Institute and studied under Don Cafasso's direction, sharing many of his interests. It was Don Cafasso who introduced Don Bosco to the slums and prisons of Turin and helped him to discover that he had a vocation to work with boys. A Salesian, John Cagliero, wrote later: "We love and reverence our dear father and founder Don Bosco, but we love Joseph Cafasso no less, for he was Don Bosco's master, adviser and guide in spiritual things and in his undertakings for over twenty years; and I venture to say that the goodness, the achievements and the wisdom of Don Bosco are Don Cafasso's glory. It was through him that Don Bosco settled in Turin, through him that boys were brought together in the first Salesian oratory; the obedience, love and wisdom which he taught have borne fruit in the thousands of youngsters in Europe and Asia and Africa who today are being well-educated for life in God's Church and in human society."

Don Cafasso inspired others as well as Don Bosco: the marchioness Juliet

Falletti di Barolo, who founded a dozen charitable institutions; Don John Cocchi, who devoted his life to founding a college for artisans and other good works in Turin; Fr Dominic Sartoris, who founded the Daughters of St Clare; Bd Clement Marchisio (20 Sept.), who founded the Daughters of St Joseph; and many more founders of charitable works.

Joseph Cafasso died on 23 June 1860. Don Bosco preached at his funeral and later wrote his first biography. He was canonized by Pope Pius XII in 1947.

John Bosco, *Biografia del sacerdote Guiseppe Cafasso* (new ed., 1960); L. N. di Robilanti, *Vita del Ven G. Cafasso*, 2 vols. (1912); J. Cottino (1947). Cardinal C. Salotti's *La perla del clero Italiano* (3d ed., 1947) is now regarded as the standard work. There is a German Life by D. W. Mut (1925). *N.C.E.*, 2, pp. 1049-50; *Bibl.SS.*, 6, 1317-21; *F.B.S.*, pp. 456-60. See also references in Lives of St John Bosco, e.g., L. C. Sheppard (1957); Peter Lappin's *Give Me Souls! The Life of Don Bosco* (1977); W. R. Ainsworth (1988; new ed., 1995).

ST JOHN THE BAPTIST (over page)
Silver Maltese cross on black field (also the emblem of the
Order of the Hospital of St John of Jerusalem).

24

THE BIRTHDAY OF ST JOHN THE BAPTIST

St Augustine of Hippo (28 Aug.) notes in a sermon on John the Baptist that the Church usually celebrates the festivals of saints on the day of their death, which is the date of their entry into eternal life. He adds that St John the Baptist is an exception, because he came into the world sinless, and that his birthday rather than the anniversary of his death has traditionally been regarded as his general feast day: "This day of the nativity is handed down to us, and is this day celebrated. We have received this by tradition from our forefathers, and we transmit it to our descendants to be celebrated with like devotion."

An account of the Baptist's life is given on the date of the commemoration of his beheading (29 Aug.). The celebration of his birth is primarily concerned with the events recorded in the first chapter of St Luke's Gospel. The narrative up to Luke 3:21-2 is built on a comparison and contrast between the nativity of the Baptist and that of Jesus.

Zechariah was a priest of the Jewish Law, and his wife Elizabeth was descended from the house of Aaron. They were both "worthy in the sight of God, and scrupulously observed all the commandments and observances of the Lord," but despite their longing for a child and their constant prayers they were childless and had almost given up hope. Then, while Zechariah was carrying out his priestly office, burning incense in the sanctuary while the people prayed outside, he had a vision in which the angel Gabriel appeared standing on the right side of the altar of incense. His first reaction was one of fear and anxiety; but the angel told him not to be afraid and assured him that Elizabeth would bear him a son, who was to be called John. It was predicted that "even from his mother's womb he will be filled with the Holy Spirit and he will bring back many of the sons of Israel to the Lord their God." Zechariah pointed out that he was an old man, and Elizabeth was "getting on in years." He was silenced and told that he would not speak again until the child was born. When he left the sanctuary, the people who had been waiting outside realized that he had had a vision because he had remained there so long, but he was unable to convey it to them except by signs.

Some time after this event Elizabeth conceived, and she kept to herself for five months. In the sixth month of her pregnancy she received a visit from her kinswoman Mary. When she heard Mary's salutation, the child quickened and "leapt in her womb," and Elizabeth knew that Mary was to become the Mother of God. The Visitation of Mary, which is a feast of the Virgin Mary, has been celebrated in different parts of the Church on a number of different dates. If it occurred early in the sixth month of Elizabeth's pregnancy and the child was born on or about 24 June, that would place it in the first or second week of April; but it is now celebrated on 31 May, which assures it an importance not overridden by that of Easter.

When the child was born and all the relatives and neighbours visited to share the rejoicing, Zechariah remained unable to speak until the eighth day, when there was an argument about the child's name. The relatives wanted him to be called after his father, but Elizabeth insisted that his name was John; and Zechariah sent for a writing tablet and wrote, "His name is John." From that moment he recovered his power of speech. The neighbours wondered and no doubt talked to their neighbours in turn, and all through the hill country of Judaea, people heard about the events and asked, "What will this child turn out to be?"

From this mixture of high spiritual experience and purely domestic detail, we learn about the forerunner of the Messiah. We know nothing more of John's life until he begins his mission, coming in from the wilderness to preach repentance in preparation for the coming of the Messiah and baptizing in the river Jordan.

John's birthday was celebrated as one of the earliest feasts of the Church, and the date is located by St Augustine in his sermon on the feast-day. He refers to the words of John the Baptist reported in the Fourth Gospel: "He must increase, while I must decrease" (John 1:30). Augustine finds the date appropriate because, as he points out, after the birthday of John the days grow shorter, while after the birthday of Our Lord the days grow longer.

John is very widely represented in art, usually as a shaggy figure from his days in the wilderness. He is the patron saint of Florence and has many representations there. He is also patron saint of the Knights Hospitaller of St John. He is frequently commemorated on baptismal fonts and in baptisteries.

Augustine, Sermon 292, *Natalis Johannis Bapt.*; *AA.SS.*, June, 4, pp. 698-705; D. Buzy, *The Life of St John the Baptist* (1947), has a good bibliography; W. Wink, *John the Baptist in the Gospel Tradition* (1968); Carl R. Kazmierski, *John the Baptist: Prophet and Evangelist* (1996); L. Duchesne, *Christian Worship*, pp. 270-1; *D.A.C.L.*, 7, 2167-84; *O.D.S.*, pp. 258-9. For a detailed account of his representation in art see the entry for 29 Aug. in the present work.

St Bartholomew of Farne (1193)

Bartholomew was one of the holy men who followed the example of St Cuthbert (20 Mar.) and became a hermit on one of the Farne islands, off the Northumbrian coast. He was a native of Whitby. His parents, who were presumably of

Scandinavian origin, named him Tostig, but apparently this name laid him open to ridicule by his playmates. The fashion was for Norman names, so he changed his name to William. He determined to go to Scandinavia, and his wanderings led him to Norway, recently Christianized by English missionaries, perhaps in search of his origins. There he studied and was ordained priest by the bishop of Nidaros, or Trondhjem.

At that time the Norwegian clergy were usually married, and he was pressed to marry a Norwegian girl by her parents. This may have contributed to his decision to return to England and become a hermit. He went to Durham, where he received the monastic habit and was given a third name, that of Bartholomew. He was inspired by the example of St Cuthbert to go to the island of the Inner Farne to occupy a cell where St Cuthbert had lived.

Human relations are seldom uncomplicated, even for those who avoid marriage and seek solitude. When Bartholomew arrived he found another hermit named Brother Ebwin or Aelwin already installed and displeased at the invasion of his privacy. Ebwin did everything possible to drive the newcomer away. On one occasion, when a monk of Durham was visiting Bartholomew, a stone came crashing down on the roof. Bartholomew said, "It is only a trick of the old enemy." The monk thought that he meant the devil, but it seems that he was referring to Brother Ebwin.

Eventually Ebwin admitted defeat and left the island. Bartholomew lived a very austere life modelled on that of the Desert Fathers; but his solitude was again interrupted by the arrival of a former prior of Durham named Thomas. The two found it impossible to agree about food. Thomas could not manage to live on as little as Bartholomew required and accused him of hypocrisy— presumably of eating their joint rations when his own back was turned. Bartholomew was deeply offended at this accusation and left the island for Durham. There he remained for a year in spite of Thomas' apologies, until the bishop summarily ordered him to go back again and to be reconciled. After that, the two hermits seem to have lived in comparative peace.

Despite these personal difficulties, Bartholomew seems to have been a cheerful and kindly man, generous to visitors, and no respecter of persons. He was ready to reprove the rich and powerful and to get them to change their ways. He wore a coat and trousers of ram's skin and never took them off or allowed them to be washed until the skins became black with sweat and dirt. "The dirtier the body, the cleaner the soul," claimed Bartholomew. The charitable monks of Durham said that he "made the island fragrant with his virtues." He passed his days in prayer and study and manual labour, singing psalms in a loud and melodious voice. Some monks from the Scottish abbey of Coldingham were with him when he had his final illness, and they buried him on the island. He had a cult in Durham and north-east England; and a stone sarcophagus, possibly identical with one he carved for himself, stands outside the chapel where he used to pray.

Contemporary Life by Geoffrey of Durham in the works of Symeon of Durham, ed. T. Arnold, R.S. 76, 1, pp. 293-325; *AA.SS.*, June, 5, pp. 713-21; *N.L.A.*, 1, pp. 101-6; Stanton, pp. 287-8; *Anal.Boll.* 70 (1952), pp. 5-19; V. M. Tudor, "St Godric of Finchale and St Bartholomew of Farne," in D. H. Farmer (ed.), *Benedict's Disciples* (2d ed., 1995), pp.195-211.

25

St Prosper of Aquitaine (c. 465)

This Prosper (not to be confused with his contemporary, St Prosper, bishop of Reggio, see below) is well known in his writings, though little is known about his life. He was neither a bishop nor a priest but a Christian theologian and historian. He may have been married, though the attribution to him of a poem "From a Husband to his Wife, expressive of trust in God wherever life leads them" is disputed. Some commentators think that the author is Paulinus of Nola (23 June).

Prosper was well known in the mid-fifth century. He was a friend of a secular priest named Hilary and wrote to St Augustine of Hippo (28 Aug.) at his suggestion. The matters raised in their correspondence led to the writing of Augustine's treatises *Concerning Predestination* and *Concerning the Gift of Perseverance*. Augustine had expressed the view that most of the human race were damned, because specific grace was necessary to lead people to salvation. In *De vocatione omnium gentium* Prosper insisted that grace was a free gift, possible for all humankind in the ultimate mercy of God. This did not solve the problem of predestination and free will, but it helped to soften Augustine's rigid attitude.

Prosper became involved in the semi-Pelagian controversy concerning the doctrine of original sin and opposed the views of the Egyptian abbot John Cassian (23 July) and possibly those of Vincent of Lérins (24 May).

Prosper went to Rome with Hilary, and they returned with a letter from Pope Celestine I (6 Apr.), a strong opponent of Pelagius, to the bishops of Gaul. This praised the zeal of the bearers and called for peace in the theological disputes that were still continuing. Prosper eventually went back to Rome, where he is said to have been secretary to Pope Leo the Great (10 Nov.). He died in Rome.

The writings of Prosper of Aquitaine, both in verse and in prose, are primarily concerned with the controversy about grace and free will. His longest poem is a dogmatic treatise of 1,002 hexameters, *De ingratis*, "A Song about the Graceless." The most widely known of his works is the *Chronicle*, a history of the known world from the creation to the capture of Rome by the Vandals in the year 455. Prosper's feast is celebrated in Tarbes as that of "the Aquitainian Doctor," and French sources sometimes refer to him as a Doctor of the Church, though this title does not appear to have been officially accorded him.

P.L., 51, pp. 67-74 and 77-90; *AA.SS.*, June, 5, pp. 53-71; *C.M.H.*, p. 255; *D.T.C.*, 13, 846-50; *N.C.E.*, 11, p. 878; *P.B.*, 7, pp. 344-50; *D.H.G.E.*, 13, pt. 1, 846-50; L. Valentin, *S.*

Prosper d'Aquitaine (1900). Many of Prosper's works have survived. They were translated into French by Lequeux (1762). Eng. trans. of the treatise on grace and free will, *The Call of All Nations* (1950), and of *The Defence of St Augustine* (1963).

St Prosper of Reggio, *Bishop* (? 466)

In his Roman Martyrology Cardinal Baronius assumed that the two Prospers were one person, but their careers were quite distinct, and there was no attempt to identify them with each other before the tenth century. Prosper of Reggio was a bishop, and his see was based not on Reggio di Calabria in the extreme south of Italy but on the lesser-known Reggio nell'Emilia in the north, between Parma and Modena. He is still venerated in that region and is the principal patron of the city.

As far as is known Bishop Prosper left no theological writings, and he was remembered primarily as a beloved pastor. There is a tradition that he gave all his goods to the poor in order to fulfill Christ's precept to the rich young man (Matt. 19:21; Mark 10:21). He is said to have died on 25 June 466, surrounded by his priests and deacons, after a beneficent episcopate which lasted twenty-two years. He was buried in the church of St Apollinaris, which he had built and consecrated, outside the walls of Reggio. In 703 his relics were translated to a great new church erected in his honour by Thomas, bishop of Reggio.

The confusion between the two St Prospers has been convincingly dealt with by Dom Germain Morin, *Rev. Bén.* 12 (1895), pp. 241-57. See also *Anal.Boll.* 15 (1896) pp. 161-256; *Histoire littéraire*, 2, pp. 369-406. The miracles attributed to Bishop Prosper of Reggio are dealt with at length in *AA.SS.*, June, 7, pp. 47-63.

St Maximus of Turin, *Bishop* (*c.* 380-467)

The historian Gennadius, in *The Book of Ecclesiastical Writers*, describes Maximus as a profound student of the Bible, a preacher well able to instruct the people, and the author of many books, of which the titles are listed. The notice ends by saying that Maximus lived in the reigns of Honorius and Theodosius the Younger. In fact, he is known to have survived both. As the first known bishop of Turin he attended the Synod of Milan in 451, when he was one of the signatories of a letter to Pope Leo the Great (10 Nov.) from the prelates of northern Italy, and he was at the Council of Rome in 465. His signature on this latter occasion comes directly after that of Pope Hilarus (28 Feb.). Precedence was determined by age, so he must have been a very old man by then. He is thought to have died shortly afterwards.

Maximus was born in northern Italy, possibly in Vercelli or in the province of Rhaetia. He writes that in 397 he witnessed the martyrdom of three missionary bishops at Anaunia, in the Rhaetian Alps. Very little is known about his life, though some inferences can be drawn from his writings. However, some caution is necessary: the collection edited by Bruno Bruni in 1784 comprises some 116 sermons, 118 homilies, and six treatises, some of which may be the

work of other writers. There has been considerable debate about the authorship of these pieces. Some have been attributed by the Bollandists to St Ambrose.
Professor C. H. Turner has edited certain Latin pieces which he is inclined to
attribute to Maximus, while Dom Capelle argues that they are the work of the
Arian bishop Maximinus; but the main corpus of the work is distinctively that
of Maximus and is of considerable interest to historians of theology.

The collection is chiefly interesting for the light it throws on the customs
and the condition of the people of Lombardy at the time of the Gothic invasions. The destruction of Milan by Attila is described in one homily. Another
mentions the martyrs Octavius, Solutor, and Adventus, whose relics were preserved at Turin, with the comment: "All the martyrs are to be honoured by us,
but especially those whose relics we possess: they preserve us as to our bodies
in this life, and receive us when we depart hence." Two homilies on thanksgiving preach the duty of giving praise to God daily and recommend the use of
the psalms for this purpose. Morning and evening prayer are to be said daily,
and a thanksgiving before and after meals is required. Christians are exhorted
to make the sign of the cross before every action, "that by the sign of Jesus
Christ (devoutly used) a blessing may be insured to us in all things."

A sermon on New Year's Day deprecates the practice of giving presents to
the well-to-do without also giving alms to the poor and denounces the hypo-
critical protestation of friendship that does not come from the heart. Elsewhere, there is an attack on "heretics who sell the pardon of sins"—pretended
priests who take money for absolving offences instead of imposing penance.

Maximus is a patron saint of Turin.

AA.SS., June, 7, pp. 43-7; C. Ferreri, *San Maximo, vescovo di Torino* (1858); E. Amann in
D.T.C., 10, 464-6; *D.C.B.*, 3, pp. 881-2; Bardenhewer, 4, pp. 610-13. Bruno Bruni's
collection of writings is in *P.L.*, 57. For commentaries, see C. H. Turner, "St Maximus
of Turin," *Journal of Theological Studies* 20 (1919), pp. 289-310, and "On Ms. Veron. L1
(49)" *Journal of Theological Studies* 24 (1923), pp. 71-9; Dom Capelle, *Rev.Bén.* 34 (1922),
pp. 81-108.

St Moluag, *Bishop* (*c.* 520-92)

Moluag (Moloc, Mollach, Lughaid) is said to have been a Scot, trained in
Ireland, who returned to evangelize parts of his native land. The chief evidence
for his life is an entry in the *Aberdeen Breviary* under the date of 25 June from
the *Félire* of Oengus the Culdee, poet and bishop (11 Mar.). This says,
"Sinchell's feast, Telle's feast: they were heights of Ireland, with Moluoc pure—
fair son of Lismore and of Alba." A translation from the Gaelic version of the
metrical hymn, which may be more accurate, describes him as "Moluag, the
clear and brilliant, / The sun of Lismore in Alba." In either case, there can be
no doubt of his importance in the religious history of Scotland.

There has been some confusion between Moluag and Abbot Molua (4 Aug.).
Both are said to have been originally called Lughaidh, and both founded mon-

asteries; but there are three versions of a Latin Life of Molua, who was the founder of the monastery of Killaloe, Co. Clare, and the teacher of St Flannan (18 Dec.). Molua is thought to have died about 609, and Moluag about 592. Moluag's missionary record is located in Scotland, not in Ireland. He is said to have been trained at Birr under St Brendan the Elder, then to have returned to his own country. He landed in Argyllshire, evangelized the inhabitants of Lismore, visited islands as far north as the Hebrides, and then devoted the rest of his life to missionary work in Ross and the province of Mar. He died at Rossmarkie, but his relics were translated to Murlach, or Mortlach, which bears his name. King Malcolm II of Scotland attributed his victory over the Danes near Murlach to the intercessions of Our Lady and of the saint. As an act of thanksgiving he founded an abbey, a cathedral church, and an episcopal see. The bishopric was subsequently transferred to Aberdeen.

The *bachuil*, or crozier, of St Moluag, a pastoral staff of blackthorn once enshrined in gilded metal and perhaps studded with jewels, has for centuries been an heirloom in the family of Livingstone of Lismore, and the head of the family is known as baron of Bachuil. A Latin charter of 1554 confirms the family's possession since time immemorial of the *Magnum Baculum* of St Moluag. At one time the crozier was placed for safekeeping in the vaults of the dukes of Argyll; but in 1973 the present duke, accompanied by the duchess, their young son the marquis of Lorne, the Episcopal bishop of Argyll and the Isles, and two ministers of the Church of Scotland, embarked in a coracle from Port Appin and returned it to its rightful hereditary keeper. Almost the whole population of Lismore was present at the ensuing ceremony. On 25 June 1992 the fourteen-hundredth anniversary of the saint's death was celebrated in Lismore. The crozier is still brought out to be carried in procession on major occasions.

K.S.S., pp. 409-11, quotes the lesson from the *Aberdeen Breviary* at length. See also *AA.SS.*, June, 7, pp. 677-80; *B.H.L.*, 2, p. 874; *Irish Saints*, pp. 259-6; *O.D.S.*, p. 343.

St Adalbert of Egmond (? 705 or after 714)

Adalbert was one of a group of young men who left the monastery of Rathmelsigi in 690 under the leadership of St Willibrord (7 Nov.) to evangelize Friesland. He came from Northumbria and may have been a grandson of Oswald, king of Deira. He was a deacon who had followed St Egbert (24 Apr.) to undertake monastic training in Ireland. St Willibrord's missionaries operated under the protection of Pepin of Herstal, and their language was so like that of the Friesians that they had little difficulty in making themselves understood.

Adalbert was renowned for his gentleness and his humility. He worked largely at Egmond, near the present-day town of Alkmaar, and seems to have converted most of the inhabitants with the support of the lord of the county. It may have been humility that held him back from offering himself for the priesthood, for he remained a deacon; but Willibrord is said to have appointed him archdeacon of Utrecht. An archdeacon at that time was, as the title suggests, a deacon supervising the work of others, and this office gave him authority for his work.

In the tenth century Duke Theodoric built at Egmond a Benedictine abbey dedicated under the name of Adalbert. This was destroyed by the Spaniards at the siege of Alkmaar in 1573 and has been revived in the twentieth century by the Benedictines of Solesmes under the same titular.

The sources for St Adalbert's Life are somewhat unsatisfactory. *AA.SS.*, June, 7, pp. 82-95, contains a Latin biography by Rupert, a monk at Mettlach, but this provides little more than generalities. *AA.SS.OSB.*, 3, p. 585, has a brief biography by a monk of Egmont. Adalbert's claim to the title of archdeacon has been queried but is supported by W. Levison: see his "Wilhelm Procurator von Egmond" in *Neues Archiv.* 90 (1916), pp. 793-804; also *D.H.G.E.*, 1, 441; *D.N.B.*, 1, pp. 73-4; Stanton, pp. 288-9; *N.C.E.*, 1, p. 112; *O.D.S.*, p. 3.

St Eurosia, *Martyr* (? Eighth Century)

Eurosia (Orosia) is a good example of a saint whose origins are very difficult to establish, though her cult is well known. There is little early corroboration of her existence, and some commentators have taken the view that she is an apocryphal character. On the other hand, there is good evidence of a widely-established cult originating in Spain in the fifteenth century, from whence it spread into Lombardy. Fr Delehaye writes: "Everything is suspect in the origins of this *cultus*, which was propagated in the north of Italy, thanks to the political relations between Spain and Lombardy. . . . A considerable number of places in the dioceses of Como, Cremona, Pavia, and Novara possess chapels, altars, images and relics of St Eurosia, who is honoured as the protector of the fruits of the field."

The cult is thought to have been spread by Spanish soldiers and by the religious Congregation of the Somaschi, whose headquarters were in the diocese of Cremona. In the sixteenth century there was an office and Mass in honour of Eurosia in the town of Jaca, on the southern slopes of the Pyrenees.

According to popular tradition Eurosia was the daughter of a noble family from the province of Bayonne. She refused to marry a Saracen chieftain, fled to the mountains, and was there killed by his followers. The basic story is not improbable, but it has been embroidered with a variety of unlikely and contradictory legends.

That there should be no early records of a martyrdom in a mountainous region overrun by the Moors is reasonable: at first the cult would be localized and not widely known. If it was taken by soldiers from the area into Italy, we might expect that repetition by word of mouth would lead to embroidery and to contradictions in detail. Eurosia was the local girl saint from the soldiers' home province. They took her into battle with them and spread her fame.

Eurosia became known not only as the protector of the crops but as a saint who could be invoked against bad weather. It may be that the cult has two strands—one the worship of some local pagan goddess of fertility in a pre-Christian era and the other an account of a Christian girl who defied the Muslim invaders.

Many places in the sees of Milan, Como, Cremona, Pavia, and Novara have chapels or altars dedicated to her, and some claim to possess relics.

AA.SS., 7, pp. 76-9; *D.H.G.E.*, 15, 1428; *D.H.E.E.*, 2, p. 886; *Bibl.SS.*, 5, pp. 240-1; *Saints in Italy*, p. 156.

St Gohard, *Bishop,* and Companions, *Martyrs* (843)

When the Norsemen raided the coasts of England and France in the ninth century they often singled out monasteries and cathedrals for attack. Religious foundations frequently held treasure, either of their own or entrusted to their care for safety, and they were unprotected. It was not uncommon for the buildings to be destroyed or set on fire and the monks to be massacred.

In the year 843 a number of Norse ships appeared at the mouth of the river Loire. They were piloted up-river by a traitor named Lambert, who had aspired to be count of Nantes and had been driven out by the citizens. When the ships reached Nantes, the people, greatly alarmed, took shelter in the church of SS Peter and Paul the Apostles; and the monks of a nearby monastery, greatly alarmed, carried their ecclesiastical treasure there. Gohard, the bishop, was celebrating Mass. He had just reached the *Sursum corda* when the Norsemen smashed in the doors and windows, forced an entry, and killed him at the altar. The priests who were with him in the sanctuary and the monks were also killed. Leading citizens were captured to be held to ransom, and the church was pillaged and set on fire. Before they withdrew the Norsemen laid waste the whole city. Gohard's body was subsequently recovered, and his relics were taken to Angers, his native town.

AA.SS., June, 7, pp. 681-2; Duchesne, *Fastes*, 3, p. 369; *P.B.*, 7, p. 362.

St William of Vercelli, *Abbot* (1085-1142)

William was born at Vercelli, north of Turin. His parents died when he was very young, and although he was kindly cared for by relatives, he seems to have made up his mind very early that he wanted to lead a penitential life. He was only fourteen when he set out for Compostela in northern Spain as a pilgrim, wearing two iron bands round his body. He had persuaded a smith to forge them so that he could not take them off. In his early twenties he was living as a hermit on the slopes of Monte Solicoli. He was reputed to have cured a blind man, and this brought him so much unwelcome publicity that he went to stay with St John of Matera (20 June) in the Basilicata, part of the kingdom of Naples. They were kindred spirits and became close friends. William proposed to go on a pilgrimage to Jerusalem, though John assured him that there was work for him closer to home. Soon after he set out he was attacked by robbers: he took this as a sign that John was right and gave up his journey.

He moved to the slopes of Monte Vergiliano in a mountainous area inland from Naples, between Nola and Benevento. The mountain was said to have derived its name from Virgil, who reputedly lived there for a time. At first William lived there as a hermit, but he was soon joined by would-be disciples, both priests and laymen. He formed them into a community. When a church was built and dedicated to Our Lady, the name of the mountain was changed to Montevergine.

William's rule was austere: no wine, meat, or dairy produce was allowed, and on three days of the week only vegetables and dry bread were served. After the first fervour had cooled there was a general demand for some relaxation. William had no desire to constrain his brethren, though he had no intention of relaxing his own Spartan régime. He appointed a prior and left, with John of Matera and five faithful followers, to found a new community at Monte Laceno in Apulia. This was in a wild and inhospitable region. The soil was barren, the site exposed to the elements, and the high altitude made it difficult for even the most hardy to survive in the winter. The monks were discussing a move when it became inevitable: fire destroyed their huts, and they had to descend to the valley. Here William and John parted, William to found a monastery on Monte Cognato in the Basilicata, while John founded another at Pulsano.

When the monastery at Monte Cognato was well established, William again appointed a prior and moved on to found fresh monasteries, this time at Conza, in Apulia, and Guglietto, near Nusco. The foundation at Guglietto was a double monastery, for men and for women. Roger II, the powerful Norman king of Naples and Sicily, was so impressed by William's personality that he drew him to his court at Salerno to have the benefit of his counsel, but some of the courtiers resented William's influence and plotted to discredit him by sending a prostitute to seduce him. The story that William dealt with the situation by parting the logs on a blazing fire, lying down, and inviting the woman to join him may be put down to local exaggeration; but at all events the woman was converted, gave up her way of life, and entered a convent. She is remembered as Bd Agnes of Venossa and numbered among the penitents of the Church. The envious courtiers were silenced. King Roger continued to support William and endowed a number of religious houses, which he placed under his control.

William died at Guglietto on 25 June 1142. He left no written Constitution, but a code of regulations bringing the Congregation of Montevergine into conformity with the Benedictine Rule was drawn up by the third abbot general, Robert. Montevergine is now a place of pilgrimage. Though the monks

194

followed the Benedictine Rule, they retained their original white habits and are sometimes known as Whitemantles. In art William is represented kneeling before the Virgin Mary. His remains were translated to the crypt of the church at Montevergine in 1807.

AA.SS., June, 7, pp. 97-121, has an account from a manuscript apparently written by William's disciple John of Nusco. This has some interesting personal touches, though the manuscript is faulty. A better text, edited by Dom. C. Mercuro, which fills some gaps in the earlier copy, was discovered in Naples and published in the *Rivista Storia Benedettina* 1 (1906), 2 (1907), and 3 (1908), with a historical commentary. See also G. Mongelli (1960); P. Lugano, *L'Italia Benedettina* (1929), pp. 379-439; *Saints in Italy*, pp. 457-8; *Bibl.SS.*, 7, 487-9. The church at Montevergine was rebuilt after the Second World War, incorporating elements and treasures from earlier churches: G. Farnedi, O.S.B., *Guida ai Santuari d'Italia* (1996), pp. 291-3.

Bd Henry Zdik, *Bishop* (1150 or 1151)

Bishop Henry Zdik's cult has never been officially approved, but the great services he rendered to the Church in his own country and beyond have caused him to be honoured as a *beatus* in the Czech Republic. He is said to have been closely connected with the rulers of Bohemia, but it is not clear what the nature of the relationship was. All that is known for certain is that he was born in Moravia and in 1126 he became bishop of Olomouc. Under his auspices, Duke Wenceslaus I undertook the building of the cathedral, and the completion and decoration of the basilica were Bishop Henry's own concern. In 1137 or 1138 he made a pilgrimage to Jerusalem. While he was there he experienced a spiritual awakening and took the Praemonstratensian habit.

When he returned to Olomouc he joined a mission to convert the Prussians, and in 1143 he was one of the founders of the abbey of Strabov. He entitled it Mount Sion and brought to it Praemonstratensians from Steinfeld, near Cologne. Later he restored the monastery of Litomerice, of which he is reckoned the second founder, and named it Mount Olivet.

Bishop Henry tried to enforce the Roman observance on his clergy, particularly in the matter of celibacy. Since this proved difficult, he set out for Rome to confer with the pope, but soon after he started on this journey he was set upon by would-be assassins and barely escaped with his life. A second attempt was unnecessary, for the papal nuncio arrived in Bohemia and gave him the support and authority necessary to carry out his reforms. He died in 1150 or 1151 and was buried in the monastery at Strabov.

AA.SS., June, 7, pp. 121-4; A. Zark in *Annales de l'Ordre de Prémontré* (1908; 1910).

Bd John the Spaniard (1123-60)

Jean l'Espagnol, as the French called him, was probably born in Almanza, east of the Spanish city of León. At the age of thirteen he went to France with a companion to study, and they were taught at Arles. When his studies were completed John went to study with a hermit for about two and a half years and was then admitted to the Carthusian monastery of Montrieu or Mons Rivi. There in time he became sacristan, an office he filled for six years, and then prior. He encouraged learning and was personally engaged in the copying and correction of sacred manuscripts.

After a time he resigned as prior and went to the Grande Chartreuse, where St Anthelm (26 June) was the superior. When a nobleman asked Anthelm for Carthusians to make a foundation on his estates near Lake Geneva, he selected John as their prior. The new foundation was called the Reposoir, a place of peace. At Anthelm's request John also drew up a Constitution for Carthusian nuns.

John was at the Reposoir for nine years. During that time he conducted the funeral of two shepherds who had been killed by an avalanche, and he asked that when he died he should be buried with them. On his death in 1160 this was done. A chapel was built over his tomb, but in 1649 his remains were transferred to the sacristy of the monastery church by Charles Augustus de Sales, bishop of Geneva and nephew of St Francis de Sales (24 Jan.). The formal instrument drawn up by him, with a description of what occurred, is still preserved. John the Spaniard's cult was confirmed in 1864.

Annales Ordinis Cartusiensis, 2, pp. 199-212; *B.H.L.*, 1, p. 652.

26

SS John and Paul of Rome, *Martyrs* (? 362)

Apart from their names and the fact that they are Christian martyrs there is little that is certain about these two saints. They have been known since the fourth century, when their relics were deposited in a house on the Coelian Hill given by St Pammachius (30 Aug.) or his father to be converted into a church. In the fifth century a new basilica was erected on the older foundations. This may have been originally dedicated to the apostles Peter and Paul, but it came to be popularly associated with John and Paul, who were said to be brothers and martyrs. Their names were inserted into the Canon of the Mass and included in the Litany of the Saints, and they were commemorated in several liturgies. In the Sacramentary known as the *Gelasianum* their feast was preceded for a time by a vigil with fast, but this was abrogated, possibly because of the proximity to the great feasts of the Birthday of St John Baptist and the Apostles Peter and Paul.

The veneration of John and Paul reached England. William of Malmesbury, writing in the first half of the twelfth century, mentions their shrine on the Coelian Hill, and the Council of Oxford in 1222 enacted that their feast should be kept as a festival of the third order. It was not a holy day, but obligation was laid on the faithful to assist at Mass before going to work.

The recorded acts of these two saints are ancient but of dubious authenticity, since they contain chronological mistakes. They are said to be taken from an account by Terentius, the captain of the guard charged with their execution, and the story is as follows: John and Paul were army officers whom the emperor Constantine assigned to the household of his daughter Constantia. She held them in great esteem and appointed one her steward and the other her majordomo. After a time they were recalled by the emperor and sent to serve in Thrace against the Scythians. When the imperial army was in danger of defeat John and Paul approached the commander, Gallicanus, and assured him of victory if he would become a Christian. He gave the required undertaking, and immediately a legion of angels appeared and put the Scythians to flight. This may be the Gallicanus who is commemorated on 25 June in some Menologies, who is said to have become a Roman consul.

John and Paul continued to serve Constantine and his family until Constantine's death; but when his nephew Julian the Apostate became emperor and rejected Christianity, reinstituting the worship of the old Roman gods, they refused to comply with his orders or to go to court. They were given ten days to reconsider their refusal. Then Terentius was sent with a body of men to carry out their execution at their own house on the Coelian Hill. They were buried in the garden.

Julian the Apostate reigned for only three years, 360 to 363. Pammachius, who was a wealthy Roman and a close friend of St Jerome (30 Sept.), died in 410, so it is certainly possible that the deaths of John and Paul occurred during his lifetime and that he gave the site of the house for a church with a dedication in their names. The emperor Jovian, who succeeded Julian for about two years before his own death, is said to have been responsible for the building of the church.

The present basilica of SS. Giovanni e Paolo in Rome, with its twelfth-century Lombard-Romanesque belfry and colonnaded apse, was bestowed upon St Paul of the Cross (19 Oct.) by Pope Clement XIV, whose pontificate lasted from 1769 to 1774. Excavations in 1887 revealed rooms of the ancient dwelling-house beneath the church. Some of these date back to the second century. The walls are covered with ancient frescoes. The great church dedicated to SS John and Paul in Venice (sometimes called San Zanipaolo in the Venetian dialect) was built by Dominican friars from the convent of SS Giovanni e Paolo in Rome.

AA.SS., June, 7, pp. 138-42, has the story of these martyrs. For its authenticity or lack of it, see H. Delehaye in *C.M.H.*, p. 256; *B.H.L.*, 1, pp. 484-5; P. Franchi de'Cavalieri in *Studi e Testi* 9, pp. 55-65, and 27, pp. 41-62; J. P. Kirsch, *Die römischen Titelkirchen* pp. 26-33, 120-4, 156-8; *Anal. Boll.* 44 (1926), p. 250, and 48 (1930), p. 16; *D.A.C.L.*, 2, 2832-70 has sketches showing reconstructions of the house on the Coelian Hill.

St Vigilius, *Bishop and Martyr* (405)

The principal patron of the Trentino and the Italian Tyrol is Vigilius, who was largely responsible for the conversion of these districts to Christianity.

He was born at Trento, south of Bolzano, of a Roman family which had lived there long enough to acquire rights of citizenship. He was educated at Athens and returned to Trento, where he was elected bishop at an unusually early age. There he founded a church dedicated in the names of SS Gervase and Protase (19 June). Ambrose of Milan (7 Dec.) sent him relics.

A letter to Vigilius from Ambrose, who was his metropolitan, is still extant. In it Ambrose urges Vigilius to oppose usury, to discourage the marriages of Christians to pagans, and to give hospitality to strangers, especially pilgrims. There were still many unconverted people in the mountain villages of the Trentino and the Tyrol, and Bishop Vigilius went to preach to them in person. Ambrose sent him three other missionaries, Sisinnnius, Marturius, and Alexander (29 May), who were martyred in 395. Vigilius wrote a short account of their death to Ambrose's successor Simplician (13 Aug.) and a longer one to John Chrysostom (13 Sept.), whom he had probably known in Athens. In these letters he says how envious he is of these martyrs, and laments that his own unworthiness precluded him from sharing their martyrdom, but he too was martyred some ten years after them. In the year 405 he was preaching in the remote valley of Rendena, and it is said that he physically overthrew a statue of Saturn, the god of agriculture. The infuriated peasants, fearing for their harvest, stoned him to death.

Trento still claims to possess the relics of Vigilius together with relics reputed to be those of his mother and brothers, but it is thought that these may have been translated to Milan in the fifteenth century.

AA.SS., June, 7, pp. 143-8, contains a passion. This, or a similar document, was sent to Rome and seems to be the basis of the statement by Pope Benedict XIV, whose pontificate lasted from 1740 to 1758, that Vigilius was the first saint to be formally canonized by the Holy See. See also Perini, *Cenni sulla Vita de S Vigilio* (1863), and *Scritti di storia e d'arte per il 15 centenaria di S. Vigilio* (1905); *B.H.L.*, 2, p. 1244; *Bibl.SS.*, 12, 1086-8.

St Maxentius, *Abbot* (*c*. 445-515)

The French town of Saint-Maixent-l'Ecole, some few miles south-west of Poitiers, covers the place where Maxentius had his cell and the adjacent monastery he ruled. He was born at Agde, on the Mediterranean coast of France north of Perpignan, and baptized Adjutor. He was brought up in a monastery and was much esteemed by the abbot; but praise was distasteful to him, and he quietly slipped away for two years, perhaps to live as a hermit. When he returned, he found himself thrust into even greater prominence, because his return coincided with rain after a prolonged drought, so he was hailed as a wonder-worker. He still sought obscurity, so he left Agde for good and made his way north to Poitou, where he entered a community in the valley of Vauclair presided over by Abbot Agapitus. In order to efface the past he took the name of Maxentius.

If he could conceal his identity, he could not conceal his sanctity. He lived so austerely that he ate only barley bread and drank only water. He prayed so constantly that his back became bent. He was elected abbot by the unanimous vote of his brethren about the year 500. During the war that raged a few years later between Clovis, king of the Franks, and Alaric the Visigoth, the monastery was threatened by a band of armed men. Maxentius reassured his monks and went out to meet the invaders. One of the soldiers raised his sword to strike the abbot down but found himself unable to do so. It is said that his arm remained as though paralyzed until Maxentius restored it through the application of holy oil.

Following the example of his predecessor Agapitus, Maxentius laid down his office at the approach of old age and went to live in a cell near the monastery. There he died at the age of seventy.

In art Maxentius is often represented with birds perched on his shoulder, or stroking a bird held in one hand. The birds were his companions in the forest.

There are several Lives of Maxentius in French and a somewhat doubtful text in *AA.SS.*, June, 7, pp. 148-55; *B.H.L.*, 2, p. 849; *P.B.*, 7, pp. 370-1. The story of Maxentius was the subject of lively discussion in the *Revue des questions historiques* in 1883 and 1888.

St John of the Goths, *Bishop* (*c.* 800).

Though he has no particular cult in the West, John of the Goths is honoured in the Eastern churches because of his resistance to Iconoclasm. He was a native of the area north of the Black Sea that includes the Crimea, and his grandfather was an Armenian legionary. In 761 the then bishop of the Goths, who subscribed to the imperial edicts banning sacred pictures and images, was rewarded by being promoted to the see of Heracles. The people of his diocese, who were more orthodox, asked that John should be appointed in his place. The request was granted, but they had to await his return from Jerusalem, where he spent three years.

John wrote a defence of the veneration paid to sacred images and relics and of the practice of invoking the saints. His arguments were supported by quotations from the Old and New Testaments as well as by references to the teaching of the Fathers of the Church. Under the regency of the empress Irene the ban against sacred images was raised, and John was able to go to Constantinople to attend the synod summoned by St Tarasius (18 Feb.). He also attended the Second Council of Nicaea in 787, when doctrine with regard to sacred images was clearly defined.

After his return John's diocese was invaded by the Khazars. He was betrayed into the hands of their chieftain and spent some time as a captive before escaping and finding a refuge with Bishop Georgios of Amastris in Asia Minor. Here he was hospitably treated and spent the last four years of his life. Upon being informed that the Khazar chieftain had died he turned to his friends and said, "And I too shall depart from hence in forty days, and will plead my cause with him before God." He died peacefully some forty days later. His body was conveyed back to his country by the bishop of Amastris and interred in the monastery at Partheniti in the Crimea.

AA.SS., June, 7, pp. 162-71, contains an account of John's activities and a near-contemporary Greek biography. See also *B.G.*, June, p. 374.

St Anthelm, *Bishop* (1107-78)

Anthelm, the son of a Savoyard nobleman, was born in the castle of Chignin, near Chambéry. He ministered for some years as a secular priest and became provost of Geneva. He was a man of methodical habits and kept excellent accounts, thereby increasing the revenues of the Church.

Some of his relatives were Carthusians, and he visited them in the monastery of Portes. He was impressed by the stillness of the valley. Its limestone crags and pines offered him a very different life from the one he led over the accounting tables of Geneva. He was also attracted by the Order and its way of life. The hermits led solitary lives in cells built around a cloister, in solitude and silence. Meals were served to them through a shutter on the cell door, and they said most of their offices privately. Communal meals and communal worship were reserved for Sundays and holy days.

Anthelm determined to join the Order. He received the habit about 1137, and before he had completed his novitiate he was sent to the Grande Chartreuse. The monastery was going through a difficult time: an avalanche had destroyed most of its buildings, with a consequent loss of morale among the monks. Family contacts, leadership qualities, and financial skills must all have played a part in Anthelm's capacity to restore the great foundation to full functioning and prosperity. On the resignation of Prior Hugh I in 1139 he was elected as his successor, the seventh prior of the Grande Chartreuse.

His first care was to restore the ruined buildings, which he enclosed within a high wall. He brought water in through an aqueduct and renewed the farm premises and the sheepfolds. He re-established the primitive Rule, which had fallen into abeyance. At that time the charterhouses operated independently, each one being subject only to the bishop of the diocese. Anthelm was responsible for summoning the first general chapter. The Grande Chartreuse was recognized as the motherhouse, and he became in fact if not in name the first minister general of the Order.

Anthelm's reputation for holiness and wisdom brought him many recruits. Among them were his own father, his brother, and William, count of Nivernais, who became a lay brother. Anthelm commissioned John the Spaniard (25 June) to draw up a Constitution for women who wished to live under the Carthusian Rule.

After governing the Grande Chartreuse for twelve years, Anthelm resigned his office and went at his own wish to live as a solitary; but he was not allowed to do so for long. When Bernard, the founder and first prior of Portes, resigned on the grounds of old age, Anthelm, who was still in his early forties, was appointed to replace him. Portes was a very wealthy monastery. Anthelm declared that its church treasures, full coffers, and overflowing barns were incompatible with the poverty enjoined by the Rule. In a time of scarcity he ordered food and money to be distributed to all who were in need, and some of the church ornaments were sold to provide extra resources.

Two years later he returned to the Grande Chartreuse, but again he was not left to live in obscurity for long. He became involved in the struggle of Pope Alexander III against the antipope, Victor IV, who was the nominee of the emperor Frederick Barbarossa. Anthelm and Geoffrey, the Cistercian abbot of Hautecombe, succeeded in influencing their own brethren and the religious of other communities in favour of Alexander, promoting his cause in France, in Spain, and even in England. When the bishopric of Belley became vacant, Pope Alexander set aside the selected candidates and nominated Anthelm.

Though Anthelm entreated the pope to spare him, Alexander was insistent, and the consecration took place on 8 September 1163.

Once consecrated, Anthelm set to work with characteristic thoroughness. He was quite uncompromising in enforcing clerical celibacy. When persuasion and warnings failed, he deprived those clergy who lived openly as married men of their benefices. He defended the rights of ecclesiastical jurisdiction against the laity: when Humbert III, count of Maurienne, imprisoned a priest accused of a misdemeanour, Anthelm sent a representative to free him, threatening excommunication if Humbert resisted. Humbert tried to rearrest the priest, and the priest was killed in the scuffle. The threat of excommunication was carried out. Even when the pope, with whom Humbert was something of a favourite, asked Anthelm to lift the ban, he refused, saying, "He who is justly bound may not be loosed unless for the wrong done penance has been made." The pope lifted the ban on his own authority. Anthelm protested that the pontiff was acting *ultra vires*—that even St Peter himself did not have the authority to take this action. He retired to Portes and was persuaded to return to his diocese only with difficulty. Even then he refused to allow Humbert to receive the Sacrament.

The pope did not, apparently, hold this against him. Probably because of his firm stand for ecclesiastical authority, Anthelm was chosen as legate for a mission to England to mediate between King Henry II and Thomas Becket (29 Dec.), though this mission never took place.

Anthelm continued to manage the affairs of his diocese and to live in Carthusian simplicity. Any time he could spare was spent in the Grande Chartreuse or the other houses of his Order. Two other causes particularly concerned him—a community of women solitaries at a place called Bons, and a leper house where he would tend the lepers with his own hands. He continued to care for the people of the diocese, and he was making a distribution of food during a famine when he was seized with a fever which was to prove fatal. Before he died, Count Humbert came to beg his forgiveness and to promise amendment of life.

Anthelm's relics were preserved during the French Revolution and are in the Chapel of St Anthelm at Belley, to which they were translated on 30 June 1829.

AA.SS., June, 7, pp. 201-19, has a Life apparently written by a contemporary, obtained from the Grande Chartreuse. See also the *Annales Ordinis Cartusiensis*, vols. 1 and 2, and vol. 3, pp. 375-406; C. Marchal, *Vie de S. Anthelme* (1878); *P.B.*, 7, pp. 375-81; *B.G.*, June, pp. 378-84; *D.H.G.E.*, 3, 523-5.

Bd Josemaria Escriva de Balaguer, *Founder* (1902-75)

José María Escribá, to give him his original Spanish name, was born in Barbastro, a town in north-eastern Spain not far south of the French border, on 9 January 1902. He was the second child of José Escribá, a textile merchant whose family came from Balaguer, some miles to the south, and his wife, Dolores Albas. José María had an elder sister, Carmen, a younger brother, Santiago, and three younger sisters who died in infancy. The family was devoutly religious. When José María was two years old he was seriously ill and was expected to die. His mother prayed unceasingly to the Blessed Virgin, and when the crisis was over his parents took him to the shrine of our Lady at Torreciudad to give thanks. He was to speak of this occasion many times in later life.

In 1915 his father's business collapsed, and the family moved to Logroño, between Pamplona and Burgos, where for a time they lived in somewhat straitened circumstances. At sixteen José María decided to study for the priesthood. He entered a seminary in Logroño and after two years of theological studies proceeded to the seminary of Zaragoza. He studied both theology and law, and qualified in both. He was ordained on 28 March 1925 and became a licentiate in law in 1927. In 1928 he proceeded to the university of Madrid to write his doctoral thesis.

This took him several years. To support himself he taught at a tutorial college for some time and then became chaplain to the Damas Apostólicas (the Apostolic Ladies of the Sacred Heart), who cared for the sick poor of the city. He learned about the conditions of the urban slums, ministering the sacraments to the terminally ill and dying. He also came into contact with wealthy and powerful people whose support would be valuable to a cause.

He had a sense of a special vocation and he constantly prayed *Ut sit* (that it may be so)—that is, may what God has designed for me come to pass. It was on 2 October 1928 that he had the inspiration for Opus Dei—"like a divine seed falling from heaven," as his biographer Vasquez says. He was making a retreat at the time at a house on the outskirts of Madrid. He heard the bells ring out from the nearby church of Our Lady of the Angels, and the plan grew from that moment.

Afterwards, he refused to talk about the experience. At its inception, Opus Dei was simply a group of men, mostly postgraduate students, who wanted to put the gospel into action. Weary of what they regarded as the elaborate and cumbersome structures of the Church, they lived in common without formal organization, without distinctive dress, and without rules, apart from a commitment of total obedience to the founder, who was the only priest. Like the Society of Jesus, they used military terminology. They were "Christ's Army," working in the world, particularly in Catholic teaching in the increasingly secularized Spanish educational system.

Fr José María's mother, sister, and brother came to live in Madrid. His mother, Dolores, had received an inheritance, and they bought a house in the Calle de Ferraz large enough for themselves and for the first residents. A chapel and an oratory were added. The structure of the community was based on the family: Fr José María was known as the Father, Dolores as the Grandmother, and Carmen as the Aunt. The group did not court publicity, but it was known that they lived a strictly religious life, including a devotion to the Virgin Mary and some extreme penitential practices. It was here that the founder wrote his *Spiritual Considerations*, published in 1934. The book consisted of a series of maxims which he enlarged and elaborated, republishing the revised manuscript in 1939 as *El Camino*, "The Way." This has remained one of the basic and revered texts of Opus Dei.

It is important to see the development of José María's thought against the background of the shattering events in Spain in the 1930s. The dictatorship of Primo de Rivera ended in 1931, when there were elections and a republican government took office. Two days later King Alfonso abdicated, and a republic was proclaimed. The Spanish monarchy had traditionally been strongly identified with the Church, and the ending of the monarchy meant the persecution of the Church. The Jesuits were expelled, crosses and sacred images were removed from schools and other buildings, ecclesiastical property was appropriated, and relations between the government and the Vatican were broken off. When the civil war broke out in 1936, monasteries and churches were burned all over Spain, and priests, monks, and nuns were executed without trial as enemies of the State. In all, some four thousand priests and two thousand religious met violent deaths.

The members of Opus Dei were scattered, and Fr José María's life was in danger. He passed as a layman and for a time posed as a patient in a psychiatric clinic. He hid in attics and closets when the militia came searching for Catholics. He spent several months in the embassy for Honduras. When his mother visited him, she did not recognize him because he had been ill and had lost so much weight. Eventually he escaped to Andorra and travelled on foot through the Pyrenees into France. He was used to hardship. It was inevitable that he should support General Franco, who promised a crusade to restore Spain to its traditional glory as the foremost Catholic power in Europe. He was with the first nationalist troops who marched into Madrid. It was from an army observation post that he used a military range-finding telescope to look for the house in the Calle de Ferraz. It was in ruins.

In Franco's Spain, Opus Dei grew rapidly. Fr José María developed a doctrine of "National Catholicism," which involved a combination of strict religious faith based on Thomist teaching with a fervent love of the traditional Spanish heritage. Protestantism, Judaism, agnosticism, atheism, socialism, and liberalism were all equally to be regarded as enemies. "National Catholicism" had the support of the minister of education, José Ibañez Martín, who had been much impressed by a member of Opus Dei when they were both in a refugee camp in France.

The defeat of the Republicans left many vacant posts in universities and schools. Catholics of proven right-wing sympathies were required to fill them, and Opus Dei was an ideal channel to provide them. It acquired considerable influence in the Spanish educational system within a few years, recruiting both teachers and students and setting up hostels in universities and colleges. From February 1950 the movement accepted women as well as men, though they were kept strictly to teaching their own sex and to separate accommodation. Most recruiting was done among students by a procedure known as "fishing." Recruits were often told not to discuss their membership with their parents.

Concern about the operations of Opus Dei grew largely because its members, now including some priests as well as laypeople, were not identifiable. They wore no special dress, they did not talk about Opus Dei practices, and most followed their own occupations. Even diocesan bishops found it difficult to discover which of their clergy were members of the movement or what was going on in their own dioceses. Secrecy led to suspicion, and opposition grew: in Barcelona *El Camino* was burned, and Opus Dei members were wildly accused of belonging to a Jewish sect allied to the Freemasons. More soberly, the Jesuits, those earlier soldiers of Christ, were highly critical of a movement which seemed to have no organizational structure and which was not responsible to any properly constituted authority within the Church.

Opus Dei's response fundamentally altered its character. In 1943 plans were drawn up for an approved organization to train its own members for the priesthood, the Sacerdotal Society of the Holy Cross. Fr José María secured the approval of Pope Pius XII, and on 25 June 1944 the first three candidates, all former engineers, were ordained. By 1946 the Sacerdotal Society had twelve priests, 250 "numeraries" or full-time members in training, and 400 "oblates." There were houses in all the principal cities of Spain.

In 1939-45, while much of the world was convulsed by war, Spain was at peace. Italy surrendered to the Allies, then Germany, and then Japan; but while other dictatorships perished, Spain had remained virtually isolated under a Fascist government. In 1943, after the surrender of Italy, Fr José María made his way to Rome in difficult conditions to seek approval for conditions in which Opus Dei could become an international movement. At a time when the whole Western world seemed to be moving to socialism or communism, the Vatican was receptive. Fr José María had two audiences with Pope Pius XII. In 1947 an Apostolic Constitution, *Provida Mater Ecclesia*, set out a framework for secular Institutes, of which there were by that time a number in different countries. The Institutes were placed under the control of the Sacred Constitution for Religious, and Opus Dei was the first to be recognized.

Fr José María was appointed a domestic prelate to the pope, which gave him the title of monsignor and the right to wear purple. On the advice of Mgr Montini, the future Pope Paul VI, and with the help of an Italian duchess, Virginia Sforza Cesarini, he acquired the former Hungarian embassy to the Holy See as a headquarters for Opus Dei in Rome. Hungary was by that time part of the Soviet bloc, and official relations with the Vatican had been broken. The building was renamed the Roman College of the Holy Cross and was popularly known as the Villa Tevere.

Rome became the headquarters of the movement. From about 1960 the founder began to sign his Christian names as one word, Josemaria, and to use the more elaborate Castilian form of his family name: Escriva de Balaguer y Albas. It became usual to render both without the accents required in Spanish. In 1968, he petitioned for and was granted the disused title of marquess of Peralta.

Financial support came from many sources in the postwar world, and he travelled tirelessly in other countries to found new branches of Opus Dei. The movement spread—to Portugal, England, France, Ireland, Mexico, the United States, Australia, New Zealand, and South America. Opus Dei became a very influential and wealthy international organization with its own publishing houses and radio stations.

The Second Vatican Council of 1962-5, convened by Pope John XXIII, brought liberalizing changes to the Church. Though Mgr Escriva had initially welcomed the setting up of the council, he was not in sympathy with many of the outcomes, identifying with the views of Pope John's successor, Paul VI, who spoke of the dangers of the "decomposition of the Church." Though Opus Dei had pioneered in the development of the work of the laity, the organization was strongly opposed to the growing movement for democracy in Church structures. To charges that it was traditionalist and old-fashioned, its supporters replied that Opus Dei sought to teach the Faith, even if it was inconvenient and currently unfashionable. They were even more strongly opposed to liberation theology when that movement developed after 1968.

In 1962 Mgr Escriva approached the Vatican with a proposal for a "personal prelature," which would exempt Opus Dei from the supervision of the Catholic hierarchy. This proposal, which drew very strong opposition from the Spanish bishops, was not approved until after his death; but in 1978 Pope John Paul II set in motion the procedure for a personal prelature, which was finally granted in 1983.

Mgr Escriva died suddenly at the Villa Tevere in Rome on 26 June 1975. The cause of canonization was introduced in Rome on 19 February 1981, and his beatification was pronounced by Pope John Paul II in Rome on 11 May 1992.

This procedure was completed with unusual haste. In the case of many canonizations, the cause takes centuries to reach the very stringent standards of proof required. It was not completed without controversy. Though he had many powerful supporters, the decree of beatification mentions "detractors" and the fact that Josemaria Escriva suffered "the weight of contradictions" during his earthly life. The prefect and secretary of the Congregation for the Causes of Saints issued a lengthy statement, published in the *Osservatore Romano*, to tell the faithful that that they were aware of "discordant voices" within the Church who had expressed opposition to the beatification and to assure them that proper procedures had been "carefully followed." Opus Dei has issued a fact sheet referring to "unsubstantiated criticisms" of "political motivation and spiritual formalism."

The controversy is increasingly concerned with the current standing of Opus Dei, which continues to evolve, rather than with the life of its founder, which was necessarily influenced by the time and place in which he lived. Josemaria Escriva's devotion to the Church and his massive contribution to the maintenance of its traditional attitudes and practices are undeniable. Some commentators have attributed his opposition to any liberalization to his experience in the polarized Spain of the 1930s, when to be left-wing or even liberal was to be an enemy of the Church. Opus Dei members are anxious to rebut the implications of what they call "the Spanish question," arguing that his move to Rome in 1946 effectively separated the movement from its Spanish roots. Catholics who have welcomed the insights of Vatican II continue to have reservations about an influence in the life of the Church which they regard as retrogressive.

The main Lives written by members of Opus Dei are those by A. Vasquez de Prada (1983); L. Carandell (1975); Salvador Bernal (1977); and William Keenan (1990). An authorized biography (unattributed) was published by Opus Dei in Rome in 1992. For a summary of critical views, see Michael Walsh, *The Secret World of Opus Dei* (1989), which has a very full bibliography. María del Carmen Tapía's *Beyond the Threshold* (1996) describes life in Opus Dei, including five years which the author spent working with the founder. William Connor's *Opus Dei: An Open Door* (Dublin 1991) is a reply to Michael Walsh. See also *Osservatore Romano*, 20 May 1992; *N.C.E.*, 10, pp. 709-10. Principal writings by Josemaria Escriva (now available in many languages, including English) are *The Holy Rosary* (1934); *The Way* (1939); *Friends of God* (1977); *Furrow* (1986); *The Forge* (1988).

ST CYRIL OF ALEXANDRIA (over page)
Gold pens, white scroll with black Theotokos *for his defence*
of the Blessed Virgin, on blue field.

27

ST CYRIL OF ALEXANDRIA, *Bishop and Doctor* (376-444)

Cyril is commemorated in the Syrian and Maronite Mass as "a tower of truth and interpreter of the Word of God made flesh." He made it a rule never to advance any doctrine which he had not learned from the Fathers of the Church, and he was a champion of orthodoxy. He defended the doctrine of the person of Christ as formulated at the Council of Nicaea against Nestorius, patriarch of Constantinople, drawing on the works of such authorities as Athanasius (2 May), Basil the Great (2 Jan.), and Gregory Nazianzen (2 Jan.).

Theophilus, patriarch of Alexandria and Cyril's uncle, was responsible for the deposition and exile of John Chrysostom (13 Sept.) from the patriarchate of Constantinople. Though Chrysostom's theology was always sound, he was creative and innovative, and he became a powerful and outspoken reformer. He incurred the emnity of the emperor Arcadius and of the patriarch Theophilus himself by his attacks on the misuse of wealth and other abuses. Theophilus, perhaps inspired by the growing rivalry between Alexandria and Constantinople and wanting the emperor's favour, found means of discrediting Chrysostom on what are now regarded as frivolous and unsustainable charges, and Cyril appears to have assisted his uncle in this.

Cyril succeeded Theophilus in 412. According to the historian Socrates, he acquired "greater power than Theophilus ever used," and his episcopate "went beyond the limit of its sacerdotal functions." His actions as patriarch seem to have been designed to secure orthodoxy at all costs: he drove out the Jews from Alexandria and shut the churches of the Novationists, a schismatic group, confiscating their sacred vessels and stripping their bishop, Theopemptus, of all his possessions. He also quarrelled with the imperial prefect, Orestes. An influential woman Neoplatonist philosopher, Hypatia, who advised Orestes on many matters, was brutally murdered in the streets by Cyril's supporters. Although Cyril almost certainly had no hand in the murder, her death is indicative of the atmosphere of intolerance and violence which was only too common in Alexandria at the time.

Nestorius, a priest-monk of Antioch, became archbishop of Constantinople in 428. The standard teaching of his school was that Christ had two natures, human and divine, and that these were joined by a "moral union." God took the form of a man, but the human body was only the temple of the divine spirit. The Blessed Virgin gave birth to Jesus, but not to the *Logos*, who always existed. She was *Christotokos*, Christ-bearing, but not *Theotokos*, God-bearing.

Cyril argued that this formulation made the Incarnation an illusion and under-mined the doctrine of redemption. The issue was referred to Rome, where Pope Celestine I condemned the teaching of Nestorius, deposed him, and threatened him with excommunication unless he retracted. Cyril was deputed to carry out the sentence, and he sent Nestorius a letter containing twelve anathemas.

Nestorius refused to retract; and Cyril convened the Council of Ephesus in 431, attended by some two hundred bishops. Proceedings were held before the arrival of the archbishop of Antioch and forty-one bishops of that jurisdiction, most of whom were supporters of Nestorius, and also before the arrival of the papal legates. In the circumstances, Nestorius refused to appear before the council, and he was again condemned. Six days later the Antioch bishops arrived, accused Cyril of heresy, and issued a decree of their own deposing him. Both sides appealed to the emperor, on whose order both Cyril and Nestorius were arrested for a time. Pope Celestine eventually confirmed the condemnation of Nestorius and approved Cyril's conduct. The result was schism—the creation of a separate Nestorian Church which carried out much missionary work in India and China before it was virtually overwhelmed by the Mongol invasions of the fourteenth century.

Commentators have differed over whether Cyril was a true champion of orthodoxy, defending essential doctrines, or whether the schism with the Nestorians might have been prevented by discussion and mutual forbearance. Certainly passions were roused on both sides. Cyril's writings on the subject are extensive. He was declared a Doctor of the Church by Pope Leo XIII in 1882.

There is a painting of Cyril by Domenichino in the Basilican church of Grotto Ferrara, near Rome. In art he is often shown contemplating a vision of the Virgin Mary, to commemorate his championship of her title as the Mother of God.

Socrates, *H.E.*, 7, 7; *AA.SS.*, Jan., 3, pp. 459-70; *P.G.*, 67-77. See also *D.T.C.*, 3, pt. 2, 2475-527, "Cyrille d'Alexandrie," and 5, pt. 1, 137-63, "Ephèse, Concile d'"; *N. C. E.*, 4, pp. 571-6; W. Burghardt, *The Image of God in Man According to Cyril of Alexandria* (1957); encyclical letter of Pope Pius XII, *Orientalis ecclesiae decus*, 1944.

St Samson of Constantinople (Fifth Century)

Some time during the fifth century, probably about the middle, a rich and philanthropic priest named Samson, or Sampson, founded at his own expense a great hospital for the sick poor of Constantinople. He is said to have been a Roman by birth, a relative of the emperor Constantine, and a physician as well as a priest. He ministered personally to those who suffered in body, mind, or spirit. The hospital was named after him, and he was honoured during his lifetime as "Samson the Hospitable" and "Samson Xenodochus" (Samson who cared for strangers). After he died he was venerated as a saint. He is listed in a number of Greek Menologies.

In the sixth century his hospital was burned to the ground, and it was rebuilt by the emperor Justinian. Early chroniclers made an earnest attempt to connect the two, saying that Samson had cured Justinian of a deadly disease and that Justinian built the hospital in thanksgiving; but Samson died before the year 500, and Justinian did not become emperor until 527. During the Crusades the hospital was taken over by the Knights Templar.

P.G., 115, 277-308, and *AA.SS.*, June, 7, pp. 233-49, include the Greek text of a biography attributed to the Metaphrast. *C.M.H.*, p. 258; *B.H.G.*, p. 230; *Bibl.SS.*, 11, 636-8; L. Miller, *The Birth of the Hospital in the Byzantine Empire* (1985), pp. 80-3.

St John of Chinon (Sixth Century)

John was a hermit, a stranger to the Loire Valley, who settled at Chinon, between Tours and Saumur, and developed a reputation as a healer and a wise man. He was said to come from Brittany, but nothing is known of his antecedents. He is also known in France as St Jean du Moustier (a corruption of *Monasterii*) or Jean de Tours. Gregory of Tours (17 Nov.) recorded the story of how Queen Radegund (13 Aug.) consulted him when she fled from her brutal husband, Clotaire I, who had murdered her brother. She feared that Clotaire would hunt her down and force her to return.

A messenger arrived at John's retreat bearing a present from Radegund and asking for his hair-shirt and his prayers. John prayed all night and sent back a message saying that Radegund had nothing to fear from Clotaire. She was later made a deaconess by St Médard (8 June) and founded the monastery of the Holy Cross at Poitiers, where she lived in peace for many years.

John died in his solitary retreat and was buried in his oratory near the church of St Maximus.

Gregory of Tours, *De gloria confessorum*, ch. 23, Eng. trans. R. Van Dam, (1988), pp. 38-9; *B.G.*, June, p. 388.

St George Mtasmindeli, *Abbot* (*c.* 1014-66)

The curious name of this saint means "George of the Black Mountain." He is also known as "George the Athonite," a reference to his connection with Mount Athos, and "George the Hagiorite." He was sent to a local monastery at the age of seven to commence his education and after three years moved to another, at Habuli, where two of his uncles were monks. One of the two went to live as chaplain in a noble house and took the young George with him. The boy was treated as a son of the house and given an excellent classical Greek education, which was to prove of great importance for his future work. He returned to the monastery at Habuli when he was twenty-five, then made a pilgrimage to Jerusalem and subsequently spent some time as the disciple of another Georgian monk, George the Recluse, who lived on the Black Mountain near Antioch.

At the age of about thirty he became a monk of the monastery of Romanos, and he was ordained priest at Mount Athos. He was for some time abbot of Ivoron on Mount Athos, where he set up a scriptorium for the copying and translation of sacred documents. George the Recluse urged him to make use of his Greek by translating Greek texts into Georgian for the benefit of the Georgian (Iberian) Church, and this became his life work. He returned to the Black Mountain and made an extensive contribution to Georgian sacred literature, translating the Old Testament, the New Testament, many apocryphal writings, and liturgical, exegetical, and homilectic works of the Fathers of the Church.

George Mtasmindeli is said to have refused to become a bishop; but he spent five years reforming the Georgian Church on the basis of the literature he had made available to his own countrymen, and he defended its autonomy against the patriarch of Antioch. According to his Life, said to have been written by a disciple called George the Little, "the patriarch and all the bishops were amazed at the acumen of his mind, and the way in which the words of holy writ flowed from his mouth like a river undammed." The patriarch was apparently won over and "treated the holy monk with great respect and generosity as long as he stayed in the land of Antioch."

George made another pilgrimage to Jerusalem, and when Georgia was suffering from Turkish invasions, he set out for Mount Athos with twenty-four orphans whom he had taught Georgian and Greek, with the intention that they should enter the monastery; but he died on the way at Constantinople, on the feast of SS Peter and Paul. He is recognized as a Doctor of the Georgian Church.

Among his writings are two treatises, *The Months* and *The Fasts*, and a revision of the biblical translations of St Euthymius the Enlightener (formerly 13 May), an abbot of Ivoron who had translated much of the Bible from Greek into Iberian. George Mtasmindeli is also known for a statement on the use of unleavened bread in the Eucharist. A few days before his death, the emperor Constantine X Dukas inquired of him why the Greeks used leavened bread, while the Latins used unleavened bread. Some years earlier the patriarch Cerularius had withdrawn from communion with Rome on the grounds that the use of unleavened bread was "a horrible disease." George answered that the Greeks used leavened bread out of humility, because they had been several times stained by heresy, but the Latins used unleavened bread because they had kept the Faith in its full purity. This diplomatic answer indicates that the hermit's sympathies were with Rome rather than Constantinople.

P. Peeters in *Anal.Boll.* 36-7 (1917-19), pp. 69-159, discusses a number of contemporary manuscripts written at the instigation of George the Recluse. *D.T.C.*, 20, pp. 643-4, has a biography in Georgian. D. M. Lang, *Lives and Legends of the Georgian Saints* (1956), has a chapter on the Georgian Athonites and includes passages from the manuscript attributed to George the Little, pp. 154-72. M. Tamarati, *L'Eglise georgienne* (1910), lists the works of George Mtasmindeli, pp. 331-2.

St Ladislaus of Hungary (1095)

St Stephen of Hungary (16 Aug.), crowned on 1 January 1000, the first day of the new millennium, established the monarchy and made Hungary a Christian nation. Ladislaus (Lazlo), also of the house of Arpád, brought a new glory to it and is similarly remembered as a champion of the Church.

Stephen died in 1038. His last years were made difficult by disputes over the succession after the death of his son Emeric, and there followed a period of political intrigue and domestic violence. Ladislaus came to the throne in 1077 and defeated his kinsman Solomon in battle. Hungary was a small country with no natural borders, so he spent much of his adult life in warfare—fighting against Slavs, Huns, Poles, Russians, and other border tribes, but he did his best to win them over by peaceful means if he could. He is said to have been the embodiment of all the virtues of chivalry—strong, courageous, and zealous for the Faith. His personal life was austere and pious, his manner was benevolent. He allied himself closely with Pope Gregory VII and governed firmly in both civil and ecclesiastical affairs. Within Hungary he allowed civil and religious liberty to Jews and Muslims but protected the Church.

Ladislaus was so well known as a champion of Christendom that the kings of France, Spain, and England sent an emissary to him inviting him to lead the Christian armies on the First Crusade. He was overjoyed and went to Bohemia, where he asked his nephew the duke of Bohemia to accompany him; but before he could lead the armies to Jerusalem, he died suddenly at Nitra in Bohemia at the age of fifty-five.

From the time of his death Ladislaus was honoured as a saint and a national hero, and his deeds have formed the theme of many popular Magyar ballads and stories. He was canonized in 1119 by Pope Celestine III or his successor Innocent III, and his relics were solemnly enshrined in 1192.

AA.SS., June, 7, pp. 284-94; S. L. Endlicher, *Rerum Hungaricarum Monumenta Arpádiana* (1849), pp. 235-44 and 324-48. There is an article, "St Lazlo," in English, trans. E. Lindner, in the *Ungarische Revue* for 1885. The best of the Lives in Magyar is said to be that by J. Karacsonyi (1926). See also *Revue archéologique* (1925), pp. 315-27, and C. A. Macartney, *The Medieval Hungarian Historians* (1953).

Bd Benvenuto of Gubbio (1232)

Benvenuto was a native of Gubbio, in Umbria, and a former soldier. He said that soldiers made good monks because they had already formed habits of discipline, endurance, and obedience. He could neither read nor write, but he came under Franciscan influence and received the habit as a lay brother. From the start he modelled his life entirely on that of St Francis. At his own request he was placed in charge of the lepers, and he treated them as though they had been Christ himself, tending their sores, washing them, and never shrinking from the most repulsive cases or the meanest tasks. He waited on them hand

and foot, and although he had serious illnesses, he bore his own sufferings with much patience.

Benvenuto lived an exemplary life as a member of the Franciscan movement. He was totally obedient to authority and was never known to merit a reproof of any sort. He often spent much of the night in prayer, stretching out his arms to the Christ-child. He died at Corneto, in Apulia, and was buried in the parish church: the convent's own church was too small to receive all the people who came to his funeral. He was beatified by a decree of Pope Innocent XI published in 1697.

AA.SS., June, 7, pp. 295-300; Wadding, 4, p. 325; *Auréole Séraphique*, 2, pp. 427-9; *Bibl.SS.*, 2, 1251; *F.B.S.*, pp. 473-5.

Bd Madeleine Fontaine and Companions, *Martyrs* (1794)

These four Daughters of Charity of St Vincent de Paul suffered during "the Great Terror" in revolutionary France. In the period from September 1793 to August 1794, when Austria, Prussia, England, and Spain had combined to attack France, the policy of "dechristianization" reached its height. All public and private worship was forbidden, and priests and nuns were arraigned and executed as "enemies of the State."

The small community at Arras consisted of seven Sisters, who nursed the sick people of the town and conducted a school for girls. Their work became endangered in 1793 when Joseph Lebon, a notorious apostate priest, seized the community's goods and imposed a lay director on the school. For a time the nuns were permitted to continue their nursing duties in secular dress. Realizing that worse was to come, the superior, Mother Madeleine Fontaine, sent the two youngest nuns to Belgium disguised as peasants. She was herself seventy-one years old. One Sister, who had taken temporary vows, had returned to her family when these expired, and the remaining three, Françoise Lanel, Thérèse Fantou, and Jeanne Gérard, were all in their forties. They joined their superior in refusing to take the oath demanded of clergy and religious by the Revolutionary Convention.

They were arrested as suspects on 14 February 1794. Evidence of their so-called "counter-revolutionary activity" was fabricated, and they were taken to Cambrai, where Joseph Lebon was in charge of investigations. They arrived on 26 June, were brought before a tribunal on the same day, and were condemned to be executed. The sentence was carried out on the following day.

The Sisters went to their death singing *Ave maris stella*. Mother Madeleine was the last to go to the guillotine, and as she approached it she turned to the crowd and shouted, "Listen, Christians! We are the last victims. The persecution is going to stop. The gallows will be destroyed. The altars of Jesus will rise again gloriously."

Her prophecy came true. France was weary of persecution. Robespierre, the architect of the Terror, went to the guillotine in July of that same year, and Joseph Lebon followed him in August. The four Martyrs of Arras were beatified with the Martyrs of Valenciennes on 13 June 1920 by Pope Benedict XV.

L. Misermont, *Les Bienheureuses Filles de la Charité d'Arras* (1920), in the series Les saints; A. Lovat, *The Sisters of Charity Martyred at Arras in 1794* (1920); *N.C.E.*, 1, p. 849. See also "Martyrs of the French Revolution," (2 Jan.) in the present work.

Bd Louisa de Montaignac, *Foundress* (1820-85)

Louise-Thérèse Montaignac de Chauvance was born on 14 May 1820 at Le Havre, where her father was a prominent financier. The family was a devout one, and at the age of seven she was sent to the boarding school of the Faithful Companions of Jesus at Chateauroux. There she developed a devotion to the Sacred Heart of Jesus. She was also influenced by an aunt who introduced her to the writings of St Teresa of Avila.

Her aunt was much concerned at the religious indifference of French society and developed a plan for a society of women devoted to the Sacred Heart who would "renew society by their example and their holy lives." She did not live to carry out this plan. Louisa had been planning to enter Carmel, but her spiritual director suggested that she should fulfill her aunt's intentions. On 8 September 1843, at the age of twenty-three, she made a vow to devote herself wholly and completely to the Sacred Heart of Jesus, and in 1848 she moved to Montluçon to found the Guild of the Tabernacle. Her aim was to establish a Congregation devoted to venerating Our Lord in the Holy Sacrament of the Altars through penance and worship. But there were many years of hard work and discouragement, in which she worked with other Congregations, before she was able to found the Pious Union of the Oblates of the Sacred Heart in 1874. Throughout the years she inspired many other people to work in meeting the needs she saw so clearly—setting up orphanages and educational establishments, cleaning and decorating poor churches, promoting Eucharistic adoration and retreats.

She died on 27 June 1885 and was beatified by Pope John Paul II on 4 November 1990.

Osservatore Romano, 5 Nov. 1990; *A.A.S.* 84, pt. 1 (1992), pp. 115-7.

28

ST IRENAEUS OF LYONS, *Bishop* (*c*. 125-202)

Irenaeus was Greek, born in Asia Minor, possibly near Smyrna. When he was a boy he was greatly influenced by St Polycarp (23 Feb.), who was bishop of Smyrna and a disciple of St John the Evangelist (27 Dec.). Eusebius quotes a letter to Florinus in which Irenaeus writes of his memories of Polycarp:

> I remember the events of that time more clearly than those of recent years, for what boys learn, growing with their mind, becomes joined with it, so that I am able to describe the very place in which the blessed Polycarp sat as he discoursed, and his goings out and his comings in, and the manner of his life, and his physical appearance, and his discourses to the people, and the accounts which he gave of his intercourse with John and with the others who had seen the Lord. . . . These things being told to me by the mercy of God, I listened to them attentively, noting them down not on paper but in my heart.

Through Irenaeus the apostolic tradition was passed on to a new generation, and to Gaul.

Irenaeus had an excellent education, which gave him a thorough knowledge of the scriptures and a good grounding in Greek philosophy and literature. He had studied in Rome under Justin Martyr (1 June), and his theology derived much from his teacher. Gregory of Tours (17 Nov.) says that it was Polycarp who sent him to Gaul, but there is no evidence to support this statement. We do know that he was one of the early missionaries to Gaul. In the second century Levantine traders from the ports of Asia Minor regularly travelled to Marseilles and up the Rhône to Lugdonum, now Lyons, which became the chief market of western Europe and the largest city in Gaul. Some of the traders settled there, and the missionaries followed. The first bishop was St Pothinus, also from Asia Minor, who, like Irenaeus, had "listened to those who heard the Apostles." Irenaeus was attached to the bishop's household, and he was evidently highly esteemed, because in the year 177 he was entrusted with an important mission to Rome.

The Church in Lyons was already under attack. Christians were insulted, expelled from public meetings, stoned and beaten by mobs. A terrible persecution followed, probably later in that same year, in which Bishop Pothinus and many other Christians were killed (see Martyrs of Lyons; 2 June). The letter which Irenaeus carried to Pope Eleutherius was not concerned with the plight of the Lyons clergy, some of whom were already in prison when he left the city. It contained a plea for the pope's clemency for their brethren in Phrygia, who were currently influenced by the Montanist heresy. The links with the Church of the Middle East were evidently still very strong. The letter described Irenaeus as a priest "filled with zeal for the testament of Christ" and, as his name implied, a lover of peace.

This mission explains why Irenaeus was not involved in the persecutions at Lyons and did not witness them. We do not know how long he remained in Rome, but when he returned it was to occupy the vacant bishopric and to rebuild the work of the Church in the Rhône Valley. The twenty or more years of his episcopate were years of relative peace. Information about his activities is sparse, but we are told that he habitually used the language of Gaul rather than his native Greek, so it seems that he made considerable efforts to identify with his people. In addition to his pastoral activities he did much to evangelize the neighbouring districts. He is said to have sent the priest Felix and the deacons Fortunatus and Achilleus (23 Apr.) to Valence; and Ferreolus and Ferrutio, priest and deacon (16 June), to Besançon. All five were to be martyred in another outburst of persecution about the year 212.

Irenaeus is best known for his writings in defence of the Faith against Gnosticism. The Gnostic movement was difficult to define and took many forms. It existed in Palestine in Jesus' day, and the Gnostics claimed Jesus as one of their teachers. By the second century it seems to have combined Greek philosophy, mythology, and some magical rites with elements of Christianity. One basic doctrine was that the visible world was created, preserved, and governed by angelic beings, while the Demiurge (or God) remained aloof from it. Tertullian tells us that Irenaeus was "a curious explorer of all kinds of learning." Gnostic tenets were very widespread in Gaul, and Irenaeus produced a treatise in five books in which he set out the doctrines of the various Gnostic sects and contrasted them with the teaching of the apostles.

He was convinced that much of the attraction of Gnosticism lay in the secrecy of its adherents and their pride in being an inner circle of initiates. He writes: "As soon as a man has been won over to their way of salvation, he becomes so puffed up with conceit and self-importance that he imagines himself to be no longer in Heaven or on earth, but to have already passed into the Pleroma [the invisible spiritual world], and with the majestic air of a cock, he goes strutting about—as if he had already embraced his angel." Irenaeus was determined to "strip the fox," as he put it—to make clear the ways in which this mix of beliefs differed from Christian belief. He sets out the Christian view of the Trinity in forthright terms: "The Father is above all, and he is the head of Christ, but the Word is through all things, and he is himself the head of the Church, while the Spirit is in us all; and his is the living water which the Lord gave to those who believe in him and love him and know that there is one Father above all things and through all things and in all things." He insists that God cares for all human beings, not only for those who follow esoteric rituals:

"God's splendour is the source of life, those who see him share this life. . . . God sustains the universe in being. His nature and his greatness cannot be seen or described by any of the creatures he has made. But he is known to all of them. The Word proclaims to all that there is one God the Father, who holds all things in being, and gives being to all creatures."

In *Adversus Haereses* Irenaeus produced a major work of Christian apologetics. Originally written in Greek, it was quickly translated into Latin and widely circulated through the Church. From that time onward Gnosticism ceased to offer a serious challenge to the Christian faith. The treatise against the Gnostics is extant in its full Latin version, and great interest was raised in 1904 by the discovery of a work entitled *Proof of the Apostolic Teaching*, of which previously only the title had been known. Though the rest of his works have not survived, these two texts provide the elements of a complete system of Christian theology.

About the year 190 Irenaeus was asked to mediate between the pope and a body of Christians in Asia Minor. This group, the Quartodecimans, refused to keep Easter in accordance with the Western use. It seemed that a schism was imminent. Irenaeus, still a peacemaker, intervened with the pope on their behalf, pointing out that they were only following their old tradition and that a difference of opinion on this point had not prevented Pope Anicetus and St Polycarp from remaining in communion with Rome. The Quartodecimans were allowed to keep to their own tradition—though they conformed to the Roman usage at the time of the Council of Nicaea in 325 without any pressure from the Holy See.

Irenaeus is thought to have died about the year 202. There was a later tradition that he had been martyred, but this is now thought to be improbable. Gregory of Tours writes that his body was buried under the altar of what was then called the church of St John in Lyons, and this church later bore a dedication in the name of Irenaeus himself. The shrine survived until 1562, when it was destroyed by the Calvinists.

The feast of St Irenaeus has long been observed in the East (23 Aug.) but has been general in the Western Church only since 1922.

Eusebius, *H.E.*, 5, 20; *AA.SS.*, June, 7, pp. 303-15; *C.M.H.*, p. 260; F. R. M. Hitchcock, *Irenaeus of Lugdunum* (1914); *D.T.C.*, 7, pp. 2394-2533 (an entry of nearly 150 columns); *B.H.L.*, 1, p. 661; *D.C.B.*, 3, pp. 255-79; *P.B.*, 7, pp. 402-16; Bardenhewer, 1, pp. 496-521. Ruinart, pp. 117-9, classifies Irenaeus as a martyr. For the arguments for and against the martyrdom of St Irenaeus, see *C.M.H.*, pp. 341-2. Eng. trans. of *Adversus Haereses: Against Heresies*, ed. F. R. M. Hitchock (1898). See also John Lawson, *The Biblical Theology of St Irenaeus* (1948).

SS Plutarch, Potomiaena, and Companions, *Martyrs*
(Early Third Century)

The school of theology at Alexandria was famous at the beginning of the third century. Though doctrines of some of its teachers (notably Origen) were later found somewhat unorthodox, it provided a training ground in Christian perfection, and many of those associated with it were martyred for their faith.

The persecutions of Severus raged from 202 to his death in 211. Plutarch was the brother of Heraclas, later bishop of Alexandria. The two brothers had been converted to the Faith together by listening to the lectures of Origen, who became catechist at Alexandria in 203. After Plutarch's arrest Origen visited him in prison, and he went with him to his execution. Origen himself was nearly lynched, because the crowd was very sympathetic to the martyrs and he was thought to be responsible for Plutarch's death. With Plutarch died six other martyrs who attended the catechetical school: three men, Hero and two named Serenus; and three women, Marcella, her daughter Potomiaena, and Herais.

Potomiaena is said to have been young, beautiful, and accomplished. She refused offers to spare her life at the expense of her chastity and died a cruel death with such patience and courage that her executioner, Basilides, was converted. He too was executed.

Eusebius, *H.E.*, bk. 6, ch. 5; Palladius, *Historia Lausiaca*, ed. Cuthbert Butler (1904), bk. 3; Ruinart, pp. 168-71; *P.B.*, 7, pp. 418-7.

St Paul I, *Pope* (767)

The immediate successor to Pope Stephen III in the chair of St Peter was his younger brother Paul. They had been educated together at the Lateran school and had been made deacons together by Pope St Zachary (15 Mar.), whose pontificate lasted from 741 to 752. Paul remained closely associated with his brother, carried out diplomatic missions for him during his papacy, nursed him through his last illness, and continued his policies after his death.

His diplomatic relations were highly competent. According to Mgr Mann, "by unceasing diplomatic effort, Paul prevented the Lombards on the one hand and the Greeks on the other from effecting anything of moment against the newly-acquired temporal powers of the supreme pontiff; he caused great events never to get beyond the eve of happening." He kept on the best of terms with King Pepin of the Franks, then the most powerful monarch in Christian Europe, sending him polite letters, presents (including an organ), and relics of the martyrs. Pepin's protection was an important bulwark against the Lombards and the Greeks. He gave the Holy See the district of Ravenna, which he had captured from the Lombards. This was of particular importance, because Ravenna had been the seat of Byzantine rule in Italy for over two centuries before its conquest by the Lombards in 712.

Some historians have suggested that Paul cared only for the temporal affairs of the Church; but it can be argued that these were the pressing problems of the papacy at the time. A contemporary, writing in the *Liber Pontificalis*, emphasizes Paul's kindness, his clemency, and his magnanimity. He was always ready to help people in distress: he is known to have visited the sick poor in their homes or in hospitals, and he frequently redeemed poor debtors from prison. He also did much to honour the memory of the early martyrs. Many of the catacombs had been destroyed or badly damaged by the barbarians, and Paul caused the relics of many saints to be transferred to churches in Rome. The relics of St Petronilla, then supposed to be St Peter's daughter, were brought to a restored mausoleum which became known as the Chapel of the Kings of France. Paul also built or rebuilt the church of SS Peter and Paul and had an oratory constructed in St Peter's in honour of Our Lady. He turned his family mansion into a monastery under the dedication of the popes St Stephen I (2 Aug.) and St Silvester (31 Dec.) and placed in it Greek monks who were refugees from the Iconoclastic persecution. He rebuilt the adjoining church for them, and this was given the name of San Silvestro in Capite. The title referred to the head which these monks had brought as a relic from the East, reputed to be the head of John the Baptist. Eleven hundred years later, that church (long since rebuilt again) was given by Pope Leo XIII to the English Catholics in Rome.

Pope Paul's useful and busy pontificate lasted some ten years. Like so many popes, he was overcome by the heat and noxious air of the Roman summer, and he died of a fever at St Paul's Outside the Walls on 28 June 767. He is buried in a tomb in St Peter's, Rome, which he had prepared for himself.

Lib.Pont., 1, pp. 463-7; *AA.SS.*, June, 7, pp. 343-8; Mann, 1, pt. 2, pp. 331-60; *O.D.P.*, pp. 92-3; *Christian Worship*, p. 102. *M.G.H., Epistolae Selectae*, 3, pp. 508-55, contains letters from Pope Paul to Pepin and his sons.

St Heimrad (1019)

Heimrad was an eccentric and a wanderer. Some of his contemporaries thought he was a saint, others that he had a demon or that he was an impostor. The story of his life probably tells us more about the social attitudes of the late tenth and early eleventh centuries than it does about his claims to sanctity.

His parents were serfs on a great estate in Swabia. He must have possessed some unusual qualities as a young man, for the noble and wealthy lady on whose estate he had been born thought he was devout, had him trained for the priesthood, and appointed him her chaplain. Her benevolence went unrewarded, because he proved quite unfitted for the post, and he was released at his own request. He decided to go on pilgrimages, first to Rome and then to Jerusalem, begging his bread as he went and sharing with other wayfarers whatever alms he received. When he returned to Europe he wandered about western Germany. There were many people on the roads, and the distinction between a traveller, a vagrant, a wandering lunatic, and a pilgrim was not a very clear one.

At one time Heimrad seemed inclined to settle in the abbey at Hersfeld, where he was given shelter, though he refused to take the habit or submit to the Rule. One day when the community was in chapter, he threw himself dramatically on the floor and asked leave to depart, saying that he was sure he could never find salvation there. The abbot made no attempt to detain him, and he was somewhat unceremoniously ejected. Outside the monastery he complained vociferously, saying that it was wrong that the abbot and the monks should treat him, an emperor's brother, in this manner. The bystanders were much amused, and the abbot directed that he should be whipped and turned away. Apparently the whipping was a fairly mild one, and he went on his travels again.

At Detmold, in Westphalia, a kindly parish priest allowed Heimrad to take over a disused church; but he soon had cause to regret it, for his congregation, attracted by the gaunt form and peculiar utterances of the newcomer, decided that he was a saint and transferred their offerings to him. The priest was a married man, as was then often the case in rural areas, and his wife took Heimrad a gift. He refused it on the grounds that she was living an immoral life. This was too much for the priest, who set the dogs on him.

Heimrad continued to wander from place to place and was generally treated with contempt, often with violence, even by people with a claim to holiness. They thought they were beating out the devil. St Cunegund (24 July), wife of the Holy Roman Emperor, had him beaten when he appeared before her. St Meinwerk (5 June), bishop of Paderborn, challenged him with being a demoniac. Heimrad replied that he did not have a devil: he was a priest, and he had just celebrated Mass that day. Meinwerk asked to see his office books. They were so dirty and dilapidated that the bishop had them flung on to the fire and ordered Heimrad to be beaten again.

Eventually this strange man found peace, perhaps because he was getting old and no longer had the strength to wander. He made a retreat for himself in a wooded area of western Germany near where the town of Wolfhagen now stands and lived there in great poverty and destitution. He died in 1019. After his death stories of miraculous happenings at his tomb began to be circulated, and it became a place of pilgrimage. He became called a saint by popular local acclaim, not by any official sanction; but the same is true of many early candidates for sainthood.

Heimrad's biographer, Egbert, was a monk of Hersfeld. He wrote some fifty years after Heimrad's death and claimed to have the story from his father and from others who had known the recluse personally. He suggests that many of the extravagant things Heimrad did were deliberately undertaken to draw contumely upon himself. This is possible: Francis of Assisi (4 Oct.) and his companions had a similar instinct to make themselves the lowest of the low, and this form of asceticism is well known in Eastern hagiology. Egbert also says that when Heimrad claimed to be an emperor's brother, he meant only that, like all men, he was a brother of Jesus Christ.

Egbert wrote in charity; it seems that the monks of Hersfeld and the townspeople had not forgotten their curious visitor, and perhaps their consciences were troubled long after he was driven out of the area. Today, he might be classified as a misfit, a drop-out, or mentally ill. Born a serf, he was subjected to a social experiment by a rich lady. It failed, and he had nowhere to go and no place to fill. He was harmless, though troublesome. Perhaps the best reason for including him in a book of saints is that he acts as a marker for our own consciences.

Egbert's account of Heimrad is published (with illustrations) in *AA.SS.*, June, 7, pp. 350-9; *M.G.H., Scriptores*, 10, pp. 598-607.

SS Sergius and Germanus of Valaam, *Abbots* (date uncertain)

These two saints are venerated as Greek monks who founded the great Russian monastery of Valaam (Valamo) on the island of that name in Lake Ladoga, Finland. The monastery was founded as a centre of evangelism, with the aim of converting the Karelians, who lived on the shores of the lake.

This event is commonly dated to the period 973-92, at the time when the evangelization of the Russians was taking place around Kiev; but there are no grounds for accepting such an early date, and a more likely one is 1329, when Russian monasteries were being planted in the Ladoga region as part of a political consolidation against the Swedes of western Karelia. The monastery was certainly founded before the fifteenth century, but when Peter the Great re-established it in 1718 it had been an unoccupied ruin for more than a hundred years. Consequently, written and oral tradition had been broken, and there is no information about the original foundation.

According to tradition, Sergius was a stranger from Novgorod or from Byzantium. One story is that he was the head of the powerful trading community in Novgorod. He came to live in the Vaaga cave, an old site of pre-Christian religious practices. From there he counselled and healed the people of the district, and for his living and a recreation he carved in stone. Gradually disciples came to join him; he was regarded as their abbot and was the leader in local affairs.

Germanus (Herman) was a contemporary of Sergius and his collaborator. The shrines of the two saints have been venerated for centuries in the *katholikon* of the Valaam monastery, which has continued to function despite the very chequered political history of the region. It is now kept by monks of the Finnish Orthodox Church, and is open to visitors.

Information from the director of the Finnish state archives at Viborg. Article by Fr S. M. Quandalle in *Russie et Chrétienté* 1 (1938); C. F. L. St George in the *Eastern Churches Quarterly* 3, no. 3 (1938); Valamo Sura Ry, *Valamo and its Message* (1982).

St John Southworth, *Martyr* (1634)

Interest in John Southworth was raised by the discovery of his remains at Douai in 1927. They were subsequently enshrined in the chapel of St George and the English Martyrs at Westminster Cathedral. The Southworths were a Lancashire family who remained staunchly Catholic through a long period of persecution and became impoverished through heavy fines. John, a member of the younger branch of the house, was sent to Douai in 1613 to be trained for the priesthood. After his ordination he tried his vocation for a time with the Benedictines; but deciding that he was not called to the monastic life, he decided to remain a secular priest.

On 13 December 1619 he was sent on the English Mission. All that is known about his activities in the next few years is that he was living in or near London in 1623. In 1624 he went back to Belgium, where he was confessor to the Benedictine nuns for a time. Then he was sent back to England, this time to his native Lancashire, where he ministered until 1627.

He was arrested and charged with being a priest. The law was not rigorously enforced at that time: Queen Henrietta Maria and many of the nobility were practising Catholics, and King Charles I was known to be sympathetic. John Southworth was sentenced to death but reprieved and imprisoned in Lancaster Castle. He was able to give absolution to his fellow Lancastrian, the Jesuit Edmund Arrowsmith (28 Aug.), as that priest was taken to his execution. After three years in prison John Southworth was taken to London and there released with some fifteen other priests at the insistence of Queen Henrietta Maria. They were ordered to leave the country, but it is doubtful whether Fr John obeyed this injunction. He was certainly living in England soon afterwards, and in 1632 he was a prisoner in the Clink. He was not harshly treated. The Puritan Prynne called him "a dangerous seducer" and complained that "he had full liberty to walk abroad at his pleasure, as most priests had during their imprisonment."

He made good use of his liberty. In 1636 there was an outbreak of plague in London, and with a fellow-prisoner, Fr Henry Morse (1 Feb.), he visited stricken houses in Westminster daily. Parish relief was denied to Catholics, and the two priests took alms from the queen and other wealthy Catholics besides hearing confessions and administering the sacraments. At one point, he was strictly confined to prison because the curate of St Margaret's Westminster alleged that he was converting people on their death-beds. The queen intervened; he was allowed to visit again, and shortly afterwards he was released from prison.

His position, and that of other priests, was precarious: though they had royal support, king and Parliament were in conflict. It was against the law, supported by the increasingly hard-line Protestant Parliament, for Catholic priests to carry out their office. The conflict between king and Parliament was rapidly reaching the point of no return. When the Civil War broke out and the king himself was executed, the priests of the English Mission were again regarded as political enemies of the realm. Challoner notes that Cromwell's party "looked upon the Papists as mortal enemies to their government, and as fast friends and devoted servants to the crown and the royal family."

There is no information about John Southworth's activities under the Commonwealth, but in 1654 he was seized at night by a party led by Colonel Worsley, Cromwell's representative. When he admitted having exercised his functions as a priest, he was condemned—though even the judge urged him to plead "not guilty" and frantic efforts to save him were made by the French and Spanish ambassadors. He was dragged on a sledge to Tyburn between two counterfeiters on the eve of the feast of SS Peter and Paul. He was seventy-two years old.

Thousands turned out to watch the execution, though it was a stormy and rainy day. They listened quietly while he made his final speech:

> Hither I was sent by my lawful superiors to teach Christ's faith, not to meddle with any temporal affairs. Christ sent his apostles; his apostles, their successors; and their successors, me. I did what I was commanded by them who had power to command me. . . . I die for Christ's law, which no human law, by whomsoever committed, ought to withstand or contradict.

Eventually, "being interrupted by some officers desiring him to make haste, he requested all present who were Catholics to pray for him and with him." With eyes closed and hands raised to heaven, he "expected the time of his execution, which immediately followed."

His body was bought by the Howards of Norfolk and taken to the chapel of the English College at Douai, where it remained until the college was seized by the revolutionary authorities in 1793. To save the relics from profanation, four students secretly removed the coffin and buried it inside the building. It was discovered by a workman in 1927 during the excavation of the foundations of the former college. The relics were identified and brought back to England to rest at St Edmund's College, Ware, which carried on the work of the old Douai seminary. Four months after the beatification of the English Martyrs in 1929, of whom John Southworth was one, the relics were brought to Westminster, to be solemnly enshrined in the cathedral on 1 May 1930. He is one of the Forty Martyrs of England and Wales canonized by Pope Paul VI on 25 October 1970.

The best source is Fr A. B. Purdie's *The Life of John Southworth* (1930); see also *M.M.P.*, pp. 504–10.

29

ST PETER, *Apostle and Martyr* (? 64)

The early part of Peter's ministry is familiar to us from the Gospels. We know that he was a Galilean, that his original home was at Bethsaida, and that he was the brother of the apostle Andrew (30 Nov.). They were the sons of John, or Jonah, and they worked as commercial fishermen in partnership with James (25 July) and John (27 Dec.), the sons of Zebedee. Peter was married and lived at Capernaum with his wife and his mother-in-law, whom Jesus cured of a fever (Mark 1:20-1). His name was Symeon in Aramaic, which was the common language of the area, and Simon in Greek. Both forms occur in the Gospels. Jesus told him on their first meeting that he should be called *Képa'*, which meant "rock" or "stone" in Aramaic. The Greek word was *Cephas* or *Petros*. The choice of this name had a great significance in Judaea, where great rock formations alternate with shifting sand dunes. Jesus used the contrast between the two in his teaching (Matt. 7:24-6; Luke 6:48-9).

It was Peter who, as the spokesman of the apostles, made the sublime confession of faith: "You are the Christ, the son of the living God"; and it was to Peter that Jesus replied:

> Simon son of Jonah, you are a happy man. Because it was not flesh and blood that revealed this to you but my Father in heaven. So I now say to you: You are Peter, and on this rock I will build my Church. And the gates of the underworld can never hold out against it. I will give you the keys of the kingdom of heaven: whatever you bind on earth shall be considered bound in heaven, and whatever you loose on earth shall be considered loosed in heaven (Matt. 16:17-19).

The key phrase "You are Peter and on this rock I will build my church" does not translate well into English. In the Latin version, which circles the great dome of the basilica of St Peter in Rome, it is *TU ES PETRUS ET SUPER HANC PETRAM AEDIFICABO ECCLESIAM MEAM*, which preserves the double meaning; but in English we still use the verb "to petrify," which means "to turn into stone."

Peter's leadership of the disciples is made clear in the Gospels. Whenever the Twelve are listed he is always mentioned first (Matt. 10:1; Mark 3:16; Luke 6:14; Acts 1:13). He asks questions in the name of the others (Luke 12:41, Matt. 15:15-16 and 21:20). With James and John he witnesses the raising of Jairus' daughter (Mark 5:37), the transfiguration (Mark 9:1-7), and Jesus' agony in Gethsemane (Mark 14:37), and his name comes first in each case. He is courageous and impulsive: he tries to walk on the water (Matt. 14:28-31); he wants to make tents on the mountain for Jesus with Moses and Elijah (Mark 9:5); and he is determined to keep faith with Jesus to the death, even if all the others forsake him (Mark 14: 29).

The story of Peter's triple denial of Jesus in spite of his assertion of faith is told by all four evangelists (Matt. 26:69-75; Mark 14:66-72; Luke 22:54-62; John 18:15-27). They tell it with an immediacy and a fullness of detail that indicate the depth of despair among the apostles: even Peter did not stand firm when put to the test. If Peter did not heed Jesus' warning before the event, we need to remember that the warning was prefaced, according to St Luke, by a prophecy implying that his inability to keep faith would involve more than human weakness: "Simon, Simon! Satan, you must know, has got his wish to sift you all like wheat; but I have prayed for you, Simon, that your faith may not fail, and once you have recovered, you in your turn must strengthen your brothers."

After the resurrection the triple denial is forgiven and replaced by a triple affirmation:

> After the meal, Jesus said to Simon Peter, "Simon, son of John, do you love me more than these others do?" He answered "Yes, Lord, you know I love you." Jesus said to him, "Feed my lambs." A second time he said to him, "Simon son of John, do you love me?" He replied "Yes, Lord, you know I love you." Jesus said to him, "Look after my sheep." Then he said to him a third time, "Simon son of John, do you love me?" Peter was upset that he asked him the third time "Do you love me?" and said "Lord, you know everything; you know that I love you." Jesus said to him "Feed my sheep" (John 21:15-17).

This is followed by another prophecy, according to John: that when Peter is old, he will be bound and taken where he would not wish to go; and the evangelist adds, "In these words he indicated the kind of death by which Peter would give glory to God."

On the day of the resurrection Peter, hearing that the tomb is empty, runs all the way to see for himself. The Beloved Disciple, who is younger, runs faster; but in deference to Peter he stands aside and allows Peter to enter first (John 20:3-10). After the ascension Peter takes a leading part in the activities of the apostles. He is named first in the group of apostles who prayed in the upper room with the women and Mary the mother of Jesus, awaiting the coming of the Holy Spirit (Acts 1:13). He leads the election of Matthias to replace Judas as one of the Twelve; and on the day of Pentecost he is the first to address the crowd in the power of the Spirit:

> Men of Israel, listen to what I am going to say. Jesus the Nazarene was a man commended to you by God. . . . This man . . . you took and had crucified by men outside the Law. . . . God raised this man Jesus to life, and all of us are

witnesses to that. Now raised to the heights by God's right hand, he has received from the Father the Holy Spirit, who was promised, and what you see and hear is the outpouring of that Spirit (Acts 2:22-3, 32-3).

When the people ask what they should do, Peter tells them to repent and be baptized, "and there were added in that day about three thousand souls."

At all the crucial decisions of the early Church, Peter takes the lead. He performs the first healing, of the lame man lying at the gate of the Temple, saying, "I have neither silver nor gold, but I will give you what I have. In the name of Jesus Christ, walk!" (Acts 3:6). He and John face the Sanhedrin, the rulers, elders, and scribes of Jerusalem, who are astonished at their assurance "considering they were uneducated laymen" (Acts 4:5-22). He takes charge of the inquiry into the fraud of Ananias and Sapphira (Acts 5:1-11). He and John go to Samaria to lay hands on those baptized by Philip the Deacon (6 June; Acts 8:14-17), the first mission outside Israel; and it is Peter who deals there with the magician Simon Magus, who wants to purchase the Holy Spirit and use it for his own ends.

It is Peter who receives the revelation that, against all his instincts as a good Jew, he must accept people who are not in the line of Abraham and Moses as Christians. He is hungry and waiting for his meal when he has a vision of all sorts of animals and birds that he has been taught to regard as profane or unclean, and he is told to eat of them: "What God has called clean, you have no right to call profane" (Acts 10:9-16). So, overcoming a lifetime of reluctance to mix with Gentiles, he baptizes the Roman centurion Cornelius and his household. Though there were debates to come over whether Gentile converts should be required to observe the Law of Moses and to be circumcised, and Paul later reproached Peter with being half-hearted (Gal. 2:11-14), this was a momentous step in the history of the Church. Leaving James (St James the Less; 3 May) in charge of the Church in Jerusalem, he visits "one place after another," including the churches in Galilee, Lydda, Sharon, and Joppa (Acts 9:31-6), carrying out a healing ministry. Paul tells us (1 Cor. 9:5) that Peter's wife usually accompanied him on these journeys.

As the Church grew, so it faced persecution. King Herod Agrippa killed James, who was administering the Church in Jerusalem, and had Peter cast into prison. He was evidently an important prisoner and one who needed a close guard to prevent his friends from rescuing him. He was assigned four teams of four soldiers to guard him in shifts and made to sleep between two soldiers, bound to them with chains. Outside, the Church prayed for him unremittingly; and on the night before his trial he was rescued, by an angel according to Acts 12:1-11, and walked past the sleeping soldiers to safety.

After that, "Peter departed and went to another place." From this point, Peter is not mentioned in the Acts of the Apostles, except in connection with the Council at Jerusalem in the year 49 or 50 to discuss the status of Gentile converts. There is an ancient tradition, recorded by Origen and Eusebius, that he was the founder of the Church at Antioch, and Paul mentions him as being in that city (Gal. 2:11). He probably went to Corinth for a time: Paul, when appealing to the Corinthians to overcome their divisions, mentions a group who say, "I am for Cephas" (1 Cor. 1:12).

The tradition that Peter went to Rome has been much debated. The first general letter of Peter to all those Christians "living among foreigners" comes from "Babylon," which was a code name for Rome among Christians (1 Pet. 5:13). The authorship of this letter has been questioned, but it is now generally thought to be authentic, though the second letter was probably written much later by another hand. Paul does not mention Peter in his letter to the Romans, thought to have been written in 57 or 58, but it may have been written after Peter's death, or while he was absent from Rome; and in any case, the two were not the closest of colleagues after Paul's angry outburst at the Council of Jerusalem (Gal. 1:11-14). It is no longer accepted by commentators that Peter ruled the Church in Rome for twenty-five years, but it is accepted that he was martyred there during the reign of Nero (54-68); though if there was a written account of his imprisonment and execution it has not survived. The story that Peter, leaving Rome at the earnest request of his flock shortly before his arrest, met Jesus going toward the city, and asked him, *Domine, quo vadis?* ("Lord, where are you going?") is first recorded in the apocryphal Acts of Peter in the second century. Jesus replied, "I am going to Rome to be crucified again," and Peter turned back.

According to a very old tradition he was confined in the Mamertine prison, where the church of St Peter in Carcere now stands. Tertullian (d. *c.* 225) says that he was crucified. Eusebius adds, on the authority of Origen (d. 253), that he was crucified head downward, at his own wish. The place is thought to have been the gardens of Nero, where so many executions took place during his reign.

Irenaeus (28 June), writing in the second century, calls the Church at Rome "the greatest and most ancient Church, founded by the two glorious apostles, Peter and Paul." Irenaeus had been taught by Polycarp (23 Feb.), who had sat at the feet of John the Evangelist (27 Dec.), so this was an oral tradition going back to the days of the early Church. Eusebius quotes Gaius, a priest of Rome in the time of Pope Zephyrinus (189-207), as stating that Peter's body was interred in the Tropaion, a memorial shrine in a cemetery on the Vatican Hill. This was thought to have been set up within twenty years of Peter's death by Pope Anacletus, whose pontificate lasted from the year 79 to 81. The relics were subsequently transferred to the catacombs for safety during the persecutions of Heliogabalus (218-22) or Valerian (253-60), when the Tropaion was destroyed. They were not returned to Vatican Hill until they were housed in the new basilica built by Constantine early in the fourth century.

The names of Peter and Paul are bracketed together from a very early date. Archaeological investigations in 1915-22 at the catacombs on the Appian Way, close to the present church of St Sebastian, revealed a large room dated to about the year 250. The plaster walls are covered with scribblings of roughly the same period. Some are now illegible, but about eighty refer to Peter and Paul, with such inscriptions as "I, Tomius Coelius, made a feast in honour of Peter and Paul"; "Paul and Peter, make intercession for Victor"; and "Peter and Paul, do not forget Antonius Bassus." These spontaneous and often semi-literate appeals, written in Latin or Greek, testify to a great popular cult of SS Peter and Paul at this spot. The inscription set up by Pope Damasus I to the two saints nearby may indicate the place of their interment or commemorate the institution of their festival.

Recent excavations at the Vatican establish beyond reasonable doubt that Peter's tomb now lies under the great basilica which bears his name but do not conclusively prove that the relics are his. However, the evidence, the result of much detailed and rigorous archaeological investigation, is very strong.

Constantine's marble edifice is known to have been built to house St Peter's tomb. The emperor is said to have dug the first spits of earth with his own hands and to have carried from the trench twelve baskets of rubbish in honour of the twelve apostles. Here Peter's body was translated from the catacombs, and the church was dedicated in his name. The present St Peter's, which dates from the sixteenth century, was built on Constantine's foundations. Twentieth-century excavations of the original site of the Christian cemetery, now some forty feet below the ground, have faced many difficulties. The search involved not a single tomb but an extended site, rather like a street in Pompeii, with tombs on either side. In the intervening centuries there has been flooding and soil slippage. There were many bones jumbled together, human and animal: Nero is known to have used part of the area for stabling his horses.

It was not until 1963 that two experts, Professor Corriente of the University of Palermo and Professor Guarducci of the University of Rome, began to study seriously a wooden box which had been put to one side in previous excavations. This had been found in a niche in Constantine's marble edifice, some four or five feet higher than the original cemetery where they expected Peter's relics to have been replaced; but it was possible that they had been interred at a higher level to avoid flooding. The two professors approached the new pope, Paul VI, who, as Cardinal Montini, had been a long-standing friend of Professor Guarducci's family, and obtained his permission to have chemical tests carried out on the niche and contents of the box. These tests indicated that the niche had been constructed in Constantine's time and had not been violated since; that in the box were a variety of bones, including most of the bones and the skull of an elderly man of heavy build, wrapped in imperial purple with gold threads; that soil adhering to the bones matched that of the original central tomb some five feet lower, indicating that it had been moved after the original interment; and that a nearby inscription in Greek reads *PETROS ENI*—"Peter is here."

The findings were greeted with much controversy, some commentators accusing the excavation team of wishful thinking, while others found them too timid in their conclusions. There was considerable debate about Roman textiles and dyes and criticism because the bones had not been carbon dated. The criticism was easily met: carbon dating is not an exact science, and since it was established that the bones had lain undisturbed since the fourth century, there was little point. Further, carbon dating processes would have damaged the bones.

On 26 June 1968, Pope Paul VI presided over a ceremony in the depths of the Vatican. Nineteen carefully-labelled boxes of bones, human and animal (including the skeleton of a mouse which had somehow been included in the wooden box), were replaced in the niche by Professors Correnti and Guarducci, a glass front was affixed, and a prayer recited. A notary read an official description of the proceedings for the records.

"St Peter's Chair," which is preserved in a casing of bronze by Bernini, is a memorial of the apostle's role in the life of the Church. Some writers have conjectured that it may have come from "the house of Prisca and Aquila" (Rom. 16:5) on the site of the church in the Aventine dedicated to St Prisca, and that this may have been the first meeting place of the small Christian community. The feast of St Peter's Chair at Rome was kept throughout Christendom on 18 January from the late sixth century.

It is significant that no place other than Rome has ever claimed the honour of being the see or the resting place of St Peter, and no chronicler through the centuries has disputed the tradition.

The best early representation of SS Peter and Paul is on a bronze medal dating from the first half of the second century. This was found in the catacomb of Domitilla and is now in the Vatican Museum. It indicates that their physical characteristics, as portrayed with remarkable consistency by artists and sculptors in many countries through the centuries, go back to very early models, perhaps even to living memory. Peter is shown as sturdy and thickset, with a curly beard, and Paul as thin and bald, with a long head, a scantier beard, and deep-set eyes.

From early times Peter has been regarded as the heavenly doorkeeper, the patron of the Church and of the papacy. His emblems in art are the keys, a fish or a boat, or a crowing cock in memory of his denial of Jesus. The Sistine Chapel has a painting by Perrugino, the *Delivery of the Keys*, and two of Raphael's works in the Vatican deal with scenes from his life.

AA.SS., June, 7, pp. 1-174; Eusebius, *H.E.*, 2, pp. 25, 27; Jerome, 2, 25; Tertullian, *De praescriptione*, 36, and *Scorpiacus*, 15; *Origines du culte*, pp. 263-9; *N. C. E.*, 11, pp. 200-5, and *Bibl.SS.*, 10, 588-650, both well illustrated; A. S. Barnes, *The Martyrdom of St Peter and St Paul* (1933), and cf. *Anal.Boll.* 102 (1934), pp. 69-72; O. Karrer, *Peter and the Church* (1963); D. W. O'Connor, *Peter in Rome: The Literary, Liturgical and Archaeological Evidence* (1969); For the excavations, see *N.C.E.*, 14, pp. 546-7; J. M. C. Toynbee and J. W. Perkins, *The Shrine of St Peter and the Vatican* (1956); A. A. de Marco, *The Tomb of St Peter* (1964); J. Lees-Milne, *St Peter's: The Story of St Peter's Basilica in Rome*; J. Smith and A. S. Barnes, *St Peter in Rome* (1975).

ST PAUL, *Apostle and Martyr* (? 64 or 67)

The feast on this day is a joint feast of SS Peter and Paul, but precedence is given to St Peter, since this is his main feast. The Church also celebrates the Conversion of St Paul (25 Jan.) as a feast.

As the invocations quoted in the notice on St Peter (above) suggest and many church dedications testify, Peter and Paul are often bracketed together as the joint founders of the Church. Peter was the leader of the apostles during Jesus' lifetime and the main authority figure in the Church after Pentecost; Paul was the intellectual who developed Christian doctrine in the Graeco-Roman world, and he was the indefatigable missionary who spread the gospel across the eastern Mediterranean.

Their personalities, like their roles, were very different. Peter was a Galilean fisherman whose first language was Aramaic, though he and the other disciples probably spoke some Greek. He had walked and talked with Jesus during his earthly life. He had lived through the horror of the crucifixion and the joy of the resurrection. Saul of Tarsus, later Paul, was a city man from what is now southern Turkey—nearly two hundred miles from Jerusalem. He was an outsider to the tight little knot of apostles: a Jew but not a Judaean and with a different social and educational background. He was a Roman citizen, which suggests that his family was well-to-do and that he collaborated with the Roman authorities. Though he earned his living later as a tentmaker, he was well educated in Jewish Law and had studied under the great rabbinical teacher Gamaliel in the Temple at Jerusalem.

Saul was a Pharisee, instructed in the meticulous observance of the Law. One does not have to look far in the Gospels to discover what the Pharisees thought of Jesus, or he of them. They complained of his activities, they watched him, they alleged that he cast out devils through the prince of devils. They said that he mixed with tax collectors and sinners. They were shocked because the disciples did not always wash their hands before eating and because they picked ears of corn on the Sabbath when they were hungry. Jesus, for his part, was scathing about their preoccupation with the external niceties of religion: "If your virtue goes no deeper than that of the scribes and Pharisees, you will never get into the kingdom of heaven," he told the disciples. He told the story of two men who went up into the Temple to pray, one a Pharisee and one a publican: it was the publican who was commended for his humility (Luke 18:10-14). There is a long diatribe in Matthew 23 (perhaps composed of sayings on different occasions) against the scribes and Pharisees, who are repeatedly described as hypocrites and finally as "serpents" and a "brood of vipers." Expressions of this kind were part of the normal language of rabbinical discourse, but they certainly express strong disapproval.

After the crucifixion, Saul was working for the Temple authorities. He guarded the clothes of the official witnesses while they supervised Stephen's martyrdom (Acts 8:59); and he "entirely approved of the killing." He "worked for the total destruction of the Church," arresting men and women Christians and sending them to prison (Acts 8:3). He breathed "threats to slaughter the Lord's disciples" (Acts 9:1). Then he asked the high priest to send him to Damascus with letters to the temple authorities there ordering them to arrest Christians.

On the way he had a shattering experience that changed his life. It may be that guilt had been building up in him for some time and that his vehemence in searching out Christians was an attempt to convince himself that he was in the right. He had never seen Jesus during his earthly life; but something like a year after his crucifixion, he met him on the road to Damascus: "Last of all, he appeared to me too: it was as though I was born when no one expected it." (*New Jerusalem Bible*, 1 Cor. 15:8). Other and perhaps more vivid translations of the Greek are "born out of due time" and "as though I were a late birth." The Pharisees, unlike the Sadducees, believed in an afterlife, so that he was at least intellectually prepared for this revelation.

To their credit the Christians of Damascus took him in, blind and confused, and showed him kindness. They baptized him, changing his name to Paul, gave him food, helped him until he recovered his sight, and let him down over the walls in a basket when he had to escape from the fury of the Damascus synagogue. Back in Jerusalem it was a different matter. The Christian community, with searing and recent memories of his activities, did not want to know him. They thought he was a spy. The Hellenists wanted to kill him because they thought he was a risk to the Church. Only Barnabas (11 June), a good man who had given all his property to the Christian community, believed him and spoke for him. Barnabas was also an outsider: his family came from Cyprus. When he accompanied Paul on his first missionary journey, their first visit outside Palestine was to Cyprus. Tradition has it that Paul was flogged at Paphos, at the pillars which still stand about half a mile from the harbour fortress.

Paul never held any authority in the Church in Jerusalem. His contribution to the Faith was to take the gospel around the eastern Mediterranean, to visit and re-visit the growing churches of Asia Minor, and to superintend them through letters. He writes of "my daily preoccupation: my anxiety for all the churches" (2 Cor. 11:28).

The Acts of the Apostles describe three great journeys (see maps on pp xvii and xviii). The first has been dated to the years 46 to 48. It took him from Antioch to Salamis and Paphos and through South Galatia. The churches at Pisidian Antioch, Iconium, Lystra, and Derbe were founded on this expedition. Paul always started by going to the synagogue to explain his mission. Like Jesus, he had come to fulfil the Law, not to abolish it.

It was probably in the latter part of the year 48 that Paul had his violent disagreement with Peter at Antioch (Gal 2:11-21). Though Peter had seen the need to take the gospel to the Gentiles, the conservatism of James and other members of the Church in Jerusalem had caused him to refrain from eating with them. "When Cephas came to Antioch, I opposed him to his face, seeing that he was manifestly in the wrong," writes Paul. "I said to Cephas in front of everyone, 'In spite of being a Jew, you live like the pagans and not like the Jews, so you have no right to make the pagans copy Jewish ways.'" It is not clear whether this breach was ever fully healed.

The second voyage, from 49 to 52, was undertaken with Timothy (26 Jan.), who came from Lystra. This time they went much farther—through Tarsus and Antioch, back to the newly-founded churches of South Galatia, on through Asia Minor to Macedonia and Greece, before coming back by way of Ephesus and Rhodes. The third journey, from 53 to 57, took them back over all this territory, visiting the new churches at Ephesus, Philippi, Thessalonica, Corinth, and many others that were springing up. It was very hard work and often dangerous. Paul writes vehemently to the Corinthians, telling them what he has endured and saying that he has done as much as any of the brethren: "Hebrews, are they? So am I. Israelites? So am I. Descendants of Abraham? So am I. The servants of Christ? I must be mad to say this, but so am I, and more than they: more, because I have worked harder. I have been sent to prison more often, and whipped so many times more, often almost to death" (2 Cor. 11:22-4).

He goes on to catalogue his sufferings: five times ritually flogged with the stipulated "forty stripes save one," three times beaten with sticks, once stoned, three times shipwrecked, once adrift in an open boat for a day and a night. He has faced danger from fording rivers, from attacks by brigands, from pagans, and from his own "so-called brothers." He has worked and laboured, gone without sleep, gone cold and hungry. He praises God, glories in his own feebleness, and blesses the name of Christ; but it is clear that he feels his work to be undervalued in Corinth, as in Jerusalem.

The dates given above indicate that each mission was longer than the previous one. There was always so much more to do; and as Paul travelled he wrote to the churches in answer to their queries, or upon receiving reports from other travelling Christians on how they were faring. He writes in very different Greek from the simply-structured accounts in the Gospels. The Greek of the four evangelists was adequate for their task, which was mainly reportage of events; but Paul was dealing with theological issues and abstract concepts. Though Jerome was to complain later that Paul's command of Greek was limited and hindered his expression of the great issues with which he was dealing, he had a much wider vocabulary and a greater facility with words than the evangelists.

Most of the letters to the growing churches were dictated, with a subscript in Paul's own hand. The preamble in the *New Jerusalem Bible* makes it clear that they were not written in the order in which they appear in the New Testament, in descending order of length; and it is suggested that they should be read in chronological order to follow Paul's career and the development of his thought. 1 Thessalonians came first and was written from Corinth in the year

50-1, during the second missionary journey. It contains encouragement for a church which welcomed him after he had "had rough treatment and been grossly insulted at Philippi." The second letter to the Thessalonians, which contains apocalyptic thought, is judged by some commentators to be a later document by another writer. The letter to the Philippians was written in 56-7 when Paul was under arrest, probably in Ephesus. There had been persecution in Philippi, and he says, "Now we can breathe again, as you are still holding firm in the Lord." The two letters to the church at Corinth are all that remain of four and are perhaps patched together from different documents. They are a curious mixture of practical advice relevant to the immediate situation and inspired passages that endure for all time. Corinth was a seaport and a garrison town, and a centre of the worship of Venus (Aphrodite). This may explain Paul's strictures on the subject of sex and the status of women; but he insists that the body is the temple of the Holy Spirit: "You are not your own property: you have been bought and paid for" (1 Cor. 6:19-20). This raises the argument to a new theological level. The passages in 1 Corinthians 12-14 on the analogy of the Church with the human body, the nature of love, and spiritual gifts, do not date at all. He must have thought long and earnestly about the difference in the spiritual gifts given to him and to Peter.

The letters to the Galatians and the Romans were written in 57-8. He explains the righteousness of God, the way in which his promise to Abraham has been fulfilled in Christ, the doctrine of justification by faith, and the new life of Christ, which transcends the Law and is offered to Jew and Gentile alike. The authorship of the letters to the Ephesians and Colossians and the letters to Timothy, Titus, and Philemon is disputed, and the letter to the Hebrews is certainly not Pauline: its authorship has been debated since early in the Church's history but remains undecided.

Paul's later movements are uncertain. He may have travelled as far as Spain. We know that he ended in Rome, where he was arrested and kept under house arrest for two years. Though he was released, he was evidently arrested again, for he was executed in Rome at Tre Fontana, probably in the year 65. The belief that he and Peter died on the same day has no evidence to support it: it seems to have arisen from the fact that they share a feast-day. As a Roman citizen, Paul would have been beheaded instead of suffering one of the crueller deaths reserved for non-citizens. He was buried where the basilica of St Paul's Without the Walls now stands. Constantine is thought to have planned a basilica over St Paul's tomb, but the building was principally the work of the emperor Theodosius I (379-95) and Pope St Leo the Great (440-61; 10 Nov.). It stood until 1823, when it was destroyed by fire. Contributions for its restoration came from all over the world. In the course of the works, a tomb was found with the inscription *PAULO APOST. MART.* It was left unopened, and the new building was constructed on the same lines as the earlier one. It was consecrated by Pope Pius IX on 10 December 1854.

Paul's contribution to the development of Christian theology would be hard to overstate. Its influence on later writers and on the councils and synods which defined Christian doctrine has been very great. At the same time, there are no grounds for the belief that Paul took the simple faith of fishermen and overelaborated it. The faith was far from simple; but it needed a theologian to bring it into coherent relation with the traditions of Israel and the thought of the Graeco-Roman world. In the letters that have survived, he takes the great events of the Incarnation, the crucifixion, the resurrection and the coming of the Holy Spirit and explains a new world-view in which these are the central and pivotal events in the drama of redemption. From the beginning of time, the whole creation has been "groaning in one great act of giving birth" (Rom. 8:22). Now salvation is at hand.

Paul's usual emblems in art are a sword and a book. In some medieval representations he appears as one of the twelve apostles, replacing Matthias: a belated act of hospitality to the man who was never at home among the Christians of Jerusalem.

Impulsive, generous Peter and moody, introverted Paul make an odd pair; but their work was complementary, which is why the Church has remembered them together through the centuries.

None of the secondary sources is a substitute for reading St Paul in the original. Lives include W. J. Conybeare and J. S. Howson, 2 vols. (1951); A. Sabbatier, *L'Apôtre Paul* (1871, Eng. trans., 1891); W. H. Ramsay, *St Paul the Traveller* (1908); A. H. McNeile (1920); D. A. Penna (Eng. trans., 1953); J. Munch, trans. F. Clarke (1960). See also G. Ogg, *The Chronology of St Paul* (1966); F. Prat, *The Theology of St Paul* (Eng. trans., 2 vols., 1927-34); Albert Schweitzer, *The Mysticism of St Paul the Apostle* (1931); J. B. Phillips, *Letters to Young Churches* (1947); E. Kirschbaum, *The Tombs of St Peter and St Paul* (1959); J. Murphy O'Connor, *St Paul: A Critical Study* (1996); *N.C.E.*, 11, pp. 1-12; *O.D.S.*, pp. 381-2. See also The Conversion of St Paul (25 Jan.) in the present work, with further bibliography.

St Cassius, *Bishop* (538)

Gregory of Tours (17 Nov.) writes in his *Dialogues* about the virtues of Cassius, whom he regarded as an exemplary bishop and pastor. His personal life was one of great simplicity: he cared for his clergy and people and was generous in giving alms to the poor. Gregory also mentions him in a special sermon.

Cassius was bishop of Narni in Tuscany, due north of Rome. The tradition is that he was told by one of his clergy that he would die in Rome on the feast of SS Peter and Paul. He composed his own epitaph and asked that he might be buried in Narni next to a lady named Fausta, who is thought to have been his wife, and near his predecessor, Juvenalis.

Thereafter, he went to Rome every year for the feast. Six times he returned to Narni, but on the seventh occasion the prophecy was fulfilled, and he died peacefully in Rome after celebrating Mass. His tomb is in the crypt of San

Giovenale in the cathedral at Narni. He is said to have prepared it himself and to have composed the verses inscribed on it.

AA.SS., June, 7, pp. 445-50, has the relevant extracts from Gregory of Tours. *B.H.L.*, 1, pp. 248-9.

SS Salome and Judith (? Ninth Century)

About the middle of the ninth century, Walter, abbot of the double monastery of Ober Altaich in Bavaria, is said to have had a cell built for an anchoress at the west end of the church with an aperture through into the choir. In it, he enclosed with the customary rites a relative of his own, a woman from England named Salome. A monk of Altaich who appears to be a contemporary has a detailed Latin narrative telling of a royal English lady, a niece of a king of England, who had made a pilgrimage to the Holy Land. On the way back her two attendants died and she lost all her possessions. She was going blind and she fell into the Danube near Regensburg, where she was rescued by fishermen. They took her to Passau, the great medieval episcopal seat at the confluence of the Danube and the Inn. There she found shelter in the house of a noble lady until the abbot of Altaich, claiming some kinship with her, offered her a cell where she could end her days in prayer and seclusion.

Some time later she was joined by another relative, a cousin or aunt named Judith, who was a widow. It was popularly believed that Judith had been sent by the king of England to find Salome, but she also decided to remain at Altaich, and a second cell was constructed for her. Eventually Salome died, and Judith remained there alone. Sometimes she had night terrors, and the monks would come running from the nearby monastery to find out if she was being murdered or attacked by the devil.

When Judith died she was buried next to Salome in Ober Altaich. The monastery was overrun and destroyed by the Hungarians in 907, but it is said that the relics of both anchoresses were translated to Nieder Altaich, where they are still venerated.

This narrative presents some problems: in 1709 the Bollandists described the author as a near-contemporary of Salome and Judith, but later critics think that the document cannot be earlier in origin than the twelfth century. There are some grounds for thinking that Abbot Walter of Altaich lived in the eleventh century, not the ninth.

The identity of Salome and Judith is puzzling. No English princess known to history in either the ninth or the eleventh century seems to tally with either. In the ninth century there was no king of England. One suggestion is that Salome may have been Edburga, daughter of Offa, king of Mercia, who was said to have plotted the death of several people at court and to have accidentally killed her husband, Beorhtric, king of the West Saxons, with poison meant for a young man named Worr, who was the king's favourite. This reputedly beautiful and wicked princess was driven out of England. Asser, the monk-chronicler who compiled his biography of King Alfred the Great in about 893, says that she was well known in Mercia "in recent times." She went to the court of Charlemagne. He was overwhelmed by her beauty and gave her the choice of marrying himself or his son. Edburga chose the son, and Charlemagne was so offended that he retracted the offer and gave her a nunnery instead. There her conduct as abbess was so scandalous that she was driven out again and reduced to wandering the streets. "She shamefully spent her life in poverty and misery until her death; so much so that in the end, accompanied by a single slave boy (as I have heard of many who saw her) and begging every day, she died a miserable death in Patavium."

"Patavium" is usually translated as Pisa, but this could be a copyist's mistake for Patavia, or Passau, where Salome is said to have stayed before going to her retreat at Ober Altaich. Edburga's end may not have been as miserable as Asser thought.

Stories about Edburga seem to have been in circulation in Wessex in the late ninth century, and it is possible that there was quite a long written narrative about her, which has not survived.

AA.SS., June, 5, pp. 493, 498, and June, 7, pp. 451-6; *M.G.H.*, *Scriptores*, 15, pt. 2, p. 847; Asser, *Life of King Alfred*, various editions, chs. 14-15; *The Annals of Roger de Hoveden*, Eng. trans. ed. H. T. Riley (1944), pp. 19-20; *B.G.*, June, pp. 455-60; R. M. Wilson, *The Lost Literature of Mediaeval England* (1952), pp. 37-8.

St Emma (1045)

Emma (or Hemma) was related on her mother's side to the Holy Roman Emperor St Henry II (13 July) and was one of the girls trained at his court by his wife, St Cunegund (3 Mar.), who had no children of her own. According to her medieval biography, Emma was given in marriage to William, landgrave of Friesach, and although this was an arranged marriage, it seems to have been a happy one. They had two sons, William and Hartwig; and when the boys were old enough, the landgrave gave them charge of the mines from which he derived part of his wealth.

Unfortunately, the management of the mines went badly. Whether the miners felt that their conditions were unbearable or the young counts were simply unable to control them, the two were driven into repressive actions that made rebellion inevitable. When William ordered the hanging of one of the men for gross immorality, the miners rose and murdered both William and Hartwig.

The effect on their parents was devastating. Emma abandoned herself to grief, and the landgrave threatened to have all the rebels executed, with their wives and children. Eventually, both turned to prayer. Emma remained in Friesach, but William, having pardoned all but the leaders, undertook a pilgrimage to Rome. On the way back he became ill, and he died only a short distance from his home.

Emma had lost both her husband and her sons. She resolved to devote the rest of her life to the service of God and people in need. She gave alms liberally to the poor and founded several monasteries, of which one was on her own estates near the Austrian town of Gurk, in Carinthia, and included her castle of Gurkhofen. This became a double monastery. There were twenty monks and seventy nuns, who were able to maintain the *laus perennis*, singing the divine office day and night without intermission. It is not clear whether Emma herself received the veil at Gurk, but when she died in about the year 1045, she was buried in the church there. Gurk later became the title of an archbishopric.

Investigations by the Congregation of Sacred Rites in the 1930s modified this medieval biography. Emma was herself a member of the Friesach family, and her husband was William of Sangrau. When he died about the year 1015 she had another son living, and it was only after he was killed in battle some twenty years later that her religious benefactions began. A process of canonization was instituted by Pope Paul II at the instigation of the emperor Frederick III in 1464, but this seems to have lapsed. Emma's cult was confirmed by the Holy See in 1938 as a *beata*, but she is commonly called "saint."

AA.SS., June, 7, pp. 456-85; *B.G.*, June, p. 461; Congregation of Rites, *Confirmationis cultus . . . servae Dei Hemmae . . .* (1937).

Bd Raymund Lull, *Martyr* (1232-1316)

Among the few Lives of the saints which have come to us from medieval times, the contemporary Life of Raymund (Ramón) Lull is exceptional for its humanity and authenticity. The identity of the chronicler is unknown, and it is not even clear whether the Latin or the Catalan text is the original; we know that Raymund himself told his remarkable story to his followers at their request. He tells it with honesty and candour in a remarkable account.

He was a vehement man—passionate, generous, dedicated, and courageous. The great conceptions that filled his mind were so clear and offered him so wonderful a vision that he could brook no obstacles to their fulfilment. If he was often reckless and lacking in worldly judgment, it was in the most exalted of causes.

Raymund was born in Palma, Majorca, in 1232 or 1235, at a time when that island was a kingdom in its own right. He was the son of one of the military chiefs who were successful in re-conquering the island from the Moors in the thirteenth century. He grew up on the island in a mixed Christian and Moorish society. As a child he was a page at court; when he grew to manhood he became marshall and high steward to King James and enjoyed the king's friendship and favour. He was wealthy, well educated, and happily married, with a small son and daughter—though he was frequently unfaithful to his wife and lived a life of luxury and self-indulgence. Behind this façade of superficial satisfactions he must have been thinking deeply about the Moors he knew and the relationship of their Muslim beliefs to his own faith. He was thirty years old when, while composing a love poem, he suddenly had a vision of Christ crucified. He tried to ignore it but could not and took to his bed. The vision was repeated five times in all before he came to accept it and to work out what it meant for him. He decided that he must abandon his way of life and devote himself to bringing the Moors to Christ.

Like Isaac of Córdoba (3 June) nearly five centuries earlier, he did not think this an impossible task. Muslims believed in one God, and they were People of the Book, like Jews and Christians. They shared the traditions of Israel and the great Jewish patriarchs, and they recognized Jesus Christ as a prophet, though they held Mohammed to be a greater one. The Church ranked them as heretics but not as pagans. They had a noble tradition of Arab scholarship. It seemed possible to Raymund that Muslims and Christians could reach a mutually acceptable understanding. Others had shared the same dream: in the eleventh century Peter the Venerable, abbot of Cluny (30 Dec.), had set up a translation school in Toledo where the Koran and works of Arab scholarship were translated into Latin. In 1219 St Francis of Assisi (4 Oct.) had made a journey to the Holy Land to evangelize the Saracens, though without success. Jerusalem had fallen to Saladin in 1187. The Seventh Crusade (1248-54) had ended, like its predecessors, in political wrangling and military disaster. It is understandable that Christians, particularly in Spain and the Balearic Islands, where they had experience of working and living with Muslims, should have been looking in the 1260s for means of reconciliation.

Once his project was decided, Raymund characteristically poured all his energies into it. He made a pilgrimage to Santiago de Compostela, and then to Rocamadour, where the twelfth-century statue of the Black Virgin was already a focus for pilgrimage. He returned, convinced of divine guidance, to make generous provision for his family and his dependents and to give the rest of his wealth to the poor. Then, after a period of seclusion and prayer, he began to prepare himself for his task. He spent nine years in learning Arabic and undertaking preliminary studies, and he made plans for the first missionary college to undertake the conversion of the Moors. This was eventually set up in Majorca in 1276, with the help of King James, and run by the Friars Minor, though its achievements were very limited.

Raymund continued his studies and wrote prolifically on theological and philosophical subjects. He also wrote a romance, *Blanquerna*, which has been translated into English; but despite his labours his great project did not win support. He was a great man in Majorca, but away from his own island his word did not carry weight in the Church. He was a layman, he was not under obedience to a diocesan or a religious Order, and he was distinctly critical of ecclesiastical abuses. The Church authorities were not prepared to authorize or assist his projects. He went to Rome in 1277, to Paris in 1286, and to Genoa in 1290 but made little or no impact. He tried to join the Order of Preachers to regularize his position, but he was not accepted. Despite this rebuff, his vision was still strong, and he was determined to follow it even at the cost of his own life.

At last the Franciscans accepted him as a tertiary; and though he was ill by that time, he had himself carried on board a galley bound for North Africa to realize his dream of preaching in the streets of Tunis. He made what he accounted a miraculous recovery, and he did preach in the streets of Tunis, but the Muslim authorities were unimpressed. He was imprisoned and roughly handled before being deported to Naples.

He appealed to Pope Boniface VIII in Rome and later to Pope Clement V in Avignon for assistance, but his pleas went unanswered. A journey to Cyprus (to convert the Great Khan of Tartary, whom he mistakenly thought to be the ruler of the Saracens) came to nothing. He went back to Africa—to Bougie, on the Barbary Coast—and preached again, but again he was imprisoned, cruelly treated, and then deported. This time he was shipwrecked on the way to Italy. He appealed again to the Holy See, and to the Council of Vienne in 1311, but without result. He lectured for a time in Paris but gained few supporters. At length he went back to Africa for a third time: he was stoned at Bougie and left for dead. Some Genoese sailors rescued him and took him by ship to Majorca, but he died within sight of Palma harbour on 29 June 1316.

Raymund is the special patron of Majorca. His life was one of great personal heroism and—from a human viewpoint—almost totally misdirected effort. He underestimated the racial and cultural elements in Islam that had brought Muslims into bitter confrontation with Christians; and he underestimated the opposition of his own Church to one who followed his own vision without regard for established ecclesiastical practices or ecclesiastical sensibilities. Only the Friars Minor gave him limited recognition, and as a tertiary of their Order he is celebrated liturgically.

His prodigious literary output combined a genuine piety with trenchant criticism of abuses in the Church. In 1928 Pope Pius XI spoke highly of Raymund in the encyclical letter *Orientalium rerum*, though without formally according him the title Blessed.

AA.SS., June, 7, pp. 581-676; Fr E. Longpré's long notice in *D.T.C.*, 9, 1072-1141, has an analysis of his life and works and an excellent bibliography; *Bibl.SS.*, 8, 372; *F.B.S.*, p. 476. A critical revision of the Latin version of the contemporary Life is available in *Anal.Boll.* 48 (1930), pp. 130-78. E. Allison Peers has published an English translation of the Catalan text, *Vida Coetània* (1927); a biography, *The Fool of Love: The Life of Ramón Lull* (1929, rp. 1946); and translations of *The Tree of Love* and *Blanquerna* (both 1926). The complete works were published in Spain, ed. M. Bataillon and M. Caldentey (1948).

St Vincentia Gerosa, *Foundress* (1784-1847)

Bartolomea Capitanio (26 July) and Caterina Gerosa were the joint founders of the Sisters of Charity of Lovere in northern Italy, which adopted the Rule of the Sisters of Charity of St Vincent de Paul (27 Sept.). Caterina, who took the name Vincentia in religion, was in her late thirties, and Bartolomea was no more than sixteen or seventeen. They were moved by the appeal of Mgr Nava, bishop of Brescia, to embark on the education and care of neglected children. Caterina had devoted herself to bringing up her brothers and sisters after the early death of their parents and was known for works of charity.

The two founders wished to affiliate their Institute to the Order of the Sisters of Charity of St Vincent de Paul, but that Order originated in France, and the part of Italy in which they lived was under Austrian rule. The provincial government refused to allow the affiliation. In a war-torn area where there was much social misery, the new movement developed very rapidly, despite the early death of Bartholomea at the age of twenty-six. Vincentia proved to be an excellent organizer: many recruits came forward, and other foundations were made. She was a very humble woman and found the respect accorded to her a great trial. Her faith was focussed on Christ's sufferings on the cross, and she used to say, "He who has not learned what the crucifix means knows nothing, and he who knows his crucifix has nothing more to learn."

After a long illness, which she bore with great patience, Mother Vincentia died on 29 June 1847. She and Bartolomea Capitanio were both canonized in 1950 by Pope Pius XII.

A.A.S. 25 (1933), pp. 300-3, includes a biographical summary. Fr Luigi Mazza, S.J., who published in 1905 a full account of Bartolomea Capitanio and her Institute, supplemented this with a Life of Mother Vincentia Gerosa; *F.B.S.*, pp. 404-7.

ST PETER (pp. 224-9)
Gold upside-down cross, silver keys
of the Kingdom of heaven,
on red field.

ST PAUL (pp. 230-4)
White book with black "Sword of the Spirit" (red initials), silver sword with gold hilt, on red field.

30

THE MARTYRS OF ROME UNDER NERO (64-8)

This feast commemorates all the other proto-martyrs of the Church in Rome who died in the same persecutions as SS Peter and Paul. Since 1969 it has appropriately been held on the day following their feast.

Nero was the first of the Caesars to persecute Christians. The Roman historian Tacitus tells the story in detail. On 19 July in the year 64, the tenth year of Nero's reign, a terrible fire broke out in Rome. It began near the Great Circus in a district of shops and booths packed with inflammable goods. In the heat of summer the flames quickly spread in all directions. The fire raged for seven days and seven nights, consuming temples, palaces, and public monuments. A great circle of buildings, mainly tenements and huts in which the poor of the city lived, was razed to the ground to contain it; but the conflagration broke out again in the garden of Tigellinus, the prefect of the Praetorian Guard, and continued for three more days. By the time it had finally died down some two-thirds of Rome lay in smouldering ruins.

For three days Nero stayed at Antium, receiving panic-stricken messages from the city but giving no orders. On the third day he went to Rome to survey the scene. It is recorded that he went to the top of the tower of Maecenas, put on his tragedian's costume, and to the accompaniment of his lyre, recited Priam's lament over the burning of Troy. His delight at the flames gave rise to the belief that he had ordered the conflagration himself, or at least had prevented it from being extinguished. In order to divert suspicion, he announced that the Christians were responsible and ordered their arrest and execution.

Those who acknowledged that they were Christians were seized, exposed to public derision, and often tortured to make them implicate others. Then the victims were put to death with the utmost cruelty. Some were crucified, some were smeared with wax and ignited to serve as human torches, some were sewn into animal skins to be devoured by animals. These barbarities took place as entertainments at public fêtes which Nero gave nightly in the gardens of his palace. They served as sideshows while the emperor diverted his guests with chariot races, mixing with the crowd or driving himself in a chariot. Hardened though the Romans were to gladiatorial shows, the savage cruelty of these tortures appalled many of those who witnessed them. A wave of uprisings followed, and Nero committed suicide four years later.

Tacitus, born about the year 56 and a Roman, says that Nero "was corrupted by every lust, natural and unnatural," but keeps an open mind on the cause of the conflagration, saying, "Whether it was accidental or caused by the emperor's criminal act is uncertain—both versions have their supporters." It is in this context that he provides the earliest reference by a classical historian to Christianity in Rome, describing how Nero "persecuted with every refinement the notoriously-depraved Christians (as they were popularly called). Their originator, Christ, had been executed in Tiberias' reign by the governor of Judaea, Pontius Pilate."

Tacitus evidently believed all the calumnies popularly alleged against the Christians, describing Christianity as a "deadly superstition" and commenting, "All degraded and shameful practices collect in this capital," but he adds: "Despite their guilt as Christians and the ruthless punishment it deserved, the victims were pitied. For it was felt that they were being sacrificed to one man's brutality rather than to the national interest."

This early recorded testimony to the historical facts of Jesus' passion and the strength of the Christian community in Rome by the year 65 is of particular importance because Tacitus is a scrupulous historian and he clearly has no motive for exaggerating in the Christians' favour. He holds no brief for them, and indeed regards them as public enemies. At the same time he records that they were made the scapegoats for the fire and that many people believed that Nero was personally responsible.

Suetonius was born about the year 69, and was thus some fifteen years younger than Tacitus. He can only have heard about the fire from his elders. By the time he wrote his account of Nero's reign, the guilt of this most depraved of emperors was evidently accepted, for he writes categorically that Nero "brazenly set fire to the City."

Edward Gibbon, a late-eighteenth-century rationalist, has complicated the history with some prejudiced views in *The Decline and Fall of the Roman Empire*. Gibbon maintains that Tacitus was an "infant" at the time of the fire and could not possibly remember the events. In fact he appears to have been eight or nine years old, and if he lived in Rome with his parents, the family would have had a very clear memory of the catastrophe he describes with such detailed knowledge. Gibbon also argues that the main point of the attack was against the Jews, not the Christians. Christians, he maintains, were so small and unimportant a sect that Nero and his guard must have confused them with the more numerous Jews. While there has been considerable debate on this point, most commentators take the view that the Christians were the main target of attack. Gibbon's views now have few supporters.

Tacitus, *Annals*, ch. 15; Suetonius, *The Twelve Caesars*, ch. 6; E. Gibbon, *The Decline and Fall of the Roman Empire* (1776–88), ch. 16. *D.C.B.*, 4, pp. 24–7.

St Martial of Limoges, *Bishop* (*c.* 250)

The story of Martial is an interesting example of the efforts of medieval French chroniclers to link the early history of Christianity in their own country with the biblical narrative of the life of Christ. This could be achieved by attributing a mission in France to a biblical character such as St Lazarus of Bethany (17 Dec.); by confusing two people of the same name, for example, identifying St Trophimus of Arles (29 Dec.) with the biblical Trophimus mentioned in 2 Timothy 4:20; or by attributing a biblical background to a French saint who actually lived centuries after the events chronicled in the New Testament.

Martial is an example of this third process. All that we actually know about him is that he was a bishop of Limoges and that he was venerated from a very early date as the apostle of the Limousin and the founder of the see. According to a tradition current in the sixth century and recorded by Gregory of Tours, he was one of seven missionaries sent from Rome to Gaul shortly before 250. Gatian (17 Dec.) went to Tours; Trophimus went to Arles; Paul (22 Mar.) went to Narbonne; Martial to Limoges; Dionysius, or Denis (9 Oct.), to Paris; Saturninus (29 Nov.) to Toulouse; and Austremonius (1 Nov.) to the Auvergne. All became bishops and are venerated as saints.

In the early liturgies of Limoges Martial appears as a confessor, but a more extravagant account of his acts appeared in 1029. This purported to be written by Martial's successor, Bishop Aurelian (16 June), but it borrows extensively from the *Historia Apostolica*, an apocryphal document first circulated under the name of Abdias. The story seems to have been fabricated by Adhémar de Chabannes with the object of enhancing the fame of the Abbey of St Martial of Limoges, where he had been educated. It represents Martial as living in Palestine during the earthly life of Christ. The question was taken seriously enough to be considered at several synods.

Martial, the faithful were told, had been converted by Jesus' preaching at the age of fifteen; he had been baptized by the apostle Peter (29 June, above), who was his kinsman; he was the boy with the barley loaves and the fishes at the feeding of the five thousand; he carried the towel when Jesus washed the disciples' feet; he was present at the raising of Lazarus, waited at table during the Last Supper, and received the Holy Spirit with the other disciples at Pentecost; he became one of the seventy-two disciples; he went to Antioch and Rome with St Peter, who sent him to preach the gospel in Gaul. With Peter's staff, he raised to life a companion who died on the journey. Thereafter he went to Tulle, where he delivered his host's daughter from an evil spirit and resuscitated the son of the Roman governor, who had been strangled by a demon. These two miracles led to the conversion and baptism of 3,600 persons. Other miracles followed: pagan priests who attacked Martial were smitten with blindness, and their sight was restored only as a result of his prayers. People who beat and imprisoned him at Limoges were killed by a thunderbolt, but when the citizens asked Martial to have pity on them he brought them back to life again. A noble lady named Valeria was betrothed to Duke Stephen but refused to marry him because she had become one of Martial's penitents and had made a vow of virginity. Duke Stephen had her beheaded, and she walked away from the scene of the execution with her head under her arm. He was subsequently converted and went on a pilgrimage to Rome, where he found St Peter teaching the people in a place called the Vatican. The duke was able to give Peter the latest news of Martial and to make a favourable report on the progress of the missions in Gaul.

Clearly imagination had run riot. It was certainly Adhémar who forged the supposed Bull of Pope John XIX authorizing the cult of Martial with all the honour due to one of the apostles, and he is gravely suspected of forging other spurious documents of similar importance.

In 1854 the Congregation of Rites refused to ratify the supposed Bull, stating that Martial was to be venerated in the Mass, the litanies, and the office only as a bishop and confessor; but some French sources, following Orderic Vitalis, have continued to insist that he was a first-century apostle "of Jewish origin, of the tribe of Benjamin," and " the first who preached to the people of the west."

P.L., 141, 89-112. The short account of St Martial given by Gregory of Tours is in his *De gloria confessorum*, Eng. trans. by R. Van Dam (1948), pp. 41-2; *Orderic Vitalis, The Ecclesiastical History*, bk. 2, trans. and ed. Marjorie Chibnall (1969), 1, pp. 296-312. Cf. Gregory's *History of the Franks*, 1, 29, in O. M. Dalton's edition, vol. 2, 20. The best text of the narrative attributed to Aurelian (probably by Adhémar) is in C. F. Bellet (ed.), *L'ancienne vie de St Martial et la prose rhythmée* (1897). See also *P.B.*, 6, pp. 516-28, which maintains the French view; Duchesne, *Fastes*, 2, pp. 104-17; *Anal. Boll.* 64 (1946) pp. 84-6; *B.H.L.*, 2, pp. 816-20; H. Leclercq in *D.A.C.L*, 9, 1063-167, which includes an extensive bibliography.

St Bertrand of Le Mans, *Bishop* (623)

Bertrand (Bertichramnus) was born about the middle of the sixth century. We do not know his place of birth, but he went to Paris, probably studied there, and was ordained priest by St Germanus (28 May). He became one of the cathedral clergy and in time was made archdeacon. In 587 he was nominated to the bishopric of Le Mans.

His new position was not an easy one, because the kings of Neustria and Austrasia were contending for power and bishops had to take sides. Bertrand supported the Neustrian princes, and his fortunes varied with theirs. On several occasions he was driven from his see, and for some time a usurper occupied it. In 605 he was finally reinstated by King Clotaire II. Clotaire thought highly of Bertrand and induced the pope to send him the *pallium*, though he was not an archbishop.

A number of landowners made over estates to Bertrand. He used them to endow religious foundations, to establish new ones, and to enrich the church at Le Mans. Among his foundations were the abbey of SS Peter and Paul, a large hospice for pilgrims and travellers, and a church, which he dedicated in the name of St Germanus. He took a great interest in the agriculture of the area and insisted on the development and good management of land that came under his control. His friend St Licinius of Angers sent him some vines bearing a particularly choice variety of grape, and these he propagated with great success.

Despite all his benefactions he was still in possession of considerable property when he died, and he disposed of this in his will, which is still extant and generally agreed to be authentic. This document has helped to correct some of the errors in his chronicler's account of his episcopate.

AA.SS., June, 1, pp. 699-714; *P.B.*, 7, pp. 629-43, from the *Histoire de l'Église du Mans*; Ambrose Ledru in *La Province du Maine*, 14 (1906), pp. 369-83, and 15 (1907), pp. 20-6, 97-108, 122-34, 142-62, 227-36, 267-71.

St Theobald of Provins (1017-66)

As a young man, Theobald (or Thibaut), the son of Count Arnoul of Champagne, was much impressed by what he read of the lives of the desert saints. The self-denial, contemplation, and purity of life of John the Baptist (24 June and 29 Aug.), Paul the Hermit (15 Jan.), Antony (17 Jan.), and Arsenius (19 July) particularly attracted him. He longed to emulate them, and when his father, who expected him to follow the normal life of a young nobleman, asked him to lead a body of troops in a local war, he respectfully told him that he had made a vow to leave worldly life.

Count Arnoul eventually agreed, and Theobald went with a companion, a young nobleman named Walter or Gauthier, to the abbey of Saint-Rémi in Reims, where they divested themselves of their worldly goods and their rich clothes. Dressed as beggars, they wandered north until they came to the forest of Pettingen in Luxembourg, where they found a place of solitude and built two cells. There they went barefoot and suffered from cold, heat, hunger, and fatigue. Manual labour is a necessary duty of the ascetic or penitential life, and since they had no skill in the tasks of making baskets or mats, they went into the neighbouring villages and hired themselves out by the day to do such unskilled work as was available—working in the fields, loading and unloading wagons, cleaning out stables, carrying stones and mortar for the builders, blowing bellows, and making charcoal for the forges. While they worked with their hands, their hearts were employed in prayer, and at night they sang the office in the hours of darkness.

As was so often the case, their solitude and dedication gave them a reputation for sanctity, and others came to see them and destroyed their solitude. They wanted to go to the Holy Land, but the way was barred by the Saracens. They went on pilgrimage to Compostela and then to Rome and visited many holy places in Italy. Then they settled in a remote and wooded place called

Salanigo, near Vicenza in northern Italy, where they found a ruined chapel. They were there for two years before Walter died.

Theobald thought that he had not long to live and allowed a number of disciples to come and join him. The bishop of Vicenza ordained him as a priest so that he could direct them better. The facts about Theobald's background became known, and his parents were informed that the hermit of Salanigo, whose sanctity had been heard of even in Champagne, was the son they had mourned for so long. They had been searching for him for years. On one occasion Theobald had seen his father in Trier, looking anxious and bent with age, but had not approached him because he knew that the old count would want him to go home again. Now they were very old, but they travelled to Italy to see him. They found him pale and wasted, his body weak from his austerities, but they rejoiced to find him alive and living a life of such sanctity. His mother, Gisela, with the consent of her husband, decided to spend the rest of her life in Salanigo as an anchoress, and a cell was built for her near the community.

Soon after, Theobald was stricken with his last illness. This was a painful and repulsive disease, possibly leprosy or one of the conditions that passed for leprosy in medieval times. He bore it with great patience. Shortly before his death he sent for the abbot of a Camaldolese community from whom he had already received the habit. He made his profession to him, recommended his mother and his disciples to his care, received the Last Rites, and died in peace. He was canonized less than seven years later by Pope Alexander II.

Theobald is the patron saint of charcoal burners and is sometimes called *Le Charbonnier*.

AA.SS., June, 7, pp. 540-6, has a full contemporary biography by Peter, abbot of Vangadizza. By some error Theobald is sometimes venerated as the founder of the church and town of Thann in Alsace, but there are no grounds for this: see *Anal.Boll.* 24 (1905), p. 159, and R. Thompson, *Two Old French Poems on St Thibaut* (1936). *P.B.*, 7, pp. 583-90, from the records of the diocese of Troyes.

Bd Philip Powell, *Martyr* (1594-1646)

Philip Powell, or Powel, was born at Trallwng, about seven miles from Brecon, and educated at the grammar school at Abergavenny. At the age of sixteen he was sent to London to study law under a distinguished lawyer, later Fr Augustine Baker, a well-known Benedictine writer and spiritual director. Philip was eighteen or nineteen when he was sent to Douai on business, and there he also became attracted to the Benedictine way of life. He studied at Louvain and was ordained priest in 1618. There is some debate about the date of his formal clothing as a Benedictine. According to the Douai Profession Book this took place in 1619, but he may have made a vow or oblation earlier.

On 7 March 1622 he was sent on the English Mission. It was usual for English seminarists and missionary priests to take an alias, and throughout his later career Philip was usually known by his mother's name of Morgan. After staying for sixteen months with Fr Augustine Baker he was sent to Devonshire with an introduction to a Catholic family. He ministered in Devon, Somerset, and Cornwall for some twenty years, being based first at Bableigh in Devon and then at Leighland Barton in Somerset. The penal laws against Catholics generally fell into disuse during the reign of Charles I, and it was possible for Catholic priests to minister unhindered as long as they used a little discretion; but the outbreak of the Civil War introduced a new era of persecution under Cromwell and a Puritan Parliament, and many Catholic families were scattered. According to Dom Robert Anderton, who later wrote an account of Fr Philip's ministry and imprisonment, Devon and Somerset were "overrunne with Parliament soldiers and the Catholiques could have no place of safety."

Fr Philip joined the Royalist forces and served as a chaplain to General Goring's army in Devon and Cornwall for about six months, until it was disbanded. He was on his way to Wales by ship when the vessel was seized and searched by order of the parliamentarian vice-admiral, Captain Crowther. Two members of the crew recognized Fr Philip and denounced him as a Catholic priest who had "seduced the greater part of the parishioners of Yarnscombe and Parkham in Devonshire from their allegiance to the Protestant Church."

He was taken to Penarth, where Captain Crowther questioned him, and he frankly admitted being a priest. He was kept on board ship and consigned to the lower deck. His clothing was stripped from him and he was "clothed in the most beggarly rags," according to Challoner. Here he stayed for two months until he was taken by sea to London. There, after a short period of being treated fairly humanely, he was confined in the harsh conditions of the common gaol of the King's Bench, crammed in a small room with other prisoners, and forced to sleep on the floor. He contracted pleurisy; but when he was brought up for examination, he defended himself with spirit.

He based his case on two main premises: first, that treason meant treason to the king, and that the court had no jurisdiction over him because it represented a rebel Parliament; second, that the law against priests extended only to the territories of England and not to the high seas. He was condemned to death and gave thanks to God for his coming deliverance. His judges petitioned Parliament to grant him a reprieve, but without effect.

His personality and his conduct in prison so impressed his fellow-prisoners that they drew up a sort of testimonial to his virtues. It was signed by twenty-three Protestants and six Catholics. One of his fellow-prisoners, a convert called John Breion or Preion, described him in verse, with a sort of awkward fervour:

Mild, patient, stout: his hand to every poor
Most open, till they blush'd to ask him more.
Most temperate and constant to his Christ,
That tongue that saith other must say to mine, Thou lyest.

The officer who came to the prison to announce the date of his execution was so much overcome that he could not read the notice, and Fr Philip, looking over his shoulder, prompted him. On the way to the scaffold an onlooker gave him a glass of sack, and he drank to "the coachman"—the carter driving the horses and cart which were taking him to his death. "Oh, what am I," he said, "that God thus honours me and will have me die for his sake?"

He died bravely at Tyburn on 30 June 1646. Dom Robert Anderton was in the crowd and gave him absolution. Subsequently he wrote an account of Fr Philip's life and martyrdom, which was published in London as a broadsheet.

Bede Camm, *Nine Martyr Monks* (1931), pp. 318-43; *M.M.P.*, pp. 474-81; T. P. Ellis, *Catholic Martyrs of Wales* (1933), pp. 100-2, and *Welsh Benedictines of the Terror* (1936), pp. 166-79.

Anchor, forming a cross, one of the most ancient
symbols of Christ, with martyr's palms.
From a wood engraving by Frank Martin.

Consultant Editors

DAVID HUGH FARMER. Former Reader in history at the University of Reading. Author of *St Hugh of Lincoln* and other biographical studies of saints. Author of *The Oxford Dictionary of Saints*. General consultant editor.

REV. PHILIP CARAMAN, S.J. Author of numerous biographies of saints and chief promoter of the cause of the Forty English Martyrs (canonized in 1970). Consultant on English Martyrs.

JOHN HARWOOD. Librarian of the Missionary Institute in London and course lecturer on the Orthodox churches. Consultant on Eastern and Orthodox saints.

DOM ERIC HOLLAS, O.S.B. Monk of St John's Abbey, Collegeville, Minnesota, and director of the Hill Monastic Manuscript Library in Collegeville, where he also teaches theology at St John's University. General consultant, U.S.A.

PROF. KATHLEEN JONES. Emeritus Professor of Social Policy at the University of York. Author of many books and articles on social policy and mental illness. Honorary Fellow of the Royal College of Psychiatrists. Translator of *The Poems of St John of the Cross* (1993). Consultant on social history and abnormal behaviour.

DOM DANIEL REES, O.S.B. Monk of Downside Abbey and librarian of the monastery library. Bibliographical consultant.

DR RICHARD SHARPE. Reader in diplomatic history at the University of Oxford. Author of *Medieval Irish Saints' Lives* (1991), *Adomnán of Iona. Life of St Columba* (1995), and numerous articles on Celtic saints. Consultant on this subject.

REV. AYLWARD SHORTER, W.F. Long experience of African Missions and author of many books on the subject. Former President of Missionary Institute, London, now Principal of Tangaza College, Nairobi. Consultant on missionary saints.

DOM ALBERIC STACPOOLE, O.S.B. Monk of Ampleforth Abbey. Fellow of the Royal Historical Society. Secretary of the Ecumenical Society of Our Lady. Editor of several works, including *Vatican II by Those Who Were There* (1985). Engaged on a study of St Anslem. Consultant on feasts of Our Lady.

DOM HENRY WANSBROUGH, O.S.B. Monk of Ampleforth Abbey, currently Master of St Benet's Hall, Oxford. Member of the Pontifical Biblical Commission. Author of numerous works on scripture and Editor of the *New Jerusalem Bible* (1985). Consultant on New Testament saints.

SR BENEDICTA WARD. Anglican religious. Lecturer at Oxford Institute of Medieval History. Author of numerous works on hagiography, spirituality, and mysticism. Consultant on Middle Ages and age of Bede.